Hispanics and United States Film:

An Overview and Handbook

Bilingual Press/Editorial Bilingüe

General Editor
    Gary D. Keller

Managing Editor
    Karen S. Van Hooft

Associate Editors
    Ann Waggoner Aken
    Theresa Hannon

Assistant Editor
    Linda St. George Thurston

Editorial Consultants
    Ingrid Muller
    Janet Woolum

Address:
Bilingual Press
Hispanic Research Center
Arizona State University
Box 872702
Tempe, Arizona 85287-2702
(602) 965-3867

Hispanics and United States Film:

An Overview and Handbook

Gary D. Keller

Bilingual Review/Press
TEMPE, ARIZONA

ISBN 0-927534-40-1 (paper)

Library of Congress Cataloging-in-Publication Data

Keller, Gary D.
    Hispanics and United States Film: An Overview and Handbook / Gary D. Keller
       p.   cm.
    Includes bibliographical references and index.
    ISBN 0-927534-40-1 (pbk.)
    1. Latin Americans in motion pictures. 2. Hispanic Americans in motion pictures.
3. Motion pictures—United States—History.
I. Title.
PN1995.9.L37K46   1994
791.43´08968—dc20   · 93-38145
                                                 CIP

PRINTED IN THE UNITED STATES OF AMERICA

Cover design by Bidlack Creative Services

Back cover photograph by Conley Photography, Inc.

CONTENTS

Introduction

The general indifference of the United States film industry toward the treatment of Hispanic themes and the presence of Hispanic participants and, to a certain extent, the neglect by those who have done research on this industry have been a source of deep emotions for me and have had a profound impact on my professional life as a scholar over the last decade. The completion of this book—it is, of course, not complete—and of its forthcoming companion volume has been both exasperating and exhilarating. The book is about five years overdue, and not for want of consistent effort!

Working over the last ten years in this field, I have not ceased to be amazed at the amount of data waiting to be unearthed. Whenever I thought I had more or less covered a certain aspect, period, film type, or theme, I would find nugget upon nugget of additional information—names of films, actors, filmmakers, and so on—of critical importance. And so the book(s) expanded and expanded! And let me be the first to observe that the work of recuperating the Hispanic participation in United States film is barely in its initial stage. Nevertheless, a decade and more of work on this topic dictates that this book and its companion be published at once, despite the blemishes, inadequacies, and lacunae in coverage they may have. I must acknowledge the due diligence—and more, the Herculean heroism above and beyond the standard—on the part of the Bilingual Press staff (Ann Waggoner Aken, Theresa Hannon, Linda St. George Thurston, Karen Van Hooft, and intern Ingrid Muller) to produce this overdue book with some semblance of a due date. And as a reward, we all get to do it over again. As the [film] historian says, the first time as tragedy, the second as pictorial!

Originally this work had been envisioned as encompassing one volume. But I had no idea, when I began my research years ago, of the extent of the Hispanic aspect of United States film, both with respect to the cinematic treatment of Hispanics and the participation of Hispanics in the industry. Even two years ago, I could not have predicted how great the Hispanic presence actually was and is, and the extent to which it has been obscured. The scope of my research has made it necessary to divide what has been produced thus far into two separate volumes. A companion volume, *A Pictorial Handbook of Hispanics and United States Film*, is currently in production and will appear within the year.

The data will be most effectively accessed by using the two books in tandem. The current volume, *Hispanics and United States Film: An Overview and Handbook*, is organized historically, and so is the companion *Pictorial Handbook*, which is designed to accompany and supplement the current volume. Whereas the current volume focuses more on character types, film types, and the effect of important historical events (e.g., World War II) or policies (e.g., the Production Code), the companion volume focuses on individual Hispanic figures who worked in United States film and, to a lesser degree, non-Hispanic actors who assumed roles as Hispanics. Similarly, numerous photographs and reproductions of film posters and other realia appear in the companion *Pictorial Handbook*.

The Hispanic figures who appear in this volume have been referenced by historical period. Thus, figures such as Anthony Quinn and Dolores del Río appear in more than one chapter because their career was long sustained and spanned different periods. However, the current volume does not provide systematic biographical data nor a consolidated entry for each Hispanic figure. The companion volume contains an extensive biographical section, "Outstanding Hispanic Figures in the Film Industry," which is alphabetically arranged and does provide one consolidated entry for each figure, together with dates and places of birth, the major films in which each figure participated, and other useful information.

Finally, the bibliography that appears in the current volume is much reduced and primarily reflects works actually cited. *The Pictorial Handbook* contains a general bibliography and a general index cross-referenced to both volumes.

Although the participation of Hispanics has been greatly obscured in United States film history, there have always been researchers working in their own niches, sometimes way outside of the mainstream of film scholarship and its professional associations. Also, in the last ten years, the pace of research with respect to Hispanics and other minorities has greatly accelerated, and my work is much indebted to many researchers. I must acknowledge the important research that richly informs this volume by Eileen Bowser, Carlos Cortés, Aurelio de los Reyes, Emilio García Riera, George Hadley-García, Norma Iglesias, Richard Koszarski, David Maciel, Carl J. Mora, Charles Musser, Kemp R. Niver, Chon Noriega, Arthur G. Pettit, Charles Ramírez Berg, Alfred Charles Richard, Jr., Cecil Robinson, George H. Roeder, Jr., Peter Roffman and Jim Purdy, Jesús Salvador Treviño, Allen L. Woll, and many others cited in the book itself. Without being able to build upon the work of so many researchers, I surely never would have been able to finish this book. Nevertheless, I do believe that the current volume cuts the data pie in a new way and is different from—more than it is similar to—the work of the researchers cited above, even the work it has the closest affinities or similarities with, such as Emilio García Riera's *Mexico visto por el cine extranjero* and Alfred Richard's *The Hispanic Image on the Silver Screen: An Interpretive Filmography* and *Censorship and Hollywood's Hispanic Image.* I am pleased with the fact that this book has an enormous wealth of data not available in one place anywhere else, data which I hope and think have been innovatively arrayed, classified, and, on a basic level, analyzed.

I need to emphasize that both volumes—this one and the forthcoming companion—are handbooks and overviews, not histories. Much of the information provided in these books appears for the first time in a systematic way. I believe that the material assembled in the two volumes will greatly aid in the writing of a history of Hispanics in the film industry as well as of the filmic treatment of Hispanics in American film. These two volumes do not constitute such a history, however, which involves an effort that requires considerable additional analysis and consideration. I see both handbooks as greatly expanding the data set for such a history, which hopefully will appear sometime in the future.

Finally, I should observe that the current *Overview and Handbook* is far from exhaustive, definitive, or complete. As is probably the case with every first compilation of data previously unavailable except in multiple, and often fugitive sources, there is certainly ample room for additions and improvements. I am sure that important films and figures that ought to appear in a work such as this are not included, simply because they haven't been unearthed thus far or because I didn't locate a source that might describe them. Nor does one have to engage in any subtlety to foresee how the material brought together here can be further elaborated. In the text I often mention such portholes for future scholarship. One can profitably envision whole books completed on the Zorro cycle, the treatment of Hispanic California in American film, the Latin musical, United States films about the Mexican Revolution of 1910, greaser films and others about half-breeds and Hispanics of mixed heritage, Hispanic animated characters, the use of interracial sex involving Hispanic character types, the history of Spanish-language productions by American studios, the reception in the United States over the decades of films from the Hispanic world, the impact of the Civil Rights movement on Hispanic-focused films, the emergence of the Chicano documentary and docudrama, or the participation of Hispanic actors, filmmakers, and other professionals in television. The list of film types beginning in chapter 4 could easily be doubled. Too bad we can't say the same about Hispanic character types!

Let me turn to the matter of dates. Films often vary with respect to their original dates, although not usually by more than a year. The variation most often reflects keying the film either on the date of completion or on the date of the film's original release. In any event, it should be recognized that often films are screened in differing versions and lengths. The dates that are provided here usually come from secondary sources such as *The American Film Institute Catalog* and film reviews in magazines and periodicals. The birth dates of actors vary considerably because there is a strong incentive, financial and otherwise, for these professionals to represent themselves as younger than they are. I have made my best effort in providing accurate birth dates, but I caution the reader that generally these dates more commonly vary from source to source than they are uniform.

Finally, I do believe that the current volume and its forthcoming companion represent a significant beginning. The wonderful thing about compilations of basic research data is that the domain can be expanded over time, corrected as necessary, analyzed and further elaborated. I believe that this volume introduces core data to the general domain for other researchers to expand, probably in some cases to correct or to modify, and to use for analysis. But at least we have made a beginning.

G.D.K.
March 1994

To, for, and with
Estela and Jack Keller

*indefatigable researchers, from whom I appear to have inherited the peculiar trait,
whose tracking down the never-ending identities and products of innumerable
Armidas, Burnus, Cheeches, Chitos, Chris-Pins, Desis, Esais, Linas, Margos,
Monas, Ninas, Pinas, Ritas, and insuperable Tin-Tanes have so materially
aided in making this book useful.*

Y para la Raza, siempre

*ai les va de cuento largo para que caigan en la cuenta y podamos iniciar
el ajuste de cuentas.*

1

The Emergence of Motion Pictures and the Depiction of Race, Ethnicity, and Other Cultures

Stereotypical depictions of various outcast races, ethnicities, and cultures, often excruciatingly derogatory by contemporary standards, were commonplace in American popular culture before the invention of motion pictures.[1] Moreover, film, because of its capacity for heightening emotions as well as its ability to communicate to mass audiences, took these depictions to new, often more extreme levels. Early films' racial and ethnic topics stemmed from the comic strip, vaudeville, the dime and nickel novels,[2] and other primarily popular forms of entertainment that predated cinema. The technology of film entertainment was so powerful, however, that one of the side effects of American cinema was often crushingly brutal portrayals of other races and cultures, depictions that spread to larger audiences than ever before possible around the nation and even around the globe.

From the beginning of the American experience, the phenomenon of racial and ethnic conflict and occasional cooperation were central to the development of American society. The facts of widespread racial and ethnic diversity in the United States were interpreted in a variety of ways including the affirmation of the "white man's burden," the proclamation of Anglo-Saxon nativism, the elaboration of a "melting pot" philosophy where different races and ethnicities would be amalgamated into newly minted Americans, and, less commonly, a "celebration of democratic pluralism and the opportunity to forge new identities" (Musser, 1991, 39). By the second half of the nineteenth century, what had been the central element of racial relations, Anglos mostly fighting with or occasionally allying themselves with American Indians (e.g., to fight the odious French), increasingly became focused to the urban experience because great parts of the country had been cleared of Indians as aggressors and because of massive immigration. At the time that film was becoming an enormously powerful medium, the number of immigrants who entered the United States had increased from approximately one hundred thousand a year in 1887 to over one million a year by 1907. The year 1896, the year that commercial cinema was launched, was also the first time that immigrants from southern Europe, the Levant, and from the Far East outnumbered the more familiar Anglo-Saxon, Irish, or German immigrants. In addition, American cities began to fill with internal migrants from rural areas, including many African Americans and increasingly, Hispanics.

The earliest cinema fulfilled a number of functions with respect to race, ethnicity, and gender. Some of these functions were contradictory, but this should not be surprising because film did not depict race and ethnicity from one ideological point of view or set of assumptions. Commercial viability was the most important consideration in the creation of films, including those that depicted race, ethnicity, and women in various stereotypical or nonstereotypical roles. Because a large number of very short films were produced that catered to various market segments, race, ethnicity, and gender were treated in a variety of ways.

Generally, the motion picture industry made overt efforts to cater to middle-class and American-born patrons, and in fact to eschew immigrant or working-class values and behaviors while not going so far as to alienate this audience. The location of theaters, the choice of subject matter, the policies with respect to attendance etiquette, and the price of tickets were all generally consistent with an industry intent on wooing a higher status audience and embracing the values of the dominant classes. Thus, the earliest films mostly catered to the dominant culture, usually the WASP power elite or sometimes farmers and ranchers, at the expense of out-groups, which at the turn-of-the century included not only blacks, Hispanics, American Indians, and Asians, but Irish, Italians, Jews, Poles, and others.

However, other films depicted white immigrants in such a way as to promote an assimilationist ideology; the flickers functioned "as a form of mass entertainment which instructed immigrant groups in the values of their new home country and provided them with a common cultural experience that contributed to the erosion of their local, insular cultures" (Musser, 1991, 40). Rosenzweig (1983) argues, with justification, that movies helped to establish class consciousness among American workers that either transcended ethnicity or which promoted collaboration among ethnicities and which led to demands on the part of workers for unionization, power, and full participation in American society. In addition, while some films might have been intended to be understood in a context agreeable to the dominant class, "they often acquired unintended and potentially subversive meanings when shown to different types of spectators or in different contexts" (Musser, 1991, 41). Thus, while filmmakers may have claimed to embrace dominant values (or even in fact consciously did embrace them) the effects of their films and their consequent popularity may have been due partially or even primarily to their subversive messages. It has become a commonplace to interpret the "dream factory's" handling of sex and violence as opposing what was moralistically claimed and what was pruriently purveyed; subterfuge and subversion also affected either the cinematic depiction of race, ethnicity, class, and gender, or the evocation of the values and attitudes by the dominant groups toward the lower classes and out-groups, and conversely, the evocation of the values and attitudes by the lower classes and out-groups toward the dominant society.[3]

Thus, the flickers served many functions, or many masters and quickly, from the point of view of attendees, mistresses as well. However, the ability of filmmakers to establish what Musser calls a "complex negotiation" (1991, 41) that could not only cater to the dominant class but to immigrants as well was strictly limited to the more assimilable and acceptable ethnic groups, that is, to white immigrants. In Musser's important paper on ethnicity in the earliest cinema he makes a telling observation:

> I have purposefully avoided examining representations of non-European racial groups such as African-Americans and Asian-Americans. The unfavorable treatment of blacks may appear similar to the treatment of many European groups, just more extreme, but this qualitative difference was great enough in degree to become a difference in kind. With the barrier to acceptance for blacks and Asians much greater,

these assimilationist comedies did not include them. Blacks and Asians were not, except in the most peripheral sense, consumers of popular amusements. They were usually not welcome in vaudeville houses and other theatrical venues catering to whites. In any case, films did not cater to these outcast groups; moreover African-Americans and Asians—unlike Jews, Italians, and the Irish—were effectively excluded from American film production in this period. (1991, 76)

While Musser does not specifically mention Hispanics (or American Indians), they had a status similar to that of blacks and Asians. The occasional exception to this, as we shall see, was when Hispanics of supposed European stock were depicted. Also, when American films adapted important classical works that reflected Spanish characters such as Don Quixote, Carmen, the Barber of Seville, or Don Juan, the treatment, often by virtue of a well-known plot, could transcend the commonplace ethnic stereotypes. Otherwise, the depiction of Hispanics on the screen (less so with respect to their acceptance within the industry) was analogous to that of blacks and Asians. However, as our review will document, even with respect to the "hard" races and ethnicities, those presumed to be so inferior that they were undeserving of assimilation, the number of early films made and the variety of types of films was such that significant and telling exceptions to the extremely harsh norms appear that are well worth review and analysis.

Motion pictures emerged as a distinct technology beginning around 1895. They were preceded by a long-standing line of screen practices that date back to the seventeenth century; the magic lantern, a precursor of the modern slide projector, was one of the most notable of the precinematic inventions. One form of motion picture that emerged around the turn of the century was cinema, which was based on the projection of motion pictures onto a screen. A second type did not involve projection; the most historically important format of this type of motion picture provided individualized viewing through a peephole. Thomas Edison's peephole kinetoscope preceded and overlapped with cinema inasmuch as the machine used film, but did not project it. The kinetoscope allowed a person to view through a magnifying lense a sequence of pictures on a band of film that moved continuously over a light source, thus creating the illusion of motion. In the early 1890s, Edison and his associates began to develop the kinetoscope commercially and, in 1893, they built a studio to produce film for the device (Musser, 1990). A competing device, the mutoscope, was peephole-based but did not use film, but rather flip cards.

By 1897, projected motion pictures had begun to take leadership among the various new technologies of screen practice, primarily in the form of the vitascope, which Edison, the self-acknowledged "Wizard of Menlo Park" and his associates had launched in 1896. In April of that year, only one theater in the United States, in New York City, used the vitascope to project films. By May 1897, about one year later, "several hundred projectors were in use across the country." Even Honolulu and Phoenix, in Arizona Territory, experienced motion picture projection (Musser, 1990, 109).

The first year or so of cinema emphasized the illusionism of everyday special effects (trains, horses, running water, etc.). However, as the result of rapid advances in technology which permitted longer and more sophisticated films, together with the fact that illusionism based on purely optical effects such as waves beating against a pier soon grew stale, cinema began to expand its repertoire. For example, in France, as early as

1897, the former magician and illusionist Méliès began to do trick and fantasy films, including "reconstructed" (that is, fake) newsreels and dramatic adaptations from literature and the stage. His most well-known works included the 1899 *Cinderella* and his famous *Le Voyage dans la Lune/A Trip to the Moon* in 1902. In the United States, the earliest filmmakers began to do fire-rescue pieces, culminating with *Life of the American Fireman* (1902-03, Edison) by Edwin S. Porter, "bad-boy" films where the bad boys were expected to engage in mischief of one sort of another, and comedies based on newspaper comic strips.

Not all of the earliest comedies were fundamentally based on race and ethnicity. For example, the famous *Personal* (1904, Biograph) features a gang of various women chasing an impoverished French aristocrat whom they wish to marry in order to obtain his worthless title. However, many of the earliest comedies *were* premised on race, ethnicity, or the degrading depiction of other cultures. The earliest depictions of ethnicity and race went hand in hand with the first comedies. The audiences, already used to ethnic stereotypes based on comic strips or vaudeville were treated to depictions of "pilfering, lazy blacks, dumb Irish maids, unscrupulously savvy Jewish storekeepers, naive Yankee farmers, and bad boys" (Musser, 1991, 43). *Chinese Laundry Scene* (1894, Edison) presents in a single twenty-second scene based on an existing vaudeville routine, the Chinaman Hop Lee ingeniously eluding the Irish policeman who chases him (Musser, 1991, 43). In *Cohen's Advertising Scheme* (1904, Edison), a savvy Jewish businessman drums up sales with the help of a vagrant and in *Cohen's Fire Sale* (1907, Edison), the astute but unprincipled Jewish businessman makes money by starting a fire in his store and collecting insurance and then selling the merchandise for extra profit through a "fire sale." The native-born American country bumpkin falls to a New York prostitute who manages to steal his money in *How They Do Things on the Bowery* (1902, Edison). *Irish Ways of Discussing Politics* (1896) shows hard-drinking Irishmen in a bar resolving a political dispute by a fistfight. *How Bridget Served the Salad Undressed* (1900, Biograph), shows how an Irish maid, when asked to serve the salad undressed, with a typical immigrant's verbal confusion (many Irish of the period spoke Gaelic as their first language) takes off her clothes before serving the salad to the White Anglo-Saxon Protestant (WASP) family. In *The Finish of Bridget McKeen* (1901, Edison), an Irish woman, played by a man in drag, blows herself up by trying to start a fire with kerosene. The "Polish" jokes of current times were preceded in the nineteenth century by analogous "Irish" jokes.

In the same year that *Chinese Laundry Scene* was produced, as evidenced by the information provided in Ramsaye (1926), two Hispanic-focused films appeared, the linguistically mangled *Pedro Esquirel and Dionecio Gonzales–Mexican Duel* and *Carmencita* (1894, both Edison). García Riera[4] observes that from the very beginning Hispanic-focused productions cultivated stereotypes: two Hispanics crossing their blades and what was no doubt a sensual Hispanic dancer, doing her wriggling "for the voyeurs of the peep show" (1987, vol. I, 16).

The 1896 Biograph films, *A Hard Wash, Watermelon Feast,* and *Dancing Darkies* were produced as comedies to "inform" curious white audiences about black culture and behaviors. Musser observes: "Even these first motion pictures of African Americans conformed to degrading, white-imposed stereotypes characteristic of American filmmaking throughout the period [from the beginning to 1907]" (1990, 148-50). *A Hard Wash* depicts a black woman scrubbing her child. The supposedly humorous "point" is that no matter how hard the mother scrubs, she can never get the child truly "clean" (white). William N. Selig, who had been a manager of a minstrel show, made films that adapted the minstrel humor of the period, including *Who Said Watermelon?* (*ca.* 1900), *Prizefight in Coontown* (*ca.* 1902) and *A Night in Blackville* (*ca.* 1900). The catalog promotion describes the last film title in the following way:

> . . . shows a "coon" dance in full swing; all the boys have their best babies; the old fiddler and orchestra are shown seated upon a raised platform; the dance is on. Six coons are shown. A bad coon starts a fight. Razor drawn, girls faint, coon with razor starts to do some fearful execution, when little coon lets fly with a large 45 gun; finale, coon seen jumping through window; big bass viola broken and dance ends in general row. The picture is simply great; one continued round of laughter. (Selig Polyscope Company, *1903 Complete Catalogue of Films and Moving Pictures,* p. 4, cited in Musser, 1990, 292)

These so-called watermelon pictures had become so popular that by 1902 Lubin's catalog description of its 1904 *Who Said Watermelon?* remake of the 1902 Selig version explained, "the demand for a new watermelon picture has induced us to pose two colored women in which they are portrayed, ravenously getting on the outside of a number of melons, much to the amusement of the onlookers" (Musser, 1990, 331).

At the same time that the early filmmakers produced comedies, including those premised on racial and ethnic stereotypes, cinema expanded into documentary work, including current events as well as travel films or exotica, and in the more elaborate or sensitive films of this type, anthropology. The very first years of cinema coincided with the growing tension between the United States and Spain beginning in 1895 and the ensuing Spanish-American War in 1898. The war also provided the first American examples of the cinematic depiction of Hispanics and peninsular Spanish and Hispanic colonial culture, as well as the depiction of Spanish-resisting Cubans and Filipinos. The war quickly revealed new roles for infant cinema, which functioned not only as a record of apparent high visual fidelity of the war, but as a powerful medium of ideology and propaganda. The very first motion pictures of the Spanish-American War revealed a great deal about the potential of the industry to create both the impression of veracity and to stir passions. The Cuban crisis quickly turned to war after the USS *Maine* blew up in Havana Harbor on February 15, 1898. One of the leading companies of the time, Biograph, did not have an image of the destruction of the battleship but relished the effect of one on its potential audience. Biograph easily solved its dilemma. The company had few months earlier produced a documentary, *Battleships "Iowa" and "Massachusetts."* They renamed the film *Battleships "Maine" and "Iowa."* The film became an instant hit. According to a prominent newspaper of the period, the *New York World*, at one movie house, "there was fifteen minutes of terrific shouting . . . when the battleships *Maine* and *Iowa* were shown in the Biograph maneuvering off Fortress Monroe. The audience arose, cheered and cheered again, and the climax was reached when a picture of Uncle Sam was thrown on the canvas" (Musser, 1990, 241). Another Biograph film, artfully made from the point of view of propaganda, depicting the Spanish battleship *Vizcaya*, actually had too raucous an effect in places like Rochester, New York. According to the *Rochester Pony Express*, when the film of the *Vizcaya* was screened: "At first the audience hissed and with every performance there were indications of an approaching storm. Finally the gallery gods showed their disapproval with potatoes and other garden truck, and as the management did not care to start a grocery, the obnoxious picture has been permanently removed" (Musser, 1990, 244). The main film companies of the period, including Biograph, Lubin, Edison, Vitagraph, and Lumière all made movies that either filmed ongoing events during the war, or purported to, or staged war scenes. The Spanish-American War pitched the Spaniards as the evildoers and the Cubans as the heroes. Some of the films produced in 1898 included Biograph's *The Wreck of the "Maine," Cuban Reconcentrados, Theodore Roosevelt, Roosevelt Rough Riders,* and *Admiral Cervera and Spanish Officers Leaving "St. Louis."* Edison produced *Cuban Ambush, Shooting Captured Insurgents, Colored Troops Disembarking,* and *Troops Making Military Road in Front of Santiago.* Vitagraph made *Battle of Manila Bay* and *Tearing Down the Spanish Flag,* the latter credited by Katz (1979, 125) as "probably the world's first propaganda film" inasmuch as it effectively played on audience emotions by featuring the removal of the Spanish flag and the raising of the Stars and Stripes to the top of a flagpole. Two weeks after Dewey's famous naval victory, J. Stuart Blackton and Albert E. Smith made *Battle of Manila Bay* in the form of a miniaturized reenactment that used a table, topside down, filled with water an inch deep, still photographs of the American and Spanish fleets nailed to lengths of wood, and pinches of gunpowder for each firing ship. Blackton is supposed to have blown cigar smoke close to the camera lens to make the reenactment more credible (Ramsaye, 1926, 390-91).

In the Philippines, the Spanish-American War developed into an insurrection by Filipinos when it became apparent that the United States was not going to leave immediately after defeating the Spanish. This was occasion for two 1899 documentaries, *Filipinos Retreat from Trenches* (Edison) and *Capture of Trenches at Canaba* (Edison).

About the same time as the Spanish-American War, filmmakers began to shoot exotic films. According to Richard (1992, 1), two of the earliest such films, produced in 1899, "of the Pueblo Indians when much of North America used the term 'Indian' and 'Mexican' interchangeably were Edison's *Eagle Dance, Pueblo Indians* and *Wand Dance, Pueblo Indians.*" In that same year, the Edison firm crossed over from Arizona Territory into Mexico and filmed *Mexican Fishing Scene, Mexican Rurales Charge, Mexico Street Scene,* and *Train Hour in Durango, Mexico.* The American occupation of the Philippines was also the occasion for exotic film including *A Filipino Cock Fight* (1902, American Mutoscope and Biograph), *Filipino Scouts* (1904, Mutoscope) and *Musical Drill* (1904, Mutoscope). The latter two became feature attractions at the world's fair of 1904 commemorating the centennial of the Louisiana Purchase (see Wall, 1953 and Niver, 1967). In 1902, Edison filmed *Great Bull Fight* in Mexico.

An additional channel through which the film industry expanded was by producing story films. This resulted in work that often both borrowed from and closely approximated the stage. This line of expansion quickly became the most profitable of all. The number of such films rapidly increased to the point that film's assumption of its role as the medium of mass preference was closely tied to the industry's production of fiction movies.

Among the first story films were passion plays, including a film version of *The Passion Play of Oberammergau* (1898, Eden Musee) and other passion plays and religious subjects. In 1900, Billy Bitzer shot *Love in the Suburbs* (Biograph), a one-shot comic story. However, French and British filmmakers took the lead in story films and soon found themselves in the favorable position of exporting them, with duped theater cards, into the American market. Films imported from France and England included fairy tales such as *The Enchanted Well* (1903, Méliès) and, particularly from England, stories of violent crime such as *A Daring Daylight Burglary* (1903, Sheffield Photo) and *A Desperate Poaching Affray* (1903, Haggal). Three films focused on Hispanic material were imported into the United States as well: *Don Quixote* (1903) and *Christopher Columbus* (1904), both from Pathé Frères, and *The Barber of Sevilla* (1904, Méliès). In the United States, Porter directed *Uncle Tom's Cabin* (1903, Edison), although a complete and coherent story was not yet the principal concern of the filmmaker who primarily strove to present the peak moments of the book (Gunning, 1991, 38-39). Porter's famous *The Great Train Robbery* (1903, Edison) presented a complete story, but with little characterization. The early film directors, including those Europeans who worked in the American market such as Méliès or those based in the United States such as Edwin S. Porter, Stuart Blackton, Sidney Olcott, and others, quickly discovered that film had a distinct advantage over the stage in presenting stories. The devices available to film could have a reality that was impossible to attain on the stage. For example, the Count of Monte Cristo need not escape from his prison through a canvas sea; the film showed a real ocean.

Just as in the case of the earliest comedies, documentaries, and travel and tourism films, the expansion of the industry to story films was the occasion for new opportunities for denigrating stereotypes of the races, ethnicities, and cultures ill-esteemed by the dominant, WASP culture. William Paley's *Avenging a Crime, or, Burned at the Stake* (1904, Vitagraph) was a notably violent film with a highly denigrating depiction of a black, played by a white actor in blackface, who loses at gambling and subsequently kills a white woman. He is chased down, tied to a stake, and burned alive, not only validating denigrating stereotypes about blacks, but legitimating the notion of vigilante justice "as effective and reliable" (Musser, 1990, 402).

The Biograph Company, where D. W. Griffith was to get his directing start in 1908 (he worked as a writer and actor for Biograph earlier), was the first in the United States if not the world to make the decisive production commitment to fiction story films. Some of the earliest Biograph productions were chase films that did not revolve around race and ethnicity such as *Personal* (1904) and *The Lost Child* (1904). Others, including *Nigger in the Woodpile* (1904) and *The Chicken Thief* (1904) were comedies that were fundamentally based on racial stereotypes. In both films African Americans are seen as

> lazy, petty thieves stealing wood for their fire or chickens for their dinner. The 'comedy' comes after whites retaliate, by either placing a stick of dynamite in a log so that a black person's home is blown apart or setting a bear trap in a chicken coop so that the thief can be trapped like an animal and successfully tracked by a group of white farmers. (Musser, 1990, 380-81)

The earliest American-produced story film currently on record that evokes Hispanics is *A Gypsy Duel* (1904, Biograph). It develops one of the most enduring stereotypes: two hot-blooded, impassioned Hispanics (in this case Spanish Gypsies) fighting to the possible death for the affection of the señorita that each suits. The 1906 Edison film, *The Life of An American Cowboy*, directed by Porter, provides a number of tableaux-like scenes that tell a story of good Indians and faithful Indians and a villainous Mexican whose capture of an Indian maiden must be redressed by Anglo cowboys and the faithful Indians.

As is apparent from the four types of examples described above of the earliest cinema—comedies, primarily based on comic strips, minstrel humor, and vaudeville routines; documentaries of current events; travel-tourism, exotica, and anthropology; and story films—the depiction of race and ethnicity went hand-in-hand with the emergence of film.

Notes

[1] See Cecil Robinson, *Mexico ana the Hispanic Southwest in American Literature.* Tucson: University of Arizona Press, 1977, and Arthur G. Pettit, *Images of the Mexican American in Fiction and Film.* College Station, Texas: Texas A and M University Press, 1980.

[2] For a discussion of the influence of the comic strip and vaudeville, see Charles Musser, *The Emergence of Cinema: the American Screen to 1907* (New York: Scribner's, 1990). See the following on the dime and nickel novels: Ralph Admari, "The House that Beadle Built, 1859-1869," *American Book Collector* 4 (November, 1933): 223-225; W. H. Bishop, "Story-Paper Literature," *Atlantic* 44 (September, 1879): 387; Warren French, "The Cowboy in the Dime Novel," *Texas Studies in English* 30 (1951): 219-234; Charles M. Harvey, "The Dime Novel in American Life," *Atlantic Monthly* 100 (July, 1907): 44; George C. Jenks, "Dime Novel Makers," *Bookman* 22 (October, 1904): 112; Albert Johanssen, *The House of Beadle and Adams and Its Dime and Nickel Novels: The Story of a Vanished Literature.* 2 vols. Norman: University of Oklahoma Press, 1950; Edmund Pearson, *Dime Novels; or Following an Old Trail in Popular Literature.* Boston: Little, Brown, 1929; Arthur G. Pettit, *Images of the Mexican American in Fiction and Film,* and Henry Norton Robinson, "Mr. Beadle's Books," *Bookman* 60 (March, 1929): 22.

[3] See Charles Musser, *The Emergence of Cinema: the American Screen to 1907;* Miriam Hansen, *From Babel to Babylon* (Cambridge: Harvard University Press, 1991); and Charles Musser, "Role-Playing and American Film Comedy: From *Chinese Laundry Scene* to *Whoopee* (1894-1930)" in *Unspeakable Images: Ethnicity and the American Film.* Ed. Lester D. Friedman. Urbana: Univ. of Illinois Press, 1991.

[4] Emilio García Riera's massive, four-volume work (thus far), *México visto por el cine extranjero,* is essential reading for the scholar who wishes to gain an understanding of the way the U.S. film industry handled Hispanic (mostly Mexican) material, as well as the work focused on Mexico done in England, France, Germany, Latin America, and elsewhere. Above and beyond the wealth of information, including two volumes of filmography (these produced before the publication of the 1988 American Film Institute Catalog for films between 1911-1920), the work is filled with intriguing and valuable observations and insights that are original to the Mexican perspective. It is to be hoped that this landmark will be translated into English soon. García Riera starts his work with a telling observation about the Mexican duel film: "The first Mexicans on film, real or made up, were called, as it were, Pedro Esquirel and Dionecio Gonzales. This got us out to a wrong start from the beginning: plausibly the first was really named Esquivel and the second one, Dionisio González, afflicted by the so common North American confusion between z's and s's at the end of so many Spanish names. Sixty years later, another Mexican character in American film, the mouse, Speedy, hero of the cartoons, would be spelled Gonzales instead of González" (1987, vol. I, 15, translation mine).

2

The Impact of Technological, Esthetic, Socioeconomic, and Cultural Factors on the Depiction of Minorities: 1903-1915

During the period primarily between 1903 and 1915, that is, from the emergence of the first epic, the twelve-minute long *The Great Train Robbery,* and the release of *The Birth of a Nation,* a number of technological, esthetic, socioeconomic, and cultural developments in the United States appeared that helped determine for decades to come how American cinema was to depict race and ethnicity as well as the selection of the story lines for and physical settings of those depictions. As we have seen earlier, the harsh depiction of race and ethnicity that prevailed in other forms of popular culture—vaudeville, popular fiction and theater, minstrel shows, comic strips—was transferred to film from the moment of its emergence. With respect to the dimension of racial and ethnic depiction, the unfortunate filmic style that emerged in the United States was much harsher when compared to the cinema of other nations. American film stereotyping was extreme and ubiquitous, the French, Soviet, German, and Italian cinemas did not share it to the same degree. American cinema came to delight in the depiction of such as "chinkers," "Micks," "darkies," "coons," "niggers," "Hebrews," "greasers," "redskins," "guineas," and similarly derogatory racial and ethnic portrayals. Of course, the circumstances of European Americans conquering the continent and pushing back American Indians and Hispanics and the phenomenon of mass immigration into America by varied ethnic groups were phenomena that had no close analog in the experiences of the other film-pioneering nations which tended to develop "national" cinemas.

Racial epithets quickly became such common stock in the American industry that they were not only embedded into the plots of the films, but were actually used in the titles, title cards, publicity, posters, catalogs, and sales materials of the movies. Denigrating descriptions of race and ethnicity did not appear merely as a required element to tell a certain story accurately, for example, to accurately portray the values of a specific community as expressed by a specific plot. Quite to the contrary, racial and ethnic stereotyping quite simply suffused every element of the film industry. Denigrating outcast groups was excellent box office in America. For example, the word greaser was commonly used in silent films. The epithet, to which Mexicans took considerable offense, but which Anglos often used unselfconsciously, emanated from the supposed use of grease by Mexicans to comb their hair. The racial epithet was originally used primarily to refer to Mexicans, and possibly "half-breeds," but was extended occasionally to other Hispanics.

Richard's extensive filmographic research (1992, 3) identified *Lost Mine* (1907, Kalem) as the first film in which the term greaser was used in the title cards. In the same year, *The Pony Express,* also produced by Kalem, evokes greasers in their stereotypical form. The following year, 1908, marks the first use found to date by this researcher of the epithet greaser in a film's title: *The Greaser's Gauntlet* (Biograph). Numerous films between 1908 and 1918 used this epithet including: *Ah Sing and the Greaser* (1910, Lubin), *Tony the Greaser* (1911, Méliès and sufficiently successful to be remade in 1914 by Vitagraph), *The Greaser and the Weakling* (1912, American), *The Girl and the Greaser* (American, 1913), *Broncho Billy and the Greaser* (1914, Essanay), *The Greaser's Revenge* (1914, Frontier), *Broncho Billy's Greaser Deputy* (1915, Essanay), *The Greaser* (1915, Majestic), and finally, *Guns and Greasers* (1918), the last film to actually use the epithet in its title. Of course, many other films, while not using the term greaser in the title, were dedicated primarily or in part to the depiction of that stereotype.

Other racial designations, highly offensive by contemporary standards were used in addition to greaser. Persons of mixed race or ethnicity, usually villainous were evoked in *The Half-Breed's Foster Sister* (1912, CGPC), *The Half-Breed's Sacrifice* (1912, Lubin), *The Half-Breed's Treachery* (1912, Lubin), *The Half Breed* (1916, Triangle, starring Douglas Fairbanks), *The Quarterbreed* (1916, Bison), *Mixed Blood* (1916, Red Feather), *The Octoroon* (1909, Kalem), and *The Half Breed* (1922, First National). Other films referred to the dark-skinned or occasionally the dirty-skinned, or to darkies. Hispanic women were variously described, depending on the plot of the film as cantina girls, cantina cuties, hot tamales, hot peppers, (hot, dark-skinned, vampish, sweet, sacrificing, et alia) señoritas, or, in the case of the more Indianized Hispanics, squaws.

In order to better understand what transpired in American film beginning around 1903, let us turn to three factors that interacted, converged, and often reinforced each other to influence and solidify a definable style of racial stereotyping in American cinema that with *Chinese Laundry Scene* had already made its appearance as early as 1894:

1. the developing technological sophistication of filmmaking and the developing film esthetics of illusionism that correlated with it;
2. the socioeconomic forces that helped create first nickelodeons and then movie palaces and that caused the U.S. film industry to produce increasing numbers of Westerns, Indian films, epic and other prestige pictures of middle-class appeal;
3. the attitudes toward race and ethnicity that prevailed among both the prominent filmmakers of the period and their white audiences and that governed the popular culture of the times.

The Increased Sophistication of Filmmaking and the Burgeoning Esthetics of Illusionism

The early years of cinema witnessed an explosion of technology similar to the contemporary emergence of the computer industry. In the case of both film and computers, the early industry was technology driven. Advances in film technology were instrumental in determining the art of the possible for pioneering American filmmakers or foreigners active in the American market, including, among others, Harry E. Aitken, Max Aronson, otherwise known as G. M. (Broncho Billy) Anderson, G. W. "Billy" Bitzer, J. Stuart Blackton, Charlie (Sir Charles Spencer) Chaplin, Cecil B. and William C. DeMille, Allan Dwan, Thomas Alva Edison and his associates, Romaine Fielding, Samuel Goldfish (later Goldwyn), D. W. Griffith, William S. Hart, Thomas H. Ince, Rex

(Reginald) Ingram, Carl Laemmle, Jesse L. Lasky, Henry Lehrman, Siegmund (Sigmund) Lubin, Georges and Gaston Méliès (active in the United States between 1903-1911), Mabel Normand, Charles Pathé and his brothers (active in the United States until around 1918), Sidney Olcott (John S. Alcott), Edwin S. Porter, Wallace Reid, William Selig, Mack Sennett, and Adolph Zukor.

The development of more powerful projection and editing technologies permitted the production of what audiences of that period perceived to be more realistic films (although the contemporary viewer of these early specimens might find it difficult to understand this). These more "realistic" and longer films were primarily story films, including epics and spectacle films. While not all of these types of films were involved in the depiction of nonwhites, as we review later, these sorts of films did lend themselves to the depiction of minority group types, including Mexicans, blacks, Orientals, and American Indians, and they did so in a way that was not technologically possible before the turn of the century.

In 1903, Edwin S. Porter produced the first edited films, the forerunner, *The Life of an American Fireman,* and the landmark, *The Great Train Robbery.* The former film was the first to combine shots filmed specifically for production at hand with previously filmed, stock footage. The latter, significantly enough, a Western, reigned for about ten years, until the emergence of D. W. Griffith's features, as the most famous and profitable American cinematic production. Its use of cuts to produce an ellipsis that allowed the audience to infer narrative continuity despite the gaps in time and space was a major stride, possibly an unconscious one on the part of Porter who never repeated his success, in the development of both a cinematic style independent of the stage and the development of the esthetics of illusionism. *The Great Train Robbery* was of epic proportions for its time, an incredible twelve minutes. Yet, by 1915, technological advances and artistic will had stretched the concept of epic to three hours with Griffith's *The Birth of a Nation.* It is traditional in epics to deal with race and ethnicity, and it was no coincidence that Griffith's most famous epic represented the most ambitious attempt to date to present a vast panoply of ethnic and racial types, albeit a flawed and racist depiction.

As the result of the reactions of the viewers of the first "flickers," filmmakers quickly came to realize the potential for manipulating emotions on the basis of heretofore unimagined optical effects. While in the earliest movies the operating element was not plot but effects never before experienced under controlled conditions: a speeding locomotive, a barrel going over a waterfall, a galloping horse, filmmakers found that they could induce fear, vertigo, suspense, and other intense emotions in the viewers through recourse to special effect shots. *The Great Train Robbery* is famous for the last shot (occasionally placed first), a complete non sequitur close-up of a bandit firing his pistol at the audience. It had an enormous effect on the audience, which reacted as if it was being shot at. Within a few years, more complex emotions were induced. Griffith's films, through their depiction of kidnappings, attempted rapes, destruction of homesteads or Indian villages, and most of all, war, were able to bring forth feelings of outrage, simultaneous horror and titillating anticipation, pity, and remorse more intensely than other available media—theater, fiction, poetry, comic strip, or journalism.

With respect to the development of story films, and within that domain, early film melodramas, the first cinematic productions often showed a close connection with the stage in the way they were structured, and it was not until the work of D. W. Griffith that this servility was genuinely overcome. The influence of the stage affected all of the major aspects of early cinema including the style of acting, the use of makeup, and most importantly, the way that films were shot.

Just as the earliest film melodramas had borrowed the plots of the stage melodrama, so the actors brought theater acting styles to the films. The style in the theater of 1908 was flamboyant, relying on the grand gesture, the carefully planned pose. Comparing still photographs of the stage plays of the 1900s with still photographs from the motion pictures, one sees that they are almost indistinguishable. The renowned Sarah Bernhardt, in her spectacle film *Queen Elizabeth* (1912), reveals the inadequacies of the manners of even the best stage actors with respect to the motion pictures.

In addition, it was customary for the actors to apply their own makeup, as they did for stage roles and as is still done today in the legitimate theater. The lack of understanding of the special problems introduced by black-and-white photography, particularly the problems created by the orthochromatic film used at the time, resulted in a highly artificial look among the early films. The normal stage makeup for 1908 depended heavily on pinkish tones, used to overcome the high concentrations of yellow light used on stage. The pink makeup was rendered in gray-to-black tones by the orthochromatic film. Apparently no one worried too much about the sometimes horrendous effects. The audiences had no standards for the films and everything was an exciting novelty. However, the moment a film did appear that set some sort of standard, the subsequent films had to meet that new standard, and the technology of lighting and within that context, makeup, progressed quickly. However, the increased technological sophistication and aspirations for realism had its limits. It was still more common in the early cinema for whites to play blacks in blackface and for whites to do the parts of Asians. With respect to Hispanics the record is more mixed, but many Hispanic roles, including the villainous greasers, were played by whites.

The first film melodramas were produced, in large part, merely as a photographic record of a stage play. If a play had twelve scenes, the motion picture corresponding to the play had twelve shots. Each shot was made with the camera in a fixed position, approximately center-orchestra, and both the actors and the setting were photographed in their entirety. While earlier, prototypical examples exist (Gunning, 1981, 1991), Griffith was the first to establish a new style of editing, parallel editing. As Griffith used it, the cut functioned not to merely fulfill an expectation by moving from the first scene of action to a contiguous or expected following scene. In contrast, Griffith began to use the cut to interrupt the action; the cut now intervened and suspended the natural unfolding of action, suspending its progression. For example, out on the range a swarthy Hispanic evildoer may be gagging and binding a beautiful blonde maiden. The action then cuts to the ranch (e.g., the popular phrase, "Meanwhile back at the ranch . . .") where the hero, a blue-grey-eyed Anglo-Saxon is drinking coffee with the maiden's father, the ranch owner.

In parallel editing the progress of one line of action is interrupted by a shot of another (plot related) line of action. Not only is *The Greaser's Gauntlet* (1908, Biograph), the first American film to use the epithet greaser in the title, it is the earliest example of parallel editing in a film directed by Griffith. In the production, the cuts move from the lynch mob dragging away the innocent José to his white advocate Mildred as she attempts to discover the true culprit. The interweaving of the two actions demands that the spectators retain their expectation from one line of action while they watch another, delaying the reappearance of the moving element which has disappeared from the shot. The psychological effect of this filmic effect on the viewer is *suspense.*

By the end of 1908, Griffith had begun to foreground his cuts (in the sense used by the Prague School of literary critics[1]) at the moment of greatest narrative intensity within the shot. In this way the cut was emphasized and attention called to it as technique. To cut on the greatest narrative intensity within the shot and subsequently to slice back and reorganize the action within that shot became a standard filmic technique in Griffith. In contrast to the scene, the fundamental building block or syntagm of filmic grammar became the shot, and various shots, possibly interrupted could make up a scene. Griffith established a style where the shot and the cut which interrupts action were incorporated into a new style of narrative which created a unity of narration characterized by heightened senses of reality where spectacle and suspense became the common coin of the realm—an esthetic "high" as it were. As later commentators were to remark, "movies were life with the boring parts cut out."

Armed with the technological resources that permitted longer and more sophisticated movies, the early filmmakers, Griffith the leader among them, soon made changes in style based on the esthetics of illusionism. The course of story films changed quickly. Film rapidly moved from a style based on special optical effects (where the camera man was supreme) to a photographic record of legitimate theater, to an emotionally heightened superrealism where the auteur/director reigned supreme. The esthetics and ideology of this change are well indexed in the motion picture column begun in 1909 in a trade journal known as *The New York Dramatic Mirror.* Writing under the pseudonym "The Spectator," Frank Woods stated the ideal, later identified as that of a transparent fiction with an appearance of reality that was so strong that it effaced the awareness on the part of a viewer of the actual production of the illusion. This caused Woods to object to the early practice, so common in the films of Porter, Méliès, and Zecca, of film actors acknowledging the camera.

> Should there not be absolute unconsciousness that the camera is there—or rather, should there not appear to be this unconsciousness? It is of course admitted that the director and players must at no time really forget the camera. All action must take place in such a manner that the camera take in the best possible view of the picture, but is it not true that the nearer the players can come to making it appear that they are unaware of the camera, the nearer to absolute realism they will attain? As has been previously explained in this column, motion picture pantomime gains its greatest effectiveness by creating the illusion that it is picturing actual and not fictitious events. (*The New York Dramatic Mirror,* July 10, 1909, pp. 15-16)

Woods was convinced that the unique power of the cinema lay in its singular illusion of reality. This illusion gave cinema a "strange" psychological power over its audience:

> . . . the strange power of attraction possessed by motion pictures lies in the semblance of reality which the pictures convey; that by means of this impression of reality the motion picture exerts on the minds of the spectators an influence akin to hypnotism or magnetism by visual suggestion; that this sort of limited hypnotic influence is capable of more powerful exertion through the medium of motion pictures than is possible in any sort of stage production or in printed fact or fiction, and that it is therefore the part of wisdom to cultivate absolute realism in every department of the motion picture art. Artificial drama and artificial comedy appear to have no attraction for the public mind when displayed in motion pictures, no matter how satisfac-

tory they may be on the stage or in printed literature. (*The New York Dramatic Mirror,* May 14, 1910, p. 18)

The philosophy of illusionism matched well with the ever-increasing sophistication of film production, and one of the results of this convergence between technology and esthetics in American film was the cultivation of ever more elaborate, longer, more complex and ambitious, prestige films. These films also met the need of the industry to gain respectability among the dominant classes of American society.

As the films increased in length, they developed from single reel products to multi-reel films, and in this distinction was born the concept of the feature film.[2] Generally, feature films were longer, but also, as a function of more money and resources being put into them, they were more complex and ambitious. As Bowser (1990, 191) puts it: "When the 'feature film' was first marketed, it meant a special film, a film with something that could be featured in advertising as something out of the ordinary run. It was not just another sausage."

The most ambitious films were even further hyped as "special" features or "big" features. Many of the more ambitious films were fundamentally involved in the depiction of nonwhite races, ethnicities, or cultures. We have referred earlier to the 1915 release of D. W. Griffith's twelve-reel, three-hour epic, *The Birth of a Nation* which, although it was a highly controversial film that was protested in the United States and Canada, was also emblematic of both the technical and technological capabilities of American film and its striving to realize complex, ambitious narratives. Griffith's epic evoked the country's development from the Civil War, its "birth," as a function of the behaviors of various social types: tender and sensitive Southern whites, vain white Northern liberals, vicious or brutal blacks, merciless Northern soldiers, heroic Ku Klux Klansmen, and evil mulattoes, the result of what for Griffith was the deplorable mixing of the races.

The Birth of a Nation did not emerge out of a vacuum. Numerous prestige films, including spectacle films and epics or material taken from Biblical or classical sources preceded it. These films fulfilled the function of gaining acceptability among the upper classes of American society by producing very elaborate productions, putting previously unheard of resources into their films, charging much higher prices, screening the films at the emerging movie palaces (and often, later producing one- or two-reel versions for nickelodeon screenings), establishing the beginnings of a glamorous star system, and dazzling viewers with exciting and often extravagant publicity. Not surprisingly many of these films used nonwhite individuals as the foils or the villains. This was a safe procedure: lambasting a black, Hispanic, Oriental, or Indian was hardly going to cause a ripple. Other examples of these prestige films were also set in other cultures, such as the *Carmen* films or the American Indian films, or in antiquity, as in the case of many spectacle films, trading on the exotic or romantic qualities of nonwhite, non-European culture. However, it should be noted that the super movies of the period, a handful of transcendent films, did tend also to transcend the negative conventions and stereotypes that governed the somewhat less ambitious feature films. Movies such as *Hiawatha, The Indian Wars, The Life of General Villa,* and to a more limited extent the versions of *Carmen* were a cut above, in part due to their unique natures, including the care with which they were crafted. These films tended to bring in members of the other culture or race into the production, usually as extras. The two American-Indian films mentioned above incorporated Indians into the cast, and it would have been incongruous to have produced a conventionally stereotypical *Villa* inasmuch as the caudillo himself was brought into the venture. On the other hand, *The Birth of a Nation* and *In the Land of the Headhunters* were among the most notorious transgressors in this period from the point of view of their denigrating stereotypes. A description of the most prestigious films up until and including the *Carmen* films of 1915 follows. This review concentrates on films primarily of interest for their depiction of nonwhite individuals and to a lesser extent of white women and is focused not on the analysis of the portrayal of race and ethnicity at this point (which is done in the following chapter), but rather on the increasing sophistication and ambition of feature films.

The enthusiasm—indeed, frenzy—for high-cost, ambitious filmmaking had set in, and each of the filmmakers and their backers began to ratchet each other up. Each successive prestige film seemed to establish for itself the goal of setting a new standard along one or more dimensions: cost, length, elaborateness, uniqueness, co-optation of public figures, location of premiere, and so on. In 1912, Helen Gardner Picture Players released a six-reel version of *Cleopatra* (director Charles L. Gaskill); Fox was to release a mammoth twelve-reel *Cleopatra* in 1917 (director J. Gordon Edwards), which equaled the number of reels of *The Birth of a Nation.* The Gardner *Cleopatra* effectively supplemented the traditional distribution system in that it was shown as a special attraction "in the local opera houses and town halls and legitimate theaters at advanced prices and stayed for as long as there was enough business to support them" (Bowser, 1990, 192).

The American industry began to feel quite a bit of competition from Europe with respect to spectacle films. Italy in particular made impressive marketing inroads in the United States with *The Fall of Troy* (1911), *Quo Vadis* (1913), *The Last Days of Pompeii* (1913), and *Othello* (1913). American filmmakers responded with *Judith of Bethulia* (1914, Biograph), *The Hypocrites* (1914, Bosworth, Inc., director Lois Weber), and others.

In 1913, *Hiawatha: The Indian Passion Play* appeared (Frank E. Moore, 4 reels), featuring a cast of 150 American Indians from New York, Canada, and the Dakotas; it was filmed near Lake Superior in New York. *A Princess of Bagdad* (1913, Helen Gardner Picture Players) was a six-reel story adapted from the *Arabian Nights.* Perhaps the success story of the year was *Traffic in Souls* (1913, Independent Moving Picture Co., director George Loane Tucker, 6-7 reels). Laemmle's company invested less than $6,000 to make this film which grossed almost $500,000, touching off a wave of white-slave products. The film featured a team consisting of Mary Barton and her policeman boyfriend who foiled a white-slave ring and saved Mary's captive sister. The film promoted itself very effectively by claiming that it was based on the Rockefeller White Slavery Report, then being conducted by John D. Rockefeller, Jr., who denied the relationship and strongly protested it.

In 1914, *The Call of the North* (Lasky, directors Oscar Apfel and Cecil B. DeMille, 5 reels) was released. It had been filmed on location in Great Bear Valley, California, and Moose Factory, Canada. The film was primarily about whites falsely accusing each other, with Indians administering a cruel punishment in the form of a "Long Journey" in the wilderness. *Uncle Tom's Cabin* (1914, World Producing Corporation, director William Robert Daly, 5 reels) was notable for the fact that it was the first "white" film in which a black actor was the star. Sam Lucas, a 72-year-old actor, recreated his role from the Broadway production of the novel. (Two versions of the novel had already been done in 1903 and two in 1910.) Also in 1914, Selig Polyscope weighed in with *Your Girl and Mine: A Woman Suffrage Play* (director Giles Warren, 7-8 reels), which was sponsored by Mrs. Medill McCormick with the proceeds from the film intended for the National Woman Suffrage Association, the film's cosponsor. *Moving Picture World* called this film "the *Uncle Tom's Cabin* of the Suffragette Movement." *In the Land of the Head Hunters* (1914, Seattle Film Co., director Edward S. Curtis, 4 reels) was an absurd tale about sorcery-practicing, head-hunting Indians of British Columbia and southern Alaska. The film cost an extraordinary $75,000 to make and was produced under the sponsorship of (the late) J. Pierpont Morgan. *Judith of Bethulia* (1914, Biograph, 4 reels) on an Old Testament topic taking place during the time of Nebuchadnezzar was D. W. Griffith's first multireel directorial work. It cost a reported lofty $36,000 dollars. *The Life of General Villa* (1914, Mutual Film Corp., director W. Christy Cabanne, 7 reels), a dramatization of the early life of General Pancho Villa, boasted, according to contemporary reviews, the participation of Villa himself, although to what extent is not clear. Certainly this was a first for the film industry. The leader of the *dorados,* the Army of the North, controlled more than half of Mexico at the time and the advertising campaign that Mutual undertook to promote the film was extensive. Probably the most elaborate film of the year, however, was *The Indian Wars* (1914, Col. Wm. F. Cody Historical Picture Co.; Essanay, directors, Theodore Wharton and Vernon Day). The film, which recreated key battles between the U.S. Cavalry and the Sioux boasted the cooperation of the Department of the Interior and the participation of over 1,000 Sioux Indians. Unfortunately, the film also ran into trouble because it was too sympathetic to Indians.

> The production, which boasted over 30,000 feet of film shot from the Bad Lands of South Dakota to the Black Hills of Wyoming, was plagued by blizzards and increasing costs and later required over six months of editing. On 27 Feb 1914, the finished film was screened for Secretary Lane [Interior] and other members of Woodrow Wilson's cabinet. The film was released theatrically in Aug 1914, but according to modern sources played only in Denver and New York because of pressure from government forces, which disapproved of its content because it showed the Indians in a somewhat favorable light. (Hanson, 1988, 452)

In 1915, *The Birth of a Nation* was released with ticket prices reaching the unheard of level of $2.00. The film was boosted by the fact that it was privately screened at the White House for President Wilson and members of his cabinet and staff and their families; Wilson was in turn soundly criticized for sanctioning the film by the many protesters of its racism. The same year also marked the debut of three separate film adaptations of *Carmen,* the Prosper Mérimée novel originally written in 1845. One of these films, starring Charlie Chaplin who also directed, was a parody of the other two. The two major productions, however, that competed for box office and for prestige were the Fox production with Raoul Walsh directing and the Lasky-Paramount production directed by Cecil B. DeMille. Both films were highly successful commercially. The Walsh and the DeMille films were also notable for the elaborateness (in some ways publicly inflated) of their productions and the amount of publicity they achieved. DeMille had previously directed *The Squaw Man* (1914)[3] for the Lasky Feature Play Company (which would grow into Paramount), a spectacular six-reel tale of "tragic" miscegenation between a white male and an Indian maiden and another example of a critically and commercially successful prestige film that was also premised on the depiction of race. The new DeMille film, *Carmen* had its premiere at the Boston Symphony Hall, the first time that a motion picture was exhibited at this site. It also was the vehicle for the debut of Cuban actor Pedro de Córdoba (in the role of the bullfighter and other love interest, Escamillo), who went on to act in many notable films, including *Rose of the Rancho* (version of 1936), *Ramona* (1936), *Juárez* (1939), and *For Whom the Bell Tolls* (1943). *Carmen* reached new heights from the point of view of spectacle and technological complexity:

> For the bullfight scene, an arena was built in Los Angeles under the supervision of the Los Angeles municipal building and amusement bureaus. Matadors from Mexico were used in these scenes, which were photographed by ten cameramen, according to a news item. Many celebrities, including a number of Paramount stars, appeared in the stands. The shooting was done with the cooperation of the Society for the Prevention of Cruelty to Animals. (Hanson, 1988, 126)

In turn, the Walsh version had its premiere at the Academy of Music in New York City. It was not to be outdone as a vehicle for impressing the upper classes. In particular the construction of the sets involved extraordinary efforts.

> The film was printed and colored by the Standard Filmprint Corp. Spanish artist Edward Velásquez was brought from Seville to supervise the technical and architectural details of the sets for the Spanish cities built for the film. Colonel Antonio Bravo of the Spanish army drilled the actors playing dragoons. According to a news item, a band of real Gypsies and an Andalusian bull from Madrid appeared in the film. Raoul Walsh, in his autobiography, wrote that the bull came from Teaneck, NJ, that newsreel footage of bullfights was used, that the actor playing the toreador was trained by a real matador named Valverde,and that he got the idea to make the film after he read about the planned DeMille film of *Carmen,* which Walsh hoped his film could beat to the theaters. (Hanson, 1988, 126)

In 1915, subsequent to the release of *The Birth of a Nation,* Griffith and his production people turned once again to "birthing," in this case, Texas, via *The Martyrs of the Alamo, or the Birth of Texas* (Fine Arts Film Co., supervisor D. W. Griffith, director W. Christy Cabanne, 5 reels). This film was in the mold of *The Birth of a Nation,* essentially developing the Battle of the Alamo and the subsequent "birth" of the Republic of Texas as a reflection of Mexican officers hassling white women and arousing their men to rebellion.

The two versions of *Carmen, The Birth of a Nation, The Martyrs of the Alamo, or the Birth of Texas, Hiawatha, The Squaw Man,* and others, all spectacularly ambitious and all fundamentally based on the depiction of nonwhite races or ethnicities were not exceptions during the period. There were many other, run-of-the-mill films that exploited the same domain.

The Nickelodeon Revolution and Its Aftermath and the Strivings for Respectability

The first decade of the twentieth century witnessed two parallel phenomena, both of which, although different, converged and reinforced each other with respect to the American cinematic manner of racial and ethnic depiction. The first, as we have partially reviewed in our analysis of the increasing sophistication of films and their philosophic goal of illusionism, was the concerted effort on the part of the industry to achieve acceptance and respectability for films among the middle class. As we shall see, this trend was further reinforced by the actions of the Motion Pictures Patent

Corporation, by self-censorship on the part of the film industry, and by practices such as "happy endings" that ultimately would become part of the Hollywood formula and ultimately Hollywood law in 1934 with the introduction of the Production Code. The second was the egalitarianism across social class, gender, and generational lines that was fostered by the physical settings of the movies, particularly the nickelodeon.

As we have observed, cinema rapidly spread around the nation after its commercial inception in 1896. Its expansion came first by means of traveling motion-picture showmen, then quickly through the establishment of nickelodeons, makeshift motion picture theaters, often converted stores, which proliferated all over the nation in the first decade of the century. They were called nickelodeons because they charged a nickel for admission and they were particularly popular in working-class areas of the major cities. At the same time, the beginning of the latter part of the first decade witnessed the building of the first "movie palaces," first along classical lines in order to emphasize balance, and order, in short, respectability. Not until the nickelodeon had been supplanted that the exotic or romantic movie palaces were built. For a period of 10 to 15 years there was considerable overlap among the different varieties of film showing: traveling showmen, nickelodeons, movie palaces, specialized theaters at amusement parks, and other formats such as screenings as part of a vaudeville show or sporadic renting of halls, saloons, churches, museums, theaters, town halls, opera houses, and so on. Nevertheless, the trend was toward upscaling the physical setting where films were projected, and this was the result of a conscious economic policy of attempting to raise the social respectability of films and consequently to attract a middle class audience.

The traveling film show waned of its own accord. The basic struggle was between the nickelodeon and the upscale movie theater, what was to become the movie palace. The cultural elite rejected the nickelodeon for a variety of reasons: they were frequented by the working classes and not by who during the period were termed the "better class of people"; they were sometimes filthy, unsanitary, fire-prone and health hazards; and they fostered values and behaviors both at the physical site and on the screen that were unsanctioned by the dominant society, even subversive or outright confrontational.

Nevertheless, the nickelodeon had a major, radical effect on audience mores and behaviors. The nickelodeons catered to immigrants, at least to white ones, and they also fundamentally and permanently gave white women and even children freedom from the kinds of strictures that characterized precinematic entertainment. The liberating effects on the outcast groups, those beyond the European pale were marginal, since blacks, non-European Hispanics (Mexicans, etc.), Asians, and Native Americans were not particularly welcome in the nickelodeons and were actively excluded from the emerging theaters built expressly for screening films. In fact, the establishment of movie palaces was another venue for racial segregation in America. For example, in 1912, the *New York Daily Mirror* reported that in Denver, a group of African Americans "resenting the treatment accorded them at some of the moving picture houses" opened their own theater under the management of one of their own, "a social leader among the negroes." (January 24, 1912, 40). The racial discrimination of the time, in both the North and the South, promoted the establishment of movie theaters owned by and catering to blacks. By 1913, according to the head of the black-owned Foster

Photoplay Company of Chicago, 214 such black theaters had been established by his company. (Bowser, 1990, 10).

In their heyday, however, the nickelodeons effected a liberation for the lower classes and for white women that could not be overturned, even after the establishments themselves had passed into history. While going to the theater or to vaudeville took an entire evening and cost from ten to twenty-five cents, working-class people could slip into the nickelodeons that were everywhere around the city and see a show that lasted from ten minutes to an hour during lunch, on the way home from work, or in the evening. While scaled admission fees gave access to vaudeville and melodrama to the working class, they also segregated the classes by ticket price.

> The single price at nickelodeons not only gave the working class ready access to the theater but, once they were inside, annihilated class distinctions on that class's terms. Those who had known only the gallery suddenly sat in the orchestra. Such economic democracy had social and political implications that the custodians of conservative middle-class values found unsettling. (Musser, 1990, 432)

Members of the upper economic strata or the cultural elite did not generally go to nickelodeons, at least in the large cities. In the smaller towns there was a more egalitarian and generalized attendance pattern from a social class perspective. In the cities, during the nickelodeon period the "better" classes saw films by attending illustrated lectures or going to vaudeville performances, but not to storefront movie theaters. However, the nickelodeons spread so widely and so quickly that when people thought of what were now being called the "movies," they associated them with the nickelodeons. The elite became more and more disturbed with this new phenomenon that had spread throughout America and which, in contrast to other forms of entertainment, was beyond their control.

> Outside of the large cities, theaters had traditionally been built and controlled by local elites. Now they were started by an ex-saloon keeper, the owner of a dry-goods store, a furrier, a car dealer, or someone who had recently left the carnival. Nickelodeon managers were often immigrants, often Jewish, and often from out of town. Established community leaders didn't know what to think about the change except to know that they did not control it. Some thought it should be abolished, others were more laissez-faire. A few embraced it, but many thought it needed to be reformed. Film fires proved they were dangerous, but there was even more concern with the way the collective though intimate experience of the screen could change— and from a certain viewpoint corrupt—the consciousness of its devotees. (Musser, 1990, 447)

The media under the control of the dominant culture, including newspapers, trade journals, and the like, soon editorialized negatively about the nickelodeons, which were typically the object of condescension, disdain, or alarm. The campaign against them was so strong that

> one might believe from the trade periodicals serving the motion picture industry that nickelodeons began to disappear about 1909-1910 in favor of movie palaces and that blue-collar crowds were being replaced by refined upper-class bejeweled audiences arriving at the theater in automobiles, while the films to be seen were all educational, high-class, and respectable. It was the task of the trade periodicals to promote this concept of improvement. (Bowser, 1990, 121)

In fact, the nickelodeons, while beginning to wane in 1910 were still a major factor in American culture. In the urban ghettos, the old-style nickelodeons continued to exist until about the beginning of World War I.

The seating of the nickelodeon not only effaced class distinctions, it offered far greater sexual egalitarianism and participation across the generations than the mass entertainment settings that preceded it. An extraordinary liberation of women was achieved through the medium of cinema. In contrast to Victorian and Edwardian re-strictions on women's activities, the opening of movie theaters around the country and the mass attendance on the part of both males and females, either singly or as couples (married or unmarried), represented a new form of freedom for American women. Peiss's research (1986, 152) concludes that immigrant parents permitted their daugh-ters to attend the picture shows more than any other form of entertainment or amusement, and that the price was low enough that working women, even with their lower wages, could afford admission. The flexibility because of continuous showing and the length of the nickelodeon programs also permitted married women to find time from their household responsibilities to attend. The nickelodeons themselves en-couraged the notion of the flickers being especially suitable for "ladies and children." Similarly, the nickelodeon became a haven for the elderly and for children. In some towns, such as Dallas, women and children provided the box office base before men. At some of the nickelodeons "the emphasis was not only on women patrons but on cultivating mixed-sex patterns of social interaction" (Musser, 1990, 432). A review of the promotional activities in Lewiston, Pennsylvania, in 1907 is revealing:

> Promotional material for Keith's Lewiston house emphasized that "Everything is clean and neat, the attendants are polite and the best of order is maintained, and the ladies and children can enjoy the pictures in comfort and peace." At the rival Bijou, the manager was soon dispensing Teddy Bear souvenirs to female patrons, in ac-knowledgment of women's increasingly important role as consumers. When a third Lewiston theater opened in June, it announced that "baby carriages will be taken care of while parents are seeing the show." (Musser, 1990, 432)

The Lewiston theaters encouraged parents to send their children after school and unaccompanied children were placed in the balcony so they would not disturb the adults. However, critics soon found this easy access for children and unaccompanied young women deeply disturbing and railed against these practices.

Another important feature that helped moviegoing to be a frequent and casual ac-tivity was the fact that the nickelodeons frequently changed their offerings.

> While new programs were being offered twice a week in July 1905, three changes a week were becoming common by November 1906. By May 1907, nickelodeons were beginning to change programs every day but Sunday. The cinema was rapidly becom-ing a site of mass entertainment and mass consumption. Although this process was not complete, the lateral expansion of motion-picture houses across the country and the vertical increase of program change caused a tremendous demand for films. (Musser, 1990, 433)

The radical departure from accepted norms is well indexed by the outpouring of concerns by conservative opinion makers of the period (clergy and religious groups, social critics, etc.) They feared the consequences of women's attendance in "darkened" environments where single men, including "mashers" abounded. They even suggested that white-slave traders preyed on single women who went into the nickelodeons.

Moreover, not only was the environment of the movie theaters either morally provocative, or liberating, depending on your viewpoint, the content of the films themselves were quickly mobilized to acutely interact with that environment. Film audiences could enter the darkened movie theater and privately and with little of the normative social controls of the nonfilmic environments experience a wide range of events and actions related to sex, violence, the suffrage movement and other feminist causes, and other behaviors with an intensity not available in any other medium.

The acceptance of white women en masse at the nickelodeons and other screening places was especially significant in the determination of the films themselves as well as the structuring of the industry. A series of films, including *The Monogrammed Cigarette* (1910, Yankee) and *The Woman Who Dared* (1911, Yankee), featured bold white female detectives who often used scientific apparatuses like dictographs for eavesdropping rather than brawn in their sleuth work. Similarly, women-centered films included *Daisies* (1910, Vitagraph), which depicted a heroine who insisted on a college education over the objections of her fiancé; *Votes for Women* (1912, Reliance) and *How They Got the Vote* (1913, Edison), which expressed support of the suffrage movement; and *Eighty Million Women Want?* (1913, Unique Film Co., starring Harriet Stanton Blatch, president of the Women's Political Union), which exposed corrupt politics in New York City. With respect to industry participation, women managed movie theaters in significant numbers, "wrote a large proportion of the film scripts, and found it easier to get into directing than [they] would in later periods of film history." (Bowser, 1990, 187). Prominent female writer-directors included Alice Guy, Lois Weber, and Gene Gauntier. At a less-exalted level, a new industry job category was introduced: "script girl," the person responsible for keeping track of the details including the props required for each of the shots.

On the other side of the ledger, filmmakers produced bolder female villains as well. In 1910, Selig produced *The Vampire* and the type caught on. Rosemary Theby portrayed the vamp in *The Reincarnation of Karma* (1912, Vitagraph), and Julia Swayne Gordon, in *Red and White Roses* (1913, Vitagraph), boldly propositions a married man and reformed candidate for governor as she reclines on a tiger-head rug, smoking. The relevant title card, referring to the man's wife, states: "She is a white rose, pale and colorless—I am a red rose—glowing and made for love." Theda Bara made a career out of vamp roles on the screen and in her publicity persona up until 1919 when the audiences tired of it. She became an overnight sensation as the ruthless vamp in Fox's *A Fool There Was* (1915), based on the Kipling poem, *The Vampire*. Born Theodosia Goodman, the daughter of a Cincinnati tailor, Theda Bara billed herself as a woman of mystic powers, born in the Sahara Desert, the love child of a French artist and his Egyptian mistress. She claimed her name was an anagram of "Arab Death." She did vamp roles in over forty films in a period of about five years, including Carmen, Madame Du Barry, Salome, and Cleopatra, surrounded herself with symbols of death, and received the press while stroking a serpent in a room filled with incense. Her command, "Kiss me, my fool!" taken from a subtitle card of her 1915 film *A Fool There Was* became a popular phrase of the period. Vamps, as we see in the next chapter, were the most common role played by Hispanic women, or by non-Hispanic women in Hispanic roles.

Early filmmakers were motivated to produce some films that depicted the interaction of sex and race and sex and class in a way that was either flattering to women or which appealed to the prurience both of men and women, not just men exclusively. In

other words, filmmakers were motivated from the start to produce films that appealed
to both sexes, as they are today, in order to expand box office potential. So they produced films that were popular with everyone but were especially appealing to women,
for whom going to the movies represented, apart from the content of the film itself, an
emancipation from traditional strictures. To go to the movies and then see women in
situations profoundly provocative for the historical moment and for the sensibilities of
the time, genuinely led to a degree of addiction to the experience. Filmmakers such as
Griffith were master purveyors of shared fantasies in the dark pitched at a level that
shook the consumer but did not go too far as to induce an emotional or intellectual
aftertaste. Clients could enter the darkened movie theater and privately and without
remorse experience forbidden thoughts of rape, ravishment, interracial sex, or on the
other hand, aggressive and effective behavior by women in nontraditional roles. At the
end of the film, when the lights came on, one could go merrily one's way without giving
the film content a worry. Besides, rarely did one actually get raped or ravished (there
were exceptions) in these films. Films featured the close call and the close encounter
and the salvation of the maiden by the white hero so that in the end, everything was
right and social decorum and the social order were tested but ultimately maintained.

The interaction effects between the actual physical attendance of women at the
movie theater and the content of the films themselves, which were increasingly cus-
tomized in order to cater to white women, has not been intensively or systematically re-
searched, although Musser has recognized the phenomenon. Musser points out that a
number of films produced during the nickelodeon era "show women assuming active
roles often associated with masculine behavior" (1990, 478).[4] These films included *The
Tomboys* (1906, Selig) where young girls behaved like the bad-boys of that genre. *The
Female Highwayman* (1906, Selig) depicted a woman with criminal daring and nerve, and
The Girl from Montana (1907, Selig) featured a woman who "saves her lover from death
and several times keeps angry mobs at bay with her revolver" (478). Concerning the
Western, Musser suggests that in these films the codes of "civilized" or traditional conduct were not fully established so that both men and women were free to assume nontraditional roles and women were provided a place where they "might forge new, more
active identities" (47).

Even less recognized has been the effect of this catering to white women on the depiction of ethnic out-groups, including Hispanics, blacks, American Indians, and
Asians. An initial review of this phenomenon, which needs to be further analyzed in
subsequent research follows.

Essentially the effect of large numbers of women in attendance at the nickelodeons
led to an expansion of white women characters on the screen, including a number who
were successful in unfamiliar roles and who imposed themselves over their enemies.
Naturally, film as well as all story forms depend on conflict. The foils against which the
early film white heroines imposed themselves were usually ethnic out-groups including
blacks, Indians, Mexicans, and Asians, but also white foreigners. On the other hand,
we occasionally see films where white women collaborate with minorities as well, either
to vanquish yet other minorities (e.g., a white female and and Indian female against
another Indian and a Mexican) or to confront a white male.

White Females Versus Ethnic Out-groups

The Fatal Hour (1908, director D. W. Griffith, Biograph) is famous for its technical innovation inasmuch as it is one of the first films that made extensive and highly effective use of parallel editing, what Griffith called "alternate scenes." However, while this element generally goes unanalyzed, its depiction of gender and ethnicity is also highly significant. The film has a transitional, mixed quality, combining an unusual female character with certain more traditional behaviors on the part of that same woman. In the film a white, female detective foils Pong Lee, who is described in the *Biograph Bulletin* advertising[5] as "a Mephistophelian saffron-skinned varlet" who has carried on an "atrocious female white slave traffic." The detective, "possessed of shrewd powers of deduction . . . exercises her natural acumen with success." However, her technique is of the stereotypical kind, she flirts with one of Pong's lieutenants and dopes his drink. Moreover, later she is captured and tied to a post. A large pistol is placed on the face of a clock in such a way that when the hands point to twelve the gun is fired and the girl will receive the charge. Certain death seems to be her fate except that her plight is found out and a wild ride is made to the house where she is incarcerated. "This incident is shown in alternate scenes. There is the helpless girl, with the clock ticking its way towards her destruction, and out on the road is the carriage, tearing along at breakneck speed to the rescue, arriving just in time to get her safely out of range of the pistol as it goes off." Thus, on the one hand the film displays an effective female detective who saves other white women and is sometimes able to get the best of the saffron-skinned villains. But *The Fatal Hour* also is a film of traditional content. The detective uses her wiles. Moreover, ultimately she is captured and put in a titillating situation and has to be saved in the nick of time by men.

Other films were more radical. *The Arizona Cat Claw* (1919, World Film Corp., director William Bertram) depicts Blossom Ruggles, the fiercely independent daughter of an Arizona cattleman and "one tough woman" who is accosted by a Mexican bandit while she is riding alone on the range. She overpowers him and delivers him to a neighboring rancher and his cowboys. Naturally they do the "right thing." They throw the bandit off a cliff. The bandit incident is the subplot of this film. The main plot involves Blossom's travails leading her to marry the rancher. The film's depiction of the white woman is not entirely untraditional, there are precedents in the "tomboy" or Amazon tradition of portraying women as well as the convention of "pioneers" as a hardy, indomitable group.

In the North Woods (1912, Biograph) features a trapper's wife who is "made of stouter stuff than the ordinary female of the species" and who foils the plot by an "adventurous Frenchman" to get her bag of money and makes him "suffer for his attempted villainy."

Ethnic Women Who Turn Out to Be White

Another type of unusual plot situation of the period revolves around white women who are initially thought to be of a different race. The convention of an individual from a surprising background is not unique to early cinema; it appears in classical and renaissance literature (a Greek thought to be of barbarian background, etc.). But the visual power of these films, the races and ethnicities that are selected, and the appeal to mass consumers of these stories, greatly distinguish the film versions from those of, say, the novel. It would appear that part of the pleasure these films provided, particularly to white women, derived from their experiencing women as racial or ethnic others, particularly in interracial love situations (with white males). The trick endings where it is "learned" that the other is actually a white woman after all, provides a certain relief and attenuates the subversion of the social order. White women can pruriently empathize with the passions of other women and experience little psychological dissonance since at the end, it's "all right" because those other women are ultimately found to be white. *At the Cross Roads* (1914, Select Photo Play Producing Company, director Frank L. Dear) features an aggressive slave woman, thought to be black, who eventually kills the white man who has abused her sexually and turned her into his maid. Her extreme behavior is justified at the end of the film when it is realized during her trial that she is actually a white woman of Spanish heritage. Similarly, *The Barrier* (1917, Rex Beach Pictures Co., director Edgar Lewis) features another strong woman, a supposed Alaskan half-breed who is able to win her man in marriage when it is learned that she is actually a white woman. *Wild Sumac* (1917, Triangle Film Corp., director William V. Mong) shows how a French Canadian falls in love with the daughter of a repulsive, half-breed crook. After numerous false arrests, fights with the Mounted Police and trappers, he learns that the daughter is not really the odious half-breed's natural offspring but is of pure European stock. Now he can love her in good stead and she can even keep her wonderfully exotic name, Wild Sumac.

White Women Collaborating With Nonwhite Women and/or Men

An interesting example of a white woman who helps an Indian woman appears in *The Red Girl* (1908, Biograph). The advertising copy states, "The Biograph Company, pursuant of its policy of studying the public's taste, produced some weeks ago, *The Redman and the Child*, a story of Western life among the Indians, and *The Greaser's Gauntlet,* a tale of the Mexican border. The unprecedented success of those two subjects induced us to present another, which in locale may be said to combine the elements of both those pictures, the resultant being the production of the most thrilling and soul-stirring film ever made." In this action-packed thriller, an American Indian woman and a white "girl miner," Kate Nelson, boldly and courageously foil a "Mexican Jezebel" and her American Indian half-breed partner.

In *Unprotected* (1916, Lasky, director James Young), a white Southern woman defends herself from her uncle who she kills. She is convicted of murder and sent to a turpentine plant where black prisoners are contracted out by the state and work under harsh conditions. She plots a mutiny with the other prisoners, one of whom sacrifices himself for her in a confrontation with the head of the plant. The prisoners mutiny and kill the plant head and the woman eventually convinces the governor to have the working conditions at the plant improved.

Even as the physical place where films were screened changed over from the nickelodeons to the movie palaces, which promoted more social acceptability, the industry itself engaged in a concerted effort to gain acceptance by the dominant classes in other ways. In 1908, the industry established the Motion Picture Patents Company (MPPC) with the goals of securing a controlling monopoly of film distribution and achieving acceptance of the flickers by the middle class. The MPPC brought to the film industry the kind of organization that had been dominating American business since before the turn of the century. Industry had moved away from a system of competition between rival firms toward a variety of pooling agreements and "trusts" that would limit competition. Through control of film project patents and distribution, the MPPC sought to stabilize the industry and also to "uplift" the motion pictures, improving their content. The MPPC eventually went out of business because of its unfair business practices as a result of a lawsuit that it lost in 1917, but not before accomplishing exceedingly well its goal of uplifting and mainstreaming cinema. The MPPC engaged in the censorship of film content in order to "improve" it and therefore attract a "better class" of audience. By preempting censorship, the film industry kept production out of the hands of the police and clergy who might deal more harshly with the films than the producers wanted. Of course, there was a subversive element in the industry's establishing and controlling censorship, since box office sales were the preeminent consideration and the goal was to make films that still catered to the working class even as they attracted the middle class. As we have seen, in order to woo the middle class, filmmakers began to produce films with more complicated narrative plots and characterization. They also censored certain kinds of scenes that had appeared earlier, such as lynchings and burnings at the stake, and strove to produce films with "educational" or "instructive" values or a "moral lesson," and films with happy endings. As an editorial in *Nickelodeon* stated: "We are living in a happy, beautiful, virile age. . . . we do not want sighs or tears. . . . We are all seeking happiness—whether through money or position or imagination. It is our privilege to resent any attempt to force unhappy thoughts on us" (Gunning, 1981, 15). Once again, as in the case of adding sophistication to plot and characterization, these moral lessons or educational initiatives lent themselves to the creation of racial antagonists (Mexicans, blacks, Indians, Orientals, Gypsies, etc.) whose defeat could be the basis of a moral lesson for both the character on-screen and the audience, and for happy endings evoking the moral and physical superiority of Anglos over the degenerate or primitive out-races.

An additional factor that determined the manner of American portrayals of race and ethnicity as well as the selection of the minority groups to be portrayed, was the production of vast numbers of Westerns and Indian films by the American film industry. The reasons for the Westerns were several. Primary, of course was that the Wild West was still an active ingredient of American life in some places, and in vast stretches of territory, only recently tamed and therefore a perfect topic for nostalgic embellishment. Despite the complaints of the film industry critics and even the aspirations of the industry itself, consumers demanded these films (Bowser, 1990, 169). Second, enormous resources were available for filmic adaptation in the form of dime novels, pulp magazine stories, and other sources, many using Mexicans or Indians as foils to Anglo heroes and heroines. Besides, the Wild West had been a show phenomenon already for years, in the form of demonstrations and entertainments by individuals like Buffalo Bill Cody, the producer of the ill-fated *The Indian Wars*.

Another important factor was economic competition at the international level. The United States film industry found a ready international market for Westerns, since there was a great demand for them in Europe as well. This genre became proprietary to the American film industry, which didn't experience the same sort of competition with European films in its marketing of other genres such as comedies, spectacle films, religious subjects, magical or special effect films, detective films, Gothic and horror, or cops and robbers. Westerns, Indian films, and Civil War films by and large did not have to compete with the film industries of other nations, although some foreigners such as Méliès came to the United States and produced Westerns on American soil.

In the early years, Indian films constituted a separate genre. Although they shared some elements in common with the Westerns, they were sufficiently different in their themes, prospective audience, and settings. Indians appeared in abundance in Westerns, usually as marauding villains or other negative roles. However, in the Indian films themselves they had a much wider range of behaviors, often emphasizing their "nobility." For example, the Biograph advertising for Griffith's *The Redman and the Child* (1908, Biograph) is a turgid paean to the noble savage.

> Alongside of a beautiful mountain stream in the foothills of Colorado there camped a Sioux Indian, who besides being a magnificent type of the aboriginal American, is a most noble creature, as kind-hearted as a woman and as brave as a lion. . . . What a magnificent picture he strikes as he stands there, his tawny skin silhouetted against the sky, with muscles turgid and jaws set in grim determination. It is but for a moment he stands thus, yet the pose speaks volumes. Turning quickly he leaps into a canoe at the bank and paddles swiftly after the fugitives. (Bowser, ed., *Biograph Bulletins,* No. 156, 5)

One should not make too much of the noble savage element, however, in the Indian films, which were capable of the most harsh stereotypes conceivable. In D. W. Griffith's *The Battle at Elderbush Gulch* (1913, Biograph), a great tragedy is caused by improper segregation of the races. Two dogs run away from white girls "into the arms of two Indians, who having returned late to their camp, have missed a great dog feast." When the girls attempt to rescue their pets a series of incidents are triggered that lead to the Indians' slaughter of most of the white inhabitants of Elderbush Gulch.

Bowser points out that the Indian films of this period

> could be made in the eastern or southern part of the United States, as well as in the Far West, without departing from authenticity. The attractions of Indian films included the beautiful landscapes and free movements of Western films plus elements of exoticism, nobility, and romance. There was also the allure of nudity (of men only), which had the same respectability as the nakedness of indigenes in travel films from distant lands. (1990, 173)

A filmmaker of the period, Fred Balshofer, head of Bison, observed about one of his actors who portrayed an Indian: he "made a striking appearance on the screen, and the ladies simply went gaga over him. Ohs and ahs came from them whenever he appeared on the screen in one of his naked Indian hero roles, so naturally most of his pictures were on that order" (Balshofer and Miller, 1967, 40).

As a separate genre, the Indian films did not survive long; Indians as characters continued in their role as villains, usually in Westerns, occasionally as faithful allies to whites, particularly in the latter's struggle against Mexicans (the reverse was also true, faithful Mexicans or half-breeds serving whites in their struggle with Indians). "By 1913 the amateur scriptwriting public was informed that Indian scenarios were not wanted by the studios. They were considered to be an exhausted vein, while the Westerns continued to be as strong as ever" (Bowser, 1990, 176).

Richard (1992) documents the great number of Westerns, at least those which featured Hispanics, usually Mexicans. His filmography and review of the Hispanic image in American films, which makes use of innovative sources that include the New York State

Archives in Albany (where over 70,000 film scripts were deposited because of censorship requirements), identifies a total of 1,814 separate films made between 1898 and 1935. Not all of these were Westerns of course. Some of these films were about Spain, Gypsies, bullfighting, Carmen, Don Quixote, the Mexican Revolution, various aspects of Latin America, and so on. Nevertheless, the majority were Westerns.

Attitudes Toward Race and Ethnicity Among the Filmmakers and Their White Audiences

As we have seen earlier, many of the plots of the early films came from existing sources including comic strips, popular fiction, theater and vaudeville, the Bible, classical or highbrow literature, opera, minstrel shows, and other forms of entertainment. The prevailing attitudes of American society that infused these formats predating cinema generally were transferred to the cinematic format, with certain exceptions, particularly involving attitudes and behaviors related to the lower classes and to white women. We have reviewed in some depth the "complex negotiation," in Musser's words, between the values of films and the white immigrant classes and the effect on the development of new plots and characters that was apparently caused by the strong attendance of white women at the movies. With respect to the depiction of nonwhite races and ethnicities, however, there were few adjustments caused by cinema from the prevailing depictions in the cultural media available to society during the period. However, one important adjustment was caused by the burgeoning travel-tourism, exotic, and anthropological films, which developed a more objective view of other cultures within the constraints of films that were primarily romantic, escapist travelogues to foreign lands. Another twist in the depiction of race and ethnicity that films provided, a minor one at that, was attributable to the new depictions of women in more aggressive roles or unfamiliar roles. As a result, white women sporadically collaborated rather than more commonly confronted nonwhites. Finally, a small but significant number of "big features" such as *The Life of General Villa* or *The Indian Wars* made a commitment to accuracy and verisimilitude which to a certain degree overrode stereotype and convention. But most of the movies maintained the prevailing stereotypes.

Moreover, the increasing sophistication of filmmaking technology which at this point had now become capable of longer narrative treatments, the developing philosophy of illusionism, and the international economic pressures to produce Westerns and epics determined that filmmakers, with nowhere else to readily turn and a need to produce films at a prodigious rate, would either turn to the prevailing literature of the day and adapt it into film, or alternatively, hire scriptwriters to produce screenplays closely modeled on that prevailing literature. Before 1908, the primary sources for films were vaudeville and burlesque sketches, fairy tales, comic strips, and popular songs. These forms stressed spectacular effects or physical action, rather than psychological motivation. Now film looked toward more respectable narrative models and the problems that they entailed. With respect to Westerns, a vast literature existed, almost all of it formulaic pulp fiction, that could be either adapted or imitated in kind.

Westerns, as Arthur Pettit observed, are "at least as rigid in their conventions as any medieval morality play" (1980, xv). The genre has a finite number of categories such as the cattle empire, the ranch, the revenge, the cowboys-versus-Indians, the outlaw, the law-and-order, and the conquest story. The depiction of Mexicans and Indians in these stories, and their adaptation to the screen by filmmakers seeking to introduce narrative and psychological complexity into their works as well as woo a new audience, matched the formulas that prevailed in the dime novel and pulp fiction. Pettit, in his review and analysis of hundreds of nineteenth- and twentieth-century popular Western novels distilled the following conclusions about the genre, conclusions which are valid in turn for the story films that emerged in cinema's first decade, and throughout the silent period and beyond. In fact, many of these films were adapted from the very popular Western novels that Pettit analyzed.

> When [the Anglo] set out to bring democracy, progress, and Protestantism to the Hispanic Southwest, he could find a place for the Mexican in what he soon regarded as "his" Southwest only if the Mexican would become, insofar as his limited talents permitted, what the American perceived himself to be: enterprising, steady, and Protestant—in a word, civilized. Yet somehow the Mexican remained something else in the Anglo-American's eye: shiftless, unreliable, and alternately decadent or barbaric. Thus, it seemed to be the American's manifest destiny to conquer and convert this errant race. In the process it was also necessary to destroy a culture the Mexican would not willingly surrender. Operating from such moral absolutes, the Anglo was able to achieve a satisfactory interpretation of his racial and cultural superiority. He could flatter himself that he was not deprecating a race but standing up for civilization. He could persuade himself, in fact, that he was not guilty of racism in any sense that we understand the term. For if the Mexican could be evaluated only in terms of the civilization to which, by the laws of nature, God, and history alike, he had to give way, then how could the conqueror be blamed for what was destined to happen? The Anglo-American thus came to see the indigenous way of life in what became the American Southwest as inherently and irrevocably inferior and hostile to his own institutions. (Pettit, 1980, xvii-xviii)

In short, white Americans believed in the superiority of the white race and depicted this superiority on the silver screen. Every other race was evaluated in relationship to the attainments of the white race and with respect to its approximation to the white race which provided the standard for emulation. A good example of the depiction of this attitude is to be found in *The Martyrs of the Alamo or The Birth of Texas* (director and screenplay, William Christy Cabanne, supervisor, D. W. Griffith). Released on November 21, 1915, less than a year after Griffith's *The Birth of a Nation,* this film reveals important similarities to the latter. For example, not only does *Martyrs* present the Texas independence movement from Mexico as primarily a racial conflict, this film introduces the fear of miscegenation as a major factor in its historical interpretation of the war to free Texas from Mexico. Mexican ethnicity is simply depicted as a debased and depraved group, morally and physically inferior to the Anglo-Saxon, and also, of course, disposed to mongrelizing the Anglo-Saxon by virtue of its untrammeled sexual instincts.

An important corollary to the belief in the superiority of the white race was the belief in the ability of the less civilized races to overcome their inferiority to the degree that they showed commitment, obeisance to and fealty to Anglo-Saxon values, and to the degree they had good, positive Anglo-Saxon role models available to them. *The Savage* (1917, Bluebird Photoplays, director Rupert Julian) provides an example of the elaboration of this attitude on film. Julio Sandoval, a base savage, "a reckless young half-breed ruled by his animal instincts" develops a passion for a white girl. He carries her away to his cabin on a mountain top but collapses from "mountain fever brought on by overexertion." Marie, consoling angel, takes pity on him and nurses him to health. Later, the grateful savage surrenders his own life to save the white fiancé of Marie.

Also notable in this regard are two of the greaser movies of this period. *The Greaser's Gauntlet* and *Tony the Greaser* (both the 1911 and 1914 versions) cultivate the theme of Hispanic redemption through obeisance to the high physical and moral splendor of an Anglo-Saxon beauty. This style of movie, in which D. W. Griffith made a significant contribution, represents the first examples of the Hispanic of low blood but good heart. In fact, D. W. Griffith's *The Greaser's Gauntlet* ends on a note eerily similar to the the famous 1935 production, *Bordertown*, where the protagonist, Johnny Ramírez eschews white society and goes back to his people. In the *Gauntlet*, José, who is first saved by a white woman and then saves her, "makes a solemn resolution, which he immediately fulfills" to leave white society and "to return to his dear old mother in the mountains in whose arms we leave him. . . ." The Mexican obeisant to Anglo-Saxons and their values, as Pettit puts it, has "an unenviable lot, as he is doomed to wander between the longed-for world of the Anglo and the stigmatized world of the Mexican, held forever in a middle position between Saxon heroes and greaser villains. It is the . . . beginning of a pattern to be developed more fully in a later generation of books and films" (1980, 135).

A third aspect of the racial attitudes of the period that had considerable play in the movies was an abhorrence of so called "mongrelization." Half-breeds, such as mulattoes, were among the worst, most deplorable human types. Part and parcel of this attitude was the great fear of miscegenation, which at the same time produced considerable titillation in films. Many of the period films have "fate worse than death" scenes, which typically used some mongrelized character as a would-be rapist. Attempted, but usually unconsummated, interracial rape was a speciality of early film. This sort of primal scene was terrific box office. The fate worse than death element of American cinema became one of the staples that spurred the careers of many actresses, usually blonds whose fairness contrasted beautifully on celluloid with the ominous, darker-hued attempted rapists. *The Birth of a Nation* contains the most famous examples of this element. In Griffith's most famous epic, a special category of villainy was reserved for the mulattoes, the alleged foul fruit of most deplorable mixing of the races.

On the positive side of the ledger appear a few films that suggest a growing interest in and even respect and admiration for other races and cultures in their "pristine state." The relationship between cinema and the development of contemporary anthropology is an engaging and complex one inasmuch as specific films reflect either the earlier evolutionistic cultural anthropology or the emerging culture-centered views. The beginnings of cinema coincide with the development of contemporary cultural anthropology—relativistic, culture-centered, and nonracist. At the same time filmmakers began producing movies in New York, Franz Boas, specialist in the cultures and languages of American Indians, was in the process of developing the fundamental concepts of contemporary cultural anthropology and training a generation of anthropologists that would extend those concepts through their fieldwork.[6]

It appears that most American films such as *Barbarous Mexico* (1913, America's Feature Film Co.) reflected the earlier evolutionary-based anthropology which persisted almost to the end of the nineteenth century, and which conceived of cultural anthropology as considerably devoted to defining the phases and states through which different societies and cultures pass. In this linear interpretation of history some groups of the "human family" were thought to progress more slowly, some faster, as they advanced from the simple to the complex and from the irrational to the rational. The progression was from savagery to barbarism to civilization. In the words of a significant evolutionary anthropologist of the period, Lewis Henry Morgan: "As it is undeniable that portions of the human family have existed in a state of savagery, other portions in a state of barbarism, and still other portions in a state of civilization, it seems equally so that these three distinct conditions are connected with each other in a natural as well as necessary sequence of progress" (*Ancient Society*, 1877). The Mexicans in *Barbarous Mexico* were seen to be way behind civilized America. Mexico, despite being in the midst of its revolution was still a land of siestas and fiestas, although either could be interrupted at any moment by much gunplay.

The influence of anthropology, both in its nineteenth century and developing twentieth century, relativistic, nonracist forms, seem apparent in the American film of the period, albeit indirectly as part of the intellectual milieu. Toward the end of the nineteenth century, the tales of missionaries, traders, and adventurers provided an abundance of lore and information for such works as Sir James Frazer's *Golden Bough* (1890) and Ernest Crawley's *Mystic Rose* (1902). These collections of customs, religious and magical practices, and other curiosities became potential source material for films; the intellectual community read them with much enthusiasm. Evolutionary-minded anthropologists appropriated them as well as data and evidence for their theories that the different groups of the human family progress through an evolutionary sequence of magical, religious, and finally, scientific thought.

In a film like *The Zulu's Heart* (1908, Biograph), savage and savagery seem not to have merely a commonplace, layperson's meaning, but seem tied to nineteenth-century, evolutionary-premised anthropological concepts. In *The Zulu's Heart*, the first shot shows a Zulu chief burying his only daughter who has died of fever. Then, the grief-stricken chief joins his tribe, described as "merciless black brutes," as they make war on the Boers. However, after killing numerous whites, they come upon a young white girl, the same age as the chief's deceased daughter, and through her intercession and the chief's own grief, "the savage becomes compassionate," and returns the daughter to her mother, even at the cost of slaying three of his own tribesman. The film appears to show the transition to white, Christian, compassionate, civilized behavior of a Zulu savage in a fashion consistent with the anthropology of the nineteenth century. A variation on the exemplary influence of white models is the depiction of blacks in the antebellum South being cared for like children by white aristocrats. Here blacks are the beneficiaries of the white man's burden. Given this mind-set of white stewardship over the less-civilized peoples, Griffith, often thought of as extremely prejudiced, was capable of producing films notable for their tenderness toward minorities. For example, in Griffith's *The Greatest Thing in Life* (1918, Famous Players-Lasky Corp.), during World War I a young black soldier offers a white man his last drop of water. Soon afterwards, the black soldier is shot, and as he lies dying and calling for his mother, the white man comforts him and kisses his cheek.

On the other hand, we now witness story films, not unlike the travel-tourism and exotic films of the period, that no matter how flawed and condescending by contemporary standards, do introduce an element of admiration and wonder for other races and cultures, particularly in their "pristine state." In *The Redman and the Child*, the noble savage whom we have earlier described is able to foil and ultimately kill two white men who have tortured a white boy, who has befriended the Indian, and killed the boy's grandfather. In this noble savage modality of movie it is perfectly acceptable for the savage to vanquish white intruders, who themselves are seen to be debased, depraved, or otherwise de-evolved.

We have reviewed and given a few pertinent examples of a number of complex and mostly converging forces and factors that strongly influenced the manner of American cinematic depictions of race, ethnicity, gender and nonwhite cultures for the first decades, and in some cases, even to the present. We are now in a position to review the overall production with respect to the image of Hispanics and the participation of Hispanics in the film industry, with a focus on the types of films that were produced and the types of characters that populated them.

Notes

[1] The Prague School employed their concepts in the analysis of literature, including folklore, but the notion of foregrounding also works well for this aspect of cinema. See: Bohuslav Havránek, "The Functional Differentiation of the Standard Language," in *A Prague School Reader on Esthetics, Literary Structure and Style,* ed. Paul L. Garvin, Washington, D.C.: Georgetown University Press, 1964; and René Wellek and Austin Warren, *Theory of Literature,* 3rd ed., New York: Harcourt Brace and World, 1956, 242-245.

[2] See Eileen Bowser, *The Transformation of Cinema, 1907-1915. History of the American Cinema.* vol. 2. Charles Harpole, gen. editor. New York: Charles Scribner's Sons, 1990, Chapter 12, 217-234 for an explanation of the different measurements of "reels" during the period and a review of "feature films," "special feature films" and similar terms.

[3] *The Squaw Man* was around for a long time. One-act versions of the play were produced as early as 1904. The 1914 version, although not the first film to be made in Hollywood, was the first Hollywood feature-length production. In 1917, Lasky produced a five-reel sequel (director E. J. Le Saint), *The Squaw Man's Son* and in 1918 yet a second version of the popular original picture was produced. In 1931, DeMille made yet another version for M-G-M starring Warner Baxter.

[4] It should also be noted that Musser identifies films which he also suggests were clearly aimed at female spectators that "placed them in a passive position and indulged their most masochistic fantasies" (1990, 482). *Mother's Dream* (1907, Lubin) evokes a mother who dreams of her death and the problems that her orphaned children will experience. Another Lubin film, *When Women Vote* (1907), was clearly not for suffragettes inasmuch as it depicted a sort of nightmare world that women control, putting men in prison for trying to kiss their wives and forcing them to do the housework. Still other films, dedicated ostensibly to the homosocial world of body building and the manly physique, appear to have had unintended erotic effects on female spectators.

[5] In this and following chapters, material describing films that appears in quotation marks and for which there is no citation generally cites the film company's advertising. The most common compendium of such advertising appears in Kemp Niver, ed., *Biograph Bulletins, 1896-1908.* Los Angeles: Locare Research Group, 1971 and Eileen Bowser, ed., *Biograph Bulletins 1908-1912.* New York: Farrar, Straus and Giroux, 1973, which collect the Biograph company trade advertisements for each of their films during the applicable periods.

[6] Franz Boas had a seminal influence on the formation and development of contemporary cultural anthropology. He found British and American anthropology in the latter part of the nineteenth century to have been evolutionary-based, arguing that some peoples have achieved higher states of culture, leaving behind, either permanently or temporarily, other peoples and cultures. This anthropology initially surmised that genetic factors may have been at work, but eventually gave up hard-core social Darwinism in favor of an explanation of the differences between civilized and primitive peoples on the basis of environmental, cultural, and historical circumstances. Boas successfully promoted the view, which has now become overwhelmingly dominant, of cultural relativism. The

cultural relativists argue that the evolutionary view is ethnocentric, deriving from a human disposition to characterize groups other than one's own as inferior, and that all peoples and cultures have evolved equally but in their own, unique ways. Professionally active in the United States between 1886 and 1942, primarily at Columbia University, Boas trained and inspired a number of prominent students including Ruth Benedict, Arthur L. Campa (the Chicano folklorist of New Mexico), Melville J. Herskovits, Alfred L. Kroeber, Margaret Mead, and Edward Sapir.

3

The First Decades: Types of Characters

Since the publication of what at the time was the first book on the U.S. Hispanic image in American film, Keller, ed., (1985, Spanish version, 1988), a considerable amount of primary filmographic research has been conducted and published, which is a fortunate thing because Cortés observes facetiously that

> *only* 21,000 feature films were produced in the United States between 1900 and 1951, and *only* 300-500 have been added each year since then. However, about half of all pre-1950 films have disappeared or been destroyed. That fact combined with the temporal impossibility of seeing all existing films makes reading about unviewed films a necessary but limiting supplement. (1992, 85).

The 1911-1920 volume of feature films of the ongoing series, *The American Film Institute Catalog of Motion Pictures Produced in the United States* (Hanson, 1988) contains coverage of Hispanic-focused material although it is only dedicated to feature films, defined as four reels or more, and therefore misses great numbers of films of the period, including many that are critical to the understanding of the Hispanic image in American film, such as most of the greaser films. On the other hand, the works of García Riera (1987-1988), Richard (1992),[1] and Keller (1993) are entirely devoted to Hispanics. The publication of the multivolume *Variety Film Reviews (1907-90)* and other such compendia of reviews have made access to these sources much simpler. In addition, we have seen the publication of important works of analysis and synthesis including Noriega, ed., (1992), Fregoso (1993), and Hadley-García (1990), although the latter is a trade book not primarily concerned with scholarship. Similarly, much work has recently been done on Mexico, including Ramírez Berg's book (1992), and an updated version of Mora's landmark work (1990). Film scholars, in contrast to the situation ten years ago, are now in a position to conduct a taxonomic analysis of the image of Hispanics in the United States.[2] A first step is entertained in this and the following chapter, which attempts an initial taxonomy at a certain level of depth and detail for the first decades of American film, although it is certainly not complete because of the extent of the data set. The number of films or their scripts, trade advertisements and announcements, reviews in newspapers and trade journals, and other data far surpasses the ability of this handbook to give more than fractional coverage of any one character type, or, for that matter, with a few exceptions, any specific type of film. For each of the types of roles that are described below, only some examples are offered of the numerous films where that character type appears. The period covered in this chapter is primarily the silent era.

However, in order to maintain continuity, some coverage of certain characters or film types extends into the sound period as well.

Further discussion of Spanish-language films produced by the American film industry appears later in this handbook, but it should be observed here that in 1929 with the advent of the sound films, Spanish and Latin American newspapers and other cultural institutions attempted to campaign against the introduction of Hollywood talking films in their nations. Essentially, some groups requested that their governments prohibit the exhibition of talking films with dialog in English. They alleged that the showing of English-speaking films would damage and even imperil the Spanish language. Hollywood during this period was unsure whether to dub films in Spanish, to use Spanish subtitles, or to create Spanish versions. The sorts of concerns that emerged in the Spanish-speaking world and other markets such as francophone areas supported the third procedure, which became the most common one throughout the 1930s. By the 1950s dubbing had risen to the forefront. In addition, for a brief period, beginning with the 1929 sound films, the American film industry made an effort to produce various language versions of their most germane films. For example, Paramount set up a complete studio in Joinville, France where foreign nationals acted in films primarily for the Spanish, Latin American, and French markets. *Film Daily* reported that Paramount had plans to produce some of their films in thirteen separate languages. This experiment ran for about five years but proved unnecessary because the Hollywood product had the most success internationally without the need to create other-language versions.[3]

A few other methodological observations are in order. It has seemed valuable to conduct a review of the types of characters that appear in this chapter by separating them by gender, inasmuch as female Hispanics and male Hispanics usually had singularly different roles in American film, although to some extent they also matched each other or functioned as counterparts. For example, the counterpart to the male "bad Mexican" was the female "vamp" or "seductress." However, as we have seen in our analysis of the previous chapter, certain forces operated on American cinema that caused the creation of white female characters in either unique roles or more aggressive roles, and this, to a minor extent spilled over to nonwhite females as well, providing them with some more positive roles from the perspective of the moral values of the period. Also, the American penchant for attempted rape scenes, interracial or potential interracial sex, sexual harassment and abuse of various kinds engaged in by either sex but through vastly different behaviors, channelled Hispanic characters into different types of roles that were gender specific. Moreover, it should be noted that some of the character types, notably the "gay caballero" and the occasional bandit had women assuming those roles. Despite the fact that these categories appear as male character types, instances of them as represented by females appear in those sections as well.

Finally, the categorizations that appear in the reviews that follow in this and the next chapter are not intended to be exclusive, for this would not work. For example, a cantina girl may also be vamp, or, on the other hand, she may be a faithful señorita. Similarly, in a specific film, a cantina girl may appear opposite a good bad Mexican. However, for the sake of economy and concision, the films, with few exceptions, are referenced only once, in the one category in which they seem to best fit. It should be emphasized that the categories that appear below are offered primarily for the usefulness in making sense of a very large data set and should not be interpreted rigidly.

General Characteristics of the Hispanic Characters in American Films of the First Decades

While a summary of the Hispanic characters found in the first decades of American film appears before each gender section some general, orienting comments are in order. As we shall see, the range and typology of Hispanic characters was very constrained. A content analysis of hundreds of films netted only three distinct female roles of any predominance and eight male roles, and even these eleven roles were interconnected. Even the names of Hispanic characters were very limited. Chiquita, Carmen, variations on Carmen, Lolita, Bonita (the alluring Latina par excellence!), María, Pedro or Pete or Mexican Pete, Pancho, López, and of course, Zorro and Cisco appear again and again.

As one might expect, Hispanic characters appear in a context that makes them either foils to or sex objects of Anglos or overwhelmingly provide material of interest primarily directed to Anglos. Anglos usually predominate in these films, either bringing Hispanics to justice or occasionally helping them. This is usually the case even of films where normally one would surmise the plot would revolve around purely Hispanic characters, such as the Mexican Revolution. However, even in Mexican Revolution films it was often the case that an Anglo character had the main role, either helping Mexicans or being victimized by them.

Heterosexual behavior plays an enormous part in these films, and in many of them, drives the plot. Much of this behavior is interracial in nature, predominantly señoritas falling head over heels for Anglo males or Hispanic males either lusting after or idealizing white women. More often than not, as in *Martyrs of the Alamo, The Spirit of the Flag, Under the Yoke,* or *The Woman God Forgot,* history is made to pivot around either feared or encouraged interracial sex. Hispanic males also are driven by greed, gratitude, revenge, covetousness for power or property, or status. Some older Hispanic characters are portrayed, usually as the fathers of young señoritas. Even here, however, they are typically engaged in attempts to leverage their daughter's good looks by marrying them off to someone wealthy or powerful. For Hispanic females, however, there are few other avenues of behavior other than the sexually charged ones, and therefore there is little importance attached to social class, and older, or nonsexually foregrounded female characters rarely appear in film during the first decades.

The Physical Setting

Most of these films are set in the American West. A smaller but significant number were set in Spain, but often a Spain that had many of the physical qualities of the American West: the hard terrain, dancing girls, vamps or temptresses, bandits, and so on. A few films are set in the Philippines. The Westerns, Mexican Revolution films, and films taking place in Spain were all actually filmed in the West. Beginning around the turn of the century, American film companies roved out West to film and by 1915, the year of the various *Carmen* productions, Hollywood had become very well established. García Riera has well reviewed the interaction of the Western setting, with the depiction of Hispanic, primarily Mexican, characters in order to create an alien and exotic domain—both physical and moral—counterposed to the WASP world.

> ... the presence of Mexican elements in the Western transcended the mere depiction of characters conceived through naiveté, racism, prejudice, and pu-

ritan apprehensiveness.The Mexican elements provided the unique qualities of the landscape: a profusion of edifices such as churches and missions, haciendas and adobe houses, and even plants that one might claim as a natural conspiracy on behalf of Mexicanness, like nopals and magueys, all establishing an often undetermined domain for a great quantity of Westerns within an extensive territory that once was Mexico proper and which generally maintained its names from Mexican times. The conflict-torn border between Mexico and this territory consisting of the current states of California, Arizona, New Mexico, and Texas would stay open until 1924, permitting free travel on the part of the characters of the Western—vaqueros and cowboys, Mexican and gringo bandits, *rurales* and rangers, Yaqui or Apache Indians, ranchers and cattlemen, fugitives—into a sort of no man's land, sometimes deserted, on other occasions brimming. (1987, vol. I, 20-21, translation mine)

Female Roles

The range permitted to Hispanic female characters was very constricted because they primarily functioned in relationship to an Anglo love interest. Most of the films have the characters contained in them placed in one of three categories. There is the cantina girl, especially if her role is primarily focused on her dancing a peak scene, perhaps on a cantina table, with great sexual allure and heavily looked forward to by the film audience. Dancing, or possibly singing, certainly behaving in an alluring fashion is the essential trait of the cantina girl. A second type is the faithful, moral, or self-sacrificing señorita. Often this character is good bad in the sense that she goes wrong in the middle of the film and at the end, realizing her poor behavior, places her body in front of the knife or bullet intended for her Anglo love interest. The third type is a vamp if she pursues her love for the Anglo to its logical conclusion from the perspective of her own self-interest. Whereas the cantina girl is a more simply and often merely physically represented sex object, the vamp uses her wiles. She is a psychological menace to males, usually white males ill equipped to defend themselves. Outside of the parameters of romance or sex, there are virtually no roles for Hispanic females. As one might imagine, given these sorts of constraints, older or nonsexual female characters rarely appear in film during the first decades.

Cantina Girls

The early examples of this type of character are that of a naughty lady of easy virtue, who is also outgoing and exhibitionistic. While the very first examples are evoked in a purely Hispanic setting with all Hispanic characters (played by Anglos), beginning with the 1913 *On the Border*, with rare exceptions the cantina girl serves an ancillary function as the love interest of the Anglo hero. She seems either to be waiting for the Anglo to enter her life, or is quick to discard her Latin suitor in favor of the Anglo. In overwhelming instances, the cantina girl falls head over heels for the Anglo. Quite often she is a dancer in the cantina and does a seductive dance that is a peak scene in the film. With the easing of the Production Code and its attendant censorship restrictions, the type evolved, perhaps devolved is more appropriate, to a harsher portrayal, sometimes as a prostitute, often as a drug addict supporting herself and/or children by selling her body. The formula for creating the cantina girl was so uniform that an incredible number of these characters are called "Chiquita," as in *Scarlet Days* (1919, Famous Players-Lasky Corp.), *Last Trail* (1921, Fox), and *The Ne'er-Do-Well* (1923,

Famous Players-Lasky Corp.). The cantinas themselves are primarily set in Mexico, usually just on the border, and to a lesser degree in Panama, catering to the various rough and ready types of the Canal Zone.

One of the first of this type appears in *Her Sacrifice* (1911, Biograph) where a barmaid loves her high caste Mexican so much that she takes the bullet intended for him, shot from the gun of the jealous lower-class Mexican who loves her. In *The Dove and the Serpent* (1912, IMP), a "cantina cutie" interferes with the love between a high-class woman, Tórtola and her swain, Pablo, but she is foiled. In *A Mexican Romance* (1912, Lubin), the cantina girl and the Latin Lover interact in a frivolous, stereotypical fashion. Don José proposes to Pepita under a big cactus in the Grape Vine courtyard. But just as he is slipping the ring on his love's finger, "with one eye" he spies the cantina dancer and is smitten. He takes his fiancée home and goes back to the cantina. The plot gets complicated at this point but José narrowly misses the traditional knife in the back from outraged Pepita and in the end this Hispanic of hot blood and loose morals returns to her after all.

In *On the Border* (1913, American), it is not a Hispanic but an Anglo cowboy who falls in love with a señorita, "as Chiquita danced merrily to the sound of her tambourine and the soft twanging of guitars." The Mexican waiter who is also in love with Chiquita tries to poison the Anglo's drink but he is foiled. This interracial formula is repeated constantly. In *The Masked Dancer* 1914, Vitagraph), an Anglo mining engineer is smitten by the local cantina girl, causing his Anglo wife to learn how to dance like the Latina in order to win back his affections. The contemporary review in *Moving Picture World* (1.24. 1914) commented that "George Cooper who is the greaser divekeeper [is] in as convincing a role as any we have seen." Unfortunately, Hispanic actors were usually barred from even doing the greaser roles that presumably, by the attitudes of the period, would be their natural forte. As Richard puts it, "Apparently it took an Anglo actor to really bring the slime out of a 'greaser' characterization" (1992, 124). Chiquita appears again in D. W. Griffith's *Scarlet Days* (1919, Famous Players-Lasky) in a supporting role, standing by her man, the good bad Mexican bandit Alvarez (loosely modeled on the exploits of Joaquín Murrieta) in this complicated plot set in a dance hall owned by an Anglo woman who is using the proceeds to keep her Anglo daughter in boarding school in Boston. Once again a cantina girl called Chiquita appears in *The-Ne'er-Do-Well* (1923, Paramount), set in Panama where an Anglo remakes his life and gains the love of the señorita.

Percy (1925, Pathé) provides the opportunity for a cantina girl to make a "real man" out of an Anglo. A "sissy" who has been raised by his mother in an unmanly fashion while the father runs for political office is sent to the border area by the father's friend who has offered to make a true man out of him. Introduced to "demon rum" and heavy drinking (in Mexico, during the Prohibition, this was an added subversive, titillating quality of the film) and taken in by the more than willing Lolita, the lovely Mexican cantina dancer, he is soon boldly challenging the local cacique who is mistreating the peasantry. Percy's father arrives and is so pleased that he permits him to marry Lolita, despite her past. A 1937 film, *Border Cafe*, essentially tells the same story with only slight variation. An odious extreme is achieved with respect to the willingness of the cantina girl to service Anglos in *The Showdown* (1928, Pathé) about two archrivals in the oil rich tropics who fight over the services of the willing cantina girl.

99 Wounds (1931, Tiffany) is another example of the cantina girl who not only falls in love with the Anglo, but helps him. This film features Tom Tyler as an Anglo investigating warring Indians attacking settlers in the border area. With the help of Carmencita, the cute cantina girl, he discovers that the culprits are actually whites dressed up like Indians. Tom and Carmencita recruit the real "redskins" and together they capture the renegade Anglos. In *Breed of the Border* (1933, Mono), advertised as a "Snappy Western of Mexican Border Bandits Has Modern Slant with Speed Car," the Anglo private detective allies himself with the cantina girl in the border café which is frequented by smugglers. He captures the whole gang and saves her from a life of crime.

Rogue of the Río Grande (1930, SonoArt) provides a twist in that the cantina girl falls in love with a Mexican. José Bohr, a Spanish actor who would later devote himself to acting in and directing Mexican movies, plays the role of "El Malo," a good bad Pancho Villa type bandit, aided by a trusty Mexican sidekick, Pedro. Among their adventures in this musical (songs include "Argentine Moon," "Carmita," and "Song of the Bandoleros") is the bandit's encounter with Chiquita, played by Myrna Loy, who loves to sing and dance and be admired by all. After capturing her heart and blaming his crimes on the sheriff (who happens to be a crook in his own right), the good bad bandit makes it across the border with his cantina girl.

The Faithful, Moral, or Self-Sacrificing Señorita

In a fashion consistent with her place in society, the faithful señorita is the analog to the faithful Mexican male. However, whereas often the faithful Mexican displays his behavior as a reflection of respect or gratitude toward the Anglo patriarch such as a rancher (it should be observed that Mexicans were also occasionally faithful to the Anglo lady that they loved, usually in unrequited fashion), the moral señorita is faithful to her Anglo love interest. Moral in this context does not refer to sexual behaviors, she may have or not have physical love with her Anglo. Moral refers to fidelity to Anglos from ethnocentric, Anglo expectations: fealty to the Anglo race, the United States and its symbols such as the flag, the sheriff, or the cavalry, or to American culture or mores. Because morality is adherence to Anglo-Saxonism, to America and its values, the señorita in these films often has to display the behavior of a turncoat, a traitor to her culture, above all, to her family. Perhaps she must turn against a member of her family—a brother, as in *Chiquita, the Dancer,* or a father, as in *A Spanish Love Song,* thus demonstrating both her loyalty to the hero and her allegiance to "the land of the free." The moral señorita gains the hero only by radically renouncing her previous formation; often she doesn't get the hero even then, but has the satisfaction of dying in his arms or seeing him on his way to his one true Anglo lady.

One of the first of these films is *The Mexican's Jealousy* (1910, New York Motion Picture Co.) featuring a dark-skinned señorita, Rita, who saves and escapes with the Anglo and his half-breed friend. They flee the Mexican lover and his gang who has not only been scorned but insulted and humiliated and kicked in the rear by the Anglo swain. *Bonita of El Cajón* (1911, American) depicts a Texas Ranger who wins the love of a dark-skinned lady, but who has an Anglo lady of his own. The father counsels Bonita to commit treachery, which she plans, but when she talks with the other woman, she realizes that the Anglos belong together. After helping them to escape the treachery that is planned and kissing the Ranger goodbye, Bonita is later killed by a bullet from her father's own weapon.

A Spanish Love Song (1911, Méliès) is a French production building upon but expanding the scope of Latin amorous passion. An Anglo boy who has problems with his betrothed is sent by his family across the border to resolve his problem. There he meets Juanita, who promptly falls for him and dumps the rich local, Don José, whom her father wants her to wed for financial gain. As a result of her loving, the Anglo becomes a genuine cowboy. Don José is constantly attempting to kill him, but Juanita keeps saving him. However, the Anglo is summoned back north to marry the white girl, thus breaking Juanita's heart. All is saved when it is found that the white fiancée has run off with another man, allowing the Anglo "to return to his Mexican therapist" (Richard, 1992, 53). In *Chiquita, the Dancer* (1912, American), the señorita turns against her dim-witted brother and others to save her Anglo lover from an evil Justice of the Peace. Chiquita also happens to be, we know of course from the name, a dancing cantina girl! In *Carmenita the Faithful* (1911, Essanay), the highly moral mexicana, with the help of an Anglo hero who loves her, foils her rich Mexican merchant father who wants to sell her in marriage for as much as she can bring. The Anglo wins the good lady but loses the use of his legs while "the bad Mexican is seen dejected and being led away to prison."

Saved by the Flag (1911, Pathé) imbues Old Glory with a sort of mystical significance formerly reserved for Excalibur. The film has a young Army officer fall in love with a señorita, marry her, and resign to become a local businessman. The reigning general who thought she belonged to him, plots his vengeance. They are warned of their imminent arrest and make a mad dash for the U.S. border with the Mexican federales in hot pursuit. As the two lovers cross over, the former officer grabs the American flag and wraps it around himself and his Mexican wife, taunting the Mexicans who are rendered helpless by the Stars and Stripes.

In *The Greater Love* (1913, American), Conchita, who has fallen in love with an Easterner who has come west to make money so he can marry an Anglo girl back home, eventually realizes that she has no realistic chance for his love. Conchita's jealous Mexican lover takes advantage of the fact that the Anglo has had an accident and is bed-ridden, but Conchita throws herself across his body and lets the knife intended for the Anglo plunge into her own back.

An Adventure of the Mexican Border (1913, Lubin), featuring Romaine Fielding who also directed, has a very different climax. A mexicana is torn between two suitors, a kind and gentle Mexican captain and a brash young Anglo lieutenant. She chooses the older Mexican and the lieutenant accepts his loss and in the spirit of fair play, apologizes for having told lies about the captain. The film, interestingly produced before Pancho Villa's 1916 execution of sixteen Americans in Mexico and attack on Columbus, New Mexico that was to turn the American public against Mexico, is exceptional in that in a specific interracial love triangle, it has the señorita chose the suitor of her own race and culture.

A number of the moral señoritas are placed in the Philippines. *The Spirit of the Flag* (1913, Bison) once again promotes the Stars and Stripes. The film anachronistically has both the Spaniards and the Americans simultaneously stationed in the Philippines, apparently from the way the plot develops, just before the outbreak of the Spanish-American War. Bonita falls in love with a young Anglo doctor but she becomes jealous when he falls in love with an Anglo teacher who is instructing the natives on how important the American flag is. At first Bonita aids the Spaniards, but they kill her father and this good bad woman realizes the error of her ways, and with the help of the doctor, they initiate the Philippine struggle for independence. Bonita willingly dies clutching the folds of the American flag. *The Quicksand* (1914, Kalem) is similarly set in the

Philippines with the same sort of plot. A native girl falls in love with a young officer and gives her life trying to save him despite her awareness of his Anglo sweetheart. The *Heart of Bonita* (1916, Laemmle) although set in Mexico has the same conclusion, except that Bonita merely saves the Anglo's life without giving up her own, permitting her to take her persistent Mexican suitor. *Desert Gold* (1919, Pathé) is true to the format of the Zane Grey novel on which it is based; these novels typically had numerous Mexican badmen and self-sacrificing señoritas who rescue the Anglos for their white ladies. In *Lasca* (1919, Universal), the primary variation is that the girl in the title role saves the Anglo from stampeding cattle.

White Gold (1927, Cecil B. DeMille Picture Corp.) was a much reviewed and highly publicized film ostensibly about sheepmen (the sheep are the white gold) versus cattlemen. It is Hispanic-focused in that it depicts a patriarch's son, an Anglo with a weak sort of personality but sufficiently good looking to attract Dolores, the Mexican cantina dancer. He takes her from "the bounteous feast" of life in the cantina to the "hollow husk" of a torridly hot Arizona ranch. With the connivance of the father, ultimately the son accuses his woman of infidelity, despite the fact that she had remained faithful to the point of defending her honor by killing the foreman who accosted her. Finally, in a scene that is a notch above in its sympathy for Hispanic characters, Dolores walks off into the desert by herself, leaving the patriarch and his weak son to their own devices.[4]

The Vamp or Temptress

The vamp or temptress was the most common female Hispanic type during the first decades of American film production. This was also a very common role for either white female characters or personages appearing in period pieces, spectacle films, and epics (French, Egyptian, biblical, classical, and so on). With respect to Hispanic vamps, however, Carmen or a character very much like her predominated, although the cantina girl character was often also a vamp. As can be seen from the review which follows, and from the earlier review of the cantina dancer, a number of films conjoin the two characters.

The vamp or temptress was the female analog to the bad Mexican. She did her work by using her wiles, often bringing men to violence, either to others or themselves. However, the Hispanic vamp tended to differ somewhat in degree from her white counterparts in that passionate sex more than psychological manipulation was more her trademark, and accordingly, she often displayed a willingness to commit physical violence rather than merely manipulate men. These character traits reflected the frequent projection by the more puritanical Anglo culture of easy sex onto both Hispanic females and males.

Partly because so many of the Hispanic vamps emerge out of the context of the Carmen plot, more films that depict the vamp are set in a purely Hispanic world than we have seen with other female characters, although there is plenty of interracial activity for the Hispanic vamp as well.

One of the first vamp films, approximately three minutes long, is *Mexican Sweethearts* (1909, Vitagraph) where a pretty señorita pretends to love an American soldier, which almost gets him killed because of her Mexican lover's temper. As the señorita looks on approvingly, the enraged Latin chases the American boy with a knife; he is unhurt but learns a valuable lesson. "The experience of Tantalus was never so chafing as a tantalizing sweetheart . . . The strength of this phrase is better understood when one realizes the impetuous nature of the Latin type of person." In the same year, *The Spanish Girl*

(1909, Essanay) featured a "Spanish" (Mexican) dancer who conspired to steal an Anglo ranch foreman from his Anglo sweetheart by enticing another man, José, to do her dirty work for her.

Both the archetypal and stereotypical grandmother of the Hispanic vamp in American film as well as the Hispanic vamp produced by other film industries surely was Carmen. Richard judges that the cycle's "influence on Hollywood productions would be difficult to overstate" and that "by 1929 there had been so many versions of this work that any ten year old could recognize the plot as the basis on which most vamp stories for the screen were founded" (1992, 364). On the other hand, while the plot of *Carmen* might have become ubiquitous in Hollywood, this version of the "eternal triangle" itself harks to numerous earlier, classical, medieval, and renaissance narrative models. The Carmen cycle primarily consists of film adaptations of the Prosper Mérimée 1845 novel *Carmen*. During the silent period alone, various versions of the film were marketed in the United States, with *Carmen* as the title. Yet other films without that specific title were clearly adapted from the story of Carmen.

A very early version, *A Love Tragedy in Spain* (1908, Méliès), is billed as "a thrilling episode in the style of Bizet's *Carmen*" in this case between a Spanish smuggler and a local "danseuse" (the production company displayed its French connection). As in the Mérimée template from which this film was inspired, the smuggler fights to the death with another love interest, killing him and then "heroically stab[bing] himself." The first film with the title *Carmen* was a French production (1910, Pathé/Film d'Art), followed by two 1913 productions, one by Monopol, starring Marion Leonard and the other by Thanhouser, starring Marguerite Snow.

Around the same period other films produced looser versions of the Carmen story, although retaining the name or one close to it, the plot based on two men fighting for the girl, and the location in Spain. *Love in Madrid* (1911, Pathé) is slightly different in that the character, Juanita María del Carmen does not vamp men, but the plot is similar otherwise. Enrique falls in love with her, and she drops him a red rose from her balcony. Later a bystander makes unwelcome advances and is killed by Enrique in a duel. The father, impressed by the daring Enrique consents to marriage. The twist in *The Test of Love* (1911, Yankee) involves the introduction of a bar girl vamping an Anglo tourist in Carmen-like fashion. Carmencita, "a wild, carefree daughter of Spain" is "the favorite dancer of Madrid's wine gardens." She vamps the North American in order to make her Spanish lover jealous, with near fatal results for the chagrined and sobered Anglo. *The Last Dance* (1914, Picture Playhouse Film Co.) depicts a young artist who is taken from his true love by a vampish Spanish dancer. He marries her briefly but things quickly go wrong. Broken-hearted, he dies in the bad woman's arms. In his memory, she performs a last provocative dance for him as he lies dead on the floor. In *The Spanish Omelet* (1914, Biograph), the owner of the Tarantula Café makes "Spanish omelets of antique eggs" while his feckless daughter (Carmen, of course) manages to get two Spanish gentlemen dueling over her, Don Bullo, a bull fighter and Don José, "a tabasco Spanish Lothario." All's well that ends well, the remorseful father pulls Carmen's wig off her head, and the "surprised duelists embrace and congratulate each other on escaping conjugal relations with one so false as Carmen."

As pointed out in the previous chapter, 1915 was the great vintage year for *Carmen* productions. Charlie Chaplin directed and acted in an Essanay production that year (which was not released until 1916 in an augmented form), *Charlie Chaplin's Burlesque on "Carmen"* with Chaplin playing "Darn Hosiery" (changed to Don José in the 1920 reissue) with Edna Puriance (who replaced Mabel Normand in 1915 and starred in almost all of Chaplin's films through 1923) as his leading lady. This film played upon and parodied the other two films that in turn competed with each other in 1915. The Fox production with Raoul Walsh directing featured the notorious vamp specialist Theda Bara, and the Lasky-Paramount production directed by Cecil B. DeMille featured Geraldine Farrar, a beautiful and talented opera star who often sang opposite Caruso. Both of these productions attempted to be high-fidelity versions of the Mérimée Carmen story.

In 1917, a Spanish production by Cine was released in the United States (it had actually been produced in 1915) with Spanish language title cards causing consternation to the *Variety* reviewer, and in 1918, Ernst Lubitsch directed *Gypsy Blood* in Germany, starring the Polish film star Pola Negri, who soon began to work in and become very popular in the United States. Lubitsch returned quickly to this story, producing for the American market in 1921, *Gypsy Blood* (First National, again starring Pola Negri). The original title was envisioned as *Carmen.* It was basically the story told in extreme: The Spanish vamp was portrayed as a "heartless, ignorant, unmoral, basely reared Spanish Gypsy, without one redeeming trait; a beautiful animal whose friendship [was] a curse and whose death at the hands of Navarro [was] richly deserved" (*Motion Picture World,* May 21, 1921). Similarly, the normally staid *New York Times* seemed to find in the Spanish archetype a predatory menace to men and patriarchs:

> Miss Negri's Carmen is not a studio puppet; she is no grand operatic queen without a vivifying voice. She is a tempestuous, intemperate, free-loving savage of capricious appetites and a consuming zest for satisfying them. Nothing is precious in her eyes. She does not seek to have and to hold; the sport is to capture and destroy, for to destroy the captured is to carry the conquest to its natural completion. She hunts and kills in disregard or ignorance of posted fields and closed seasons. She possesses all of the natural artfulness of the female of the variety. (May 9, 1921)

Richard makes the following observation about the *Times* review: "One must assume that was so, because she is Spanish. Certainly not a little flapper to bring home to meet mamacita in the suburbs, but if you could just get a chain around her neck and tie her to the bed, Oh! You Kid! The characterization of silver screen Carmens and most of the other chiquitas remained basically unchanged as they wiggled their way down to present days" (1992, 237).

In 1927, Raoul Walsh returned to the subject with *Loves of Carmen* (Fox), starring Dolores del Río and the former boxer, Victor McLaglen, the great white hope made famous by being knocked out by the famed black boxer, Jack Johnson. McLaglen did the part of Escamillo, the toreador. *Motion Picture World* described the female stereotype as "the woman who has the heart of a wanton, the mind of a child and the soul of a woman" (cited in Richard, 1992, 351). Yet again in 1928 Dolores del Río and Don Alvarado did *No Other Woman* (Fox) in which a nonpredatory Carmilita is betrayed by a transient male. Del Río plays a Spanish aristocrat and the sweetheart of Alvarado, this time cast as a Frenchman, Maurice, and is stolen from his arms by a sophisticated South American fortune hunter who leaves when the money is gone. Realizing her mistake, she returns to the arms of the Frenchman. By the late 1920s, Dolores del Río had become a marketable commodity and Don Alvarado was one of the leading "Latin Lovers" of the period.

Finally, the last of the silent films that this research has identified with the actual title of *Carmen* was the French version of 1928, which was appreciated, if not for its vampishness, at least for the most realistic bullfight. The cycle has continued on including renditions by director Charles Vidor, *The Loves of Carmen* (Columbia, 1948), starring Rita Hayworth, and Otto Preminger's *Carmen Jones* (1954, Fox), starring Dorothy Dandridge. This production, based on a long-running, wartime (1943) Broadway play was a modernized, all-black version of the Bizet opera, *Carmen.* Outside of the United States, other film industries have been active with this plot as well. Examples include Carlos Saura's Spanish version, *Carmen* (1983), Jean-Luc Godard's *Prenom Carmen* (1983), and Francesco Rosi's direction of *Bizet's Carmen* (1984), a French-Italian production.

In 1918, the Carmen type story moved to Asia. *Under the Yoke* (1918, Fox), starring no less than the archetypal vamp herself, Theda Bara, but playing out of her normal character, continued the interracial Carmen version, this time against the background of the North American occupation of the Philippines. Once again, Hollywood made history the consequence of interracial love. The female, María Valverde, in this case not a vamp but a moral Hispana fresh from the convent school, prefers an Anglo officer instead of the rich Spanish planter, Diablo Ramírez, whom her grandee father wants her to marry. The Spaniard retaliates by fomenting a revolution against the Americans so that he might capture her, which he does. However, the occupying troops come to the rescue, initiating, it would seem a historical moment of the Spanish American War, at least in the Philippines, and permitting the true love of the interracial pair its full reign.

Richard (1992, 340) judges that the Carmen cycle also was the vehicle for the establishment of the "classic cliché in which two incredibly tough Marines with good hearts fight the enemy fiercely but would much rather fight each other for fun and for the affections of ready and willing women all over the world just waiting to nurse their wounds." The film that so honored the first elaboration of this commonplace was *What Price Glory* (1926, Fox, director Raoul Walsh), a top-grossing and extremely popular World War I movie with a Carmen twist that featured Victor McLaglen as one of the Marines, once again opposite Dolores del Río as the sexy French country girl who is the object of the Marines' rivalry, as well as a second girl, a hot-blooded temptress. This film which was on the *New York Times* 1926 list of the ten best films of the year was so successful that it generated a number of sequels, including *A Girl in Every Port* (1928, Fox) and *Women of All Nations* (1931, Fox).

The Black Mantilla (1917, Universal) takes the vamp to new extremes in the form of Marachita, "the Señorita Shrew." Jealous and callous beyond redemption, Marachita toys with four separate lovers, and through her actions causes one to steal a valuable painting from a mission church and lose his life at the hands of an enraged mob. Fatty Arbuckle's last film before he was banned from working in the industry, *Crazy to Marry* (1921, Famous Players), was a very popular comedy that included the señorita vamp with all the accepted stereotypes. *The Temptress* (1926, MGM), starring Greta Garbo in the role of vamp and based on a work by Vicente Blasco Ibáñez, tells the story of an Argentine who goes to Paris and is vamped by the sexy Elena. Only when it's too late does he discover that she's married and responsible for the suicide of at least one other man. He returns to Argentina, but she follows him, seducing every man she meets just to get his attention. Finally beaten, he tells the vamp that he loves her; she realizes it's too late because of the type of person she is, and she returns to Paris and addicts herself to absinthe. A number of years go by and in the final scene the two are reunited for her death scene.

Male Roles

Just as the range available to Hispanic female characters was limited primarily to cantina girls, faithful señoritas, or vamps, Hispanic male characters were limited primarily to bandits or otherwise badmen, good badmen, greasers, faithful Mexicans or other Hispanics, Latin Lovers, and two aggressively positive roles, both closely connected, the Hispanic avenger and the gay caballero, a type of Latino Robin Hood. Whereas the Hispanic female primarily functioned in relationship to an Anglo love interest, the Hispanic male is usually a foil to an Anglo hero. He is almost always either the physical antagonist of that Anglo or his loyal and subordinate partner. When the Hispanic and the Anglo are antagonists, they struggle over power, money, property, or a woman, usually a señorita. As collaborators, the Hispanic is usually either the loyal, often inept sidekick or he is a good badman who has come to appreciate Anglo values, or he may be a faithful Mexican or other Hispanic, repaying a debt of gratitude. The relationship between Hispanic males and Anglo women tends almost always to revolve around sex or romance. The Hispanic either lusts for the Anglo woman or he worships her abjectly. Even while interracial sex or romance often drives the Hispanic male character, in contrast to the circumstances of the Hispanic female, who operated almost exclusively within the context of romance or sex, various Hispanic males do appear in roles that cast them as covetous, greedy, lusting for power, property, and the like, rather than driven by sexual passion or romance. Also, in contrast to the situation obtaining for Hispanic females, older Hispanic males appear sometimes, but almost never in appealing roles. They are usually among the most evil Hispanics, typically bent on selling into marriage or otherwise realizing financial or property gains from their daughters. It is worth noting that within the typecast world of Hispanics executed by the American film industry the behavior of Hispanic fathers to daughters embodies patriarchal tyranny.

Social class and socioeconomic status distinguish Hispanic male roles much more than Hispanic female roles. Some Hispanic characters are of the "better class of people," as it was phrased contemporaneously, in fact the aristocracy. The gay caballero is usually a Don or the son of an aristocrat. The Latin Lover tends to be a man of financial means. Even the bad Mexican is frequently an opportunist intent on leveraging his resources; he is a landowner more often than a tramp. The greasers are usually the lower class or outcast individuals: faithful Mexicans, bandits, peons, tramps, and the like.

Greasers

The categorization of greaser as a Hispanic male, or for that matter, occasional female role (e.g., in *The Red Girl*), presents a special kind of difficulty. The greaser appeared in American film with an ascribed status from birth. Greaserhood was primarily associated with *mexicanidad*. It was a condition of life, primarily of the lower social status Mexican, although examples appear among the higher classes of Mexicans and even Spaniards when they engage in behaviors odious to the Anglo way of life. Pettit has observed how wide a range of characters fell within the epithet:

> Some greasers meet their fate because they are greasers. Others violate Saxon moral codes. All of them rob, assault, kidnap, and murder. . . . Greed plays a primary role in the early movie greaser's misconduct. Occasionally, as in *The Mexican,* a covetous Mexican landlord demands too much rent from the heroine and gets his "yellow cheeks" slapped by the girl's fiancé. More often, the greaser attempts to steal horses or gold. . . . The greaser of the early films is as lustful as he is greedy. In *The Pony Express* a bandido abducts the Saxon Heroine. The hero summons a posse and in one of the first of many cinematic chases, pursues the bandido and his henchmen, shooting them down one by one without sustaining casualties. In the final showdown the greaser leader tries to stab the hero several times but is overcome by a knockout blow (1980, 133).

This phenomenon of assigning innate greaserhood by both American film and American society permitted the production of films where greasers appeared in various occupations and in various roles, ranging from bandits to bullfighters to generals to tramps to peons to landowners. Similarly, because the status of greaserhood was ascribed, there appeared in American film both evil greasers, the most common variety, and what on the surface would appear to be an oxymoron, "good" greasers, those who were faithful to Anglo morality, such as Tony the Greaser in the film with the same title, or José, the protagonist in *The Greaser's Gauntlet.* "Good greaser" films allow the greaser to reform or redeem himself, usually by saving a beautiful Anglo heroine. *The Greaser's Gauntlet* and *Tony the Greaser* cultivate the theme of Hispanic redemption through obeisance to the high physical and moral splendor of an Anglo-Saxon beauty and the Americanism she represents. This style of movie, to which D. W. Griffith made a significant contribution, represents the first examples of the Hispanic of low blood but good heart. "His is an unenviable lot, as he is doomed to wander between the longed-for world of the Anglo and the stigmatized world of the Mexican, held forever in a middle position between Saxon heroes and greaser villains. It is the faint beginning of a pattern to be developed more fully in a later generation of books and films" (Pettit, 1980, 135).

If interpreted widely, many of the male roles described below could be identified as greasers. I have not done this because the focus of this handbook is analysis, namely to distinguish between character and film types, to find the differences among them, even though those differences arc sometimes subtle. On the other hand, another alternative, eliminating the greaser as a character type and putting all of the greasers who were bandits in that category and those who were faithful Mexicans in the relevant slot, also is not an appropriate procedure. The fact is that quite a few films were produced where the primary tag was greaser, that is, where the title of the film foregrounded this odious epithet, or where the title cards, dialog, or plot construction emphasized the fundamental condition of greaserhood. My procedure has been cautious and conservative. I have identified productions as greaser films when the epithet was overtly used and had a major function in the film itself. Otherwise the character of the bandit, the badman, the general, and so on, even through he too could be viewed as a greaser, appears in one of those other categories.

Richard (1992, 55) has suggested that films that show obeisant greasers in a sympathetic light have been inaccurately cited by researchers as examples of negative stereotyping. He views *Tony the Greaser* (version of 1911) as clearly displaying sympathy for the Mexican. However, the lamentable production of greaser films by the American industry in my judgment is not ameliorated by the depiction of a handful of "good greasers" who either start out in the film fully transculturated (although the Anglo film characters don't quite know it yet), or spend film moments beating the Hispanic element out of themselves in order to Americanize. Quite to the contrary, the creation of this seemingly contradictory type points to an underlying, pervasive, and morally devastating cultural chauvinism. The Horatio Alger story for greasers is that if with great efforts they can overcome their own cultural identities and embrace the WASP view of Americanism, then, and only then, can they become good. (They also usually become dead or at the least return to the Mexican world in their new, exalted state.) In a very tangible sense, the way out of greaserhood that these films point to lays bare a very deep-seated racial prejudice, even among favorably disposed whites. W. E. B. Du Bois in *The Soul of Black Folks* (1903) pointed out this phenomenon among sympathetic whites toward his negritude, and his consequent difficulty with dealing with this form of totally unselfconscious and reflexive prejudice, inhaled and exhaled like the American air we breathe:

> Between me and the other world there is ever an unasked question: unasked by some through a feeling of delicacy; by others through the difficulty of rightly framing it. All, nevertheless flutter round it. They approach me in a half-hesitant sort of way, eye me curiously or compassionately, and then, instead of saying directly, How does it feel to be a problem? They say, I know an excellent colored man in my town; or, I fought at Mechanicsville; or, Do not these Southern outrages make your blood boil? At these I smile, or am interested, or reduce the boiling to a simmer, as the occasion may require. To the real question, How does it feel to be a problem? I answer seldom a word.

However, despite creation of a few "good" greaser characters, the analysis of the moral qualities of most greasers and the putative response to them by the great majority of the American film viewing public does not require any great subtlety. According to Lamb (1975), the crowds loved these films and reacted to them in the movie theater along lines common to theatrical melodrama.

> To appreciate fully the brown-white moral dichotomy established in these early movies, one would probably have to be able to view them with a contemporary audience. *Moving Picture World*, the leading trade journal of the first two decades of the century, reported that audiences viewing *Across the Mexican Line* applauded almost every move made by the good Americans, while the actions of Castro, the bandido, met with loud hisses (Lamb, 1975, 8).

As pointed out in the previous chapter, *Lost Mine* (Kalem, 1907) appears to be the first film in which the term greaser was specifically used, in this case in the title cards. The film opens with numerous greasers easily identified as Mexicans playing dice in front of a saloon. Two of them have knives. Quickly a sheriff disperses the sleazy Mexicans and the scene shifts to inside the saloon where the owner and his Mexican henchman plot to illegally acquire the rights to a mine owned by a hurt man. In the end they are thwarted by the Anglo sheriff and the sweetheart of the disabled mine owner. In the same year, *The Pony Express,* also produced by Kalem, evoked greasers in their archetypal form. The Mexican greaser makes an advance on an Anglo woman, is rejected and swears revenge against her and and her Anglo lover. The greaser is foiled by the Anglos. *Mexican's Crime* (1909, New York Motion Picture Co.) depicts a Mexican who is scorned by a Mexican dancing girl. He first attempts to stab her suitor and then shoots her. An Anglo posse is organized and chases after him but is surrounded by other Mexicans who come to the criminal's assistance. In the fight many individuals are hurt, but the villainous Mexican is brought to justice.

The Greaser's Gauntlet (1908, Biograph, director D. W. Griffith) has a greaser of the faithful kind first helped by a white woman and then helping another before he realizes that he should return to his mother and his culture. *Tony the Greaser* (1911, Méliès, remade in 1914, Vitagraph) is cut from the same cloth: "From force of habit some might call him a greaser. True he is a Mexicano [but also] a man of noble instincts and chivalrous nature." At the end, Tony grabs the flag that a gang of "dissolute Mexicans" who attack the ranch are about to desecrate and races to sound the alarm. He fights these "black hearted devils" who slay him as he clutches his white woman's bandanna, evidence of his devotion and love. *The Greaser* (1915, Majestic) takes the obeisant image of self-sacrifice to new extremes. Manuel, a ranch hand loves an Anglo woman who is nice but very distant; he's just another greaser to her. One day her father kicks the greaser because he had the impertinence to kiss a discarded rose she had once touched. This causes the greaser to plot revenge and when the Anglo love interest of the white woman accidently kills someone, he personally leads the lynching party. However, seeing that the white woman he loves is so upset, he puts on the clothing of the pursued Anglo, thus fooling the posse and causing it to come his way and shoot him dead.

In *Ah Sing and the Greaser* (1910, Lubin), two of the major foils to Anglo heroes are brought together: the Oriental and the greaser, and in *Across the Mexican Border* (1911, Powers), an old Mexican greaser is depicted as trying to sell his daughter to a young Mexican but foiled by Jack Armstrong, a North American soldier who is the señorita's true love interest. *Across the Mexican Line* (1911, Solax) has the Mexican revolutionary agent, Juanita, at the cost of betraying her cause, rescue her Anglo lover, Lieutenant Harvey who has been tortured by the greaser Mexican general to get information out of him.

The Greaser and the Weakling (1912, American) depicts a Mexican greaser "generally disliked for his bullying ways" who is the only one unmoved when the Anglo owner dies. Subsequently, he tries to gain control of the ranch by attempting first to marry one and then the other daughter, then abducting one when his other plans fail. He is shot dead by the Anglo avenging hero. On the other hand, *The Prayers of Manuelo* (1912, Vitagraph) is exceptional in that the greaser epithet is used in what might be considered a sociological or socially critical mode. Manuelo attempts to steal a few beans to feed his family and is called a "lazy greaser." He is given a job by a sheep man, which turns out to be a form of slavery. Attempting to return home to his pregnant wife, Manuelo takes a horse and is pursued and wounded. But when the cowboys enter his mud hut to finish their work they discover him with his good arm around his wife and child and the picture of the Virgin above the bed. They decide that they've punished Manuelo enough and leave him to his own devices.

Pedro's Treachery (1913, Lubin) continued the formula by featuring a Mexican who is evil in a variety of ways: after being beaten by the Anglo hero, he implicates the former in a robbery/murder, he is later caught being cruel to an animal, and he mistreats his "squaw." Eventually he is put away.

The Girl and the Greaser (1913, American) has one of those plucky white women beat back a greaser who invades her home while the husband is somewhere else, ill. At first the greaser is successful in stealing money but when he decides to burn the house, the white woman is able to put out the fire and hold him at bay with her revolver until help arrives. *The Greaser's Revenge* (1914, Frontier), also released with slight variations as *Dolly's Deliverance,* depicts a greaser with the effrontery to try to "make love to a lady." White males intervene and he is fired from his ranchhand job but steals a horse. After various plot complications the greaser is overpowered and brought to justice. In *Fool's Gold* (1915, Biograph), a greaser attempts to rob an old man who mistakenly thought he struck it rich but simply found fool's gold. In *The Heart of Texas Ryan* (1917, Fox), Tom Mix is captured by dirty greasers and saved by a lady who pays his ransom. In *Guns and Greasers* (1918, Artcraft), the last film with the derogatory epithet in the title, the greasers are bad Mexicans in charge of the business of running guns across the border. A similar type plot is found in *Wolves of the Border* (1918, Triangle) except that in this case the greasers are border cattle rustlers who are wiped out by righteous Anglos.

In *Fool's Paradise* (1921, Lasky), a DeMille extravaganza that commanded an extraordinary Saturday night top ticket price of $2.20, greasers were part of the subplot as inept kidnappers sent by "Roderiguez," a bad Mexican who owned a cantina and was in danger of losing his principal vamp to an Anglo. *The Killer* (1921, Pathé) features a respectable Anglo, Henry Hooper, on the Arizona-Mexico border who is a secret serial killer. His accomplice is Ramón, a greaser and willing dupe who does much of the dirty work, making the murders look like accidents. Eventually Hooper fixes on the daughter of a rancher. He wants to gain control of the ranch but she refuses the advances of this "Machiavellian villain" until he threatens to give her to "his lecherous Mexican as a victim of his lustful desires." Before the fate worse than death can be consummated, a neighboring ranch owner rescues her. *The Great Divide* (1924, MGM) features the tale of a woman regenerating the worst of men. "Three grim unbroken centuries of Puritan ancestry had made Ruth Jordan what she was, a girl uncompromising in her standards, high principle, intellectual and deeply religious." Going out west she encounters the man she must regenerate, a burly man named "Dutch" (played by Wallace Beery). But she also is confronted by a "short, dirty and viperous" man, a "Mexican of low order" who is simply called Greaser. The film was remade in 1930 (First National), however, as a brighter vehicle for Hispanics. There was no greaser, but Myrna Loy played Manuella, who spoke broken English and did the dancing cantina routine.

By 1922, the term greaser was capable of being generalized to all Hispanics. The description of *The American Toreador* (1922, Anchor) in the trade journal, *Movie Picture World* documents this:

> Bill, a husky Western cowboy determines to visit the land of romance and bull throwing and vamping señoritas—Spain. Bill finds the wild and woolly west tame in comparison with Spanish everyday life, but he finds no hardship in acclimating himself. He runs into Mose, a high brown from the home of prohibition, who was a member of his regiment during the recent war. Mose elects himself Bill's valet, more for protection than anything else. So Bill finds himself given every attention, but unconsciously assuming the role of bouncer for the darkie. Bill falls in love with a señorita who spends most of her time trying to persuade a greaser, who admits he's the champion bull thrower of Spain, that the place for bull throwing is inside the ring. But then bull throwers are bull throwers, and Bill has the time of his life trying to propose to the señorita. But toreadors are not to be cast off and in time Bill finds himself fighting the greaser. Of course he wins. But the climax is staged at the arena, where the supposed champion is pinned to the ground by a

rushing bull. Bill rushes into the fray and shows the greaseball how cows, bulls and such are tossed in America—and he does and saves the champion himself. That's the beginning of the end for the champion who is licked at a duel, kicked around like Jim Casey's dog, and otherwise made to understand his business is bulling the bull. (*Motion Picture World*, September 2, 1922, p. 63 cited in Richard, 1992, 244.)

Yankee Señor (1926, Fox) stars Tom Mix as a soldier of fortune of mixed blood, the son of a "high caste" and therefore acceptable Mexican mother and a New England father. Mix stops a band of Mexican bandidos from robbing the company payroll and later decides to cross the border and visit Mexico. He finds out that the head of the bandits, a "foxy greaser," is also his uncle. The greaser uncle decides to murder Mix, spread-eagling him in the desert sun, but Mix's horse saves him. Still later, Mix falls in love with a señorita who happens to be the uncle's daughter. Really enraged now, the uncle hires another Mexican "dancing dame" to vamp Mix. It seems to be effective, but Mix eventually rejects the vamp, and now both the hired woman and the uncle want his skin. But all ends well for Mix in the last reel.

Richard has reviewed the script of one of the most famous Hispanic-themed films, *Bordertown* (1935, Warner) and has found that

some of the lines that the PCA censored from the second and third copy of the script, would have been harsh even for a scenarist of some twenty years before: "Gimme that ball, *chili*." A policeman speaking: "On your way, greaser." "Tough little greaser." Davis in anger screaming, "greaser—greaser." To Johnny: "I guess you're not used to associating with white people." "You lazy greaser," "You greasers are all alike." And, Johnny admitting in disgust, "I'm a greasy little Mexican." There were fifty or so more uses of such terms, not one of which Joe Breen's office allowed into the final script. That script cast Muni as a semisympathetic character, the victim of his race, circumstance, and fate. (1992, 499.)

In the following chapter a few additional films that use the greaser epithet in their titles can be seen in the review of the Broncho Billy films.

The Bandit

The bandit was the most common Hispanic male character, and he is almost always Mexican or a Gypsy (for films about the latter, see the following chapter). The bandit was so overused as a Mexican that according to Richard: "By [1913] the Mexican as a bandit was firmly ingrained in the viewer's mind. The terms were thought to be interchangeable, Mexican equalled bandit" (1992, 109). Some of the bandits did their deeds purely within the Hispanic community, but the primary mode of banditry was against Anglos. Several of the bandit films featured white women in heroic roles against these villains as can be documented by the material that follows in this section and in the following chapter in the "Anglo Heroines" category.

A Cup of Cold Water (1911, Selig) has the bandit José abduct a baby girl from the hacienda. Pursued by the rurales, he is killed before returning the lost child and the film moves to tracing her life into adulthood. *A Fair Exchange* (1911, Selig) has Mexican bandits capture an Anglo because one of theirs has been taken prisoner by the sheriff. An Anglo girl, Madge, the "spunky sweetheart" then captures Carita, one of the bandits' women and exchanges her for her own Anglo love interest. *The Long Arm of the*

Law (1911, Kalem) features a clever Mexican outlaw who outwits Mexican authorities and crosses over into the United States. However, his lust is his downfall, for he makes a play for an Anglo woman but is rebuffed. Later, at a fiesta he is recognized and takes the Anglo woman as his shield but is eventually driven off the edge of a precipice by the posse in his pursuit.

Betty's Bandit (1912, Nestor) is primarily about a white woman torn between love and duty. A Mexican bandit attempts to rob an Anglo with his jeweled dagger. The Anglo is wounded but successfully resists and keeps the bandit's dagger. He is helped by Betty who nurses him to health and notices the dagger, thinking it belongs to the wounded Anglo. When a reward is posted for the owner of this dagger she is torn between her love for the wounded man and her sense of duty. She chooses love, but is overjoyed at learning that the Anglo is innocent when the evil Mexican is brought to justice.

The Outlaw's Sacrifice (1912, Essanay) features a Mexican marauder so bad that he is shot by a "good" Anglo outlaw as the Mexican attacks the sheriff's wife. In *The Ghost of the Hacienda* (1913, American/Mutual), Anglos buy a hacienda south of the border and Mexican bandits, learning that they have gold hidden away there, decide to raid it. Meanwhile, the Anglo woman learns from her peons that the hacienda is reputed to be haunted by the ghost of "señorita Ysolda" who had been killed by El Capitán, the Mexican bandit. She remembers how "superstitious the lower class Mexicans are" and dons the garb of a ghost as the bandits burst into the house. Her appearance on the veranda sends the Mexicans scrambling in all directions. *The Jealousy of Miguel and Isabella* (1913, Selig) has a Mexican maiden, Isabella, arrange for Pedro, the local bandit, to capture two Anglos, a man and a woman, to ensure that her own Anglo love interest is free to woo her. The señorita's plans go awry and the remorseful Isabella releases one of the captives, and the remorseful bandido, seeking atonement for his sins, lets himself be captured and jailed.

To the Brave Belong the Fair (1913, Nestor) is a remarkably insulting remake of a fairy tale, set south of the border during the Mexican Revolution. An Anglo offers his daughter's hand to whomever can cross the border and capture a Mexican. Hiram, John, and Eddie, the suitors, start out. Eddie at first captures a Mexican general and, realizing the danger of his action, then makes him exchange clothes and leaves the hapless Mexican in the bushes. He then encounters a band of bandidos who mistake him for their leader and he heads the band north. In the meantime, John dresses a tramp as a Mexican and for this is awarded the girl. However, at the marriage ceremony, when Eddie is seen with all of his captive bandits, the girl is given to the proper hero.

At Mexico's Mercy (1914, Victor) has Romero, a Mexican bandit, attempting to extort an Anglo mine operator by threatening to close his business. He is helped in the film by a General Cardillo, a supposed revolutionary but actual bandit. The Anglos are saved at the end by the U.S. Cavalry.

The Caballero's Way (1914, Eclair), based on a story by O. Henry, is possibly the first film in which the main character is called Cisco, although he does not yet have the salient features of the Cisco Kid. This bandit takes what he wants from the general store, shoots the sheriff "through the badge" and is very jealous about the behavior of his love, Tonia, a temptress. The army is assigned to deal with this menace and a handsome Anglo lieutenant falls for Tonia. When Cisco learns of the affair, his spirit is broken and he is brought to justice submissive and seeking punishment.

'Cross the Mexican Line (1914, Nestor) is another film where a disappointed Mexican woman plots revenge and repents. She has fallen in love with a wounded Anglo whom she has nursed to health, but when events don't go her way, she arranges to have him and his Anglo love captured by Mexican bandits. Repenting of her actions, she tries to have them freed but is unable to do so; the U.S. Cavalry succeeds where she fails.

Girl of the Golden West (1915, Lasky-Belasco, director Cecil B. DeMille) was a major film production with major plot complications to go with it. The Anglo woman, Nora gets involved with the bandit Ramerrez; however, he actually is a city-bred man named Johnson. Eventually Nora leaves behind the Anglo sheriff as well as the town with the pseudo-Mexican bandit to begin a new life. This very popular film, based on the play with the same title by David Belasco (it was also made into a notable Puccini opera, *La Fanciulla Del West),* was remade in 1923 (First National) causing the *New York Times* (5.12.1923) to criticize the Mexican bandit as too classy to be convincing: "In those golden days of '49 there may have been Beau Brummell bandits, but Mr. Kerrigan outdoes the usual conception of a handsome beguiling bandit. His face is too wavy for anyone who runs a band of highwaymen. . . . When he is wounded by the sheriff and kept in bed by the girl, his chin is wonderfully free from any sign of a beard. Mr. Kerrigan is a most unusual Mexican." The film was made yet again in 1930 (First National) in a sound version and released as an operetta with the same title (1938, MGM) starring Jeannette MacDonald, Nelson Eddy, and Walter Pidgeon.

The Grudge (1915, Broncho), starring William S. Hart, who some critics have supposed to be anti-Mexican and who would replace Broncho Billy as the premier Western genre hero, had a Mexican bandit engaged in a grudge with an Anglo youth. However, revenge according to the Mexican's code of ethics had to be deferred until the Anglo, who became ill, could recuperate. By that time the bandit was ready to forgive and the two became fast friends. *The Heart of a Bandit* (1915, Biograph) depicts a cowardly half-breed who tries to capture a bandit with all sorts of odious ruses such as using the bandit's wife and child. The half-breed is killed but the bandit dies honorably, sacrificing his life for the Anglo rancher's family. *The Obstinate Sheriff* (1915, Lubin) is a classic example of one of the most common Hollywood plots directed against Mexican bandits or any other hated group of the moment. Steve loves the sheriff's beautiful daughter, but is spurned by the father. However, when the bandit Mexican Pete kidnaps the lady and uses her as a "human shield," Steve uses his ingenuity to save her and his reward is the woman's hand in marriage.

The Patriot (1916, Triangle) features William S. Hart as an Anglo who initially feels wronged by his government and participates in a Mexican bandit raid on a U.S. settlement. But when he discovers an orphan boy, he comes to his senses and helps defeat the attacking bandits. *Headin' South* (1918, Famous Players-Lasky) is among the earliest good badman films, featuring Douglas Fairbanks going south of the border and teaming up with Spanish Joe and his gang of bandits. Fairbanks put brains into Joe's border bandit operation but a dispute over a pretty señorita puts a violent end to the partnership. Besides, in the end Fairbanks reveals himself not to be a bandit at all, but an officer of the Northwest Mounted Police. Richard observes, "one might consider this film to be the very early beginnings of the 'Good Badman' genre, an anti-hero who makes his own personal distinction between good and evil and never betrays his honor by violating this conception. As a bandit, 'Doug' was a perfect gentleman" (1992, 211). The film was advertised as a "dizzy debauch of daring deeds and startling stunts."

Heart of the Sunset (1918, Goldwyn) is about another strong white woman, the film was advertised as one in which "real humans do real human deeds." Alaire owns ranches on both sides of the border, but she is afflicted with a dissolute husband "whose fancy ran free among the native Mexican women" and "left free to her own devices" she falls for a local Anglo lawman. However, the lustful Mexican rebel chief, Longorio, who aspires to be Mexico's president, no less, wants the woman for himself. He steals some of her cattle to lure her into Mexico and captures her and kills her husband. She refuses his offer of marriage and when the Anglo law enforcer who has come for her is also captured, they are both to be executed. Again, the U.S. Cavalry arrives in time to save them.

The Knickerbocker Buckaroo (1919, Fairbanks/Famous Players-Lasky), starring Douglas Fairbanks during a period when American grievances over Pancho Villa and Mexican bandits of the Revolution of 1910 had begun to ease, is a transitional film, one of the earliest where an Anglo hero uses the Mexican bandit more as a comic foil, a buffoon with humorous possibilities. Fairbanks jumps, rides over, and shoots his opposition with derision and athletic ease, and at one point the bandit, López, saves him from a lynching. *The Double O* (1922, Arrow) features a ranch managed by an odious Anglo character who with his best friend, a Mexican, Cholo Pete, is in league with Mexican cattle rustlers. When the pretty new Anglo owner of the ranch arrives, the manager makes advances on her which she rejects. The manager arranges to have Cholo kidnap her, which causes Happy Hanes, a brash Anglo hero to try and find her. However, he too is captured by the Mexican bandits. Even so, the two Anglos are able to defeat the Mexican bandits and ultimately are married.

In *Somewhere in Sonora* (1927, First National), one Anglo saves his Anglo buddies from joining up with a really bad bunch of bandits, some from south of the border. In *Desert Rider* (1929, MGM), Western star Tim McCoy rides for the Pony Express and saves Dolores, the beautiful señorita, played by Raquel Torres, who has just been robbed of the deed to her hacienda by a bunch of bandits, an ethnically mixed group led by Anglos. *The Lawless Region* (1929, First National) has Western hero Ken Maynar and his faithful horse Tarzan save a group of small-time cattle ranchers from Ramírez and his gang of Mexican cattle thieves. Richard (1992, 386) observes about this film: "There was a bit of a bad moment when the Hispanics heavily doped the hero, but that horse was almost human and certainly a match for any Mexican. Licking his master's face to revive him, man and horse go on to bring the bandits to justice."

Rio Rita (1929, RKO) was the first musical Western, featuring not only "all dialogue" as the industry called it, but songs as well. In this very successful film, Bebe Daniels played Rita, a carefree señorita filled with singing affection for good bad bandits and Mexican generals. The plot revolves around the search for Kinkajou, a mysterious and notorious bandit in whose honor a song and dance has been created:

> They have a dance in Mexicola
> It's all the natives do,
> You'll have it on your pianola
> It's called the Kinkajou.
> They dance every night,
> It is dynamite, Yea!
> It has a bit of Española
> A bit of Chile too, Señor.

The Show of Shows (1929, Warner/First National) was a mechanism for presenting the stars of the Warner Studio, enabling them to show off in the talking roles of the new sound era. This was a musical that had one Hispanic-themed musical number that the Mexican government protested for its insulting implications. The number featured Douglas Fairbanks, Monte Blue, Noah Beery, and others in a "line them up against the wall and execute them" scene with Mexican bandits, set in the badlands of Mexico.

The Land of Missing Men (1930, Tiffany) was the vehicle for the first appearance of the distinguished Mexican director, Emilio "El Indio" Fernández in a Hollywood production, naturally in the role of the murderous bandit for which he received praise for his "realistic appearance" and for his speaking "with a Spanish accent that sounds real and no doubt is so" (cited in Richard, 1992, 410). With respect to other cultures and language groups, Hollywood has always had a challenge in deciding how much other than English to include and what accent to emphasize. How much German should a Nazi speak in order to support an appropriate characterization? What language should Romans of antiquity speak? Usually British English. In the case of Mexicans, the answer was usually broken English during the first decades. In this film, however, it was noted that realism was enhanced "particularly in the use of Spanish when one of the bandit group speaks to another." When López, the bandit leader was brought to justice, his Spanish cursing required no translation.

Beyond the Rockies (1932, RKO) was a popular Western featuring one of Hollywood's most successful cowboys, Tom Keene, whose modus operandi was enhanced by the addition of Julián Rivero, the loyal and womanizing sidekick. Rivero was typically seen in these films leering through a window at a cook or other domestic and offering to steal something that she might want. The comic angle provided strong counterpoint to the rough activities of Keene in catching badmen. Rivero's character was advertised to have "robbed many banks," "killed many men," and "loved many women, but had never forgotten to be a gentleman." *Law and Lawless* (1933, Majestic Pictures) similarly features Jack Hoxie teamed up with Julián Rivero, beating up bandits who in turn are made up of both Anglos and Mexicans to save a sweet señorita from sure death. *Outlaw Justice* (1933, Majestic Pictures) had Jack Hoxie permit himself marked as a bandit in order to readily enter the guild and capture the real badmen. The Mexican American actor from Tucson, Chris-Pin Martin, who often provided comic relief as Pancho or Gorditor in the Cisco Kid series and many other Westerns, here provided the same as an inept, bumbling Mexican bandit. *Somewhere in Sonora* (1933, Warner) featured John Wayne, who is framed for fixing a stagecoach race and has to cross the border where he falls in with local bandidos who he pretends to join. Eventually thwarting their designs on a silver mine, he heads for home with the pretty señorita.

Two interesting films feature mexicana bandits, consequently with different plots. The most interesting of these films is *Female Bandit* (1910, New York Motion Picture Co.), where poverty drives a peasant's wife to banditry so she can feed her family and sick husband. When her home is raided she escapes but her husband is taken away and blamed for the crimes. About to be hanged, la bandida returns just in the nick of time to save him from the noose, then saves the governor's daughter from a fire. *The Señorita's Conquest* (1911, Lubin) features Dolores, a Mexican bandida, who "in the spirit of dare-deviltry" decides to turn against her bandit chief, Juan, for a reward of $500. Falling in love with the Anglo sheriff brings complications however, as both are captured by Juan. Nevertheless, Dolores helps her Anglo lover escape and is rescued and the Mexican bandit chief killed.

The Bad Mexican

In the following chapter we review additional badmen; however, the bad Mexican was pervasive in the first decades of American film, as was the Western film itself or its cousins such as those taking place during the Mexican Revolution. In light of this phenomenon, I have chosen to label the badman role as the "bad Mexican," who stands here by antonomasia for all of the Hispanic villains. The bad Mexican is, of course, very close to the bandit. However, there is an occupational difference. In contrast to the bandit, the bad Mexican opportunistically engages in some evil, almost always against Anglos. They are crooked gamblers, generals or other soldiers, hangers-on, merchants, lurkers, tramps, or landlords. While sometimes he simply wants money, power, or property, more often than not the bad Mexican is interested in satisfying his sexual desires in the basest manner. Usually the object of his lust is a white woman. In several of the bad Mexican movies, the villain is prepared to accept the woman as payment for a debt of one kind or another.

A Mexican's Crime (1909, New York Motion Picture Co.) has a Mexican scorned by a dancing cantina señorita. He attempts to stab her suitor first, and then he successfully shoots her. After a fierce chase, an Anglo posse is surrounded by many Mexicans who come to their evil compatriot's assistance but they are vanquished and the foul Mexican is brought to justice. In *A Tale of Texas* (1909, Centaur), "a bad Mexican, Valdéz" cheats Anglo cowboys at poker, but Tom finds him out and kicks him around. First Valdéz attempts to stab Tom in the back, and when failing that, steals money and blames the Anglo. But Tom pursues the Mexican to the river where he drowns. Eventually the Anglo clears his name. In *A Cowboy's Generosity* (1910, Bison), an unscrupulous old Mexican demands the mortgage payment from an old couple who he knows can't pay. In place of payment he offers to accept the daughter, who refuses and enlists the help of an Anglo cowboy who comes to her rescue.

Western Justice (1910, Lubin) features a Mexican who sees two prospectors dividing their profits. He ambushes one of them and pushes him off a cliff. This action is witnessed by an Indian girl who the Mexican had, according to the title cards, earlier "insulted"; this, as Richard puts it, was "a then accepted euphemism which covered everything from kissing to rape" (1992, 30). The Indian girl seeks help from her Indian husband and some local Anglos. They collaborate to hunt down the Mexican, tie a rope around his neck, and administer "western justice of the summary kind." The film's lynching scene predates the 1922 establishment of self-censorship by the Motion Picture Producers and Distributors of America, organized in that year.

What Great Bear Learned (1910, Méliès) is a production by the French group that may not have been plausible to U.S. production companies inasmuch as Indians are pit against Mexicans. Great Bear is the victim of a scheming bad Mexican and learns to never again trust one since he "was deceived as many others have been before and will be after." *The Mexican* (1911, Lubin) depicts a Mexican landlord who tries to cheat an Anglo woman who is defended by her daughter's suitor, Tom. The Anglo disciplines the Mexican who leaves only to return with a group of Mexican bandits intent on killing the family. The daughter takes one of the bandit's horses and brings the cavalry to dispose of the evildoers.

In Old Arizona (1909, Selig Polyscope) depicts a young woman on her way to an Arizona homestead who rejects the advances of a Mexican suitor. Enraged, he frees all of the horses in her camp, leaving the campers at the mercy of the dreaded Apaches;

however, they are saved by the U.S. Cavalry. Similarly, *The Poisoned Flume* (1911, American) features revenge by the bad Mexican through evildoing to the livestock. The film depicts the plight of a pretty widow and her daughter who are trying to keep the ranch going on their own. Martínez, the bad Mexican offers to marry first the mother and subsequently the daughter in order to control the property. When the avaricious opportunist is rejected by both, he seeks revenge by poisoning some of their cattle. Joe, the Anglo ranch hand kills the Mexican for the ladies, thus ridding them of this blight.

The Ranch Man's Daughter (1911, Lubin) features the bad Mexican as a migrant worker. José tires of his wife in Mexico and crosses the border for employment. He falls in love with the daughter of the owner of the ranch where he is employed. He makes advances to this Anglo woman, but she rejects him. Nonetheless, José steals her picture and brags about "how he got it" in the saloon where the Anglo woman's love interest overhears all and is devastated. At this point José's wife, who has been tracking the wayward Mexican, enters the saloon and, in the complications that follow, fatally shoots him, eliminating the menace to the Anglo lovers.

The Ranch Woman (1912, Champion) depicts Peggy, an Anglo woman lamentably fallen in love with a bad Mexican gambler, Juan, who has a beautiful señorita on the side, another "string to his bow." Unaware of this, the lady gives Juan money, which he squanders. The plot reaches the point where Juan decides to kill Peggy, but Black Cloud, her faithful Chippewa friend, saves her and throws him off the cliff. *The Wayfarer* (1912, Selig) has an itinerant Mexican opportunistically waiting for his chance to steal the family treasure but is foiled by the Anglo family. *A Western Child's Heroism* (1912, Champion) is similar. Here a wounded Mexican begs to be hidden. The Anglo mining family takes him in, and when the father strikes it rich, the ungrateful Mexican tries to steal the gold. He is stopped and driven off but comes back with a band of marauding Indians who attack the cabin that once was the bad Mexican's refuge. The child manages to steal one of the Indian ponies and gets help. The Mexican is captured, and the Indians beaten back.

In *The Mexican Gambler* (1913, Patheplay), a swindle is effected on the Anglo father by the Mexican, who offers to take the daughter in lieu of cash payment of the debt. Clara agrees, but on the way to the altar, the father discovers the duplicity and with the help of Clara's true Anglo love and a posse, they bring the Mexican to justice. In *A Yankee in Mexico* (1913, Patheplay), a young American sees a Mexican "brutally maltreating a peon woman" and beats him up. The Mexican demands a duel, which he tries to rig, but the woman overhears his designs and the Mexican is publicly shamed.

Captured by Mexicans (1914, Kalem) has a Mexican named Pete rescued from sure death in the desert and then "with supreme ingratitude" betray the Anglo couple in every possible way before he is finally brought to justice with the aid of the Anglo wife, a faithful dog, and the American consul. *Dolores de Aranda,* also released as *The Lady of Sorrow* (1914, Bison), has an evil hacendado, Don Miguel, impregnating one woman, kicking her in the stomach, and leaving her to die while he places Dolores in the convent to keep her a virgin. When he is rejected by the arranged bride, he rampages through the town killing many before the Anglo sheriff shoots him down and wins the girl for himself. *The Miner's Peril* (1914, Reliance) features a close encounter with death through a diabolically conceived apparatus. Two disreputable Mexicans are fired by the Anglo foreman for stealing ore. When they bother a Mexican girl, Nina, the foreman rescues her and eventually marries her. This causes the Mexicans to attack the couple's cabin, tie them up, and set up a trap designed to dump enough ore to crush their cabin. At the last moment, Nina knocks over a board, which disrupts the apparatus. The following morning the newlyweds are found safe and the Mexicans brought to justice. In *The Renegade's Vengeance* (1914, Selig), a hard-working, righteous Anglo encounters a Mexican beating his wife and physically punishes the perpetrator and takes the woman home to be cared for by his own wife. The Mexican embarks upon a series of vengeful actions against both wives, the husband, a small child, and the ranch animals but in the end is punished for his sins.

Crossroads (1922, William Smith) has an Anglo eager to become sheriff prevented from the job by a cunning Mexican who frames him to get the job for himself. The Mexican continues to harass the Anglo but when he plots his outright murder he alienates his Yaqui servant who turns against him. The Mexican is properly punished and the Anglo gets the job and the girl. *Just Tony* (1922, Fox) features Tom Mix's horse in the title role. The poor animal is beaten by his owner, a "brutal" Mexican, Manuel, in order to break his spirit. With Mix's help, the horse is saved, and in the end Tony justifiably tramples the Mexican to death just as he appears with the whip for the last time. In *King of the Arena* (1933, Universal), Western hero Ken Manyard is personally recruited by the governor of Texas to find the horrible Masked Death, who shoots people with chemical bullets that turn them into blobs. As it turns out, the lethal gunman is a bad Mexican who works at a Wild West show and is unmasked and put to death.

The Gay Caballero, Including Zorro and the Cisco Kid

The gay caballero is essentially a Latino Robin Hood. Or a pseudo-Latino one: occasionally the plot has the masked man turn out to be an Anglo in Latino disguise. The specific allusion to the Hispanic Robin Hood was common in the trade advertising or the reviews of the films, and particularly so after Douglas Fairbanks's 1922 *Robin Hood,* which, however, postdates the first Zorro film. Fairbanks did *The Good Badman* in 1916 which has some of the qualities of his Zorro role.

The Robin Hood connection is understandable in light of the fact that Douglas Fairbanks, who was closely associated with the Sherwood Forest, was the first Zorro, simply transferring his persona which featured cheerful exuberance, courage, a devil-may-care attitude, and extraordinary physical agility to the Southwest. Koszarksi points out that "what might have been a wrenching change of image for a lesser star only served to increase Fairbanks's popularity, for his new Don Diego character was simply Doug's old American aristocrat dressed up for a costume party. Behind Zorro's mask was the Fairbanks his fans had come to adore, now fully liberated through the simple expedient of the period setting" (1990, 271).

Gay caballero films primarily were set in colonial California under Spanish rule and featured conflicts between the corrupt peninsular Spanish administrator on the one hand, and on the other, the oppressed, who ranged from rich Creole hacendados to the peasant class. As the film type caught on, the setting began to vary quite a bit, and films even set in Argentina were produced. The gay caballero is similar to the good badman, but generally the essential difference is skin color and/or social class. The good badman is more often than not, a bandit. The gay caballero is, of course, an aristocrat. He also tends to be white, European, that is Castilian, even though his arch-enemy is the Spanish administrator. Interestingly, the role also developed into a vehicle for a few Latina Robin Hoods.

The White Vaquero (1913, Bison) is one of the first examples that depicts the type, but still in the garb of the bandit. Richard's research led him to conclude that "this film introduced a new characterization and represents the earliest appearance of the love-able rogue, a good badman, something of a Cisco Kid" (1992, 109). The reviewer of *Movie Picture World* noticed the difference: "The White Vaquero, a very romantic Mexican bandit, is a character who will win many friends" (November 29, 1913, p. 1009).

The year 1914 with *The Caballero's Way* (for a description see the bandit category) marked the first fully developed prototype of these films. The caballero cycle owed its inspiration to the North Carolina-born writer O. Henry (pen name of William Sidney Porter). The Cisco Kid was directly modeled on the writer's story (1907), "The Caballero's Way." O. Henry, who spent a number of years in Austin and Houston, Texas, and went to jail for embezzlement of an Austin bank, was among the last of the American writers to present Mexicans in a totally prejudicial and stereotypical manner. His usual method when writing about the West, only partially reflected in the caballero film cycle, was to spice up his stories with Spanish characters and motifs and to have pure-blooded Castilians thwart the mestizos and Indians. O. Henry's short stories, ex-tremely popular at the time, were ideal for movies since they were a type of formula fic-tion based on contrived plots, shallow characterization, strange turns of events, and surprise endings. Many of his stories were turned into films.

The first of the Zorro films was produced only a year after the character was cre-ated in 1919. *The Mark of Zorro* (1920, Fairbanks/United Artists) featured Douglas Fairbanks as Don Diego Vega/Señor Zorro, characters based on Johnson McCulley's 1919 short story, "The Curse of Capistrano." When Don Diego returns to Old California from school in Spain, he discovers the tyrannical governor Alvarado in abso-lute control. He assumes the role of a fop while secretly masquerading as Zorro, at-tempting to restore justice as a masked California Robin Hood. Zorro, the "Fox," outwits his enemies, wins over the soldiers to his cause, forces the governor to abdi-cate, and wins the love of Lolita, a lovely aristocrat who is delighted to learn that the fop to whom she has been promised but scorns is actually the dashing Zorro.

Among the many other films that were based on McCulley's story or that used the character of Zorro were *Don Q, Son of Zorro* (1925, United Artists), starring Douglas Fairbanks and Mary Astor, and *The Bold Caballero* (1936, Republic), starring Robert Livingston. A series of Republic produced serials in the 1930s and 1940s included the 1937 *Zorro Rides Again*, with Hispanic actor Duncan Renaldo, the 1939 *Zorro's Fighting Legion*, starring Reed Hadley, *The Mark of Zorro* (1940, Twentieth Century-Fox), starring Tyrone Power, and the 1944 *Zorro's Black Whip*, featuring a young girl taking the place of her brother, the murdered Zorro. Following the serials came the 1957 ABC-TV series, *Zorro*, starring Guy Williams and produced by Walt Disney, and more recently *Zorro the Gay Blade* (1981, Twentieth Century-Fox), starring George Hamilton, and Henry Darrow in the 1983 television comedy, *Zorro and Son*.

Don Q, Son of Zorro was a successful sequel to the first *The Mark of Zorro*, with Douglas Fairbanks at his athletic best, playing both Zorro, the father, and Don Q, his son. This film featured Fairbanks forswearing his sword for a bull whip. The villain is the Spanish governor who is attempting to tax the peasant population into slavery.

Richard judges the characterization as providing "audiences with a Spanish person-ality they could identify with, one whose adventures they would have enjoyed sharing. He was a Spaniard on the screen, but all knew him to be the number one swashbuck-ling Anglo star. The tyranny he fought against was still a 'greasy Spanish' captain, but Zorro, the Fox, was a good Hispanic hero who understood the meaning of democracy, justice and the North American way" (1992, xxvii).

The Cisco Kid series was the most popular of the gay caballero films. Warner Baxter starred in three such film episodes from 1929 to 1939 (note that as typical with Hollywood, at first Anglos did the role, Hispanics only later); César Romero did six between 1939 and 1941; Duncan Renaldo did eight between 1945 and 1950; and Gilbert Roland did six in 1946-1947 (Zinman, 1973). The Cisco character stressed the amorous side of the gay caballero, a charming brigand who prized a beautiful woman as a gourmet savors a vintage wine. Like his Anglo counterparts of similar Western series, his method was to ride in, destroy evil, and ride out, leaving a broken heart or two. If Cisco flirted with Anglo women, his status as a serial hero made marriage inconceivable—it would end the series! The formula worked tremendously well on television as well, since this syndicated serial garnered the largest receipts of its time.

In Old Arizona (1929, Fox, directors Raoul Walsh and Irving Cummings) officially began the Cisco Kid cycle of films. It was the first Fox all-talking feature film. Voted one of the ten best films of 1929, it featured Warner Baxter as a "jolly, romantic Mexican badman." Once again, a variation of the Robin Hood theme, it depicted a loveable bandit who specially selected the rich to rob and kept only enough of his take to live on, giving most of his loot to the poor. Cisco's woman, Chiquita, was the typical faithless and easy, sexy señorita.

The Arizona Kid (1930, Fox) chronicled the further adventures of the Cisco Kid, but here called "Arizona" and hiding out in Utah. The Argentine actress Mona Maris played Lorita, whom the Kid abandoned for the Anglo vamp played by Carol Lombard. When he realizes how bad the Anglo woman is, he returns to Lorita. Essentially this film was a remake of *In Old Arizona.*

The Cisco Kid (1931, Fox) featured this "swashbuckler with a heart," "a rogue who lived for romance," a "villain only to men" but a "hero to women," "a rough-riding, quick-shooting, hard-living son-of-a-gun" in a new format, with the usually inept sidekick, in this case, Gorditor, who in this production was played by the Mexican American, Chris-Pin Martin. This episode features the Latino Robin Hood helping a pretty widow with a lot of children keep her home with money that he steals.

In one film the gay caballero actually gets the girl. The exception actually proves the point that Hispanics within the plot of the film (as well as in the film industry itself) can only succeed if they are willing to deny their own culture and identity in favor of Anglo mores. Cornel Wilde as Don Arturo Bodega, "is a silk-suited grandee who joins Fremont's Freedom Forces in *California Conquest* [1952, Warner] and helping defeat the greaser scum of the Pacific province," proposes to his Anglo bride-to-be. The heroine mulls over the proposal by Don Arturo and responds, "You *would* give a lot to be an American, wouldn't you?" (Pettit, 1980, 140).

A female counterpart of the gay caballero also was very popular. *The Avenging Arrow* (1921, Pathé, serial with 15 episodes) featured Ruth Roland in the role of Anita, the "athletic but feminine" daughter of Don José Delgado and an Anglo mother. An offspring of this "fine old Spanish family," she had inherited the "proud blood of her race [while] at the same time having acquired many warm and human American traits." In the first episode Anita, in collaboration with Ralph, the handsome young Anglo she would fall in love with, act to save her father, Don José who has been shot and captured by a Mexican bandido. Most of the problems in these fifteen episodes are provided by a Mexican bandit. Another female counterpart appeared in *Lady Robin Hood* (1925, FBO). As the title indicates, the formula was the same, only the gender changed. Here a Spanish aristocrat's daughter fought for justice in Old California and was pitted against the evil Cabraza, the power behind the weak provincial governor. The female Robin Hood featured athletic ability as well.

The Spider and the Rose (1923, Principal) takes place in Old California before the days of the Anglos. The young Don, played by Noah Beery, overthrows the nefarious Mendozza and reestablishes justice. *Tiger Love* (1924, Paramount), based on the popular light opera *The Wild Cat* and featuring Antonio Moreno, had the same formula, except set in Spain.

The Cavalier (1928, Tiffany-Stahl) was, according to Richard, the "first feature film with a Hispanic theme that employed sound" (1992, 365). The process used synchronized records to match the actors lip movements and was never successful and was quickly supplanted by more sophisticated technology. The film was one more poor version of the masked avenger saving the poor and romancing a lady.

The plot of *The Gay Caballero* (1932, Fox) has a former football hero return to his ancestral estate in the West to fight the villainous Paco Morales, a hidalgo with an insatiable appetite for land who is aided by assorted goons like Jito, a giant who the locals fear. The Easterner allies himself with Conchita, the cantina cutie, and "El Coyote," a Robin Hood type, to make things right. *Man from Monterey* (1933, Warner Brothers) had John Wayne in the very incongruous role of an aristocratic Don, owner of a Spanish land grant, who North Americans hungry for such holdings didn't want to honor. He defended the Hispanics against this sort of oppression.

Under the Pampas Moon (1935, Fox) had Warner Baxter and Rita Cansino (before she changed her name to Rita Hayworth) in a Cisco Kid film where the Kid travels to Argentina. According to Richard (1992, 520), it was considered so awful that it was camp even before the concept had been coined. *The New York Times* (cited in Richard, ibid.) called it "antique humor" from the early days of the talkers (a mere six years earlier). *The Devil on Horseback* (1935, Grand National) featured another Hispanic Robin Hood bandit type in Argentina who wins the heart of Lili Damita (Liliane-Marie-Madeleine Carré), a French actress who played a number of Hispanic roles, sometimes opposite Errol Flynn to whom she was married for a period.

The Good or Faithful Mexican

As we have pointed out earlier, the good or faithful Mexican is usually either an obeisant greaser who has turned away from his former mores and internalized the values of WASP America, or he acts out of gratitude for some saving action by an Anglo hero. Of course, the Mexican is always faithful to a white male or female. However, the role mostly evolved into the sidekick of the gay caballero. Zorro, the Cisco Kid, and other gay caballeros were high class, and the usually bumbling, buffoon-like sidekicks were commonly from the lower class. (See the gay caballero category for a depiction of several sidekicks.)

A Mexican's Gratitude (1909, Essanay), the first film of its type uncovered by this research, was produced with G. M. Anderson as the star, before he assumed the role of the famous Broncho Billy. The Mexican is saved from a wrongful lynching by an Anglo sheriff. He writes the word "Gratitude" on a card, rips it in half, and gives one piece to the sheriff. Later, the Mexican is able to pay back the debt and save the sheriff's life. *The Mexican's Faith* (1910, Essanay) has Tony Pérez, a Mexican unjustly fired from one ranch but given a chance on another where he falls for the owner's lovely daughter. Attempting to force his affections on her, she refuses what she considers an insult and as a result he is almost horsewhipped. However, she saves him from the beating and he becomes her faithful servant. Tony saves her from an evil Easterner attempting to abduct her with the help of a different "dirty greaser." This variation on the *Tony the Greaser* plot of an obeisant Mexican had G. M. Anderson in the role of the Mexican.

The Two Sides (1911, Biograph, director D. W. Griffith), subtitled "A Vivid Contrast of the World's Prosperous and Poor," which surely must have caught the attention of the lower socioeconomic status nickelodeon crowd, portrays a Mexican laborer who "is discharged from the ranch with others, simply to reduce expenses to enhance the proprietor's already ample profits. Deprived of his revenue, the poor Mexican is in desperation as to the recovery of his sick child." Then a fire occurs which the Mexican discovers and he "is inclined through malice to allow it to burn." But when he realizes that the rancher's child is inside, he saves her and is duly rewarded.

The Mexican (1914, Selig), starring and directed by Tom Mix, depicts a Mexican who crosses the Río Bravo to seek employment at an Anglo ranch so he can feed his impoverished family. He is mistreated by the cowboys and gains revenge by burning the bunkhouse and engaging in other malicious activities. However, the owner's daughter is bitten by a rattler and turning from his vindictive ways, he rides for help to save the child. The grateful ranch owner rewards him by providing for his starving family. In *Within an Inch of His Life* (1914, Eclair), Pablo, a "Mexican snake charmer," plays a supporting role on behalf of his Anglo friend. With the help of his snakes, he breaks up a crowd who want to lynch a falsely accused Anglo.

The Good Badman

The Hispanic good badman has primarily one of two possible characterizations. One form is similar to the persona created by Douglas Fairbanks in his Anglo versions of the character, or even in his version of Zorro. However, the good badman, while he may have the agility and roguishness of Zorro, is not an aristocrat. The other style of characterization tends toward the bumbling buffoon. Here the good badman is typically a bandit, but because he is "bad" at his craft of banditry, he tends to be seen as a good or at least a good-hearted person. The good badman is usually a bandit or a pirate.

One of the first examples of this type on film appears in *The Good Bad Man* (1916, Triangle), starring Douglas Fairbanks. Although it does not have any Hispanics, the film and others like it starring Fairbanks helped to establish this characterization. The film depicted Fairbanks in the customary role of loveable rogue operating in the West. In the same year, Fairbanks starred in *The Half Breed* (1916, Triangle) based on a Bret Harte story in which a "good badman" rights the wrongs inflicted on a poor Indian girl. Fairbanks's persona was so strong and so well-known that he could play the role of a Mexican bandit, Zorro, or a half-breed and not be typecast in those roles. His followers simply accepted him in his customary athletic, daring-do role, despite whatever costume or make-up he might don.

The Bad Man (1923, First National) was the first major example of the genre of the good badman, "a genial border bandit," "a very bad hombre" but under his brown skin, good "when he gives a white man a wife, a fortune and a diamond-studded future." This production was a spectacular box office success, coast to coast. The format of the good bad bandido would be remade numerous times even into the present. In *The Bad Man*, the villain boasts with a greaser's diction, at least on dialog cards:

> I keel ze man sis morning,
> Heem call me dirty crook.
> I keel some more zis noontime
> And steal ess pocketbook. (Roeder, 1971, 21)

Reformed in the end, this low, cartoon-like bandido ultimately returns stolen cattle to their upright Anglo owners.

The sound version of *The Bad Man* (1930, First National) featured Walter Huston of *Treasure of the Sierra Madre* fame (as the prospector) as "a swaggering, gleaming-toothed flashing-eyed Pancho López, the Robin Hood of the border." Reviewers of the film were particularly impressed with the effectiveness, in their mind, of the bandit's language, spoken in broken English with an alleged tinge of Spanish. For example: "Oh, but Mexico ees no good place for me no more. Ees too civilize. Everywhere is law and order. . . . Then no go back. Ees much better United States." While *Motion Picture Guide* characterized it as the worst made movie that year, the formula was so popular that the film was remade in 1937 as *West of Shanghai,* using a Chinese bandit, and again in 1941 back in the Southwest with Wallace Beery. A Spanish language version of the same film was also produced, *El hombre malo* (1930, First National), for the Hispanic market in both the United States and abroad. The script was significantly rewritten in order to eliminate most of the negative stereotypes. Here Pancho López was primarily a protector of ruined ranchers and secondarily a bandit. All he asked for as his reward was that a child be named after him, Panchito or Panchita.

That Devil Quemado (1925, FBO) features Quemado "a bold bandit of the Robin Hood order, who helped the oppressed of Mexico in their struggle against the richer folk." It turns out, as in the case of other mistaken identity films where audiences could empathize with a different race or ethnicity but learn at the climax that the character is white after all, that Quemado is really Jim Fairfax, a Yalie who was merely "letting the steam of the ancient Dons from his veins." *Prairie Pirate* (1925, producers Distributing Corp.) has a "suave Mexican bandit who would always attend to things personal," such as seek the killer of his sister.

The Delightful Rogue (1929, RKO) an early sound or "all dialogue" movie as they were referred to contemporaneously, featured a good bad "Languid Latin" pirate. In this light comedy, he takes over a yacht and heads for the South Seas. At the end the wimpy, rich Anglo proves to be a coward and the Hispanic gets the white woman.

Beau Bandit (1930, indep.) has Rod La Rocque as Montero, a loveable, Mexican Robin Hood type bandit. In this depression-era film, Montero has a purely platonic admiration for an adorable Anglo woman who in turn is enamored of a dirt farmer about to be foreclosed on by the Anglo banker. When the banker offers money to Montero to get rid of the farmer, Montero plays Cupid and takes the money and gives it to the loving couple.

One Mad Kiss (1930, Fox) was produced primarily for the Latin American market and featured the good badman and others with the use of Latino actors: José Mojica, Mona Maris, and Antonio Moreno. Leo Carrillo was featured in *Broken Wing* (1932, Paramount) as Captain Inocencio of El Suelo, a good-natured killer who was "a man not to scoff at" since he was the chief of police as well as "the mayor, the prosecuting attorney, the judge and the Lord High Executioner when it pleases him to snuff out a life." The plot, which also featured Lupe Vélez as the good badman's woman secretly in love with an Anglo flyer (Melvyn Douglas), featured the usual complications: a love triangle, the Anglo suffering amnesia and being nursed to health by the señorita, and the interracial lovebirds facing the firing squad but saved at the last moment from el capitán.

An example of the good badman who is a buffoon is in *A Demon for Trouble* (1934, Steiner) which has Don Alvarado in the role of a notorious Mexican bandit who speaks Mexicanized English and takes time off of his usual activities to help an Anglo clear his good name, accomplishing all of this in a bumbling manner.

The Hispanic Avenger

The character of the Hispanic avenger provided some counterpoint and counterpunch to the negative stereotypes. Set against the bulk of over 2,000 Hispanic-focused films from the beginning to the mid-1930s, most of them with negative stereotypes, were a score or so that were sympathetic to Hispanics. The Hispanic avenger character is the most energetic and aggressive of the sympathetic characters. Obviously, there is a connection between the Hispanic avenger and the gay caballero, or even the good badman. The fundamental, defining feature of the avenger is, obviously, that he has been slighted or hurt personally, and thus he obtains satisfaction at one level or another for what has been done to him. I have chosen not to include in this category revenge films purely among Hispanics. Those films revolve around different behaviors such as lust, greed, and so on. In this category appear purely Hispanic avengers who are hurt by Anglos or Anglo society. They are primarily the victims of racial prejudice or the immoral use of power on the part of Anglos.

The Thread of Destiny (1910, Biograph, director D. W. Griffith) is an interesting and unique film. Taking its cues from Griffith's *The Greaser's Gauntlet,* where the Anglo heroine Mildred saves José from a lynching, the film goes much further, ending in interracial marriage. Myrtle is bringing flowers to a sick friend when she "meets a Mexican stranger, Estrada." Startled, she drops some of the flowers and the Mexican helps her recover them. Their hands touch and "she experiences a thrill, such as she had never felt before." Subsequently, Gus, a drunken Anglo who lusts after Myrtle accosts her and Estrada saves the lady. Infuriated, Gus gathers some locals together and they set out to lynch Estrada. The Anglo heroine protects the Mexican and keeps him hidden in her house. The two run off and are married at the local Spanish mission to the consternation of Gus who is told by the local boys who "awaken to their better selves" to leave the mixed-race newlyweds alone.

An unusual film in that it deals with racism as its theme is *The Mexican* (1911, American). Joe Curvey, a Mexican finds a baby girl in a basket and adopts her. Eighteen years later racist local toughs attack the father and daughter. An Anglo, Clarence and some of his more enlightened cowboy friends save the two. However, the enraged father enlists the aid of other Mexicans who have also suffered racial attacks and together they attack a neighboring Anglo ranch. People are killed and the father is captured along with the daughter. Both are to be hanged, but they are both rescued by Clarence who has fallen in love by now with the daughter. *The Ranchman's Vengeance* (1911, American) depicts how a Mexican half-breed finds an Anglo near death and brings him to his home in Mexico where his wife Marie nurses him back to health. While Pedro is toiling in the fields, the Anglo begins to have an affair with the Mexican wife. When Pedro finds out, with the patience and compassion of a saint, he sends her off with the Anglo, but with the admonition to him that he must be good to her. Five years later, Pedro learns that the Anglo has been living a life of debauchery and is beating his Mexican woman. He finds them. The weakened Marie dies and Pedro beats up the bully and ends up throwing him off a cliff. Avenged, he cries and recrosses into Mexico.

The Lash (1930, First National), also released as *Amigo* and based on the Lanier Virginia novel of the same name, was a different sort of California film in that it evoked the plight of the Hispanics immediately after California came under the control of the United States. "El Puma," the masked avenger, fights for the Hispanic population against the tyranny of United States officials who think that all property in Spanish California belongs to the new ruling Anglos. Despite the sympathy for Hispanics depicted in the film, all of the Hispanic characters were played by Anglos, with Richard Barthelmess as the young Don from Mexico City who finds his homeland overrun by ruthless americanos. This film has Mary Astor in the señorita role explain "gringo" according to a common, albeit incorrect, folk etymology, having it come from a song, "The Green Goes Over the Hill."

The Avenger (1931, Columbia) was about Joaquin Murieta (traditional English spelling) played by Buck Jones, who becomes the Black Shadow to exact revenge against three Anglo prospectors and to win the hand of Helen, the daughter of Captain Lake of the U.S. Army. *South of Río Grande* (1932, Columbia), a spin-off of the Cisco Kid, again had Buck Jones playing an avenging Mexican officer of the rurales and exposing Mona Maris as the evil Consuella.

The Latin Lover

The Latin Lover was usually an aristocrat or a person of means. He also embodied the stereotype among WASPs that Hispanics and other continentals had a certain grace, style, or savoir faire in matters of love, as well as readiness to engage in such activity without qualms, or at least puritanical ones. The phrase "continental morality" which was common in the first decades of the twentieth century was often associated with Latin Lovers, Hispanic, French, Italian, or otherwise. For these reasons many of the Hispanic Latin Lover roles are set in Spain or Argentina, and less often in Mexico. There is an indirect relationship between the Latin Lover and characters of classical literature such as Don Juan (see next chapter), Casanova, and others.

In the Land of the Cactus (1913, Lubin) features a Latin Lover who is outside of the formula for this role. The film depicts a Mexican who falls in love with an American girl who thinks that she is gravely sick. The Mexican's loving provides her cure; he is perhaps the first cinematically depicted sex therapist, certainly the first Hispanic one to exercise his therapy on a white woman. It is important to note that Romaine Fielding, who had established himself as Lubin's premier actor/director played the role of the Mexican. This was a common ethnic characterization for Fielding, as it was for Douglas Fairbanks. In the case of both of these actors, their film persona transcended the usual ethnic stereotypes associated with Hispanics, and thus, on the basis of their stardom, which was much more the "character" with whom the film viewers identified than the particular role specified by the plot, they exercised the privileges of daring, charisma, sexual attractiveness, and other qualities associated with a film celebrity.

Antonio Moreno played in a twenty-episode serial for Pathé, *House of Hate* (1918) as the Latin Lover opposite Pearl White, the immensely popular female counterpart to Douglas Fairbanks. The athletic and charming American had gained international fame with her episodic series, *The Perils of Pauline* (1914) and *The Exploits of Elaine* (1914-15). The addition of the Latin Lover to the repertoire of the acknowledged leader of the

"Dauntless Damsels of Distress" made for very successful box office. In *My American Life* (1922, Famous Players/Paramount), Antonio Moreno played opposite Gloria Swanson as an Argentine macho sportsman who loved his horses and loved his lady but had to beat back the other machos who were attracted to his Latin temptress. In *The Sainted Devil* (1924, Famous Players/Paramount), a similarly aristocratic Rudolph Valentino had to struggle with an Argentine bandit, "El Tigre," for his woman.

Four Horsemen of the Apocalypse (1921, Metro), starring Rudolph Valentino, was a major production themed around the Latin Lover. This adaptation of the novel by Spanish author Vicente Blasco Ibáñez was the most spectacular film of the year, costing a staggering $800,000 and utilizing more than 12,000 extras. Evoking the horrors of war, the film depicts the loves and intrigues of an Argentine patriarch, Julio, and other members of his family. One of the scenes, in an Argentine dance hall, with Valentino giving a notable performance, "popularized the tango and gave birth to a generation of 'Latin Lover' look-alikes that lasted well into the thirties. Because of the film's great popularity, making over three million dollars, its influence in reaffirming Latin stereotypes would be difficult to overestimate" (Richard, 1992, 235).

In Cradle Snatchers (1927, Fox), a comic version of the Latin Lover prevails. A wife teaches her erring husband a lesson by hiring a boy to play the role of a hot-blooded Spaniard. The lesson is that "just the fear of a little Latin love will keep those inattentive husbands in line, every time" (Richard, 1992, 347). *A Certain Young Man* (1928, MGM) had Ramón Novarro rejecting many willing women for the love of an innocent maiden. Novarro played an affluent Spanish college student whose only subject appeared to be señoritas in *In Gay Madrid* (1930, MGM). The film featured an early screen credit for Xavier Cugat playing the song, "Santiago." *Captain Thunder* (1931, Warner) featured a cross between the Robin Hood type and Don Juan, not too difficult to achieve. Captain Thunder was advertised as a "Hot Tamale Heartbreaker" who broke "Mexican Heads and Hearts" and the "grandest lover on the Río Grande! Kid Casanova on horseback!" Fay Wray played the loveliest of the señoritas.

Notes

[1]Richard, *The Hispanic Image on the Silver Screen: An Interpretive Filmography from Silents into Sound, 1898-1935* is not your everyday compilation. On the one hand the book is so filled with typographical atrocities, misspellings, mangled data, inaccurate plot summaries, incorrect identifications of the ethnicity of actors, and missing explanations of abbreviations, that it must be handled with the most extreme caution. *Caveat emptor* lest the tergiversated data in Richard become the cant of the ingenuous researchers who imprudently make use of it. On the other hand, use it we must. Richard has done an arduous task of research for which there is no analog; his is a gold mine of information. With respect to his opinions about the films themselves, they range from eccentric (perhaps cranky is more apt) to genial. As they say, when he is good, he is very good.

[2]For review and analysis of other races, ethnicities and cultures, see the following: Donald Bogle, *Toms, Coons, Mulattoes, Mammies, and Bucks: An Interpretive History of Blacks in American Film*; Thomas Cripps, *Slow Fade to Black: The Negro in American Film, 1900-1941*; Daniel J. Leab, *From Sambo to Superspade: The Black Experience in Motion Pictures*; James R. Nesteby, *Black Images in American Films, 1896-1954*; Gary Null, *Black Hollywood*; Gretchen Bataille and Charles L. P. Silet, *The Pretend Indians: Images of Native Americans in the Movies*; Ralph E. Friar and Natasha A. Friar, *The Only Good Indian; Indians in Film*; Lester Friedman, *Hollywood's Image of the Jew*; Lester D. Friedman, ed., *Unspeakable*

Images: Ethnicity and the American Cinema; Patricia Erens, *The Jew in American Cinema*; Sarah Blacher Cohen, ed., *From Hester Street to Hollywood.*

[3]See "Screen Credit for Dubbed Foreign Voices by UA," *Variety*, 11.27.1929, "Must Talkies Stay at Home," *Literary Digest*, 12.29.1930, Charles Ford, "Paramount at Joinville," *Films in Review*, November 1961, 541-550; "Joinville Makes 110 in 12 Languages," *Film Daily*: 8.26.30, "French-Spanish Versions for 20 Paris Pictures," *Film Daily*: 9.5.30, and the *Variety* issue, 11.10.1931.

[4]The end of the silent period witnessed the production of a group of films, *White Gold* (1927), *The Wind* (1928), and *City Girl* (1928-1930) which share the premise of an urban woman who is up-rooted and forced to relocate to a farm. In each case, "this traditional heart of American culture is pictured as a patriarchal tyranny, with madness and murder the inevitable outcome." (Koszarksi, 1990, 343, n. 55.)

[5]The most accepted etymology of gringo is as a variation of *griego*, used commonly in phrases during medieval times both in the Romance languages and in English that communicated foreign-ness, e.g., "It's Greek to me." Gringo appears in the *Quixote*, published in 1605, with that meaning hundreds of years before Anglo-Mexican contact on the U.S. border and is commonly used in Argentina to refer to non-Anglo foreigners, usually Italians.

4

The First Decades: Film Types

In the previous chapter we focused on the eleven Hispanic roles that we were able to discern, which, when taken together, account for most of the *character types* who appear in the first decades of United States film production.

Another useful way of conducting an analysis of Hispanic-focused films is to review them by *film type*, understood liberally. Reviewing the data set in this fashion, the material which follows includes films categorized either by cycle or series (Ramona films, Broncho Billy films), setting (the border, the jungle), historical events (the Mexican Revolution, the Battle of the Alamo, California's independence), plot features (Anglo marries señorita), the activities of ethnic or racial groups (Gypsies, half-breeds), communication features (bad or broken English), classical Hispanic figures (Don Juan, Don Quixote), Hispanic activities (bullfighting), and a few other film-type categories. While numerous films are reviewed within each of the categories that have been established, these represent only a sample of the films produced that could have been entered. However, in the case of a few categories such as the Ramona and Don Quixote films, where not many examples were identified, all those uncovered by this research are included. There is no aspiration for, nor for that matter, possibility of completeness. Also, as in the case of the material reviewed in the previous chapter, while many films could be cross categorized (e.g., the Ramona films also evoke half-breeds and are related to California's independence), with very few exceptions, simply for the sake of space and expedience, they are entered only once, in the category in which they appear to best fit. Finally, the categories that are presented here hardly exhaust those that could have been entertained, and are simply provided for their heuristic value in order to get a semblance of the breadth and depth of U.S. film production and to review some of the more notable film types. This point, hopefully should answer natural questions such as, why in view of a category, California's independence, no category on California more generally? An entire book could easily be produced on all of the Hispanic-focused California films. Many more categories could have been included such as Arizona, New Mexico, Texas, Panama, padres and missions, torture, revenge, Yaquis, Philip II, pirates, federales, fiestas, siestas, or Porfirio Díaz. For readers interested in isolating categories that do not appear in this handbook, the first places to go are the *American Film Institute Catalogs*, Richard (1992), and García Riera (1987).

As in the case of the material in the preceding chapter, coverage goes more or less through the silent period and the beginning of the sound period up to the social consciousness era. However, in those cases where it made more sense to extend further, even through to the present (e.g., The Alamo films), I have done so. The coverage that follows in this chapter does not include the several Mexican or other Latin American productions that were dubbed into English and released in the United States with English titles, *except for* Villa and Zapata films where it was important to do so. Nor is coverage extended in this chapter to the Spanish-language productions of the U.S. film industry intended for the Spanish-speaking market. (See Richard, 1992 for a beginning filmography of both of these categories of films.)

The Impact of the Mexican Revolution on Hispanic-Focused Film Production

Just as the Spanish-American War was serendipitous to the earliest development of U.S. film and its nascent film industry, the Mexican Revolution provided an extraordinary opportunity for film production in the United States. In 1913, President Francisco I. Madero was murdered on the orders of General Victoriano Huerta, which prompted Woodrow Wilson to withdraw American recognition of the Mexican government (even though ambassador Henry Lane Wilson was at least a tacit party to the murder, as well as an active plotter in Madero's removal). This began a period of several years when there was almost continuous confrontation between Mexico and the United States, and during which Mexico was often front-page news in the print media. Richard concludes from his interpretive filmography of the Hispanic in film which begins in 1898 and runs through 1935:

> There can be little doubt that events in Mexico fueled the growth of the motion picture industry and conversely, moving pictures helped solidify established Hispanic stereotypes. Of the total seven hundred and fifty films surveyed in these pages which were produced between 1910 and 1919, approximately fifty-five percent of them dealt specifically with Mexico. From 1911 to 1920 the percentage dropped dramatically until it solidified to less than ten percent in each of the last three years of that decade. Of the ninety-eight films with Hispanic themes which were shown in 1930, only ten of them could be considered to have a Mexican orientation. By then other Hispanic regions occupied more screen time. (1992, xxv)

Conventions Governing Hispanic-Focused Films in the First Decades of Production

Roeder (1971) analyzed eighty-three story films between 1907-1912 and found a number of primary, formative conventions in the way Hispanics were treated. In addition, Pettit (1980) has made some telling observations about interracial male-female relationships in U.S. film. Some of these generalizations, expanded upon and adapted by my research appear here inasmuch as they well apply to the films that I have reviewed in this book up until the emergence of the social consciousness era and the social problem films.

1. Violence and crime. Of the eighty-three story films identified by Roeder, at least sixty showed one or more Hispanic characters engaging in acts of violence, and in all but a half-dozen of these films, the Hispanic is shown to be clearly in the wrong. Jealousy and vengeance are the primary cause of violence. Moreover, over three-fourths of the films analyzed by Roeder depicted a Hispanic either robbing, assaulting, kidnapping, smuggling, cheating, killing, or attempting murder. Several of the Hispanics are not only violent, but perversely so. In *The Cowboy's Baby* (1910, Selig) the Mexican throws a baby in a river. The Mexicans in *A Western Child's Heroism* (1912, Champion) and *At The End of the Trail* (1912, Vitagraph) turn on Americans who have saved their lives. In the earliest films, such as *Western Justice* (1910, Lubin), *The Half-Breed's Treachery* (1912, Lubin), and *A Ride for Life* (1912, Bison) before the development of the production code, Mexicans are lynched for their crimes against Anglos. Violence and crime, of course, are staples of U.S. film and the cinema of other countries. Nevertheless, the disproportionate propensity toward violence of Hispanics on the silver screen is characteristic of U.S. film production not only of the first decades, but right up through the present.

2. Hierarchical, superordinate/subordinate relationships between Anglos and Hispanics of opposite sex. Generally, Anglo men can fall in love with and marry Hispanic women, but Anglo women rarely fall in love with Hispanic men. Hispanic men who show sexual, romantic, or marital interests in Anglo women pay dearly for their forwardness unless they merely idealize or faithfully serve their beloved from a distance. In the Roeder analysis, Anglo men won the love of Hispanic women in at least thirteen of the eighty-three story films, and married the women in over half of these. Moreover, Anglo men often attract Hispanic women away from their Hispanic lovers or suitors, families, nation, and culture; occasionally the converse, Hispanic women attracting Anglo men from their Anglo women is depicted, but it is very rare for this to occur permanently. The Anglo usually goes through a good-bad phase with the Hispanic woman and returns to his Anglo woman. Utilizing the character type, "dark lady" (we have preferred either vamp which is an epithet used generally in film criticism for both Hispanic-focused and other sorts of film, or señorita), Pettit observes that

> Blood and caste reign supreme in the dark lady film just as with the gay caballero. If the dark lady, with her hip swinging and amusing difficulties with the English language, encountered female Anglo competition, she surely went down to defeat. If, however, as in *Border Café*, there were no blondes in sight, she could eventually win her hero as long as her "Hispanic" heritage was pure Spanish. (Pettit, 1980, 141)

Pettit's research also led him to an interesting conclusion about the mixed blood or ancestry of Hispanic females with respect to their potential for learning and assimilating Anglo culture. He finds that the assumed ability to accomplish this feat is primarily dependent on her blood line:

> . . . by far the most popular type of dark lady is only half-Spanish and therefore must undergo a long apprenticeship before gaining the Saxon hero. These tests of loyalty invariably require the dark lady to desert her race, her native country, or both. Dozens of films exploit her precarious position. She may fall in love with a captured American and rescue him from imminent execution at the hands of the Mexican army. Perhaps she must turn against a member of her family—a brother, as in *Chiquita, the Dancer,* or a father, as in *His Mexican Sweetheart*–thus demonstrating both her loyalty to the hero and her allegiance to "the land of the free." Whatever the variations on the theme, the outcome is the same. The dark lady gains the hero only by renouncing her past. (1980, 142)

3. Bad Anglos can become rehabilitated or "good" again through violent or intrepid acts against Hispanics. In other words, the "good" phase of the Anglo good badman is often realized through violence against a Hispanic which is simultaneously redemptive for the

Anglo. This is the case, for example, in *Broncho Billy's Redemption* (1910), *Under Mexican Skies* (1912, Essanay), *A Mexican's Gratitude* (1909, Essanay), *The Outlaw's Sacrifice* (1912, Essanay), and *The Sheriff and His Man* (1912, Essanay) where a sheriff and his prisoner are attacked by Mexicans but the prisoner becomes a hero and is forgiven for his crimes when he chases the Mexicans down. *Brand of Cowardice* (1916, Rolfe/Metro) and *The Taint of Fear* (1916, Universal) have equally germane plots.

4. Hispanics, primarily Mexicans, are shown to be profoundly superstitious or ignorant and Anglos, particularly women, avail themselves of this in order to overcome Hispanic villainy. In *Under Mexican Skies* (1912, Essanay), an Anglo girl frightens off an aggressive Mexican by waving a crucifix, what would later become the primary antivampire prop, to ward him off. *The Ghost of the Hacienda* (1913, American/Mutual) features an Anglo woman who saves her family by donning the garb of a ghost and warding off the bandits. *The Ghost of the Rancho* (1918, Pathé, supervisor D. W. Griffith, director W. Christy Cabanne) made use of this same artifice. In *The Lamb* (1915, Triangle), a group of "Mexican half-breeds" (apparently Yaquis) are foiled by a machine gun which they see as useless junk and which permits the Anglo couple to escape. The film is notable in that it is the first with Douglas Fairbanks as the star and appears to have been written by Griffith using his pseudonym, Granville Warwick (see Hanson, 1988, 498). In *The Evil Eye* (1916, Paramount, starring Blanche Sweet), superstitious and ignorant Mexican workers consider that the light that a doctor uses to examine the throats of patients suffering from an epidemic of diphtheria is an evil eye causing the disease itself. They try to burn her eyes out but she is saved by her Anglo boyfriend. In *Lieutenant Danny, USA* (1916, Triangle), Mexican bandits execute the Anglo officer, but he is saved because the bullet is stopped by his St. Christopher's medal. Believing they are fighting a dead man, the bandits scatter.

Film Types

Anglo Dallies with Señorita

The mores of the first decades of film production were on the side of interracial romance between Anglo males and Hispanic women culminating in marriage (see *Anglo Marries Señorita* section), although virtually none of these film plots got past the actual wedding if that. Nevertheless, a significant number of films depicted mere dalliances, although more often than not, they did not end well for the Anglo cad.

Taking its cues from pulp novels, particularly those of Ned Buntline, *The Señorita* (1909, Selig) cultivated the concept that no dark-skinned woman could resist any Anglo's charms, which permitted the Anglo considerable latitude of behavior, including discarding such questionable if not inferior affection (Richard, 1992, 17). In this film, an American is saved from death in the desert by a young Mexican couple and repays this generosity by dallying with the girl. After using her, he returns her to the grateful Mexican suitor, who is happy to have his girl back. The film ends with the two Mexicans standing in front of their humble home waving goodbye to the Anglo who heads north. Similar is *Carmelita's Revenge* (1914, Selig) where an Anglo loves, gets, and discards Carmelita, who in a very rare plot twist successfully puts a knife in his back and does him in. *The Mission in the Desert* (1911, American) is a "seduced and abandoned" film. The Mexican girl, Nell, falls in love with Ned who gets her pregnant. José, Nell's hot-tempered brother, kills Ned when the latter refuses to marry the girl. Nell resolves to do penance and atone for her sins by entering the convent. *A Devil With Women* (1930, Fox) is notable in that it casts Victor McLaglen versus Humphrey Bogart struggling for the affections of Mona Maris against a Central American backdrop filled with bandits, revolutionaries, soldiers of fortune, and vamps. At the end, McLaglen, playing the main part, gives his blessing to the characters represented by Bogart and Maris (Tom and Rosita) and goes out to search for another war (and woman).

Anglo Heroines

In chapter II, we reviewed the emergence of films that depicted Anglo heroines who overcame Hispanic or other ethnic villains, as in *The Arizona Cat Claw,* or who collaborated with ethnics as in *The Greaser's Gauntlet* and *The Red Girl.* Some additional examples of Anglo heroines interacting with ethnics follow.

The Substitute (1911, Lubin) is described in the publicity as "a very commendable picture in which the heroine, who will strongly appeal to spectators, saves a large invoice of gold from Mexican bandits." The woman finds her male colleague in a drunken stupor and on her own initiative climbs a pole and successfully calls for the cavalry. *A Western Heroine* (1911, Kalem) has an Anglo woman entrusted with a large sum of money that is coveted by a Mexican thief. With considerable effort and daring, she thwarts the evildoer and returns the money entrusted to her. *A Child of the Rancho* (1911, Bison) has a Mexican suitor who has been rebuffed attempt to force the Anglo girl to elope. Using the simple ploy to trick the Mexican of shouting "Don't shoot!" to an imaginary person behind the suitor, she distracts him, get his gun, and keeps him at bay until help arrives. The premise of *El Diablo* (1916, Mustang) is that the bandit with that moniker hates sheriffs and no one in Sagebrush, Arizona wants the job. Some newcomers open up a restaurant and one of the boys takes the sheriff's job. His sister worries about that and decides to rid the region of El Diablo herself and is successful in this endeavor.

By 1916, serials had became enormously popular although they soon became associated with the juvenile market and were relegated to lesser movie theaters (see Bowser, 1990 and Koszarski, 1990 for good discussions of this), and as might be anticipated a few serials were introduced that featured Hispanic motifs. The two most important for this research featured white women accomplishing athletic and intrepid deeds that were considered contemporaneously as on a par with the feats of Douglas Fairbanks. The *Liberty–A Daughter of the USA* serials were introduced by Universal in 1916. This nineteen-part serial featured Liberty, played by Marie Walcamp, as the female Anglo heroine "struggling against the dark forces of revolutionary evil at work in Mexico" during the Mexican Revolution of 1910. Many of Liberty's efforts are directed against López, the evil bandit. "A unique feature of this adventure serial was Liberty's right-hand man, a sympathetically portrayed Mexican named Pedro who provided protection and broke her out of rat-infested prisons in almost every episode. In the final sequence, the Mexican bandit López is killed and the remainder of the revolutionaries mopped up and all the good people, Liberty, Major Winston, Pedro, and so on, reunited at the hacienda where the insurrection all began" (Richard, 1992, 179). Another serial, produced during World War I, that cultivated an Anglo heroine was *Pearl of the Army*, featuring Pearl White. Some of these episodes take place in the Hispanic world against Hispanic evildoers. The most historically interesting is *Pearl of the Army, Episode 8, International Diplomacy* (1917, Pathé), where Pearl foils the evil designs of "Bolero" and his "Boleroistas" who wish to acquire the plans of the Panama Canal so that they can destroy it for the wartime foreign powers who want it out of commission.

In *The Bird of Prey* (1918, Fox), a white woman's Anglo lover commits suicide in her presence. The man's friend blames Adele and threatens to implicate her unless she commits a penance of his design. She agrees and for her punishment he installs her as one of the ladies of a Mexican dance hall. Unhappy with her plight, she soon becomes one of the leaders of a band of bandits. However, when they plan the murder of the Anglo owner of a mine, she warns him, but Pedro, the rival bandit chieftain threatens to kill the wife and daughter of the mine owner unless she gives herself willingly to him. She agrees but manages to put off the fate worse than death until she is saved by the original man who brought her to the dance hall. Exhibitors recommended that the film be advertised with the following: "American Girl Leads Mexican Outlaws on Tour of Vengeance" or "Thrilling Story of Mexican Bandit Queen."

Señorita (1927, Paramount) had Bebe Daniels score a resounding success with her version of *Mark of Zorro*. Audiences saw her as a combination of Douglas Fairbanks and Tom Mix. The female masked avenger did her work on the Argentine pampas in this film.

Anglo Marries Señorita

Most of these films follow the formulas we described in the preceding chapter as well as the review of the conventions of interracial romance that we made at the beginning of this one. Because interracial romance was so ubiquitous there are large numbers of "Anglo marries señorita" films. While the following mostly follow the conventions they are notable in one or more lesser respect. There are two that develop the marriage and depict negative outcomes.

A Spanish Romance (1908, Manhattan/Vitagraph) featured an Englishman who clandestinely won the affections of a dark-skinned señorita, and with the intercession of a sympathetic clergyman, married her against the will of her father who wanted to save her for one of the local rich. In *Fighting Bob* (1909, Selig Polyscope), an Anglo carried off his señorita who had been promised to a wealthy Mexican with the help of Fighting Bob and other sailors who throw the police into the sea, permitting the lover to take off in his boat. According to the exhibitors the audiences were pleased to see a "Yankee lieutenant outwit a whole set of Spaniards."

The Mexican's Revenge (1909, Vitagraph) has the captain of a North American cruiser fall in love with Rosita, the local beauty. This fires the jealousy of her Hispanic swain who attempts to kill him, but because "there is a strain of Indian blood in his veins, he would first torture" his hapless victim. Rosita saves her lover by leading on horseback, the U.S. Cavalry no less. They marry, in Mexico, under the protection of Old Glory waving in the wind.

In *His Mexican Bride* (1909, Centaur), an actual marriage is developed and it is seen to not work well. An Anglo from back east goes to work in Mexico. The boss's daughter falls in love with him and the father attempts to stab him in the back as a result. He disarms and spanks the boss which gets him fired. The daughter marries him anyway, but the Anglo soon discovers that his eastern woman wants him back. Thinking she has been deceived, the Mexican plans to poison him, but then decides she is too much in love with him and stops him from drinking the poison at the last moment. Not only is the mexicana frivolous and hot tempered, but irresolute as well. *Never Too Late to Mend* (1911, Solax) also depicts the poor results of interracial marriage. Jack is on military duty on the border long enough to marry and father a son with a Mexican woman. He leaves the woman for twenty-five years, during which his son grows to manhood and becomes a Mexican horse thief. Upon his return to the area with the cavalry, the father captures his own son and upon recognizing him, remembers his errant ways. Given the circumstances he both leaves the military service and releases the young man.

The Vow of Ysobel (1912, Selig) appears to assume that Mexicans were not white because this film, set in Mexico, is advertised: "With the advent of the Gringo, or white people, into old Mexico, many picturesque, and often-times, thrilling romances took place." The film uses the stock formula of the señorita who spurns Juan for the handsome Doctor Livingston. Juan is almost able to treacherously kill the Anglo but instead falls to his death. The doctor survives to marry Ysobel. *The Rose of California* (1912, IMP) featured a wealthy Spanish ranchero who objected to a young government official's love for his daughter. Love triumphed and the two were married by the local padre, only after the enraged father unsuccessfully attempts to plunge his dagger into the bridegroom's back.

The Penalty of Jealousy (1913, Lubin) goes against the formula in certain respects. Here an Anglo fugitive crosses the border to escape the law. He steals the lovely Carmelita from her lover, Ramón, and marries her. However, his bad treatment of his wife causes her to commit suicide. When the Anglo crosses back into the United States, he finds none other than Ramón romancing his old girl. In the fight that results, both the Anglo and the Mexican, who has justly been seeking revenge against the Anglo, are blown to bits in a dynamite blast.

The Spanish Parrot-Girl (1913, Selig), notable only for its name, is pure stock formula featuring a wealthy Anglo who falls in love with the parrot girl and foils a rich Spaniard who has demanded her in lieu of the father's debts by paying those debts himself and taking the girl to the altar. *The Mexican Rebellion* (1914, Ammex) is one of several films where Anglos actually win the Mexican Revolution for the Mexicans. Billed as a "thrilling adventure of an American in Mexico" and "a sensational story of romance and war, showing how an American soldier of fortune joined the Mexican rebel army and had many narrow escapes from death," this film also has the Anglo win the heart of the señorita, Mercedes, the daughter of the Federalista general. She goes against her evil father because she "longed to lead a desperate charge . . . and transform retreat into victory."

Good Men and Bad (1923, F. W. Kraemer) is the eternal fairy tale set in the Argentine pampas. The indebted father offers the hand of his lovely daughter to whoever can ride and break a wild mare. The cowardly Don Esteban can not but Steve, the Anglo cowboy does so and wins the señorita. *Too Many Kisses* (1925, Paramount) has an Anglo touring Europe. Everything is fine until he gets to Spain, the land of el amor, where he falls in love with the dark-skinned señorita and has to best Julio, a Spanish captain and expert knife thrower. He does and takes his señorita back home. According to Richard (1992, 324), this film featured Harpo Marx in his first silent role as the Spanish village idiot.

The Dove (1928, United Artists), based on a David Belasco play, had a white-skinned Anglo, played by Norma Talmadge, wooed by the good/bad Don José, played by Noah Beery. The only Hispanic actor in this film is Gilbert Roland who curiously enough plays the Anglo who the girl loves and to whom Don José, with a big heart, gives the girl at the end. This very popular film changed its location to the republic of "Costa Roja" as the result of the protest of the Mexican government. The location wasn't half of the problem: the *New York Times* described the character of Don José:

> Taking it by and large, José is perhaps a screen character to which the Mexican government might have objected for he is greedy, sensuous, boastful, cold-blooded, irritable and quite a winebibber, but he does dress well. His top boots are always like a mirror, his riding breeches are spotless, and he is a good figure of a man. He hates to have his luncheon spoiled by a noisy victim of his shooting squad. He adores beauty, but is inconstant. (January 3, 1928)

As Richard puts it, the attitude of the *Times* would appear to be "What was Mexico objecting about?" (1992, 366). The film was very successful and remade as *Girl of the Río*, released in Great Britain as *The Dove* (1932, RKO, starring Dolores del Río).

Morals of Marcus (1935, Real Art Gaumont) featured Lupe Vélez who escapes from a harem and ends up in the cabin of an English lord. He takes his dark-skinned prize back to the ancestral estates. There are complications. Lupe runs to Paris because she thinks he only wants to marry her out of pity. In the last reel he finds her singing her broken heart out with that "foni" accent of hers and it's okay.

Aztecs

Aztecs functioned in U.S. film in one of two ways, generally. Anglos sought Aztec treasure and had to confront the particularities of contemporary Mexico in order to do so (willing señoritas, bandidos, siestas and fiestas, etc.) or films were made showing the conquest of Mexico by the Spaniards, in which case interracial romance carried the film, with the Castilians occupying the white man role.

The Fall of Montezuma (1912, Essanay) appears to be the first of this kind and apparently was filmed in Mexico during revolutionary times, with Francis X. Bushman playing Hernán Cortés (see García Riera, 1987, vol. 1, 57). Not much is known about the plot. *The Aztec Treasure* (1914, Eclair) combines the Mexican Revolution with the hunt for Montezuma's hidden treasure. The Mexican revolutionaries are dependent on their Anglo leader, Dick Henshaw. They struggle against Miguel, the tyrant of Mescalito who knows that the treasure of Montezuma is hidden somewhere in his province. He enslaves and tortures to death peons to learn where, but to know avail. Then Miguel captures Juan, the local headman who knows where the treasure is, as well as Juan's beautiful daughter, Dolores, who has fallen in love with the Anglo. He tortures Juan to death, but the latter reveals nothing. Finally, he captures the Anglo too, but out of respect for the Yankee, his own men rebel against him. Miguel dies by a snake bite trying to escape through a trap door, and the treasure is found.

The Lost Ledge (1915, Bison) features two Anglo engineers, one good, one bad, both trying to find the lost ledge of a once rich mine as well as win the hand of the girl. The good Anglo befriends an old "Aztec" (the media, including tabloid newspapers often used the term to refer to Mexicans when they wanted to emphasize Mexico's Indian background). Through various plot complications, the Aztec helps the good Anglo find lost treasure and win the girl. The bad engineer is punished, and the Aztec, having filled his function for the good Anglo, "is seen no more."

The Captive God (1916, New York Motion Picture Corp., starring William S. Hart) has a young Spanish boy washed ashore and picked up by the native "Tehuans" early in the sixteenth century. Having never seen a white man before, they raise the stranger and revere him as a god, calling him Chiapa. Their tribe prospers after Chiapa joins them, and hearing of this, the Aztecs raid the Tehuans and capture him. Montezuma's daughter, Lolomi, promptly falls in love with him. Montezuma sentences Chiapa to have his heart cut out despite Lolomi's protests, but she sends word to the surviving Tehuans, imploring them to attack her tribe. This they do, rescuing their god just as Cortés lands at Vera Cruz.

The Woman God Forgot (1917, Famous Players-Lasky), directed by Cecil B. DeMille and featuring Geraldine Farrar as Tecza, Raymond Hatton as Montezuma, and Wallace Reid as Alvarado, one of Cortés's chief lieutenants, is another elaborate DeMille production featuring a set that included an entire Aztec city complete with a temple over two hundred feet high as a center piece. One of the big scenes, said to be worth the price of admission on its own, showed a staircase built up the side of a mountain. Similar to *Martyrs of the Alamo,* the film industry's version of Aztec history was based primarily on interracial, female-male relationships. Whereas Texas had been depicted as born as a result of Mexican officers harassing white women, in this film Tecza falls in love with Alvarado, who is to have his heart torn from him at the temple. She opens the city gates to hordes of Spaniards who rescue Alvarado and storm Montezuma's castle. Tecza is cursed by her dying father who tells her that she shall wander the earth deserted by the gods of all peoples. On the other hand, Alvarado offers her his love and the consolation of Christianity, both of which she embraces to her salvation.

The Mayans and the Incas got much less play in American cinema. However, *The Mojave Kid* (1927, Joseph P. Kennedy/Film Booking Offices of America) is a standard Western featuring Anglo bandits and Anglo heroes, except for two factors. The first is that the bandits hide out in an old Incan temple. How this temple got to be situated in the American Mojave desert, several thousand miles north of the Incan culture in South America, defies the imagination, nor is it of any consequence in the film. More interesting, the film was presented (equivalent to produced) by Joseph P. Kennedy, the patriarch of the family and father of John Fitzgerald Kennedy. Kennedy functioned as presenter in the production of dozens of films during the 1920s, ranging from *Clancy's Kosher Wedding* (1927, Film Booking Offices of America), an urban interethnic comedy to *The Cherokee Kid* (1927, Film Book Offices Pictures), a Western featuring a hero with a hidden identity.

Bad or Broken English or Other Language Misunderstandings

The quality of the English spoken by an actor or expressed in a film often was highly important. A number of film stars and lesser actors based their careers partly or primarily on the quality of their spoken English. In a few movies the essential conflict revolved around linguistic misunderstanding (as it does in the Chicano film, *The Ballad of Gregorio Cortez*).

Leo Carrillo was considered highly adept at both broken English of the Hispanic and of the Italian kinds and thus as one of the busiest character actors of the 1930s and 1940s. He played a Mexican in various Westerns and was often cast as either an Hispanic or Italian mobster. Lupe Vélez's constant malaprops and idiosyncratic use of English were a hallmark of her persona, both in the Mexican spitfire series and the films which preceded them such as *Lady of the Pavements* (1929, United Artists, Presented by Joseph M. Schenck, director D. W. Griffith) and *The Half-Naked Truth* (1932, Radio Pictures, Inc.). Emilio "El Indio" Fernández was cast as a more realistic bandit in *The Land of Missing Men* (1930, Tiffany Productions) because he was able to snarl and curse in true Spanish, a novelty for the time. Accent was also a fundamental component of certain fictional personas such as the Mexican bandit or the Cisco Kid and his sidekick and associates, who often were required to speak broken English.

On the other hand, in *Ridin' Law* (1930, Big 4), the cantina dancer, Carmencita, played by René Borden, is criticized by *Variety* (July 9, 1930) for having forgotten her "spick accent" and reverting to perfect English.

Often the Hispanic persona is caused to resort to onomatopoeia as did Dolores del Río to her Anglo love interest in *Girl of the Río* (1931, RKO): "My heart is thump thump thump when I see you." Sometimes, in counterpoint fashion, the difficulty that Anglos might have (in character or out!) is used humoristically as in *The Kid from Spain* (1932, Goldwyn) where Eddie Cantor is confused with a Spanish matador and is forced to enter the arena. He is admonished that if he can only say the word "Popocatépetl" (the famous Mexican volcano), he will stop the bull dead in its tracks, but Eddie just can't accomplish that.

In *Two Gun Caballero* (1931, Imperial), an early talkie, the new Anglo in town has the following dialogue with the local cantina girl which serves as a paradigm for countless films of this ilk:

Rosita. You look sad señor. Come, Rosita will make you laugh. . . . You are an Americano, yes? Rosita likes very much the Americano. Does not the Americano like Rosita?
Bob. The señorita dances very charmingly.
López. What are you doing here? If you know who López is, then you do not make flirt with this woman.
Rosita. No! No! The Americano does not flirt with me. I flirt with him. You do not come and I am so lonesome. I flirt with him. Why? Because he look just, almost like my López. Of course, he is not quite so handsome as my López.

García Riera (see "Problemas de lenguaje: el *broken English,*" 1987, vol. I, 171ff) has an interesting discussion of this aspect of U.S. films with the conclusion:

> Hollywood made use of other languages with a system of conventions that was as effective as it was unreal. These conventions might offend the ears of a foreign public but they didn't disturb the North American routine. The commonplace of any public (not only the North American) is to register the foreign as the extravagant. Therefore, foreign languages were an occasion for laughter, especially for a Hollywood that was focused primarily on its less-cultured spectators. (In this procedure as in many others, Mexican cinema would follow Hollywood.) (García Riera, 1987, vol. I, 173, translation mine)

The linguistic component of Hispanic stereotyping has continued into the present, although it is more often used in the form of parody of earlier films, as in *¡Three Amigos!* (1986, Orion). However, as recently as *Treasure of Sierra Madre* (1948, Warner), the Mexican bandit played by Alonso Bedoya uttered his famous line, "I don't have to show you no stinking badges," which was to become the ironic title of the Luis Valdez 1986 drama. Issues of accent actually preceded the film sound era. The highly successful film, *The Bad Man* (1923, see preceding chapter, in *good badman* section) featured a good badman with crowd-pleasing broken English (I keel se man sis morning, etc.) that was conveyed by the dialogue intertitles inserted in the film.

In *Mexican As It Is Spoken* (1911, Méliès), a film that probably would not have occurred to an American production company, an Englishman finds himself "in the predicament of a man who cannot understand Mexican" spoken by two bearded "horrid men" who gesticulate violently at him and end up tying him with a rope. He discovers that he was in a blasting zone and that they saved him from injury. *The Unexpected* (1916, Rex) has a similar plot, depicting an Anglo woman who decides to go for a walk even though she is warned that there may be Mexican bandits in the area. Suddenly a Mexican comes up behind her and is quickly joined by others who can not speak English. Their wild gesticulations frighten her and when she realizes that there is dynamite in some boxes she tries to escape but is prevented from doing so by the men. After numerous plot complications she realizes that the Mexicans were merely at work and restraining her for her own safety.

The Battle of the Alamo Films

The cycle of The Battle of the Alamo movies, both theatrical and those produced for television since 1911 through 1988, is so extensive that when added up surely they surpass the entire production of the film industry of a minor South American or Asian producer nation. The number of films is so extensive that they have produced a good book solely devoted to the topic: Frank Thompson, *Alamo Movies.*

The Immortal Alamo, also released as *Fall of the Alamo* (1911, Méliès), is the first recorded Alamo picture. However, little is known about the film for which no prints are known to survive. It was advertised as both "a correct representation of the Alamo insurrection, famous in history" (Thompson, 1991, 18) and a love story. In chapter II of this book we referred to the second film in the cycle, *The Martyrs of the Alamo or The Birth of Texas* (1915, Fine Arts Film Co., director W. Christy Cabanne, supervisor D. W. Griffith); in chapter II it is discussed as a film that based the birth of Texas as primarily occurring because Mexican officers sexually harassed white women, thus causing white men to rebel. The film was advertised as a Griffith production (Cabanne was never mentioned), although Griffith was actually hard at work on *Intolerance* (released in 1916), and gave only cursory attention to *Martyrs.* The producers tried to further capitalize on Griffith's involvement by using the subtitle, *The Birth of Texas* thus implying that it was a sequel to *The Birth of a Nation,* which had been released earlier that year. The similarities were much more than publicity hype however. Thompson points out:

> *The Martyrs of the Alamo,* playing on the racial hatred which characterized *The Birth of a Nation,* presents the Texas Revolution as a conflict of skin colors. Like the arrogant Reconstruction-era Blacks of *Birth, Martyrs'* Mexican soldiers are damned in the filmmakers eyes not for their political threat, but for their disrespect for white men and mindless lust for white women. Cabanne invokes *The Birth of a Nation* with a canny bit of casting: Santa Anna is played by Walter Long, the same actor who, in *Birth,* portrayed the renegade Negro Gus whose rape attempt drives the pure Little Sister (Mae Marsh) to her death. (1991, 26)

One of the first incidents in the film sets up the conflict. A white woman on her way home through the San Antonio streets is accosted by a Mexican officer who flirts with her. She sweeps past him angrily and when her husband comes home to find her still shaken from this incident, he immediately goes and seeks out the officer and shoots him dead. His subsequent jailing is seen as the rallying point for other Americans who have been living under similarly intolerable conditions: not political oppression but the threat of miscegenation. The battle scenes of the Alamo themselves are well-staged and exciting in a manner befitting the Griffith production group and in fact the massacre's aftermath uses the same technique of tableaux showing the dead bodies of Alamo defenders that was used effectively in the "War's Peace" scenes of *The Birth of a Nation.* In the final reel, Houston defeats Santa Anna at the battle of San Jacinto. While Houston prepares for attack, the foul and heavily drugged Santa Anna—García Riera describes him as portrayed as a *mariguano* (1987, vol. I, 92)—is spending his time watching a number of sexy women dance around his camp tent, presumably preliminary to a night of debauchery. The final scene evokes the martyrdom of the fallen heroes whose efforts helped create the Lone Star State. The film dissolves on the flags of Texas. According to a 1915 review in the *New York Times,* this was the first film in which Douglas Fairbanks acted, although *The Lamb* in which the actor starred was released earlier (Hanson, 1988, 594.)

The extremely successful Cabanne/Griffith production was followed by a long line of Alamo movies: *With Davy Crockett at the Fall of the Alamo* (1926, Sunset Productions) was an uninspired version centered this time on Crockett. *Heroes of the Alamo* (1937, Sunset Productions) was even worse, a low-budget sound production that cobbled together silent footage from Sunset's earlier "epic" productions about Daniel Boone, Kit Carson, General Custer, and others with new shots. *The Man from the Alamo* (1953, Universal, director Budd Boetticher, starring Glenn Ford with Chill Wills and Dennis Weaver) is less about the Alamo than about John Stroud, a fictional character who earned the undeserved reputation of a coward because he agreed to escort women and children out of the mission turned fort which saved his own life. Part of making things right has Stroud join up with Sam Houston at San Jacinto.

Davy Crockett, King of the Wild Frontier (1955, Disney, director Norman Foster, starring Fess Parker and Buddy Ebsen) created a national phenomenon. The film was a low-budget vehicle originally produced in technicolor but broadcast in three black and white segments for the new *Disneyland* television series in 1954. As Thompson (1991, 49) points out:

> The resulting television episodes, hastily-shot and crudely constructed, were never meant to be anything but weekly series fodder, enjoyed this week, forgotten next. But when the first of them aired in December, 1954, a craze of epic proportions was born. Almost immediately, children all over the United States, and eventually, the world, tossed away their outer space paraphernalia and began wearing coonskin caps, dying heroically in backyard Alamos and endlessly crooning their new anthem, "Davy, Davy Crockett, King of the Wild Frontier!"

The film itself, as well the television segments it was based upon, had Crockett last seen alive, using Ol' Betsy, his rifle, as a club, swinging it against the charging Mexicans. The film was more effective in displaying the desperate, siege conditions of the defenders of the Alamo than lavish films such as the John Wayne production. On the other hand the battle scenes were notably threadbare.

The Last Command (1955, Republic, director Frank Lloyd, starring Sterling Hayden, Anna Maria Alberghetti, and Richard Carlson with Arthur Hunnicut, Ernest Borgnine, and Slim Pickens) added to the standard fare teen idol types who were allowed to escape the Alamo as couriers. Sterling Hayden's participation in the film is instructive in a number of ways, not least of which was the potential that defending the Alamo as an American shrine and heroically dying at the hand of despised enemies could have for rehabilitating one's tarnished image. He took on this "flag-waver" he claimed later, to atone to the film community for his membership in the Communist party earlier in life. Hayden had escaped the blacklist of the late 1940s and early 1950s by testifying before the House Un-American Activities Committee and naming several Hollywood personalities as known "Communists." He was commended by the committee "for speaking out as an intensely loyal citizen" and was spared blacklisting. He had hoped that his role as Jim Bowie would help reinstate him as a patriotic American. According to his autobiography *Wanderer* (1963), he suffered considerable remorse and loss of self-esteem by his actions before the Committee.

The Alamo (1959, Batjac, released through United Artists, director John Wayne, starring John Wayne, Richard Widmark, Laurence Harvey, Richard Boone, Frankie Avalon, and Linda Cristal with Chill Wills and bullfighter Carlos Arruza) was produced as a paean to "American" heroism, not history, and in part as an antidote to a then-perceived threat by Wayne of burgeoning communism around the world. Wayne told columnist Louella Parsons, "These are perilous times, the eyes of the world are on us. We must sell America to countries threatened with Communist domination. Our picture is also important to Americans who should appreciate the struggle our ancestors made for the precious freedom which we now enjoy" (Thompson, 1991, 80). Something else again was the long-winded mess that was produced, based on the awful script written by James Edward Grant. Thompson observes that "there isn't an instant in the film that corresponds to the historical event of 1836 in any way, except coincidentally" (1991, 67). Most egregious from the point of view of historical fidelity, for the purpose of expanding the range of possible viewers, was the full-fledged addition to the plot of teen idol Frankie Avalon in the role of Smitty and Linda Cristal as the love interest, Flaca.

Even in its own time, *The Alamo* had a mixed reception at best. The publicity campaign on its behalf which equated one's esteem for the film with the quality of one's patriotism mostly backfired so that generally the film was not taken seriously. That was not the only factor that made it easy to patronize the film. Although this lavish epic featured well-mounted and executed action scenes, the struggle between the foppish, aristocratic Travis and the hard-drinking Bowie, with normally bull-headed and fiery John Wayne in an uncomfortable, atypical role as Davy Crockett, *homo conciliator*, was tedious. The film was filled with sententious, interminable speeches and irrelevant, melodramatic subplots.

The Alamo was named as one of the "Best American Films of 1960" by the National Board of Review (originally founded in 1909 as the National Board of Censorship) and received the Harvard Lampoon "Movie Worsts" award for the same year with the following citation: "The 'Along-the-Mohawk Grant' to that film with the most drummed-up publicity campaign." Probably the film will be best-known for the largest film budget of record to date at $12 million (it recouped about $8 million in its original release) and for turning Texan's Happy Shahan's Bracketville ranch into a tourist attraction, "Alamo Village" and occasional movie location (films on Sam Houston, a couple of Alamo productions, the 1968 *Bandolero*, the 1980 *Barbarosa*, the 1989 *Lonesome Dove*, among others).

Following the pretentiousness of the John Wayne affair, the Alamo was the occasion of *Viva Max!* (1969, Commonwealth United, director Jerry Paris), a screwball comedy featuring a Mexican general's attempt with an inept group of fighters to retake the Alamo (he marches out from Laredo) in order to prove himself to his girlfriend. He is met by an equally bumbling American militia and various other wacko groups such as right-wing loonies convinced that Max's army are Chinese Communists. This production had no Hispanics in major roles with Peter Ustinov as General Maximilian Rodrigues De Santos, John Astin as Sgt. Valdez, Jonathon Winters as General Billy Joe, and Pamela Tiffin as Paula. Although the film was hardly as offensive as the Wayne vehicle, in contrast to the patriotic froth that the former generated, the latter film inspired minor demonstrations in several cities where it played. Thus *Viva Max!* is a good index of the progress of the civil rights movement during the 1960s.

Thirteen Days to Glory (1986) was a television production that aired on the NBC network in 1987 and did feature one Hispanic in a major role, Raúl Julia as Santa Anna. *Alamo . . . The Price of Freedom* (1987) is an IMAX (image maximization) production in a 48-minute version that plays continuously at the San Antonio IMAX theater and in a 39-minute version that played in various IMAX theaters around the country. The docudrama makes an attempt at giving a balanced account of the Battle of the Alamo, but the film, which primarily emphasizes battle scenes and other action, is primarily a vehicle for the IMAX production values. Dan R. Goddard of *The San Antonio Express-News* (March 6, 1988) described it as "looking like a Frederic Remington painting with an image six stories high and cannons shooting off in a six-channel wall of sound. . . ." The film used Hispanic actors in a number of roles with the major ones going to Enrique Sandino (Santa Anna) and Derek Caballero (Juan Seguín). The film has never been accepted by the Mexican community of San Antonio or elsewhere, particularly so since the Chicano production, *Seguín* (1982, Jesús Salvador Treviño, screened on Public Broadcasting System) attempted to deal with the Alamo with considerable more historical depth (see chapter 7). The Alamo has also been the topic of many television films (see Thompson, 1991).

Black Legend Films

The Black Legend is a concept that refers to the negative image of Spain and Spaniards that arose from the reign of King Phillip II (reigned 1556-98) and his anti-Protestant policies. The Black Legend particularly focuses on the alleged cruelty and intolerance of Spaniards. As might be expected, the Legend gets primarily play in those U.S. films, beginning with the earliest productions, that treated the Spanish-American War or related aspects of Cuban or Philippine life. Elements of the Black Legend are also prominent in pirate and privateer films and in other period pieces that reflect rivalry or war between England and Spain. Several of the films, notably *The Penitentes,* in addition to using Spain or Spanish elements as foils for conflict, also promote the exoticism of their material.

A Spanish Cavalier (1912, Edison) was advertised as evoking "the shadow of the Spanish Inquisition with all the cruelty and ignorant conception of misguided Christianity." The film features the Grand Inquisitor whose vast powers over life and death are misused to torture a confession from the maid of a lady who the Inquisitor secretly loves, in order to allow him to condemn the lady to death. In the last scene, the maid manages to escape and tells the Spanish cavalier, the genuine love interest, who is able to rescue the lady from the *auto-da-fe.*

Under the Black Flag (1913, Gold Seal) features the exploits of a few good-bad pirates sailing the "Spanish Main," particularly Sir Henry Morgan, whose violent deeds are justified because he commits them against the genuinely evil Spaniards.

The Penitentes (1915, Triangle, supervisor D. W. Griffith, director John Conway, based on the novel, *The Penitentes* by R. Ellis Wales) depicts Indians who come and kill everyone in a seventeenth century New Mexico village, except two monks and a baby named Manuel. The Penitentes, a violent, fanatical Catholic sect, lay claim to all property of the family estate. Achieving manhood, Manuel is chosen as the annual sacrificial victim to be crucified on Good Friday. However, troops save him at the last moment. The Penitentes are so extreme even by Hispanic standards that they need to be overcome by Spanish troops. *In the Palace of the King* (1923, Goldwyn-Cosmopolitan, starring Blanche Sweet and Edmund Lowe) has the Spanish monarch, Philip II, with whom the Black Legend originated, play a jealous, evil villain who personally stabs his half-brother, Don Juan of Austria, whom he leaves for dead.[1]

The Sea Hawk (1924, First National) has an English noble first shanghaied and, while at sea, captured by Spaniards who make him a galley slave. He escapes to the Moors and becomes a pirate, particularly devoted to revenging himself against the odious Spaniards. The film was redone again with the same title in the sound era (1940, Warner), starring Errol Flynn and Claude Rains with the same emphasis on preying on the Spanish. *The Black Pirate* (1926, United Artists) provides counterpoint to the usual stereotype, but only because it stars Douglas Fairbanks, known for his good-bad Hispanic persona. Fairbanks plays the role of Michel, a Spanish duke whose vessel is captured by pirates who kill all but him and his father, whom they maroon. He becomes a good-bad pirate himself, and after excelling at his trade eventually saves a princess, and by leveraging his status as Spanish nobility wins her hand. The film contains what might be considered the finest cinematic sword fight of the silent era.

Captain Blood (1935, Warner, starring Errol Flynn, Olivia de Havilland, and Basil Rathbone) pits any number of brigands from the point of view of nationality against each other (French, English, etc.), but the Spanish are clearly at the lowest spot on the totem pole: bad, Catholic, despotic, retrograde enemies of democracy and piratical egalitarianism. An earlier, lesser-known version of this film with the same title was done in 1924 (Vitagraph, starring J. Warren Kerrigan and Jean Paige). The Black Legend continues into later decades with films such as *Captain from Castile* (1947, Twentieth Century-Fox, starring Tyrone Power, Jean Peters, César Romero, and Antonio Moreno). While this film is primarily about Cortés and his men, the first half has Tyrone Power unjustly persecuted for heresy by the Spanish Inquisition and escaping Spain to become a recruit of Cortés.

The Border (and Drug or Alien Smuggling on the Border)

As we cited García Riera in chapter III, the border functioned in United States film as a no man's land where Puritan values were severely relaxed and anything was possible in the way of sex or romance, violence, drugs, conspiracy, desertion, or hide out. Richard, on the basis of his extensive filmography judges: "From the very earliest times, the 'border' came to be associated with all forms of violence. It was a zone in which anything could, and would take place, a place free from the responsibilities and restrictions of North American law. . . . Here it was understood by actors and audiences alike that men must take the law into their own hands and adapt it to the particular situation various problems required" (1992, 16). The number of films set on the border is prodigious, and a book could easily be written focusing on this setting. Some notable examples of films set on the border follow.

On the Border (1909, Selig), the first border story film of record, sets the tone for this type. It depicts an Anglo "Vigilance Committee" that takes law into its own hands, frees the town from the badmen, and secures the Mexican border. As Richard (1992, 16) observes, ". . . it was probably the first production to present Mexico as the refuge for those hardened criminal types of any nationality or breed that required a place to hide out for a while until things cooled off." This was possible, the reviewer explained because "under the peculiar laws then existing between the United States and Mexico, our officers were not allowed to follow a culprit across the Río Grande." So from the very first flickers, one might read an intertitle that told the boys to "head for the border."

The Toll of Fear (1913, Lubin, director Romaine Fielding) evokes the nefarious qualities of the physical place itself. The brash younger brother of the local sheriff pursues Mexican rustlers south of Nogales, Arizona. He becomes disoriented and when he discovers a note pinned to a tree that warns: "Go Back or You Die with the Sun," this warning grows on him until "worn to a raw edge by the fear which the words signify" he shoots himself in the head. When his older brother goes looking for him, he has a similar reaction.

In *Brand of Cowardice* (1916, Rolfe/Metro), the border provides the setting for a rite of passage to manhood. Starring Lionel Barrymore as a "pantywaist" and a "he butterfly," the film shows the weakling become a man by saving his commandant's girl who has strayed across the border and been captured by the Mexican bandit chief. Similarly, *The Taint of Fear* (1916, Universal) governs the moral rehabilitation of a dispirited Anglo. Young Bob suffers because he has had the spirit beaten out of him by his cruel father. He joins the National Guard and soon is sent to the border to capture Lopes, the bandit leader. Now finding himself in the Mexican desert, at first it seems too much for the spiritless coward. But when he realizes that his company is threatened by annihilation, he rediscovers his manhood and although mortally wounded, the new found hero rides for rescue. The last scene shows his ghost appearing before his grief-stricken parents and his father too late lamenting his brutality.

The Pilgrim (1923, First National) features Charlie Chaplin leaving prison, getting into various complications as a fake minister, and being found out by the sheriff who takes him to the border and kicks him across to the Mexican side. He is pictured in the final scene walking in his usual gait toward the horizon with one foot on either side of the border; on the Mexican side bandits are having a shootout with each other. This film, as well as the immensely popular *The Bad Man*, prompted a complaint by the Mexican government and an ineffective attempt at embargo, as described in a brief article in *Motion Picture World*, "Mexico Bars Any Film of Charlie's or Doug's [Fairbanks], Punishing for Kidding Country in Past Pictures" (1/27/93).

From the first films the border and drugs appeared to go together like Soy Sauce and Wasabi—Bogart and Bacall?—whatever. If it wasn't drugs being smuggled, it was illegal aliens, often Orientals.

The Border Detective (1912, American) is the first film discovered by this research that depicts drug smuggling and the interception of drugs on the Mexican American border. The story describes the work of the Secret Service and border customs officers in stopping opium from crossing the border. In *On the Border* (1915, Selig), a Mexican is caught bringing opium across the border in the tire case of an automobile. Things changed little in this time-warped locale. The same title was used fifteen years later, *On the Border* (1930, Warner), this time featuring Rin-Tin-Tin sniffing out Chinese aliens and foiling the Anglo smugglers who are attempting to get them across the border using Don José, the owner of an impoverished Mexican hacienda, as their dupe.

The Border Runner (1915, Kriterion-Navajo) has a Mexican smuggling opium in water canteens and using his guardian, an Anglo girl as his unsuspecting "mule." The Anglo ace government agent brings the evildoer to justice and saves the Anglo girl. *The Perilous Leap* (1917, Gold Seal), has Mexicans, half-breeds, and Chinese running the fruit of the poppy into Texas from their headquarters in Mexico. As in *Ah Sing and the Greaser* (1910, Lubin), two (or three, depending on your perspective) bad ethnic groups are brought in together as an efficiency of scale. Some nine years later, *The Border Sheriff* (1926, Universal) is notable for having Jack Hoxie as the sheriff break up not only illegal traffic flowing out of Mexico but out of San Francisco's Chinatown as well. This might have been another example of batching the baddies together, or perhaps the film is the first with an inkling of drugs as a reflection of international cartels.

The Loaded Door (1922, Universal) has Hoot Gibson find that his former employer has been killed by Tex-Mex Blackie López and his gang who are running a drug smuggling operation on the border. When Gibson begins to interfere, López captures his woman and threatens her life. Gibson stops the drug flow, cleans up the bad hombres, and gets back his girl.

Quicksands (1923, Paramount Famous Lasky Corp.), produced and written by Howard Hawks, already had Hollywood extolling how the "government troops were waging an incessant battle against the insidious traffic" of drugs. It appears that the United States has been winning the war on drugs at least since 1923! The film itself is the usual cliché depicting an Anglo who foils an evil drug dealer with the help of the daughter of a U.S. Customs official whom at one point he thinks just might be a drug dealer herself, but who turns out to be a secret agent. *The Drifter* (1929, Radio) had Tom Mix on the scent of drugs. The film was also a vehicle for Mix, an accomplished pilot, to capture the smuggler, an aviator, by literally forcing him out of the sky.

In the 1930s, the number of drug and other smuggling films increased. *Soldiers of the Storm* (1933, Columbia, starring Regis Toomey) has an Anglo thwarting smugglers and saving the daughter of a politician who was involved with these desperados. As in *The Drifter,* the film is notable for combining the border, smuggling, and stunt flying. *Riding Speed* (1934, Superior) featured silent film star Buffalo Bill, Jr. (Jay Wilsey) in one of his last film roles, neutralizing the customary border smugglers. *Lawless Frontier* (1935, Mono) features John Wayne clearing his name when he is falsely accused of smuggling guns across the border. The actual smuggler was a bad Mexican who also had evil designs on the señorita that honest John was protecting. A similar plot appears in *Paradise Canyon* (1935, Mono) where Wayne slays a government agent who foils counterfeiters operating on the Mexican border.

According to Richard (1992, 397), the first film to move the locus of drug traffic from the Mexican border to South America is *After Many Years* (1930, Metro/Goldwyn), premised around the son of a murdered police officer uncovering the killers and their drug-smuggling operation.

Broncho Billy

G. M. Anderson (Max Aronson) was a leading entrepreneur and actor who became prominent after playing several roles in *The Great Train Robbery*. He founded the Essanay Company with George K. Spoor in 1907, the year he starred himself in the role of a cowboy, Broncho Billy in a highly successful two-reel Western, *The Bandit Makes*

Good (Essanay). Over the next seven years, he directed and starred in close to 400 Broncho episodes (the spelling was later changed to Bronco). Producing them at an average of one a week, Broncho Billy was one of the first recognizable characters in film history and the enthusiastic viewer response made Anderson one of the screen's first stars and the first cowboy hero. Broncho Billy was usually a noble character who occasionally played the good badman who William S. Hart was also to personify well, an outlaw who reformed himself through the intercession of a beautiful woman who believed in him or an innocent child. Because Anderson made so many films, he enacted just about every Western plot available, which he drew from dime novels, pulp magazines, and stage melodramas. The Broncho Billy films overwhelmingly depicted Hispanics in a negative light and some of these films are among the most egregious of the period. The term "greaser" appears in some of the titles and was frequently used in the films themselves, most often in the intertitles and in their advertising. However, the plots of some of these films, notably *Broncho Billy's Mexican Wife* and *Broncho Billy's Way,* where the Anglo hero is aggressively cuckolded by his Mexican wife, are among the most unique and counterintuitive of the early decades of Hispanic-themed cinema in the United States. Even though some of the films run against the formula and conventions of the time, the Hispanic characters fare no better than in the more conventional Broncho Billy vehicles.

Broncho Billy's Redemption (1910, Essanay) has Broncho as a good badman fleeing vigilantes and encountering a sick adult and child in an abandoned prairie schooner. He redeems himself by going for medicine, but because he is a wanted man he agrees to have a Mexican who he has encountered do the purchasing. The "thieving Mexican" promptly betrays Broncho who regains his honor by saving the two by himself.

In *Broncho Billy's Mexican Wife* (1912, Essanay, reissued in 1915), the feckless Mexican wife marries Broncho to please her father but is set upon keeping a lover. She deceives Broncho with a Mexican and when her affair is discovered, cuts herself with a knife and accuses Billy of stabbing her. Put behind bars, she "tantalizes her imprisoned husband by kissing her Mexican lover [and] expresses the lowest depths of woman's self abandonment and fiendish cruelty." However the Mexican's first woman slays both of the illicit lovers and clears Billy. "In the final scene, our hero forgives all and places the dead lovers hands one in the other and walks away without ever looking back" (Richard, 1992, 143). The film was the occasion for an evaluation of female versus male cunning: "Billy's Mexican wife makes him appear like a deuce spot, when measuring his craftiness against hers." By 1912, G. M. Anderson in his role as Broncho Billy "could claim to be the nation's most easily identifiable and popular moving picture star" (Richard, 1992, 61).

Broncho Billy's Strategy (1913, Essanay) features an Anglo who is corrupted by a "Mexican greaser" and steals money from his wife and loses it gambling. When the greaser wants help in robbing the express office, Broncho Billy intercedes and saves the errant husband from further evildoing. The greaser is sent to prison. *Broncho Billy's Way* (1913, Essanay) is amazing in that a heroic Anglo loses his wife to a Mexican. Broncho had been warned that a Mexican lusted for his wife but he trusted her completely. Upon returning home unexpectedly, he discovers the Mexican hiding in the closet. Broncho shoots up the closet, above the head of the Mexican, but allows the scoundrel to leave, placing "the weeping form of his wife upon the horse" with the Mexican, telling her never to darken his door again.

In *Broncho Billy, Outlaw* (1914, Essanay), Broncho is captured by a sheriff he respects, along with a greaser. Broncho learns of the evil Mexican's plan to revenge himself and escapes in time to save the sheriff's wife. Grateful, the sheriff obtains a pardon for Broncho and sends the greaser back to jail. *Broncho Billy and the Greaser* (1914, Essanay) has Broncho kick a greaser out of the post office for being rude to a young woman. The half-breed swears revenge and attempts to stab Billy in his sleep, but is foiled by the grateful woman.

In *Broncho Billy's Greaser Deputy* (1915, Essanay), Broncho loses in love to another Anglo suitor, a no good drunk and thief who marries and beats his wife. Eventually, Sheriff Billy arrests the husband but the wife pleads for him with her former love and Broncho lets the husband escape. However, the wrongdoer is saved for but a moment because the greaser deputy barges in and shoots him. *Broncho Billy's Brother* (also *Broncho Billy's Cowardly Brother*, 1915, Essanay) features a series of quarrels between two badmen, the brother and a greaser. At one point the drunken brother returns home and beats up his mother. Broncho then beats up the brother, but the greaser, who has secretly witnessed the beating, shoots the brother and frames Broncho Billy. Eventually, under pressure from other Anglos, the greaser breaks down and confesses his crime and is punished while Billy goes free.

Bullfighting

The interest in bullfighting shown by the U. S. film industry and the public continues the orientation toward the exotic, which we discussed in chapters 1 and 2. While the first bullfighting films were documentaries, story lines were soon adapted around them, combining the inherent violence of the corrida, totally overemphasized by the Anglo mind-set to the exclusion of the craft, pageantry, and religious dimensions, with sex and romance. Accordingly, many of the bullfighting films are wed around plots featuring love triangles. The films mentioned in this chapter do not include direct versions of the Carmen story that we have reviewed in chapter 3, although some of these pictures do reflect the influence of *Carmen*. The French term toreador is used almost universally, to the exclusion of torero or matador; this is presumably because of the influence of Mérimée's *Carmen* as adapted into opera, drama, and cinema.

The first bullfighting film of record is *The Great Bullfight* (1902, Edison), a documentary shot in Mexico. *A Mexican Courtship* (1912, Lubin) is a fairy tale set in the Juárez area where a famous matador loves a señorita who in turn loves a poor worker at the bullring. On the day when the matador is to fight the fiercest bull in all of Chihuahua he arrives drunk. The humble Mexican worker offers to fight the bull instead and despite derision at first, wins the day, the bull, and señorita.

For the Love of a Toreador (1913, Kleins-Cines) involves a love triangle between Francisco, the famous bullfighter, and the two women who love him, Lolita and Carmen, the dancer. Francisco receives a knife wound in the shoulder from Carmen that was intended for Lolita.

The Lovely Señorita (1914, Edison) is a parody that is also a good index of the stereotypes that Hispanics suffered at the hands of Hollywood. The film features "Wood B. Wed" who inherits money and meets and weds Paprika, a fiery "dusky señorita." She puts him through Gringo hell as he is forced to be a number of Hispanic types: a lousy revolutionary, a vaquero, and a toreador. The señorita's former suitors, Tomale and Tobasco, threaten Wood B. with knives but he does the right thing, buying them off with his wealth.

The Toreador's Oath (1914, Pathé) is another triangle; two brothers in love with the same Spanish beauty. They fight to the death in front of a crucifix, falling over each other and forming a cross. In this sense it is reminiscent of the famous ranchera song, "Llegó borracho el borracho," cultivated by the 1960s border singer and actor, Eulalio González "El Piporro" and others.

The Blood of the Arena (1917, Cosmos-Kinema) appears to have been the first of the bullfighting films aspiring to be "authentic" representations of the life stories of Spanish toreadors. It depicts the rise and eventual fall of the bullfighter who is ultimately killed in the ring. *The Brand of López* (1920, Hayworth) continues this line, featuring the Japanese star Sessue Hayakawa as a Spanish bullfighter noted for his coarseness. He brands his lover's back with a cigarette before they marry, and as he goes downhill as a bullfighter he ends up a bandit, finally raping a young woman and dying defending the child he had so odiously procreated. *Blood and Sand* (1922, Famous Players-Lasky) was one of the most notable of the bullfighting films, starring Rodolph Valentino (it was also spelled Rudolph) and based on Vicente Blasco-Ibáñez's novel, *Sangre y arena*. The film once again describes a triangle. A young matador, Juan Gallardo, marries Carmen, his childhood sweetheart, but later succumbs to the charms of Doña Sol. He eventually meets disaster when distracted by the sight of a handsome stranger with his lover, he is gored by the bull. As he dies in his wife's arms, the sound of cheers for a new hero are heard in the ring.

The Spaniard (1925, Paramount, director Raoul Walsh, starring Ricardo Cortez [Jacob Krantz] and Noah Beery), based on Juanita Savage's 1924 novel, has an exotic romance story line with a Spanish grandee and bullfighter pursuing an English girl who resists his advances in England, Spain, and elsewhere. Finally convinced, she makes plans to become his wife. *The Siren of Seville* (1924, Producers Distributing Corp.) is another set of triangles with ample opportunities for bullfighting and vamping and a repeat of the artifice of a fighter gored while he spies his woman in the stands with another man.

The Bull Fighter (1927, Pathé) was a Mack Sennett comedy with a pair of brave boys bested by the bull at every nonstop turn of action. *El Terrible Toreador* (1930, Disney) is the first cartoon this research has identified on the topic. The usual stereotypes prevail, a fierce, terrible toreador who is bested by an even fiercer bull, highly adept at literally "kicking butt." *Bull Fight* (1935, Educational) was a Terry-toon with the same kind of punch. *Mixing in Mexico* (1935, Screen Attraction Co.) did the same with Mutt and Jeff in the arena.

The Kid from Spain (1932, Goldwyn-United Artists) is a romantic comedy and musical, perhaps the first that incorporates a corrida, which in this case takes place as the final, culminating scene. The film starred Eddie Cantor and Robert Young. Julián Rivero had a minor part as did the Goldwyn girls of 1932, Betty Grable, Paulette Goddard, and Jane Wyman as beautiful señoritas.

The Classics

This section discusses a few films about classical Hispanic topics, Don Juan and Don Quixote, in order to provide some coverage in this domain and give some sense of the films that were produced. (See the preceding chapter for extensive coverage of the Carmen cycle.)

Don Juan: Or a War Drama of the 18th Century (1909, Film Import and Trading Company) was an early nine-minute version of the Don Juan story, lauded at the time for its portrayal of "the typical Don Juan of literature." It is the first Don Juan film of record to be made available to the American market. *The Lucky Horseshoe* (1925, Fox) is only loosely and partly connected to the Don Juan cycle. It has a diffident Tom Mix kidnapped and hit on the head and dream himself in sunny Spain, functioning as the nation's greatest lover in a fashion imitative of Douglas Fairbanks' persona, not in any way reminiscent of the traditional Don Juan. When he wakes up he realizes he must stop the imminent wedding of the character played by Billie Dove, which he does, shaking off his wishy washiness and marrying the girl himself. *Don Juan* (1926, Warner) starred John Barrymore as the Latin Lover but operating at the Borgia court, staying in good graces with Cesare and Lucrezia while he pursues Adriana, played by Mary Astor. In his last appearance in a feature film, Douglas Fairbanks starred in *The Private Life of Don Juan* (1934, a British production) with Merle Oberon. It was the customary Fairbanks formula of intrepid daring-do: "Suceptible Seville femmes . . . not loathe to two-timing their señors [threw] rope ladders down from their balconies to facilitate the ingress and exit of the trepidacious Don Juan" (cited in Richard, 1992, 489).

As was common for one-reelers, the first *Don Quixote* (1909, Gaumont), as was common for one-reelers, presented the peak moments of the story with an emphasis on the "many pictures of Spanish life" and "promiscuous adventures." Apparently anything Spanish, even the Quixote had to be "promiscuous." *Don Quixote* (1916, Triangle, supervisor D. W. Griffith, director Edward Dillon) featured a number of the notable adventures of the knight but takes considerable liberties, having him shot and dying in the arms of Dulcinea and Sancho Panza.

Gypsies

The earliest, pre-1910 Gypsies often functioned as odious rogues, noted for, among other things, kidnapping babies. However, the earliest group are not recognized as Spanish or Hispanic. (See Musser, 1990, for a good discussion of Gypsies in the cinema up to 1907). The films that follow only reflect Gypsies who are identifiably Hispanic. The most common Gypsy persona was the hot blooded, vengeful sort. The Carmen cycle (see preceding chapter) should also be consulted for more films with Gypsy characters of this type. Hispanic Gypsies also functioned as soothsayers (often with small roles, in which case they are not reviewed here) and in musicals in a supporting role. As in the case of Aztecs, bullfighters, and certain kinds of bandidos or smugglers, the focus is not only on the violent but on the exotic. Gypsies don't exercise violence in normal ways, at least from the Anglo point of view. They use whips, knives, or, if women, cunning psychological traps.

A Gypsy Duel (1904, American Mutoscope and Biograph) is the first story film on record thus far to record Hispanics, in this case in the form of hot-blooded, lustful Spanish Gypsies dueling to a possible death in suit of a señorita. *Gypsy's Revenge* (1907, Lubin) evoked the usual stereotype of hot temper and the need for vengeance at all costs. *A Gypsy's Revenge* (1908, Pathé) crosses the vamp with the typical Gypsy vendetta motif. A Carmen-like Gypsy girl seeks revenge against the father by seducing the son. She captivates the son with her cigarette smoking by the garden gate. When the father learns what has happened, he provokes a fight with the son that causes the parent's death. Then the Gypsy vamp informs the police of the killing. As they take the son away, cursing the girl, she is seen "puffing coolly at her cigarette," vengeance fulfilled.

Romance in Old Mexico (1909, Vitagraph) features a Gypsy in the role of soothsayer, informing a young woman that her lover, a well-known bullfighter will first fight with her and then be unfaithful. After all of this occurs, the señorita decides to make her lover jealous, using his best friend to accomplish this. This causes the bullfighter to be careless and severely gored (a standard artifice, as noted in the *bullfighting* section above). In the last scene, in his lover's arms he swears eternal fidelity, should he recover.

The Spanish Dancer (1923, Famous Players-Lasky) featured Pola Negri as Rosita, the Spanish Gypsy dancer opposite Antonio Moreno as Don César. The film was often shown with its alleged rival, *Rosita* (1923, United Artists), another film described as a "Spanish Romance" featuring Mary Pickford, not as a Gypsy but as a Spanish street singer. Both film productions were based on the play by Adolphe Philippe Dennery and Philippe François Pinel, *Don César de Bazán* (1844). *The Night of Love* (1927, United Artists, featuring Ronald Coleman and Vilma Banky) had a Gypsy Robin Hood exercise that *Variety* called "the traditional vendetta [of] the Latin races" (January 26, 1927).

The semi-sound film, *Revenge* (1928, United Artists) has Dolores Del Río play the Gypsy daughter of an animal trainer who knows a lot about whips. She uses one against a Gypsy rogue, Jorga, who has cut off her braids and those of other Gypsy girls, a sign of disgrace. Jorga kidnaps her and takes her to a mountain cave where she comes to love him.

The Squall (1929, First National) featured Myrna Loy as "Nubi," the Gypsy vamp of all males who appear on site and who produces the squall in the family that she preys on. One reviewer judged that the "Gypsy was a gyp out for jewelry, etc., [and] probably the queen of the dirty skinned gold diggers" (*Variety*, 5.15.1929). In 1930, Gypsies were featured in the musical, *Song of the Caballero* (1930, Universal). Ken Maynard romanced señoritas and fought off señores in Old California set in the days of the Dons with Gypsies providing musical accompaniment.

Half-breeds and Other Mixed Bloods

The half-breeds and other mixed bloods of U. S. film are depicted in a fashion similar to greasers and in some cases the term half-breed is simply synonymous to greaser. However, in contrast to greasers, where males overwhelmingly predominated, there were numerous half-breed women. Just as in the case of greasers, half-breeds attain this usually negative status at birth and cannot overcome it. Half-breeds, of course, are almost always of mixed Hispanic-American Indian ancestry, very rarely of Anglo-American Indian background in the films that are Hispanic-themed. While almost all male half-breeds are villainous, there are a few exceptions, either the usual one of gratitude to whites and obeisance to Anglo culture, or very special reasons such as a unique role reflecting the screen persona of a transcendent actor like Douglas Fairbanks. The connection of mixed bloods to Indians is sometimes highlighted. They either collaborate with Indians or arouse them against whites, or because they are expert in their Indian ways, betray them to the white man. Female half-breeds are cast in the usual women's roles as surrogate señoritas, and are usually the simultaneous object of the attentions of an Anglo and an ethnic—Hispanic, half-breed, American Indian, whatever the case may be. With minimal exceptions, the prevailing view, one strongly held by many prominent filmmakers of the time, such as D. W. Griffith, was that mixed bloods inherited the worst traits of each of the contributing races.

The Octoroon (1909, Kalem) has the owner of a turpentine distilling plant of Spanish descent, "a cruel, vindictive brute of little principle" lust after a beautiful octoroon.

Rejected, he attempts revenge, but the octoroon's lover kills him in what is billed as a"unique duel."

The Indian Maid's Sacrifice (1911, Kalem) features a Spanish gentleman who saves an Indian girl and places her in a mission. A local half-breed seeks vengeance against the Spaniard and the Indian maiden for an assumed slight and riles up the local Indians to exterminate the mission. The Indian maiden disguises herself as a boy and kills the half-breed and saves her benefactor. Thus the film features a collaboration between an Indian and a Castilian to foil a half-breed.

The Half-Breed's Foster Sister (1912, CGPC) has a beautiful Mexican half-breed heroically save the child of a rich Castilian family. She is rewarded by being adopted. The son of the governor falls in love with her immediately. But considering her former station, she refuses to "sacrifice his life" for her own happiness and enters a convent. A similar climate of obeisance appears in *The Half-Breed's Sacrifice* (1912, Lubin). Manuel, the child of a Mexican and an Indian mother, is saved by the governor of Sonola [sic] and becomes his obedient server, eventually dying in his zeal to save the governor from various evil sorts. *The Half-Breed's Treachery* (1912, Lubin) is the converse of *Sacrifice*, with an evil, drunken, Mexican half-breed attempting to get the girl and kill her suitor. He receives his just, impromptu Anglo punishment at the end of a rope.

The Apache Kind (1913, Lubin) features Joe, a bandit of the "Apache kind" whose woman is Loretta, an attractive Mexican half-breed. Joe is a gambler and gets in trouble with the law. He escapes, leaving behind his woman who has fallen in love with the sheriff. *Episode of Cloudy Canyon* (1913, Essanay) featured G. M. Anderson, not as Broncho Billy, but rather as a totally despicable Mexican half-breed who not only did the usual vicious acts but actually beat his horse. Publicly admonished for this offense, he conceives a cunning revenge, shoots the sheriff's son and frames a drunk for the behavior. The son revives just in time and the odious Mexican is meted out swift Western justice.

Flaming Arrow (1913, Bison) is very unconventional because it does not promote the view that a person of mixed race inherits only the worst characteristics of both races. In this film, White Eagle, a half-breed Apache who has been educated among white men, returns to his tribe. He falls in love with the white colonel's daughter, provoking an alliance between the evil white colonel and an even more nefarious Mexican. These two are foiled, the Mexican killed, the girl saved from the Mexican, and the colonel relieved that his daughter is safe.

In the Amazon Jungle (1915, Selig) appear, apparently cast in accordance with Hollywood ignorance about Brazil, a pure-blooded Spaniard and two "Spanish half-breeds" (instead of Portuguese). Because of a jaguar attack one of the half-breeds abandons the Spaniard who subsequently saves him. The half-breed gratefully acknowledges the moral superiority of the Spaniard: "And in return for my treachery you saved my life." *Crooked Trails* (1916, Selig) had Tom Mix single-handedly overcome not only the Mexican half-breed who had taken offense because he lost a bronco-breaking contest, but the half-breed's gang of "desperados" as well.

The Half Breed (1916, Triangle), based on the Bret Harte novel *In the Carquinez Woods* (1883), featured Douglas Fairbanks as a good badman. He is an outcast living with his adopted Indian grandfather and rights the wrongs inflicted on a poor, outcast Indian girl. At the end they marry. Concerning *The Quarter Breed* (1916, Bison), Richard asks, only semifacetiously: "If being a half-breed was bad, was being a quarter-breed only half as bad? It is difficult at times to understand why individuals considered such things, but . . . the reality was that people were judged by their ancestry" (1992, 186). In this film, the quarter-breed falls in love with a lady but sacrifices his self interest and tells a pure blood to honor her, for he has come to understand that he is good for nothing better than driving a stagecoach.

Mixed Blood (1916, Universal) depicts Nita Valyez, half-Spanish and half-Irish, for whom Carlos represents potential violence and danger, to which she is both attracted and repelled. On the other hand, the Anglo sheriff is in love with her. When Carlos kills a faro dealer, she runs away with him to the border but Carlos contracts the plague. When the sheriff comes to get them, Carlos dies of his malady, and the Anglo takes Nita back to civilization to try to convince her to love him.

The Man Above the Law (1918, Triangle) is about a fugitive easterner who comes to the border area to open a trading post, selling "Pain Killer" to the locals, "half-Indian, half-greaser." He takes up with one of the locals, thus becoming a "squawman" and sires a quarter-breed daughter. Eventually he regenerates and decides his daughter should attend school. He takes his family back east, leaving the locals in need of a new supply of drink.

The Half Breed (1922, First National) features a good-bad half-breed in a complex plot. Essentially, the half-breed's cause is just, to regain lands that belong to his Indian mother. However, he is thwarted by a racist judge and other Anglos and commits evil deeds of all kinds. The unusual end does not feature a clear-cut moral outcome: he and a white woman he has encountered catch a freight train and avoid the sheriff's posse. *The Crow's Nest* (1922, Sunset Productions) featured the story of Esteban who was raised by a "squaw" and thought to be a half-breed but who was actually an all-white illegitimate child. He falls in love with a white girl and is rewarded with her hand in marriage and an inheritance when his true bloodline is finally revealed.

The Valley of the Hunted Men (1928, Pathé) has the usual border smuggling conventions, with one exception. According to Richard (1992, 375), it was produced at a time when the Mexican consul was threatening to have any film with negative Mexican characterizations banned in Mexico. As a result, half-breeds, together with renegade North Americans take all of the negative stereotyping. These were the only villains in the film.

Historical Films

Various films were produced on different historical events or personages within the Hispanic world. The three films that follow give some sense of these sorts of production.

A Message to García (1916, Edison) was based on Elbert Hubbard's influential 1899 essay with the same title. Much of the film, shot in Cuba, depicts events shortly after the explosion of the U.S. *Maine* in Havana Harbor. With the help of a Cuban insurgent sympathizer, Delores, who sacrifices her life for the cause, Lieutenant Rowan is able to get a message from President McKinley to Emanuel García, the leader of the Cuban insurgents that the United States will support the revolution against the Spanish.

Christopher Columbus (1910, Gaumont) was advertised as representing important scenes in the life of the "Portuguese" navigator. *The Coming of Columbus* (1912, Selig) was a highly successful, expensive production and the first serious attempt to bring Columbus's voyage to America to the screen. The film has the Indians who so loved the great white father having to be stopped lest they kill the new Spanish governor who had Columbus arrested and placed in chains.

Independence of California

The films which follow only depict aspects of California's independence from Mexico. (See Richard, 1992, for a wider filmography of Hispanic-themed California films.) The independence of California films fall into two broad categories: those that depict the actual takeover, usually featuring a señorita in love with and aiding an Anglo officer, and those involved with the issue of land rights in one form or another.

The California Revolution of 1846 (1911, Kalem) was a love story featuring a young Anglo hero and thirteen North American settlers who proclaimed independence from Mexico and "seized the pueblo of Sonoma." The Anglo also takes control over the Spanish commandant's lady in the process. It is another example of politics as usual, that is, as interracial sexual politics and as war as a function of an interracial love triangle. Similarly, *When California Was Won* (1911, Kalem) has the state join the Union as the result of the governor's daughter Manuelita falling in love with and helping Commander Sloat of the American Navy. Once again history is made on the basis of dark-skinned señoritas doing anything to win white males.

Against the background of California at the middle of the nineteenth century, a cycle of films revolve around either the problems of the Spanish rancheros or their alleged greed for land. *Rose of the Rancho* (1914, Lasky, director Cecil B. DeMille) was the first major film of this sort. The U.S. government sends secret agent Kearney to California to investigate land fraud. Kincaid, a land jumper, attempts to steal Señor Espinoza's ranch, but in a raid that he masterminds the ranchero and one of his daughters die. Later, Kearney falls in love with Juanita, the "Rose" of a different ranch, although she is engaged to Don Luis. When Kearney discovers that Kincaid plots against this ranch as well, he foils the Anglo, saves the ranch, and is able to take Juanita away from Don Luis and wed her. This film was the first cooperative feature of Jesse L. Lasky and David Belasco, who had already become preeminent before the cinema age as a New York theater empresario, producer, and playwright. (*Rose of the Rancho* was remade in 1936 by Paramount.) The film featured the strong production values associated with Cecil B. DeMille: the use of forty Mexican or American Indians in the "roles of Vaqueros, Caballeros, and Mexican Indians." These extras used their own native costumes. On the other hand, *A Sister of Six* (1916, Triangle) turns reality completely on its head. Taking place during California's transitional period from Mexican territory to statehood in the United States, it depicts a Hispanic, Don Francisco García who is not satisfied with his vast holdings but wants those of the Anglo next to him and resorts to Mexican bandits to try and get his way. The Anglos bring on the cavalry and have the Don jailed.

The perverse plot of *A California Romance* (1922, Fox) features an aggressive group of Mexican women who join patriotic officer Don Juan Diego to resist the Anglos who want to deliver California into the hands of the United States. However, when the women find that Don Juan is a worse tyrant than the prospective new landlords, they revolt against him and in favor of the Anglos. One of the final scenes shows the Mexicanas and the Anglos joining hands in their support of the red, white, and blue. *Daughters of the Don* (1922, Arrow) follows the usual formula of a señorita who falls in love with the North American soldier, thus premising the takeover of California as a function of Hispanic women infatuated with white soldiers and betraying their family and national/ethnic identity.

In *California* (1927, MGM, starring Tim McCoy), the conquest of California is a function of Manifest Destiny and righteous Anglo morality outraged by the odious behavior of the brutal Mexican overlords of Mexican California. Otherwise it was the usual cliché as advertised: "The war with Mexico serves to bring together American officer and Mexican señorita, the former all ardent and the latter defiant because of the fact that their countries are at war. Coincident with the American victory is the successful conquest by the 'Gringo' of the girl's heart."

Don Mike (1927, Film Booking Offices of America, presented by Joseph P. Kennedy) continues Hollywood poppycock history by having a Spanish grandee first fight back a group of thieving Anglos who want to set up an Empire of California only to then turn over the territory to General Fremont who arrives just in time. What more could Hollywood ask of its Hispanics? *Señor Americano* (1929, Universal, starring Ken Maynard) brought Manifest Destiny into the sound age. This film with "85% dialogue" justified in the first, silent reel, the conquest of California:

> California belongs to us by the right of conquest! The people of California right now are eager to become Americans. What right has the Spanish King to give land he ain't never seen? If we're going to make this a God fearing country . . . Our government knows best. (Cited in Richards, 1992, 391)

Intervention in Mexico during Wilson's Presidency

In addition to minor incidents or skirmishes, the United States intervened significantly twice in Mexico during the Wilson presidency, in 1914 and in 1916. On April 21, 1914, the American government began its occupation of the port of Veracruz. On March 15, 1916, General John J. Pershing, in retaliation for the *villista* raid on Columbus, New Mexico (March 8-9, 1916), led three brigades into Mexico with the acquiescence of Carranza, who after several weeks of American incursions in Mexico turned more and more negative. (See Knight, 1986, vol. 2 for an account of these interventions and the Villa incursion). It was only after Villa "invaded" the United States that the Mexican Revolution itself (as contrasted to the standard negative image of Mexico per se in Westerns where greasers, Mexican bandits, and badmen always abounded) was perceived in a very negative light, as well, of course, as Villa himself. This view of the Mexican Revolution changed again somewhat with the partially sympathetic portrayal of the Mexican revolutionary in the 1934 *Viva Villa!* (Warner). The films that follow are productions that depict the actual U.S. intervention itself.

War in Mexico (1914, Al Dia Feature Co.) depicted the North American reaction to the Tampico crisis just prior to the occupation of Veracruz (the latter city was occupied although the inciting incident took place in Tampico) and *War With Huerta* (1914, Mullin and Tisher) featured the positioning of U.S. war ships off Tampico just prior to the taking of Veracruz.

Uncle Sam in Mexico (1914, Victor) featured battle scenes in the vicinity of Veracruz. *The Battle of Vera Cruz* (1914, Sawyer) was advertised as "the *real thing* in the *real place* . . . taken on the spot during the fiercest fighting amid a hail of bullets and showing 'our boys' taking the city. . . ." *Under Fire in Mexico* (1914, Warner's Features) is notable for having obtained permission to utilize "the 4,000 Mexican prisoners being held at Eagle Pass" in the film billed as a "thrilling, stirring story of Mexican warfare to the staccato accompaniment of hair-breath escapes, dark conspiracies, wholesale massacres and daring rescues. . . . A powerful story of guerilla cruelty and American heroism. It will thrill the heart of every American patriot."

Watchful Waiting (1916, Gaumont) is a parodic criticism of Woodrow Wilson's policy of "Watchful Waiting" in Mexico rather than intervention; it depicts Uncle Sam "dreaming in blissful ignorance until a few unpleasant probes from the Mexican side, and from Germany arouses him to exasperation" (*Movie Picture World,* 4.22.16, p. 647). The film proved prophetic inasmuch as Villa attacked Columbus, New Mexico, in March 1916, before the publication of the *Movie Picture World* review, prompting the Pershing intervention in Mexico.

Following the Flag in Mexico (1916, State Rights) is a propagandistic documentary taken shortly after the Columbus, New Mexico, raid containing such scenes as an alleged American and an Englishman executed by Villa's troops and hanging in trees, General John J. Pershing posing in Columbus, and American troops passing by the Alamo as they leave for the border to punish Villa.

Jungle Films

The jungle was yet another place where the exotic reigned and moral values were severely relaxed and even the perception of physical reality was greatly altered. One could find or contract anything in the jungle: lost temples, jungle fever, cannibals, strange monsters, and so on. Above all the quality of male-female relationships was looser, more instinctual, kinky. These films often drew a fine line between silliness and titillation, awesomeness and inverisimilitude. Often Brazil is used or confused as a Spanish-American country.

Classmates (1914, American Biograph) has a few West Point cadets outdoing each other in a South American jungle in order to impress a pretty girl. The film was remade with the same title in 1924 (Inspiration Pictures). *The Black Box* (1915, Universal) was an episodic series with an intrepid anthropologist in South America, Professor Edgar Ashleigh doing research and finding exotic treasures in the jungle. *The Jaguar Trap* (1915, Selig) is a tale of rivalry between two Anglos set against the menace of a jaguar that terrorizes the South American jungle. *A Tragedy in Panama* (1915, Selig) has a righteous husband track down an adulterous wife and his man who have fled into the jungle where the lover contracts jungle fever.

The Jungle Child (1916, Triangle) as was often the case, misrepresented Brazil as a Hispanic country. It recounts how a badman from the United States encounters a Brazilian jungle village whose leader, the lost child of a rich Spanish family, is a beautiful Amazon. *The Planter* (1917, State Rights), featuring the senior Tyrone Power, folds every possible cliché into this jungle romance: enslaved Yaqui Indians, yellow fever epidemic, the white man spying on a native swimming nude, and two Europeans struggling for the affection of a native girl who at the end is revealed as European herself.

In *Framed* (1927, First National), an Anglo who has been framed finds himself in the Amazon jungle and is framed again, this time against an exotic background of jungle fever, mosquitoes, and snake infestation. When the culprit contracts a fever and repents on his death bed, the hero is free to happily embrace his loved one amidst the mud slides and the diamond fields.

Set against the subtext of the original Sandino and the first sandinistas, *Slightly Used* (1927, Warner Brothers) evokes the love complications in the United States of Major John Smith serving with his regiment in Nicaragua. Also set against Sandino and his guerrilla insurgents who didn't fight fair was *Flight* (1929, Columbia), which featured the rehabilitation of football player gone wrong and joining the flying squad of the

Marines and combatting sandinistas and giant jungle ants, not necessarily in that order. Harry Cohn produced and Frank R. Capra directed this film.

The Gateway of the Moon (1928, Fox) has Dolores del Río, the beautiful half-breed fall in love with and save the incorruptible Walter Pidgeon, who has been sent to inspect a railway being built in the Bolivian jungle through the use of cruel methods toward the construction crews.

Stark Mad (1929, Warner) has an expedition in the jungle encounter it all: a haunted Mayan temple, a strange monster with great hairy talons, a demented hermit, and so on. *Untamed* (1929, MGM) was a musical comedy starring Joan Crawford as Bingo, an American girl reared in the uninhibited jungle tropics by her father, finding her man, and singing tunes, such as "Song of the Jungle." *Kongo* (1932, MGM) took exotica to new extremes, featuring Lupe Vélez as a seductive primitive of the jungle who lived by her instincts; these naturally putting her in the arms of another white man. Her husband, played by Walter Huston, has gone completely native. He attempts to exact vengeance through some cannibalistic locals.

Fury of the Jungle (1934, Columbia) was a particularly insensitive film placing what Richard describes as "some of the world's worst white scum, the refuse of mankind" (1992, 485) on the edge of a rain forest with a South American native girl who they use at will. When the first white woman in memory arrives, the white men "gone native" fight over her and the Latina, "apparently fond of having been misused for so many years, went crazy with jealousy, tried to kill her competition, but failed" (Richard, 1992, 485).

Mexican Revolution

According to Richard (1992, xxvi) almost one new two- or three-reel film featuring Mexico or the border was produced for every week of 1914 through 1916. Sixty-four were made in 1914, forty-seven in 1915, and sixty-five in 1916, the largest number for any year in the silent era. Including some of the newsreel coverage, Mexico's revolutionary hero Pancho Villa was the major character (seen or unseen) in thirty-six of these productions. Villa had actually dared to invade the United States. Once called a "revolutionary" after the raid on Columbus, New Mexico, he was typed a treacherous and bloody bandit in the daily press and in the movies (see the *Villa* section for a sampling of these films). Films started to be produced almost at the beginning of the revolution and began to wane after 1916, but some films have been produced throughout the course of U.S. film production.

Although there are exceptions, in most films set around the Mexican Revolution the main part is given to an Anglo, either a revolutionary leader, or opponent of one group or another of Mexicans, or someone caught up in the revolution because of a woman or work. The early years of the revolution tended to produce films with sympathetic revolutionaries All of this began to change around 1914, so that in the two years before the Pancho Villa raid on Columbus, New Mexico (March 9, 1916) there was a more mixed picture. After that New Mexico raid, the Mexican Revolution was overwhelmingly seen as bad, until around 1920 by which time intense interest had peaked and the revolution was viewed more reflectively and retrospectively. (See García Riera, 1987, Vol. I, for an excellent review from a Mexican perspective of Mexican Revolution films produced by the U.S. film industry. Also see in this chapter the section *Intervention in Mexico during Wilson's Presidency.*)

In *The Mexican Joan of Arc* (1911, Kalem), only Mexican characters are featured, a relative rarity. A woman whose husband and son are arrested and murdered by a colonel and his *federales* turns into a rebel leader in order to take the evildoer prisoner and execute him in a similar fashion. Similarly, only Mexicans figure in *The Mexican Revolutionist* (1912, Kalem) which features a rebel named Juan who is captured but escapes the *federales* only to help the revolutionaries capture Guadalajara. Films with only Hispanic characters were rare because among other reasons, American film usually operated on the basis of stark moral conflicts where whites represented good and nonwhites represented evil. More typical was to have the Mexican Revolution provide the vehicle or backdrop for an Anglo actor as in *Along the Border* (1916, Selig) where Tom Mix fights rebels who are really *bandidos* in masquerade. The Anglo hero outwits them with the help of a willing señorita.

In the following early films, the Mexican Revolution is seen sympathetically, however, the heroes are North Americans. *A Prisoner of Mexico* (1911, Kalem) identifies the Revolution with the North American struggle for freedom in 1776 and romanticizes Madero. A North American youth joins the rebels and forms an "American Legion" to help them. The complicated plot has first his Anglo girlfriend then himself captured by the *federales,* but eventually they are both rescued by the American Legion. *The American Insurrecto* (1911, Kalem) has an Anglo soldier of fortune helping the Mexican revolutionaries. *The Mexican Rebellion* (1914, Ammex) was billed as "a sensational story of romance and war, showing how an American soldier of fortune joined the Mexican rebel army and had many escapes from death" before winning the señorita for himself. The variation in *A Mexican Defeat* (1913, Patheplay) is that a federalist captain rebuffed by an Anglo married woman frames her and her husband with alleged evidence that the two were conspiring against Mexico. They escape to the U.S. side of the Río Bravo and taunt the Mexican on the other side of the river. In *The Mexican Sleep Producer* (1913, Apollo), described as "a burlesque on the Mexican Revolution," an Anglo hero saves three North American lovelies from General Youhurter and the entire Mexican army by putting them to sleep with his "medicated bombs."

In the following films, the rebels are viewed as the enemies. *Mike and Jake in Mexico* (1913, Joker) has a comedy duo learn that the wicked Bumbo, leader of the rebels has abducted Chilita, daughter of the general of the federales. No problem, they save her. After being ineffectively tortured, the two clowns use their secret red pepper concoction to have most of the rebel forces sneeze themselves to death. *The Battle of Ambrose and Walrus* (1915, Keystone) is a burlesque in the same mold, featuring a Keystone comedy team against inept peon soldiers. *The Clod* (1913, Lubin) features a simple-minded Mexican farmer "so dull mentally as to be called a clod." He joins the revolution because it comes to his home, burning it and causing the death of his wife and mother. The clod understands nothing of what is transpiring.

A Mexican Tragedy (1913, Lubin) had it both ways; it was essentially a remake of an earlier film taking place during the American Revolution of 1776 where a father and a son are on different sides of the revolution, the father because of avarice, the son because he was dedicated to the cause. The usual amorous/treacherous complications arise. *The Eternal Duel* (1914, Lubin) is a similar film except that the rivals fight over a woman as well as for the *federales* or *insurrectos*, respectively. *The Terrible One* (1915, Lubin) is in the same line with the notable feature that one of the rivals uses the *ley fuga* to terminate his rival.

Madero Murdered (1913, Universal) has the status of being the first film identified by this research to be officially protested by a representative of the Mexican government, ironically, by the Victoriano Huerta government. The film, which is a documentary of the murder of Madero and the immediate aftermath, was protested by Mexico because it entered the controversy about where Madero had been shot and buried and because it was claimed that the individual represented as Félix Díaz was not the genuine counterrevolutionary at all. *Barbarous Mexico*, also advertised as *A Trip Thru Barbarous Mexico* (1913, America's Feature Film Co.) is part documentary, part patronizing travelogue of Mexican scenery and resorts. The documentary chronicles the first years of the Mexican Revolution up to and including the inauguration of Madero as president.

The Mexican Hatred (1914, Warner) has a unique plot. A Mexican woman hates the U.S. soldiers who have executed her son as a spy. One day the officer responsible for her son's death comes too close and she hits him with a rock. When he awakens, his memory is gone and she brainwashes him, filling him with hatred of Gringos and turning him into a fierce rebel leader. At the last moment, however he regains his memory and does not fight against his own men.

By 1915, with the Mexican Revolution going into its fifth year and circumstances changing, U.S. films took a more overt stand against the rebels. *The Americano* (1915, Komic) is interesting because it reflects the American government's recognition of Carranza's government after Huerta's departure in 1914. The film casts the "Constitutionalists" as good and the Americano, manager of an oil company as their ally. They struggle against a "worthless Mexican," Tonio and his "bandit soldiers" who raid the oil works, kill the Americano and kidnap his daughter, who the Constitutionalists eventually save. *The Gringo* (1916, Overland Feature Film Corp.) chronicles a wealthy young American joining the U.S. Army and being shipped to Mexico where civil war is imminent. He helps the battered wife of a Mexican renegade leader, which provokes the latter's revenge. Mexicans capture the American and storm his cell to lynch him, but he is saved by a señorita who has fallen in love with him. The American learns of his mother's death and leaves for home, witnessing many battles and meeting several Mexican generals, including Pancho Villa, on the way. Heartbroken, the señorita drowns herself.

Sometime after the white hot events of the Mexican Revolution itself, *Río Grande* (1920, Pathé, director Edwin Carewe) used the event for a family romance. Felipe López, who hates all Gringos despite the fact that his wife, Alice, is an American, takes his young daughter María and crosses into Mexico, leaving Alice and their adopted son, Danny O'Neil behind. Years later María fights at her father's side against the Mexican government and Danny becomes a member of the Texas Rangers. Many complications later, María returns to Mexico to teach the schoolchildren to love their American neighbors and her penitence thus accomplished, accepts Danny's love.

Mexicans Seen in a Sympathetic Light

A few films during the first decades of production depicted Mexicans in a sympathetic light, providing counterpoint and exceptions to the conventions. We have referred earlier to Griffith's *The Thread of Destiny;* some other notable examples follow.

The Biograph Company was notable for its production of several one-reelers that portrayed Mexicans in a sympathetic light. *The Fight for Freedom: A Story of the Southwest* (1908, Biograph) has Pedro shoot and kill an Anglo card cheat and the sheriff who pursues him. When the town accuses the sheriff's wife of the murder, Pedro breaks her out of jail and together they make their escape. Pedro falls in love with the Anglo lady, but she is killed in an ambush designed to capture him. Remorseful, he gives himself up to the authorities for a sure death. *The Two Sides* (1912, Biograph) in part described the plight of a Mexican worker fired from his job at a ranch so that the owner could reap greater profits; even so, the worker saves the owner's daughter from a fire.

The Mexican (1914, Selig) has a Mexican treated so harshly by Anglo cowboys that he finally loses control and attacks the foreman. After he loses his job, he saves the ranch owner's daughter from a snake and is compensated. *Her Last Resort* (1912, Bison) also involves hungry Mexicans at their wit's end. The husband is almost arrested for a crime he doesn't commit.

In *Fighting Fury* (1924, Universal), silent screen star Jack Hoxie was cast as a "Spanish-American" boy reared by his Mexican servant who fulfills a vow to revenge himself against the three disfigured ranchers who murdered his parents: "Two-finger" Larkin, "Scarface" Denton, and "Crooked Nose" Evans. After he eliminates them and saves an Anglo woman's cattle from being rustled, he gets a job and settles down on her ranch. The implication of this film would appear that a grievously offended Hispanic does have a higher status in the hierarchy of being if those offenders are physically disfigured Anglos.

Ramona

Helen Hunt Jackson (1831-1885) was a New Englander, who after the tragic death of her first husband and her two sons turned to writing. She married William Jackson in 1875 and moved to Colorado. A prolific writer, she gained considerable recognition for her efforts on behalf of the American Indians. *A Century of Dishonor* (1881) strongly criticized government policy toward Indians and her most famous novel, *Ramona* (1884), was written with material that she gathered as a result of having been appointed to a federal commission investigating the plight of Indians on missions. *Ramona* aroused public sentiment for improving conditions on behalf of Indians, but this aspect of both the novel and the various film versions has been somewhat obscured by the public response to another element in the work, the romantic picture of Old California. Helen Hunt Jackson's immensely popular chronicle of the problems and challenges faced by the orphaned daughter of the great house of Moreno, a powerful California Spanish family, was the object of four films.

The films in various manners depict the cruel mistreatment of the mission Indians by white settlers in southern California during the nineteenth century. Ramona learns that she is not a high-caste Hispanic but instead, half-Scot and half-Indian and chooses to leave white society and marry her childhood friend, Alessandro, a full-blooded Indian. However, secretly she remains in love with the young, handsome Don of the hacienda. Harassed by prejudiced townspeople, the couple move from community to community until one of the settlers murders Alessandro, and Ramona loses her child. Suffering from temporary amnesia, she wanders aimlessly in the countryside until she is discovered by the Don who restores her memory by reminding her of the song they loved as children. The first film (1910, Biograph, starring Mary Pickford) was a mere one-reeler directed by D. W. Griffith. However, shot on location in Ventura County, California, it was noted at the time for its breathtaking outdoor photography and innovative camera work. The second production was released in 1916 (Clune Film Producing Co.) and was a full-length feature (10-14 reels) that was one of the longest films of its times, running three hours and twenty-two minutes when not trimmed. It starred Adda Gleason and Monroe Salisbury. In 1928 (United Artists), as the novel was going through its 92nd printing, appeared the third version starring Dolores del Río and Warner Baxter. A later, fourth version starring Loretta Young and Don Ameche followed in 1936 (Fox).

Spanish-American War

As we have seen in Chapter I, the depiction of Hispanics in U.S. film began in part with newsreels and documentaries of the Spanish-American War. The film industry continued to produce an occasional dramatic feature that used the war, as exemplified by the films that follow.

The Bright Shawl (1923, Inspiration Pictures), starring Richard Barthelmess and Dorothy Gish, was a popular film about a wealthy young Anglo who goes to Cuba, helps the cause of Cuban independence, uses the information that a Spanish dancer, La Clavel, who has fallen in love with him provides, and escapes to the United States with his lover. *Masters of Men* (1923, Vitagraph) evokes the destruction of the Spanish ships in Santiago Harbor from the point of view of an Anglo hero who has been shanghaied. *The Rough Riders* (1927, Paramount, presented by Adolph Zukor and Jesse L. Lasky, starring Noah Beery) tells of the rivalry that turns to friendship between two heroes who vanquish the Spaniards in Cuba.

Villa

More pictures have been done about Villa than about any other Mexican. Most of these films have been newsreels or documentaries produced between 1914 and 1916, but there have been a number of dramatic films as well. From the first years of the Mexican Revolution through 1934, Villa was depicted alternatively as an intriguing revolutionary and possible social bandit to an outrageous rogue bandit to, in *Viva Villa!*, someone akin to a cross between the Marquis de Sade and Robin Hood.

Battle of Torreón and Career of General Villa (1914, Mutual) was a documentary claimed to be taken on location of the battle of Torreón, but the accuracy of which was strongly questioned by *Variety* (5.15.14). *The Life of General Villa* (1914, Mutual, codirector W. Christy Cabanne; codirector and starring Raoul Walsh as the young Villa) is a documentary and biography that included footage of the battle of Torreón (probably taken from an earlier short, *The Battle of Torreón* filmed by Raoul Walsh) and depicting alleged events from his early life and his revolutionary career. This seven-reel film was usually separately projected in two parts: *The Battle of Torreón*, a documentary, and *Life of Villa*, a story film. Villa was supposed to have participated in this production, but to what extent is unknown. *The Outlaw's Revenge* (1915, Mutual, director W. Christy Cabanne) was probably a reissued or re-edited version of *The Life of General Villa*, although Pancho Villa is not mentioned in the film itself (Hanson, 1988, 689).

Villa–Dead or Alive (1916, Eagle Film Mfg.) was probably the earliest film release resulting from Villa's raid into the United States and its aftermath. "Villa–Dead or Alive . . . that's what President Wilson said and that's what *we* are going to do. Is the United States prepared? GO AND SEE Uncle Sam's troops in action. SEE *your* flag cross the border to punish those who have insulted it" (*Movie Picture World*, 4.1.16, p. 149). *In the Land of the Tortilla* (1916, Beauty) was a contemptuous parody of Villa during the aftermath of his raid on Columbus, New Mexico. The American consul in Mexico receives a communication from Washington that "Veeha was captured by Caperanza and was about to be executed" because the latter is angry that the former beat him to the "generalship of the Tortillan army." The consul tries to get photographs of the scheduled execution but fails because it can only be attended by invitation. "What did all this mean? It might have meant that the United States public was so anxious to have the bandit that had actually invaded their country dead, that even seeing it happen in this humorous fantasy would be soothing to the psyche. It certainly worked for revising who really won the war in Vietnam" (Richard, 1992, 177-78).

Colonel Heeza Liar Captures Villa (1916, Paramount-Bray Animated Cartoons) was one of a series of Heeza Liar cartoons. The colonel accomplishes his feat as billed and delivers Villa across the border into the United States. In a similar film, *Colonel Heeza Liar and the Bandits* (1916, Paramount-Bray Animated Cartoons), the hero rescues Pershing and his troops who have been surrounded by Villa and his men.

Stars and Stripes in Mexico (1916, Powers) was a profoundly racist production done at the height of Villamania: "The scenes in this release show, first of all, the American army making ready to go after the notorious bandit Villa after his raid . . . in which many American civilians and soldiers lost their lives . . . the houses where Villa slaughtered sleeping Americans . . . where Uncle Sam's troops made their stand against Villa's bandits. There follow views of the ignorant young half-breeds treacherous and vicious, who supported Villa in his murderous campaign. These young bandits will be tried before judge Rodgers in New Mexico" (*Motion Picture World,* 5.13.16, p. 215).

William Randolph Hearst had been responsible for the smash hit serial, *The Perils of Pauline* (1914, Pathé) and he attempted to duplicate his success with *Patria* (1916, International) premised on the paranoiac notion of Japanese and Mexican collaboration to retake the American Southwest. It should be remembered that Hearst controlled vast portions of Mexican land at the time and his film represented an attempt to influence public opinion in order to cause the U.S. government to more actively intervene in the Mexican Revolution. A previous, comparable campaign by his newspapers had successfully influenced public opinion on behalf of intervention against Spain, leading to the Spanish-American War. In *Patria,* a fictional Japanese baron and Mexican official forge a secret alliance against the United States. In one of the *Patria* episodes, Wallace Beery (who later portrayed Villa in the 1934 *Viva Villa!*) plays the revolutionary "as an arch villain willing to conspire with little yellow men (including Warner Oland as one of the more militant Japanese barons) to put the lily white American men in the place they truly deserved, beneath the feet of the conquering avengers" (Richard, 1992, 184). By 1917, Japan was an ally in World War I and the series was proving to be a profound embarrassment for the Wilson Administration. It became the subject of a 1918 congressional hearing that was ostensibly directed at the effect of German propaganda during World War I just prior to the United States' entry.

Villa of the Movies (1917, Mack Sennett), produced after sentiment had begun to wane a bit, was a Keystone-style parody on Villa that laid him to rest as a formidable foe.

Viva Villa! (1934, Warner) has been to date, the most culturally significant Hollywood production about Pancho Villa. This is indexed by the fact that the film was not only reviewed in the usual sources such as *Variety* but in *The New York Times, Literary Digest, New Outlook, Commonweal, The Nation,* and *Scholastic.* The film was nominated for an Academy Award as the best film of 1934. Produced over a decade after Francisco Villa's death, this film represented a timely reinterpretation of Pancho Villa and the Mexican Revolution for the contemporary period, although by current standards, one that continued to be dominated primarily by negative stereotypes. This work of "rehabilitation" as it were, was aided by a Mexican production, *The Shadow of Pancho Villa,* that had also been screened in 1934 in the United States and had been well received in New York and Los Angeles.

In the Warner 1934 production, essentially Villa was portrayed as an ignorant and cruel bandit, but a highly patriotic and motivated one. *Commonweal* described the portrayal as "a fictional character . . . an inconceivably childish person of deep loyalties and great disinterestedness who fought brutally because of ignorance and of the single-minded intensity of his devotion to a cause" (April 27, 1934). Villa was simultaneously portrayed as ignorant, cruel, homicidal, childish, savage, and embracing the attitudes and behaviors of the peasant class; at the same time he was seen as filled with patriotic hatred for the oppressors of the Mexican people, and intensely loyal to martyred president Madero. The selection of Wallace Beery, usually cast as a comic type, was offensive to some, yet it was generally judged that he gave one of the great performances of his career.

The Shadow of Pancho Villa (English-language version of *La sombra de Pancho Villa),* a Mexican production distributed by Columbia, focused on the general's military career from the battle of Zacatecas where Villa vanquished the old regime through his defeat some years later by Obregón at Celaya. The film was far removed in atmosphere from the Hollywood fantastical approach to the revolutionary.

Zapata and Zapatismo

Until the famous *Viva Zapata!* (1952, Fox) very few films were available to the American public that depicted Zapata, and what was screened came from Mexico itself, except for a minor pose or view here or there in a newsreel. Zapata, of course, operating deep in the South, did not attack the United States and his cause was less amenable to stereotyping than those who could be viewed as involved in the revolution primarily for personal aggrandizement or material gain. Although Zapata has become the most influential Mexican role model for Chicanos, other Hispanics, and even the progressive mainstream population in the United States, the spread of his influence was not due to film productions during the first decades of the industry.

The Patriot (1916, Triangle, directed by and starring William S. Hart) is about an embittered Spanish-American War veteran who joins the forces of Pancho Zapilla (Zapata and Villa rolled up in one) but who reconsiders at the last moment and rather than fight his own people, attacks and beats the Mexicans. García Riera (1987, vol. I, p. 75) points out that the villain in *The Heart of Paula* (1916, Paramount) is named Emiliano and the bandit in *The Arizona Cat Claw* (1919, World) is named Zapatti.

My Friend Mendoza, an English-language version of the well-known Mexican film *El compadre Mendoza* (Aguila) was released in the United States in 1934; this was a dramatization of agrarian Zapatistas (Zapata does not appear in the film) and their struggle against the *latifundistas* who want to keep the land for themselves. The film was a critical success in the United States, transcending, in the opinion of the *New York Times* (11.19. 1934), the excessive use of histrionics or melodrama, which was the frequent criticism of Mexican films. Praised along the same lines by the *Times* (8.18.1934) was *Enemigos* (Atlántida), released as *The Enemies* in 1934, which depicts an imaginary incident about a Zapatista leader devoted to the cause of the peasants who falls prey to an aristocratic lady, a *porfirista,* who is responsible for the death of many of his comrades. When she offers him his life in return for his services, he refuses. It is instructive to note that both of these Mexican films were released in 1934, the same year that *Viva*

Villa! was released. Presumably the interest in Villa had a ripple effect that made the Mexican films viable.

Hispanics Who Figured in the Movies through 1936

Although no specific work has been dedicated primarily to the participation of Hispanic actors and other professionals in U.S. films, a number of works provide some information including the filmographies in the ongoing *American Film Institute Catalogs* (see bibliographical note), Richard (1992), Keller (1993), García Riera (1987), and Noriega (1992). We are now in a position to attempt to consolidate some of this information, albeit in a very preliminary fashion, and to make some very preliminary observations about the professional participation of Hispanics in U.S. cinema as well as to make a first attempt at recuperating the names and identities of many of these individuals.

Even as the conventions for representing of Hispanics were established during the first decades, this period in the U.S. film industry was better for foreigners, including Hispanics, at least up until the sound era (for Hispanics additional opportunities opened up in the sound era for roles or other jobs in Spanish-language Hollywood productions) than at any other time. This is a phenomenon that needs additional research and analysis, but several factors seem to be involved in this relative openness. One is that the silent era was still an embryonic period for film and as such permitted more crossovers and hybridization than at later periods. The medium did not yet impose the great obstacle of spoken language and the nascent film industries competed with each other world wide for markets. If Méliès and Pathé would come to the United States to do films, even Westerns, it made cultural and economic sense for the American film industry to be open and embracing of foreign talent. A second factor is that the United States still felt insecure about its status (or more open to other literatures or art, depending on your perspective) and looked to Europe, "to the continent" for cultural values and literary, cinematic, and other artistic ideas to some extent. This provided a premium for foreigners. With respect to Hispanics, very few actors who were "Mexican" in a highly ethnic sense made it, in contrast to debonair, cultured, and exotic types reflecting "continental morality" or its Argentine surrogate version. By the end of World War II, the tilt toward nativism as well as the overarching position of the United States in the world appears to have carried with it a consequent reduction in such a premium on the foreign or exotic. A third factor is that in the first decades more films were produced than later, more ideas and characters were needed and this made for a wider, more open U.S. film industry. Part of this factor was the motivation (partly forced through competition with continental film industries, notably Italy) to do the classics, the Bible, historical and period pieces, all of which, of course were fresh and new at the time. A commitment to such productions, including Don Juan, Don Quixote, Carmen, Black Legend films (even when they were among the most stereotypical) carried with it opportunities for different, foreign, exotic types. Yet another factor was that typecasting just was in its beginning phase, so more diversity was possible. More films were made, the cost of films were such that each did not represent a corporate entity of its own, and more risks could be taken. During this period the Hispanics who did get roles often got to play other than Hispanics as well, although they rarely were cast in a nonexotic part.

Exotics, including Latin Lovers if male, or Latin vamps if female, were among the most popular parts during the 1920s because of an insatiable demand for these types. The Italian Rudolph Valentino, the Mexicans Ramón Novarro and Gilbert Roland, the Spanish-born Antonio Moreno, and Ricardo Cortez, a Jewish Austrian who changed his name from Jacob Krantz, were counted among the major stars of Hollywood. Dolores Del Río and Lupe Vélez were the most successful Mexican actresses ever to work in Hollywood.

As Hadley-García has pointed out, during this period, "foreign names created audience interest, and although Luis Antonio De Alonso changed his to Gilbert Roland, Winnifred Hudnut became Natcha Rambova, and Muriel Harding evolved into Olga Petrova" (1990, 27).

The credits which follow generally go through 1936. See the final part of succeeding chapters for information for those figures whose careers went past 1936. Also see the concluding section, *Outstanding Hispanics in the Film Industry*.

María Alba was a Spanish actress who appeared in *Blindfold* and *Roadhouse* (1928), *Joy Street* (1929), and *Hell's Heroes* and *Olimpia* (1930). No further information on her is currently available.

Don Alvarado (born José Paige), also known professionally as Don Page, got his first role as an extra in *Mademoiselle Midnight* (1924) and soon became an established Latin Lover type in many late silents and early talkies, particularly musicals. He was cast in non-Hispanic parts as well. His films during the first decades included: The *Pleasure Buyers* (1925, Warner Brothers), *The Night Cry* (1926, Warner Brothers), *Loves of Carmen* (1927, Fox), *The Battle of the Sexes* (1928, United Artists, presented by Joseph M. Schenck, director D. W. Griffith), *The Apache* (1928, Columbia), *Río Rita* (1929, RKO), *The Bridge of San Luis Rey* (1929, MGM), *The Bad One* (1930, United Artists), *Captain Thunder* (1930, Warner Brothers), *La Cucaracha* (1932, Pioneer), *The Devil is a Woman* (1935, Paramount, starring Marlene Dietrich and César Romero), and *Rose of the Rancho* (1936, Paramount).

Armida (Armida Vendrell) was singing and dancing in a Los Angeles restaurant when she was discovered by promoter Gus Edwards and appeared in a short, *Mexicana* (1929) and was signed on by Warner Brothers. She was a Gypsy in *General Crack* (1929, Warner Brothers, starring John Barrymore) and appeared in *Border Romance* (1930, Tiffany), *On the Border* (1930, Warner Brothers), *The Texans* (1930, Paramount, starring Gary Cooper and Fay Wray), *Under a Texas Moon* (1930, Warner Brothers, the first Western totally in technicolor), and *The Marines are Coming* (1935, Mascot).

María Calvo primarily did Spanish-language versions of Hollywood productions. Occasionally, as in *A Devil with Women* (1930, Fox), she appeared in English-language films. Although no more biographical information is available, more information on her Spanish-language credits can be obtained in Richard (1992).

Rene Cardona, according to Ríos-Bustamante (who spells it Cordona; 1992, 27) appeared in supporting roles in over thirty films, including *Prince of Wales* (1934) and *Gentlemen Prefer Blondes* (1935). No further information about him has been unearthed.

During this period Leo Carrillo did, among others, *Mister Antonio* (1929), *Hell Bound*, *Homicide Squad*, *The Guilty Generation* (1931), *Girl of the Río*, *The Broken Wing*, *Deception* (1932), *Parachute Jumper*, *Racetrack*, *Obey the Law* (1933), *Four Frightened People*, *Viva Villa!*, *The Gay Bride*, *Manhattan Melodrama* (1934), *In Caliente*, *Love Me Forever* (1935), and *The Gay Desperado* (1936).

Pedro de Córdoba performed in *Carmen*, *Temptation* (1915), *María Rosa* (1916), *The New Moon* (1919), *The World and his Wife* (1920), *When Knighthood Was in Flower*, *The Inner Chamber* (1922), *Enemies of Women* (1923), *The Desert Sheik*, *The Bandolero* (1924), *The Crusades*, *Captain Blood* (1935), *Rose of the Rancho*, *Anthony Adverse*, *Ramona*, and *The Garden of Allah* (1936).

Mona Darkfeather, according to García Riera (1987, vol. I, 59) and Ramírez (1972), despite her American Indian name, was Mexican. She was cast in *Juanita* (1913, Nestor) and *The Oath of Conchita* (1913, Nestor). She was married to Frank Montgomery who directed *A Spanish Madonna* and *The Western Border* (1915), in which she appeared. After his death, she married the Mexican cowboy and stuntman Art Ortega (spelling according to García Riera, 1987; only spelled Ortego in *American Film Institute Catalog, 1911-1920*).

Chico Day worked as an assistant director to Cecil B. DeMille in *The Plainsman* (1936), and later, *The Ten Commandments* (1956), see Thomas (1971, 19-21). No further information is known.

Juan de la Cruz is presumed to be Hispanic but no specific information has been uncovered on him except that he appeared in *The Gentleman from Indiana, Peer Gynt* (1915), *The Flirt, Hop, The Devil's Brew, The House of Lies, The Making of Maddalena* (set in Rome), *Where Are My Children?* (1916), *A Gentleman's Agreement* (1918), *An Adventure in Hearts* (1919), and *Food for Scandal, For the Soul of Rafael,* and *Pegeen* (1920).

Dolores del Río got her first break in *Joanna* (1925, director Edwin Carewe). Her career peaked during the silent period as she became the victim of increasing typecasting in ethnic and exotic roles, particularly during the sound era, because of her Latin accent. She appeared in *What Price Glory* (1926), *Resurrection, The Loves of Carmen* (1927), *The Gateway of the Moon, No Other Woman, Ramona, Revenge* (1928), *Evangeline* (1929), *The Bad One* (1930), *The Girl of the Río, Bird of Paradise* (1932), *Flying Down to Rio* (1933), *Wonder Bar, Madame Du Barry* (1934), *In Caliente, I Live for Love,* and *The Widow from Monte Carlo* (1935).

Andrés de Segurola acted in twenty or more Spanish-language Hollywood productions and crossed over into English-language films in *The Love of Sunya* (1927, United Artists, opposite Gloria Swanson) as a Spanish impresario, and in *General Crack* (1929). No other information has been found on him.

Beatrice Domínguez may be Hispanic but no information on her has been obtained except that she appeared in *The Light of Victory, The Sundown Trial* (1919), and *Under Crimson Skies* (1920).

Escamillo Fernández (spelled with many variations including E.L., Escamilo, Escarmillo) almost certainly was Hispanic; no other information has been found about him except that he appeared in some twenty films including *The Two Orphans* (1915), *Audrey* (1916), *Heart of the Wilds, Woman* (1918), *Hit or Miss* (1919), *The Fortune Teller* (1920), *Love's Redemption* (1921), and *The Man from Glengarry* (1923).

Emilio "El Indio" Fernández, the famous Mexican director, appeared as a Mexican bandit in *The Land of the Missing Men* (1930, Tiffany) and *Western Code* (1933, Columbia).

Martin Garralaga was introduced in *The Gay Caballero* (1932, Fox) and would appear in some fifty more Hollywood films, almost all of them Spanish-language productions. No other information is known about him.

Recent information has been uncovered about Myrtle González (see Ríos-Bustamante, 1992), a native Mexican Californian who appeared in numerous films including *Captain Alvarez* (1914), *The Masked Dancer* (1914, Vitagraph), *The Chalice of Courage* (1915), *The End of the Rainbow, The Girl of the Lost Lake, It Happened in Honolulu, A Romance of Billy Goat Hill, The Secret of the Swamp,* and *The Heart of Bonita* (1916, Laemmle), *God's Crucible, The Greater Law, Mutiny, The Show Down,* and *Southern Justice* (1917). Unfortunately, her career was cut off by her untimely death in 1917 from the influenza. In *Captain Alvarez,* she is Bonita, beautiful by antonomasia. This film is yet another where Anglos make Latin American history. In this case an Anglo operating under the name of Alvarez defeats the Rosas Argentine dictatorship and liberates the provinces from this tyranny. In *The Heart of Bonita* (1916, Laemmle), González played a señorita in love with an Anglo.

Carmen Guerrero, born in 1911 in Mexico, appeared in some Mack Sennett shorts and in *Girl Shock* (1930); she worked primarily in Hollywood Spanish-language productions and in Mexican cinema.

Rita Hayworth began her film career using her original name, Rita Cansino in films including *Under the Pampas Moon, Charlie Chan in Egypt, Dante's Inferno* (1935), *Rebellion, Human Cargo,* and *Meet Nero Wolfe* (1936).

George Hernández (also George F. Hernández) was most probably Hispanic. Although no further information has been found on him, he appeared in over thirty films, including *The Making of Bobby Burnit* (1914), *The Rosary* (1915), *The Secret of the Swamp* (1916), *Broadway Arizona* (1917), *The Vortex* (1918), *Tin Pan Alley* (1919), *The Daredevil* (1920), *The Road Demon* (1921), *Bluebeard Jr.* (1922), and many others. Similarly, a Mrs. George Hernández appeared in a half-dozen films during the same period including *The Servant in the House* (1921) and *The Pride of Palomar* (1922).

Margo (well-known stage name of Marie Marguerita Guadalupe Teresa Estela Bolado Castilla y O'Donnell), who was originally a dancer, began her career usually typecast as a tragic, suffering woman in *Crime Without Passion* (1934), *Rumba* (1935), *The Robin Hood of Eldorado*, and *Winterset* (1936).

Mona Maris (María Capdevielle) did *Romance of the Río Grande* (1929), *Under a Texas Moon, The Arizona Kid, A Devil With Women* (1930), *The Passionate Plumber, Once in a Lifetime* (1932), *The Death Kiss, Secrets* (1933), *White Heat, and Kiss and Make-Up* (1934), as well as various foreign films including German and Mexican productions. For further information on the foreign films, see Katz (1979, 777).

Chris-Pin Martin did *The Rescue* (1929), *Billy the Kid* (1930), *The Squaw Man, The Cisco Kid* (1931), *Girl Crazy, South of Santa Fe* (1932), *Outlaw Justice* (1933), *Four Frightened People* (1934), *Under the Pampas Moon, Bordertown* (1935), and *The Gay Desperado* (1936).

Beatriz Michelena was the daughter of an opera singer in San Francisco and by 1900 was a star on the San Francisco musical stage. She appeared in *Mrs. Wiggs of the Cabbage Patch, Salomy Jane* (1914), *The Lily of Poverty Flat, Mignon, A Phyllis of the Sierras, Salvation Nell* (1915), *The Unwritten Law, The Woman Who Dared* (1916), *The Heart of Juanita, Just Squaw, The Price Woman Pays* (1919), and *The Flame of Hellgate* (1920). Her cover appeared on the January 1915 *Motion Picture World* with the caption, "Beatriz Michelena, Greatest and Most Beautiful Artist Now Appearing in Motion Pictures." (See Ríos-Bustamante, 1992). No further information about her has been unearthed following 1920.

Fox promoted José Mojica as a major Spanish-language star. He also did at least one English-language film that I have unearthed, *One Mad Kiss* (1930, Fox).

Conchita Montenegro, an extremely attractive actress from Spain played in over twenty films during these years, primarily in Hollywood Spanish-language features. She crossed over into English-language films as well, playing the señorita in *The Caballero* (1930, MGM), *The Cisco Kid, Strangers May Kiss* (1931), and *The Gay Caballero* (1932, Fox).

The noted star Antonio Moreno did *Voice of the Million, Two Daughters of Eve, The Musketeers of Pig Alley* (1912), *By Man's Law, The House of Discord* (1913), *His Father's House, Strongheart, The Song of the Ghetto, Memories in Men's Souls, Politics and the Press, The Peacemaker, In the Latin Quarter, Sunshine and Shadows* (1914), *The Quality of Mercy, Love's Way, The Dust of Egypt, The Gypsy Trail* (1915), *Kennedy Square, Rose of the South* (1916), *The Magnificent Meddler, Aladdin from Broadway* (1917), *The House of Hate* (serial), *The House of a Thousand Candles* (1918), *The Invisible Hand* (serial) (1920), *A Guilty Conscience* (1921), *My American Wife, The Trial of the Lonesome Pine, The Spanish Dancer* (1923), *Flaming Barriers, Tiger Story, The Border Legion* (1924), *Learning to Love, Her Husband's Secret* (1925), *Mare Nostrum, The Temptress, Love's Blindness* (1926), *Venus of Venice, It* (1927), *The Whip Woman, Adoration, Nameless Men* (1928), *Careers, Romance of the Río Grande* (1929), *Rough Romance, One Mad Kiss* (1930), and *The Bohemian Girl* (1936).

Rosita Moreno, born in Pachuca, Mexico (see García Riera, 1987, vol. I, 168) played in *The Santa Fe Trail* (1930) and *Her Wedding Night* (1930), but mostly worked in Spanish-language productions. No other information on her has been found.

Carlos Navarro (also Carlos de Navarro) was a Mexican who also directed the Mexican film *Janitzio* (1934). He wrote the script for two Vitagraph films, *Mareea, the Foster Mother* and *Mareea, the Half Breed*, both in 1914.

Barry Norton (born Alfredo Birabén) was a romantic lead and supporting player of late silent and early sound Hollywood films. He also appeared in various Hollywood produced Spanish-language films and Mexican productions, sometimes directing them as well. During these years he starred in *The Lily, What Price Glory* (1926), *Ankles Preferred, The Wizard, The Heart of Salome, Sunrise* (1927), *Mother Knows Best, Fleetwing, Legion of the Condemned, Four Devils* (1928), *Sins of the Fathers, The Exalted Flapper* (1929), *Dishonored* (1931), *Cocktail Hour, Lady for a Day*

(1933), *Unknown Blonde, The World Moves On, Grand Canary, Nana* (1934), and *The Criminal Within* (1936).

Ramón Novarro did, in addition to a number of bit parts prior to 1922, *The Prisoner of Zenda, Trifling Woman* (1922), *Where the Pavement Ends, Scaramouche* (1923), *The Arab, Thy Name is Woman* (1924), *A Lover's Oath* (1925), *Ben Hur* (in the title role, his most notable part, 1926), *The Road to Romance, The Student Prince* (1927), *Across to Singapore, A Certain Young Man, Forbidden Hours* (1928), *The Pagan* (1929), *In Gay Madrid, Call of the Flesh* (1930), *Daybreak, Son of India, Mata Hari* (1931), *Huddle, Son-Daughter* (1932), *The Barbarian* (1933), *Laughing Boy,* and *The Night is Young* (1934). By the mid-1930s, Novarro's career was waning as a Latin Lover. He occasionally directed the Spanish versions of films in which he starred and in 1936 he produced and directed a Mexican film as well, *Contra la corriente.*

Manuel Ojeda (also Michael R.) was Mexican and worked in the Mexican film industry in addition to having appeared in the following films: *The Law of the North* (1918), *The Man Who Turned White, Rustling a Bride* (1919), *A Double Dyed Deceiver, Pinto,* and *The Scuttlers* (1920).

Nina Quartaro (as spelled in *The American Film Institute Catalog, Feature Films 1921-30,* p. 641, but spelled Nena Quartero in Adams and Rainey, 178, p. 118) exclusively played Hispanic women in the films uncovered by this research. I think she was Hispanic but have not been able to confirm this. She was in *The Red Mark* (1928, Pathé) and *The Eternal Woman* (1929, Columbia), where she played a wife, Consuelo, of loose ways and easy morals. In *The Fighting Sheriff* (Columbia 1931), she was a lovely señorita opposite Buck Jones. In *Man From Monterey* (1933, Warner Brothers), she played a señorita opposite John Wayne who played a Hispanic avenger.

Anthony Quinn began his film career in 1936 with *Parole!, Sworn Enemy,* and *Night Waitress.*

Duncan Renaldo did *Clothes Make the Woman, The Naughty Duchess* (1928), *The Bridge of San Luis Rey, Pals of the Prairie* (1929), *Trader Horn* (1931), *Trapped in Tia Juana* (1932), *Public Stenographer* (1933), and *Moonlight Murder* (1936).

Mona Rico (María Enriqueta Valenzuela) was an actress born in Mexico who appeared as a dancer in *A Devil With Women* (1930) and a prostitute in *Thunder Below* (1932). No additional information has been discovered about her.

Julián Rivero played primarily in B films but obtained a considerable number of roles. He also did Hollywood Spanish-language films. According to Richard, "Rivero would be many a Western hero's loyal and humorous Hispanic sidekick. Always acceptably lecherous but a devoted tonto to the end" (1992, 431). He appeared in *Border Whirlwind* (1926, FBO), *Dugan of the Bad Lands* (1931, Monogram), *God's Country and the Man* (1931, Syndicate), *Beyond the Rockies* (1932, RKO), *The Kid from Spain* (1932, United Artists), *Law and Lawless* (1933, Majestic, opposite Jack Hoxie), and *Cowboy Holiday* (1934, Beacon).

Gilbert Roland did *The Plastic Age* (1925), *The Campus Flirt, The Blonde Saint* (1926), *Camille, Rose of the Golden West, The Love Mart* (1927), *The Dove, The Woman Disputed* (1928), *New York Nights* (1929), *Men of the North* (1930), *Monsieur Le Fox* (1931), *The Passionate Plumber, Life Begins, No Living Witness, Call Her Savage* (1932), *She Done Him Wrong, Our Betters, Gigolettes of Paris, After Tonight* (1933), *Elinor Norton* (1934), and *Mystery Woman* (1935).

César Romero began his career in 1933. During this period he did *The Shadow Laughs* (1933), *The Thin Man, British Agent* (1934), *Clive of India, The Good Fairy, Cardinal Richelieu, The Devil is a Woman, Diamond Jim, Metropolitan, Rendezvous, Show Them No Mercy* (1935), *Love Before Breakfast, Public Enemy's Wife,* and *15 Maiden Lane* (1936).

Soledad Jiménez (usually misspelled Solidad Jiminez) was a Spanish actress who appeared in *The Cock-Eyed World, In Old Arizona* (1929), *The Arizona Kid, A Devil With Women,* and *The Texan* (1930). No additional information has been discovered about her.

Raquel Torres (born Paula Osterman, November 11, 1908), a Mexican born in Hermosillo, chose to change her name, emphasizing her Hispanicity. She debuted and made a vivid impression in *White Shadows in the South Seas* (1928, MGM) playing a beautiful native girl opposite

Monte Blue in a film that had the unusual message that white men corrupt and destroy native civilizations. She was known for her exotic beauty. After a brief film career, she retired from the screen to marry a wealthy businessman. Widowed, she married actor Jon Hall in 1959. Other films in which she appeared included *The Bridge of San Luis Rey, The Desert Rider* (1929), *Under a Texas Moon, The Sea Bat* (1930), *Aloha* (1931), *So This Is Africa!, The Woman I Stole, Duck Soup* (1933), and *Red Wagon* (United Kingdom) (1934).

Lupita Tovar, born in Oaxaca, Mexico, 1911, her father Mexican, her mother Anglo, appeared as a cantina girl in *Border Law* (1931, Columbia) opposite Buck Jones and as a señorita in *Yankee Don* (1931, Capital). She did the 1932 version of the famous *Santa* (Compañía Nacional Productora), with Antonio Moreno directing, and she appeared in *Storm over the Andes* (1935, Universal) about the Gran Chaco war between Bolivia and Paraguay, starring opposite Antonio Moreno and Jack Holt. In addition to the films above, she did many more Spanish-language films.

Lupe Vélez broke into films in 1926 in Hal Roach comedy shorts, including a Laurel and Hardy production, *Sailors Beware,* and made her mark the following year opposite Douglas Fairbanks in *The Gaucho* (1927). Additional films she did during this period included *Stand and Deliver* (1928), where she played a Greek, *Wolf Song, Lady of the Pavements, Tiger Rose* (1929), *Hell Harbor, The Storm, East is West* (1930), *Resurrection, The Squaw Man, The Cuban Love Song* (1931), *The Broken Wing, Kongo* (1932), *Hot Pepper* (1933), *Palooka, Strictly Dynamite, Laughing Boy* (1934), and *Gypsy Melody* (1936, a British production).

It may be stretching it to have Raoul Walsh listed as a Hispanic, but he was part Spanish on his mother's side (see García Riera, 1987, vol. I, 66). Of his affinity for Hispanic subjects there is no doubt. During the period he codirected *The Life of General Villa* (1914) and directed and sometimes acted in, produced, wrote the story, or earned other credits in the following: *The Mystery of the Hindu Image, The Double Knot, The Greaser, A Bad Man and Others, Carmen* (1914), *Pillars of Society, The Serpent* (1916), *The Conqueror, Betrayed, The Silent Lie, The Innocent Sinner* (1917), *The Woman and the Law* (1918), *Evangeline* (1919), *The Deep Purple* (1920), *Serenade* (1921), *The Thief of Bagdad* (1924), *The Spaniard* (1925), *What Price Glory* (1926), *The Loves of Carmen* (1927), *Sadie Thompson, Me Gangster* (1928), *In Old Arizona* (1929, codirected), *The Big Trail* (1930), *Women of All Nations* (1931), *For Me and My Gal/Pier 13* (1932), *The Bowery, Going Hollywood* (1933), *Under Pressure* (1935), and *Klondike Annie* (1936).

In addition to the actors above who did work in English-language Hollywood productions, numerous other Hispanic actors worked in Spanish-language Hollywood productions, and often Mexican or other Latin American productions as well, some of them released in English language dubbed form in the United States. These actors included major celebrities such as the Argentine tango singer, Carlos Gardel. While a review of the films that they worked in is beyond the scope of this book, I do want to recognize a number of these actors. Hopefully, future research will be able to begin to piece together their contributions to cinema. The Hispanic actors who follow earned film credits that range from several to over twenty films (see also above, for some actors who crossed over into English-language productions but were primarily Spanish-language players): María Alba, Luis Alberni, Luana Alcániz, Manuel Arbo, Catalina Barcena, María Luz Callejo, Rene Cardona, Miguel Contreras Torres, José Crespo, Alfredo del Diestro, Carlos Gardel, José Mojica, Martin Garralaga, Carmen Guerrero, Juan de Homs, Juan de Landa, Elena Landeros, Carmen Larrabeiti, Miguel Ligero, Luis Llaneza, Delia Magaña, Paco Moreno, Rosita Moreno, Ralph Navarro, Vicente Padula, Valentín Parera, Manuel París, Manuel Peluffo, José Peña "Pepet", Julio Peña, Ramón Pereda, Carmen Rodríguez (spelled with other variations), Enrique de Rosas, Raúl Roulién, Enriqueta Soler, Romualdo Tirado, Juan Torena, Antonio Vidal, Ernesto Vilches, Carlos Villarías, Julio Villarreal, and Lucio Villegas. Some additional, sporadic information is available about them primarily in Richard (1992).

Finally, we want to note that during the period a number of Anglo (in the commonly understood meaning that included U.S. citizens of other ancestries but assimilated into American culture and not subject to strong racial prejudices) actors represented Hispanics. Among the most notable: Mary Astor, Richard Barthelmess, Noah Beery, Wallace Beery, Warner Baxter, Frank Borzage, Edwin Carewe (primarily known as a director), Ricardo Cortez (Jacob Krantz), Bebe Daniels, Douglas Fairbanks, Sr., Geraldine Farrar, Romaine Fielding, William S. Hart, Alice Joyce, Henry King, Frank Lloyd, Walter Long, Myrna Loy, Margueritte de la Motte, Mary Pickford, and Fay Wray. Among the actors of other nationalities who represented Hispanic figures should be noted Vilma Banky (Hungarian), Greta Garbo (Swedish), Sessue Hayakawa (Japanese), Pola Negri (Polish), and Rudolph (also Rodolph) Valentino (Italian).

Note

[1] The plot of *In the Palace of the King* is apocryphal. Although at times Philip harbored suspicions about Don Juan, he never attempted his murder. On the other hand, he appears to have consented to the murder of Juan de Escobedo, Don Juan of Austria's personal secretary.

WILLIAM FOX PRESENTS ~

DOLORES DEL RIO
AND
VICTOR McLAGLEN
IN **LOVES OF CARMEN**

BASED ON THE STORY BY
PROSPER MERIMEE
adapted for the screen by GERTRUDE ORR
RAOUL WALSH
production

N-3100-514

María Montez

Pedro Armendáriz in *Captain Sindbad*

5

The 1930s through the 1950s and the Era of Social Consciousness

Beginning in the 1930s, several developments significantly impacted the depiction of Hispanics in United States film, as well as their participation in the industry. Among these were the conglomeration of the film industry and the consolidation of the Production Code; the impact of protests against U.S. films in the Spanish-speaking world, which grew stronger with the sound era and which were taken ever more seriously as the globe headed toward World War II; and coincident with the development of sound films, the initiation and subsequent abandonment of Spanish-language productions.

The period also witnessed and filmically responded to major technological and sociopolitical changes. The most important new genre of Hispanic-focused films was the Latin musical, made possible through the creation of the "talkies." The Latin musical, together with the production of more jungle and other exotic films, provided the only substantive new opportunities for Hispanic actors and other professionals. The Great Depression and other social upheavals helped create the social problem film and closely allied types, the "message" biographies, and the Good Samaritan films where Anglos helped Hispanic and other defenseless or inept minorities. These films were a mixed blessing, but on balance Hispanics were portrayed more positively. From the point of view of industry participation, however, these films did not provide many opportunities because not many socially conscious films were made, and those that were often used Anglo actors (often white ethnics such as Jewish actors John Garfield and Paul Muni, or Italian actor Sal Mineo).

Some of the previous genres continued to be robust, most particularly the Western. In addition, border, bullfighting, Latin Lover, and Mexican Revolution films continued to be made, although not in the numbers of the previous decades. However, opportunities for Hispanic and other exotic or allegedly "foreign" talent were severely reduced between the 1930s and the 1950s. The United States turned inward in its films for a variety of reasons; technological and social developments conspired against exoticism and diversity (particularly of speaking style, accent, and diction) and the improvement of the image of Hispanics also had the consequent effect of reducing opportunities for Hispanics to portray greasers, vamps, bandidos, cantina girls, and other types.

Conglomeration of the Film Industry and the Production Code

The wave of ethnic stereotyping, including the stereotypification of Hispanics that we have reviewed in the preceding chapters was to a certain extent reinforced by the development of film as big business. However, other forces, including the protests of Hispanic nations and U.S. film industry initiatives to enter the Spanish-language film market, also served to temper the negative stereotypes. By the early 1930s, capital investment in the American film industry had become centered not in production but in distribution, particularly in the form of movie theaters. In contrast to the earliest period during which film companies proliferated, a long, often bitterly competitive process of concentration took place so that by the early 1930s power rested with eight major, vertically structured corporations that had consolidated production, distribution, and exhibition in monopolistic fashion: MGM, Warner Brothers, Paramount, Twentieth-Century Fox, Universal, RKO, Columbia, and United Artists. This outcome determined that the industry gave a steady priority to making a large quantity of pictures than to making good pictures. A steady turnover of product was needed in order to ensure revenue at the box office, which depended on regular attendance at many theaters on a continual basis, not on high attendance for any one movie during a single run. From an industry point of view, making good pictures was secondary to making many pictures.

The vertically integrated and managed studios operated on an assembly-line basis, similar to the contemporaneously established Detroit automobile industry. Writers and directors were assigned projects to be started Monday morning. The various departments—costume, make-up, art construction, musical scores, and so on—concentrated solely on their specific spheres of activity from film to film. The assembly-line method expedited large quantities of product into the theaters, but unlike most assembly lines, the studios did not mass-produce exactly the same product over and over. While each car off the assembly line is the same as all the others, each movie was unique, within a highly circumscribed organizational grid. Studios quickly developed means for the mass production of different products. A series of basic conventions—character, narrative, theme, style—was established as a standard mode of expression. These formulas were broad enough to be applied in a wide variety of ways and flexible enough to shift with changing times and tastes, yet fixed enough to serve as a pattern for production and marketing.

This assembly-line methodology or homogenization of craft that governed U.S. film distinguished the American film industry from those of other nations, none of which produced nearly as many films, attained a similar big business status, nor realized the vertical consolidation of production, distribution, and exhibition to the same degree. Moreover, this homogenization, usually known as the Hollywood Formula, had a profound influence on the plots, themes, performers, and other constituents of U.S. film. In particular, the effect was to significantly truncate the range of films that were made from the point of view of plot and theme as compared to the earlier decades, and consequently, to reduce the diversity of individuals who could obtain roles in the films. There were certain exceptions: those who had already attained status, those who performed in the Latin musical usually as singing and dancing seductresses or spitfires or as Latin Lovers, and those who found work in jungle or other exotic films. Otherwise, this was not a good period for a Latina or Latino to be in the movie business.

With respect to plot, film was produced and marketed to the public by genre: Western, musical, screwball comedy, horror, gangster, social problem, message biography, women's films, and others. The easily identifiable genres provided variations on familiar movie experiences and made moviegoing a sort of ritual or habit-forming pastime. Repetition of this sort ensured a basically effortless participation by the audience. There was absolute trust, for example, that the hero would prevail and get the girl. It was just a matter of how and when. With respect to performance, type-casting (the human resource analog to the production of standard fenders or automobile bodies) led to the highly salesworthy star system. After several films, the public came to know a star very well, so much so that it became difficult for actors to stray beyond their screen personae. Moviegoers all knew clearly what to expect from a Bette Davis or James Cagney, or for that matter Lupe Vélez or Fernando Lamas vehicle and the studios protected the stars' screen personae by developing film scripts that would enhance the consecrated performance qualities of each star. The star system was the most important aspect of film marketing. Character, story line, and production qualities were built around the star. The hyperbole derived from advertisements to magazines and press coverage about the glamorous world of Hollywood served the same function. Given the circumstances of marketing by the star system, it is small wonder that Hispanic film actors and actresses had the option of either being typecast negatively if they retained their Hispanic identity, or denying that very identity, by what the industry euphemistically called "repositioning" themselves. Examples of the former include the vamps or cantina girls such as Armida (Vendrell), Dolores del Río, Rita Hayworth (before she repositioned herself), and Mona Maris, or the simplistic sidekicks, Chris-Pin Martin and Julián Rivero. Leo Carrillo did both sidekicks as well as badmen as called for by the film. Lupe Vélez, dead at thirty-four in no small measure due to the humiliations of the Hollywood star system, played to perfection a comic variation of the seductress stereotype with her hip swinging and her amusing difficulties with the English language. Vélez would go down to defeat when confronted with female Anglo-Saxon competition in the struggle to infatuate an Anglo male star. The most notable example of the repositioned actor was Rita Cansino who changed her image to an Anglo Rita Hayworth in order to greatly expand the range of roles that she could obtain.

The influence of the formula on the development of a movie's theme or message did further damage to minority and other out-groups, including Hispanics. The two fundamental components of the formula in celluloid thematics were that the movie should provide wish-fulfillment and that it should communicate Americanism. Often films combined both notions—nationalism and hedonism—at the deleterious expense of out-groups. Even the confines of the United States did not present much of a constraint. In the Latin musical, Hollywood went abroad and created an American playground or theme park that was as safe and seductively predictable as it was exotic. As Roffman and Purdy observe:

> The dramatic conflict was always structured around two opposing poles definitively representing good and evil, with a readily identifiable hero and villain. But since the hero was also the star, his goodness must conform to the star's personality. Absolute virtue, however, is generally unexciting and inhibits many of the star's qualities of illicit wish fulfillment. Thus the hero often embodied slightly tainted moral traits. As long as there was no doubt as to the hero's ultimate allegiance to the side of good, the audience could indulge in his minor transgressions. By subtly combining moral uprightness with an endearing toughness, the star was made more provocative and the hero a more effective combatant of villainy. He had the air of having been everywhere and seen everything. He was the Indian fighter who was raised by the Indians, the marshal who used to be an outlaw gunfighter, the police agent who once was one of the mob, and the ultimate good bad guy, the private eye who skirts between the world of law and the underworld of crime. This helped rationalize the hero's use of violent, even immoral means to

achieve righteous ends. In the same way (though not nearly as often) sympathy could be extended to the criminal without ever upholding criminality. (Roffman and Purdy, 1981, p. 6)

Given the arrangement just described, in U.S. films the ethnic *other* almost invariably played the outcast and the evildoer. Film, and subsequently television in its early period, were instruments of socialization that now displayed even more rigidly as their guiding premise the assimilation of all racial, ethnic, and religious differences into the harmonizing credo of the Anglo-American melting pot. In contrast to the productions of the nickelodeon era when films catered to immigrants and in fact subverted the ethos of the dominant class, now films appeared that depicted non-Anglos negatively because they either attempted to subvert the melting pot notion (*Washington Masquerade, I Married a Communist*), resist it (*Right Cross*), or they were the dupes of Communists or other leftwingers (*Trial*). This new phenomenon of depicting "subversives," "resisters," or "dupes" as seen from a militant melting pot perspective contrasts with the depiction of other races and ethnicities of the earlier film period. The earlier depiction (which of course, in parallel fashion extends as well into the 1930s and beyond) had the races and ethnicities who could not be readily assimilated because of their difference of color and physiognomy—blacks, Hispanics, Asians, and Indians, drummed into the fold of evildoers and outcasts because they couldn't be American a priori, and without recourse. Now, in addition to nonwhites functioning in their tradition role as evil aliens, as non-Americans, we see them functioning as the slag and the scoria in the melting-pot alchemy of U.S. film as "bad" Americans.

Moreover, by the 1930s, Hollywood had already richly earned its description as a "dream factory." The "dreams" or usual components of wish fulfillment that were apparent in the earliest films—romance and true love, destroying evil (even as we relish it fiendishly depicted on the screen), rewarding good and realizing vengeance against villains, happy endings, and so on—now were produced in U.S. films on something genuinely characterizable as a "factory" or assembly-line basis. The Hollywood dream factory's manufacture of these wish-fulfillment elements ensured that Hispanic and other out-group characters who had traditionally provided conflict would now provide this function in innumerable plots of little difference, distinction, or range. Hispanic seductresses, exotics, Latin Lovers, and badmen came off the assembly line in industrial quantities.

The formula became law in 1934 with the introduction of the Production Code (see section below, *The Impact of Protests in the Spanish-Speaking World and the Effect of the Good Neighbor Policy*), which states the ideologized basis of the very formula. The code expresses in pontifical and hypocritical fashion the moral value system behind the Hollywood formula, decrying criminal violence and intimate sexuality, upholding the sanctity of marriage and the home and other traditions that had already become heartily compromised in the movies. The code states that entertainment is "either HELPFUL or HARMFUL to the human race." Because of this, "the motion picture . . . has special MORAL OBLIGATIONS" to create only "correct entertainment" which "raises the whole standard of a nation" and "tends to improve the race, or at least to re-create or rebuild human beings exhausted with the realities of life" (Roffman and Purdy, 1981, 6). Among the specific dos and don'ts of this document were:

"Illegal drug traffic must never be presented."
"Seduction or rape should be never more than suggested. . . . They are never the proper subject for comedy."
"Miscegenation (sex relationships between the white and black races) is forbidden."
"Sex hygiene and venereal diseases are not subjects for motion pictures."

As a result of the pressure for social change by civil liberties groups and Supreme Court decisions concerning obscenity, the code was radically revised in 1966. In 1968, a rating system was put into effect, classifying films according to their suitability for viewing by the young.

In a very broad sense, an ideological vision of the world was acted out in each formula movie. Each individual—of the correct ethnic background, this is—can aspire to success. You are limited only by your own character and energies (if you are of the correct ethnic background, of course). Wealth, status, and power are possible in America for everyone (Anglo, that is), the land of opportunity where the individual (Anglo) is rewarded for virtue. Americana such as home, motherhood, community, puritanical love, and the work ethic are all celebrated. Issues are reduced to a good and evil, simple and clear-cut conflict, a them-and-us identification process where good equals us, the American (Anglo) values and social system. Them, the villains, are defined as those who reject and seek to destroy the proper set of American (Anglo) values. Conflict is typically resolved through the use of righteous force, with Anglo values winning out. "Them" not only includes blacks, Hispanics, and Indians, that is, those ethnics whose color and racial features overtly identify them as "others," but usually any ethnic group when it is depicted ethnically, with Italians being particularly harshly represented among whites. "Them" includes not only many foreigners, aliens by definition but subversive, resisting, or duped ethnic Americans.

The Impact of Protests in the Spanish-Speaking World and the Effect of the Good Neighbor Policy

The tendency, particularly with American social problem films (as reviewed later in this chapter) to depict ethnics who were either bad or naive Americans paradoxically was further reinforced by international protests against U.S. films. These protests helped cause the industry to either go inward, finding ethnic evil in the United States itself rather than in, say the Philippines or in revolutionary Mexico, or to go nominally fantastical, creating nonexistent foreign settings that usually were transparently identifiable but which also provided a fig leaf for both the industry and censors in Mexico and many other countries, where the demand by local exhibitors (often controlled by the United States in any event) for U.S. film conflicted with the sense of outrage or humiliation that those films caused in certain sectors, particularly the Hispanic intelligentsia.

Protests against U.S. films have a history that predates the 1930s by decades. As early as 1913 (see p. 98) Mexico protested a film, *Madero Murdered.* García Riera (1987-88) provides extensive review of the protests of the depiction of Hispanic characters undertaken by Mexico, beginning during the Carranza administration.

Partially founded because of the protests of foreign countries, the activities of the Motion Picture Producers and Distributors of America (MPPDA) also worked toward a more sensitive portrayal of Spanish-speaking peoples, particularly during the pre-war and World War II period. Before the tense international period of the 1930s, however, the effectiveness of the MPPDA was at best nominal, and the methods used by the film industry to depict the Spanish-speaking and other foreign nationals more sensitively were as shallow and as cosmetic as possible, and even then, involved primarily snipping segments from films for the foreign market.

The major Hollywood studios formed the MPPDA in 1922 to coordinate industry policies and practices and to represent the industry in its dealings with public, official, and private organizations. The MPPDA was originally created in the wake of widely publicized scandals involving the private lives of film personalities (e.g., Roscoe "Fatty" Arbuckle), because of growing demands by various groups to institute some sort of censorship on films, and because of complaints by countries such as Mexico, which was particularly active in 1922, concerning the characterization of peoples and cultures outside of the United States. Under the leadership of Will H. Hays, a former United States Postmaster General, the MPPDA created the Motion Picture Production Code, a strict self-regulatory censorship charter, popularly known as "The Hays Code," which for years to come governed the shape and content of Hollywood films. In the mid-1940s, the organization changed its name to the present Motion Picture Association of America, but the production code remained unchanged until 1966 when it was replaced by a much mitigated self-censorship system involving ratings.

We have made some observations about how the code tended to hurt U.S. citizens or residents who were not white (see section above, *Conglomeration of the Film Industry and the Production Code*). The code of ethics that was developed did have a section related to the nondefaming of foreign nationals and the nondistorting of any nation's history. A similar code had recently been adopted by the International Committee of the League of Nations. However, in practical terms, little attenuation of the image of Hispanics resulted from the code until the establishment of the Good Neighbor policy of the Franklin Delano Roosevelt administration, and subsequently, the wartime creation of the Office for Coordination of Inter-American Affairs. Rather, in the early decades, at least prior to the 1934 inauguration of Roosevelt, it was more common for small portions of a film, particularly with respect to religious scenes, to be removed from the version destined for foreign markets, as deemed relevant or appropriate.

In addition, as a result of foreign protests or other market considerations, from time to time the U.S. film industry would make some minor revision or attempt to preempt controversies by placing the action in an imaginary country. *Captain Alvarez* (1914) takes place in an imaginary country that is clearly Argentina down to the "tyrant" Rosas, and in the Douglas Fairbanks vehicle, *The Americano* (1916), the hero arrives in Paragonia, a place intrinsically similar to revolutionary Mexico. García Riera (1987, vol.1, 84) notes four films placed in an imaginary country in 1915, two in 1916, two in 1917, one in 1918, and three in 1919 and 1920.

In the 1920s, the same technique of using an imaginary setting proliferated: Bargravia, San Mañana, Santa María, Costa Blanca, Costa Casaba, Centralia, and so on were place names used where Hispanic-focused plot action took place. García Riera found over thirty films with imaginary Hispanic place names between 1921 and 1928 (1987, vol. 1, 111). A location like San Mañana would appear to be a perfect place to set a Hispanic-focused film. Surely with a name like that, one surmises, Hollywood would rest assured that there wouldn't be a hint of opprobrium among the Spanish-speaking, even as the film could capitalize on the stereotypes of Hispanic laziness and such! The film in question was the comedy adventure *The Dictator* (1922, Paramount) starring

Wallace Reid as an American son of a millionaire who falls in love with Juanita, daughter of the revolutionary leader.

However, even the facile consignment of Hispanic-focused action to what García Riera has ingeniously described as a "Ruritania of cactus and adobe"[1] was the exception rather than the rule and protests accelerated in the 1920s. In 1922, Mexico announced an official ban on all films produced by two production companies, Famous Players-Lasky and Metro. One of the four films that Mexico specifically criticized was *Bachelor Daddy* (Famous Players, 1922), which featured a wealthy American's trip to Mexico to look into his mines which were in danger of being ruined by a band of guerrillas. The American's partner is killed by bandits who are depicted as able to operate in barbarous Mexico without fear of reprisal. Upon his return "to civilization," the American inherits his partner's children. Another of the films causing indignation and the protest of Alberto J. Pani, Mexican secretary of foreign relations, was *I Can Explain* (1922, Metro), depicting a kidnapping outlaw called El Pavor. *Her Husband's Trademark* (1922, Paramount) featuring Gloria Swanson chased by a lustful general and having to cross the Río Grande and be saved by the U.S. Cavalry was another film that elicited a protest by Mexico, particularly upset because of the violation of international borders.[2] However, prohibiting entry of a specific film here or there was ineffective and the occasional attempts to ban the production of whole companies were not realized. The Hollywood control over not only production but even exhibition in places like Mexico (see Contreras Torres, 1960) militated against major or concerted efforts to address negative stereotypes of Hispanics by Latin America, including Mexico.

However, the level of American sensitivity to the Hispanic nations greatly increased as the world headed toward World War II and the United States began to feel a need to court every possible ally. García Riera (1987, vol. 1, 197-199) notes the great liberalization of attitudes and foreign policy toward Latin America during the Roosevelt administration prior to 1939. In his first inaugural address (March 4, 1933), Roosevelt made a commitment "to the policy of the good neighbor." The Good Neighbor policy became a popular name for the Latin American initiatives pursued by his administration. Concrete results of that policy, which represented a great departure from traditional U.S. interventionism, included the renunciation of the right to intervene in the internal affairs of other nations at the Montevideo Conference (December 1933), the abrogation of the infamous Platt Amendment (in 1934) which had earlier sanctioned U.S. intervention in Cuba, and the withdrawal of the Marines from Haiti (August 1934). The Good Neighbor policy is generally considered by historians to have successfully mediated in part the rapidity with which Latin American states rallied to the Allies during World War II. However, U.S. postwar concerns in Europe and Asia led to renewed distrust of the United States in the Americas. García Riera (1987, vol. 2, 199) goes on to conclude that beginning in 1934, "Hollywood spent millions of dollars in its support— somewhat forced and not exactly heartfelt of the Good Neighbor policy" (translation mine). He primarily relies on the following for this conclusion: *Viva Villa!* (1934), as a "more or less benign" depiction of the Mexican revolutionary; the depiction of Joaquín Murrieta in *Robin Hood of El Dorado* (1935) as an apology of a figure who had been considered a mere bandit; the "edifying," "professional" status of the hero of *Bordertown* (1934); the positive roles of Lupe Vélez as a "ciudadana neoyorquina" even though simultaneously a Mexican Spitfire; and on the newly exemplary and debonair image of the Cisco Kid, which he correctly points out must have caused the reactionary, archracist O. Henry, the authorial father of the Kid, to turn in his grave.

There is some truth in García Riera's assertion and his ingenious collation of films. Something was in the air. On the other hand, he stretches the point. *Bordertown* is a better example of, in this instance the positive power of the censor, eliminating dozens of "greaser" passages from the original Hollywood script (see p. 53), and in any case, the final result was hardly edifying. Lupe Vélez is very hard to justify as representing an advance over previous Hispanic stereotypification, and the examples of Villa, Cisco, and Joaquín Murrieta represent sweet and sour, amour-odious, nominal advances at best. *El Dorado,* starring Warner Baxter and Margo (director William Wellman) was a poor movie and too action-driven to attach much social advancement to it, although García Riera certainly finds material to cite to that effect, both in the 1936 *New York Times* and in Mexican newspapers (1987, vol. 1, 221). The very mixed response to the highly controversial *Viva Villa!* in Mexico itself gives a good indication of how much of an advance that film was (see García Riera's excellent recounting of the Mexican reception, 1987, vol. 1, 212-220). Also, as García Riera himself suggests, "there were hairs in the soup," including "the Alamo films" to which we should add, here focusing exclusively on the films of the mid-1930s, the border and border smuggling films, for example, *Soldiers of the Storm* (1933), *Riding Speed* (1934), *Lawless Frontier* (1935), and *Paradise Canyon* (1935), and the jungle films *Kongo* (1932) and *Fury of the Jungle* (1934) are the most egregiously disparaging of this or any other period. Also, in the early 1930s, Hollywood began to produce a number of gangster films and, as we might have predicted, there quickly appeared a few greaser-gangster forms of this subgenre. Leo Carrillo played the stereotype in *Girl of the Río* (1931, RKO), where he attempted to steal the hand of the glamorous Dolores del Río, a cantina dancer called "The Dove." That particular film earned a formal protest on the part of the Mexican government, especially because it portrayed Mexican "justice" to be a reflection of who could pay the most for the verdict of their liking. Similarly, *In Caliente* (1935, Warner), featuring an avaricious Leo Carrillo was prohibited entry into Mexico.

While García Riera's magnanimous conclusions about Hollywood's more positive Hispanic-focused films of the mid-1930s are not entirely convincing, in 1939 with the film *Juárez* (see below, *Socially Conscious Films*) which made every possible attempt to affiliate the Mexican president with Abraham Lincoln, the pursuit of a more benign depiction of Hispanics who were foreign nationals as well as the cultivation of potential wartime allies among the Spanish-speaking countries went into a higher gear. García Riera points out that Jack L. Warner, head of Warner Brothers which produced *Juárez* and who probably ran the most socially progressive or at least politically sensitive of the studios during the period, managed Roosevelt's California presidential campaign and remained a close friend until Roosevelt's death. The Mexican film critic, without going so far as to allege direct U.S. government involvement in the film, views *Juárez* as emerging from the political crucible just prior to World War II and serving political ends as filmic reparation to Mexico, a political act of goodwill, an initiative consistent with the Good Neighbor policy, and a historical allegory of European despotism that might be seen as antecedent to the Nazi meddling in the affairs of Central European countries (1987, vol. 1, 236). The year 1939 also marked the importation from Brazil of Carmen Miranda, who was billed as an "ambassadress" of goodwill and Pan-Americanism.

During the war itself, Nelson D. Rockefeller's Office for Coordination of Inter-American Affairs asked Walt Disney to make a goodwill tour of Latin America in support of the Good Neighbor policy.[3] This resulted in two films, *Saludos amigos* (1943), oriented toward Brazil and *The Three Caballeros* (1945), set in Mexico. The latter film featured Panchito, a sombrero-wearing, pistol-packing rooster. Some of the stereotype remained in this fowl but he was also a likeable, fun-loving, and highly assertive type who showed *el Pato Pascual* (a Hispanic Donald Duck) and José Carioca (a Brazilian parrot from *Saludos amigos)* the wonders of Mexico, such as piñata parties, Veracruzan *jarochos, posadas,* and other celebrations of Mexican folklore. Mexico had never been given such a benign and positive image by Hollywood. The theme of Pan-Americanism was sounded in the film's title song (set to the music of "¡Ay Jalisco no te rajes!"):

> Oh, we're three caballeros
> Three gay caballeros
> They say we are birds of a feather . . .

Thus in the persons of Donald, José, and Panchito, the United States, Brazil, and Mexico were three pals, none more equal than the others. These films were highly successful both in the United States and in Latin America where they were generally appreciated for both the homage that was given to popular culture, primarily of Mexico and Brazil, the two most important allies, and for their attempt at authenticity. As García Riera describes *The Three Caballeros:* "the visible efforts toward genuine documentation were appreciated and, despite the conventionality of its folklore, the Mexican profiles used the same sorts of commonplaces that Mexico's own complacent nationalism were used to." (García Riera, 1988, vol. 2, 20, translation mine). The two Disney films were part of a spate of Latin musicals that marked the pre-war and World War II period (see the section *Proliferation of Latin Musicals).* Another of these films, *Springtime in the Rockies* (1942, Fox) starring the irrepressible Carmen Miranda with Betty Grable, John Payne, and César Romero was emblematic of the Good Neighbor nudge that was exerted by the film industry. *Time* magazine observed:

> *Springtime in the Rockies* ends with a song called 'Pan-Americana Jubilee' and attempts to be just that by whipping together (1) Latin America (César Romero, Carmen Miranda and her band), (2) the U.S. (Betty Grable, John Payne, Harry James and his band), and (3) Canada (large technicolor hunks of Lake Louise, where the action takes place). The addition of an Eskimo and a penguin would have made the show still more hemispheric in scope. ("Springtime in the Rockies," *Time,* 9 November 1942, 96)

The Initiation and Subsequent Abandonment of Spanish-Language Productions

By the early 1930s, shortly after the advent of the sound era, the Hollywood film companies had gained close to a monopoly not only over U.S. film production and exhibition but in Latin America and other parts of the world as well. However, the silent era presented minimal problems with respect to the export of U.S. films. All that one needed to do was translate the intertitles into other languages.

The United States hegemony over film production was threatened by the advent of the sound era. A limited number of options were available: dubbing, the use of subtitles in the foreign language, or the creation of films in other language versions. The technology of dubbing was not developed sufficiently during the early sound era for it to be the solution, although eventually it predominated and helped cause Hollywood to abandon foreign language versions of film. Subtitles were problematic in several ways. They introduced a new phenomenon that the public was not used to. They required literacy and in many countries many of the filmgoers were not readers. In order to perpetuate its control over the Spanish-speaking and other-language speaking worlds, Hollywood began producing, in the beginning of the sound era, Spanish-language films for distribution in Latin America and Spain. Production continued between 1930 and 1938, and in the first five years 113 such pictures were made; a total of about 150 Spanish-language films were produced in all.

Numerous problems caused the abandonment of Spanish-language films by Hollywood. For one, the star system worked against foreign language films. The public resisted seeing films where lesser-known or unknown actors speaking in Spanish substituted for consecrated, international stars.

Another major factor was the inability to create one Spanish-language film that would please the Hispanic public from Madrid to Mexico City to the River Plate. Certainly Hollywood producers were not even knowledgeable enough to understand the problem and they often compounded it by throwing together actors with a mélange of accents in the same film: Spanish, Cuban, Mexican, Argentine, Chilean, and others.

> . . . the cinema exposed mass audiences to a sort of collective culture shock; they heard their own language emerging from the screen images' lips, but a language that sounded bizarre and alien—even if understandable. Part of the problem was the American producers' assumptions—even if they knew a little Spanish—that so-called Castilian Spanish, the language as spoken in the central plain of Spain, was acceptable everywhere in the Western Hemisphere. The immediate result of this linguistic confusion was that Argentina declared that she would not permit the importation of multiaccented films or those in "Castilian." Spain, for its part, stated that its moviegoers "could not bear to listen to the irritating Latin American accents" and that if the "c" or "z" were not "orthographically pronounced," the American studios "need not bother" sending their films. (Mora, 1982, 32)

The situation was so vexed that even films produced in France featuring the renowned Argentine singer Carlos Gardel were objected to in Argentina because the singer used *tú* instead of the Argentine *vos*.

Spanish-language Hollywood films quickly declined: over thirty were produced in 1930, over forty in 1931, but only about fifteen in 1932, and by the end of the 1930s the production phenomenon had disappeared (García Riera, 1987, vol. 1, 174). Ultimately, the Hollywood initiative for control over Latin American Spanish-language films (English-language Hollywood films have always had their successes in Spanish America) succumbed in the marketplace to the resurgence of Mexican films during the Cárdenas and Avila Camacho administrations and to a lesser degree to Spanish and Argentine productions. Moreover, Hollywood soon realized that the rest of the world would readily accept its product either in the original English, or, as these technologies developed or became more familiar, through dubbing and subtitles in the non-English language. Only a small portion of the market was to be lost to films produced in Spanish, French, Italian, German, Bengali, Japanese, and other languages.

Some important Hispanic stars of English language films did appear in these Spanish-language films including Ramón Novarro, Lupe Vélez, and Gilbert Roland (see Hanson, 1993, García Riera, 1987, vol. 1, and Richard, 1992, for additional information).

Proliferation of Latin Musicals

The production of Hispanic-focused musicals immediately followed the advent of the sound era. In fact, the stereotype of the Latin world as lively and musical, characterized by fiestas (when not siestas) and even music and dancing in the cantinas carried such sway that beginning with sound, it became commonplace for music to enter Hispanic-focused films even if they were not musicals per se. In 1929, a number of sound shorts were produced: Warner's *Lerdo's Mexican Orchestra* and *Mexican Tipica Orchestra,* based on the famous Orquesta Típica founded by Miguel Lerdo de Tejada, MGM's *Mexicana* starring Armida and Columbia's *The Gay Caballero*.

The shorts were quickly followed by a number of feature films. *The Cuban Love Song* (1931, MGM, starring Lupe Vélez) was an undistinguished musical melodrama. *The Kid from Spain* (1932, Goldwyn) about a simpleton mistaken for a celebrated bullfighter, with choreography by Busby Berkeley, was noted for its kaleidoscopic and geometric top shots that took the cinematic musical into a new dimension unapproachable by the theatrical musical. *Flying Down to Río* (1932, RKO) starred Dolores del Río but Fred Astaire and Ginger Rogers, united for the first time in film, stole the show as did the finale, in which girls appeared to dance on the wings of moving airplanes. The film has become a recognized period piece. Even Emilio "El Indio" Fernández appeared in the film, indistinguishable from other mustachioed dancing Latins.

Fernández was not the only one who profited from the Latin musical. Tito Guízar, the famous Mexican ranchera singer and star of the Mexican film, *Allá en el rancho grande* (1936) also had some play in Hollywood, appearing in *Under the Pampas Moon* (1935, Fox), *The Big Broadcast of 1938* (1937, Paramount, starring W. C. Fields, Martha Raye, and Dorothy Lamour), *Tropic Holiday* (1938, Paramount), *St. Louis Blues* (1938, Paramount), and *The Llano Kid* (1939, Paramount). *The Big Broadcast of 1938,* which featured among its songs "Thanks for the Memory," also represented the debut of the indefatigable Bob Hope. (There were four of the loosely annual *Broadcast* series of films between 1932-1937.) *Fiesta* (1941, United Artists) a 45-minute feature was about amorous complications on the rancho and had Jorge Negrete in his only American film role singing (in Spanish and English) and appearing in the credits as "George." Poor guy. The Latin musical also provided opportunities for opera stars. *The Gay Desperado* (1936, Mary Pickford Production, starring Ida Lupino with Leo Carrillo) featured the opera tenor Nino Martini singing "Cielito lindo" and several other Mexican standards. This was also the moment for a new version of *The Girl of the Golden West* (1938, MGM) with Nelson Eddy as Ramírez opposite Jeanette MacDonald.

The most notable of the Latin musicals after *Flying Down to Rio* was *La Cucaracha* (1934, RKO, starring Don Alvarado) which, even though it was only a short, had a significant impact on film history. This film, which won an Oscar for its cinematographic innovations, was produced in a newly developed, high quality, trichromatic version of technicolor. It was a big success in the United States and in Mexico, where its advances in color were appreciated despite the disconcerting effect produced in the Mexican viewing public by the film's anomalous, nonauthentic garb, choreography, and musical numbers. *Dancing Pirate* (1936, RKO, with songs by Richard Rodgers and Lorenz Hart) was a full-length film also produced in the new technicolor. It featured a male dance teacher taken by pirates and deposited in the isthmus of Tehuantepec where he conquests the love of Serafina. It was a box-office failure, however, and as a consequence for several years thereafter the Latin musicals appeared in black and white.

What did impose itself in Hollywood was the song, "La cucaracha," popularized by the film with the same title. The song was overused and often used incongruously. Even as this song of the Mexican Revolution did in fact emerge from the Villista camp, it was played, anomalously, almost as if it were the national anthem or funeral requiem of the Villistas at the end of the film (and simultaneously demise of the revolutionary) in *Viva Villa!* A young Judy Garland sang it in the short, *La Fiesta de Santa Barbara* (1935, MGM); it was the background for the cartoon *Picador Porky* (1937, Warner Brothers); Armida sang it and danced to it in *La Conga Nights* (1940, Universal); and in *Six Lessons From Madame La Zonga* (1940, Universal, starring Lupe Vélez), an Anglo mailman did a rumba to it (see García Riera, 1988, vol. 2, 202).

While Dolores del Río was not known for singing, she made her entry into the Latin musical as well, playing Inez, a Latina without specific nationality, in *Wonder Bar* (1934,Warner Brothers), opposite Al Jolson and Ricardo Cortez, with choreography by Busby Berkeley. In the film, *In Caliente* (1935, Warner Brothers), she was a Mexican although her film name was La Españita prompting García Riera (1988, vol. 2, 204) to observe that her nationality and name combined "like a baseball team called the British of Brooklyn." In both films she danced the tango in musical numbers. Despite whatever progress, or nominal, pseudoversion of it Hollywood might have made generally with the receptions its films received in Latin America, *In Caliente* was prohibited entry into Mexico because of its negative view of the Mexican border, featuring an avaricious Leo Carrillo, people with their hands out constantly for "mordidas" and other such non-endearing elements. The Busby Berkeley numbers were a great hit as were songs like "Muchacha" with lyrics the likes of:

> Muchacha, at last I've gotcha
> where I wantcha, muchacha
> I've watched ya
> like a cat watches a little cucaracha
> in the lingo of the gringo
> I'm so hotcha.

By the middle and late 1930s, ersatz Latin music, inauthentically combining rumbas, tangos, mambos, and so on with each other, or with American fare such as country music or even Hawaiian music, had become the order of the day for the Latin musical. Musical Westerns, either featuring or significantly including ersatz Hispanic music began to predominate, particularly facilitating the careers of Gene Autry, Tex Ritter, and Roy Rogers. Among the Gene Autry films were *Gaucho Serenade* (1940, Republic, with Duncan Renaldo), *South of the Border* (1939, Republic, with Lupita Tovar), *Mexicali Rose* (1939, Republic), and *Down Mexico Way* (1941, Republic). Roy Rogers did *In Old Caliente* (1939, Republic) and Tex Ritter appeared in *Song of the Gringo* (1936, Grand National), *Starlight Over Texas* (1938, Monogram), and *Headin' for the Río Grande* (1936, Grand National). Hopalong Cassidy didn't sing, but the natives did in *In Old Mexico* (1938, Paramount).

Down Mexico Way was the most popular of this type of film, which intermingled action, romance, comedy, and musical numbers. Also, the Autry song, with its bilingual features (code-switching) became very popular. The first line went: "En la frontera de México fue" and then went into English. The plot had Gene Autry and his sidekick, a reformed Mexican badman played by Harold Huber trail crooks into Mexico where they were victimizing a Mexican a rancher. Autry figures out the crooks' scam and chases them down in a cinematic finale featuring automobiles, horses, and wildly careening motorcycles, but not before romancing, engaging in humorous repartee, and singing several songs.

Many of the "B Westerns" also took in Latin music. Often these films revised for sound the Mexican cantina, dance hall, or cabaret of the silent period. Among the B Westerns with Latin music were *Sing Dance, Plenty Hot* (1940, Republic) and *Mad Youth* (1940, Atlas).

In addition to the Latin musicals or musical Westerns that fundamentally focused on Hispanic elements, the 1930s was marked by the introduction of Latin local color with singing or dancing into a number of films under almost any pretense. A young Katharine Hepburn went Latin in a sequence of *Morning Glory* (1933, RKO; Don Alvarado had a secondary role), a film about an innocent country girl wanting to make it big in the theater; the film was later made in a new version, *Stage Struck* (1957, RKO, starring Susan Strasberg and Henry Fonda). Frances Drake played Chulita as a Mexican dancer and bullfighter's girlfriend in *The Trumpet Blows* (1934, Paramount); a declining Bebe Daniels appeared in *Music Is Magic* (1935, Twentieth-Century Fox) where one of the numbers had a Mexican restaurant featuring the less-than-memorable song "Honey Chile"; Jean Harlow did a cantina dance number in *Reckless* (1935, MGM); Al Jolson put on a serape and a broad-brimmed hat for a number in *Go Into Your Dance* (1935, Warner Brothers), and on and on (see García Riera, 1988, vol. 2, 203).

The number of Latin musical productions accelerated in the 1940s, spurred on both by government encouragement and the need for escape during the war years and their immediate aftermath. The dream factory began to work double time to produce a filmic Latin American theme park for Anglos, exotic enough for them to be romanced and visually seduced, but totally impregnable to the peril of Montezuma's revenge.

Encouraged by government wartime policy, Darryl F. Zanuck produced a number of escapist vehicles for Fox. These included *Down Argentine Way* (1940) starring Betty Grable, Carmen Miranda, and Don Ameche), the film which brought both Grable and Miranda to star stature and set Fox off on its successful run of Latin-focused and other extravaganzas. *That Night in Rio* (1941, starring Don Ameche, Alice Faye, Carmen Miranda, with María Montez) and *Weekend in Havana* (1941, starring Alice Faye, John Payne, Carmen Miranda, and César Romero) were part of the same group. Actresses like Betty Grable or Alice Faye resonated to gorgeous settings and striking Latin Lovers (John Payne, Don Ameche) sometimes even played by Latins (César Romero), but always dressed, as García Riera puts it, "in white smoking" (1988, vol. 2, 18). The Office of the Coordinator of Inter-American Affairs (directed by Nelson Rockefeller) paid close attention to these films. Reportedly, Zanuck was paid $40,000 to refilm some scenes of *Down Argentina Way* that might have been offensive.

Republic, a poorer studio than Fox weighed in with lesser extravaganzas: *Brazil* (1944, with Tito Guízar in a principal role, also featuring Roy Rogers), *Song of Mexico*, also released in Spanish-language version, *La canción de México* (1944, starring Adele Mara with Tin Tan), and *Mexicana* (1945, starring Tito Guízar, Constance Moore, and Leo Carrillo). Paramount did *Masquerade in Mexico* (1945) starring Arturo de Córdova as a Latin Lover opposite Dorothy Lamour as the Gringa he woos.

One of these films and also one of the most extreme was set not abroad but in New Mexico. However, this supposedly Mexican American setting might have been Mars for its recognizability. *Too Many Girls* (1940, RKO, starring Desi Arnaz as an Argentine football player opposite Lucille Ball, and featuring Richard Rodgers and Lorenz Harts songs) took place at a New Mexico college. The film, notable as the set where Ball and Arnaz first met, was a witless mishmash of Latin American elements: one student dresses as a bullfighter, the kids dance the Cuban conga, and one of the professors looks into his microscope and sees the microbes doing the same. In this "Mexican American" setting were the Mexican Americans inside out, or outside in, along with the Cuban microbes dancing under the microscope?

In the early 1940s, the chief stars of the Latin musicals were Carmen Miranda and Xavier Cugat. Other figures included Andy Russell (né Andy Rabajos) who sang solos and duets in various 1940s musicals but ended his career in the 1947 production, *Copacabana*, moving to Argentina where his singing career thrived. In 1942, two Latinas debuted through the Latin musical. Acquanetta (Burnu Acquanetta), the "Venezuelan Volcano," first appeared in *Arabian Nights* (1942, starring María Montez) but subsequently appeared in jungle and exotic films. Lina Romay (Elena Romay, born 1922), the Brooklyn-born daughter of a Mexican diplomat was billed as "Cugie's Latin Doll" and sang with the bandleader for a few years, making a screen debut as part of Cugat's act in *You Were Never Lovelier* (1942, Columbia, starring Rita Hayworth). She emerged as a singing star in *Weekend at the Waldorf* (1945, MGM) and *Love Laughs at Andy Hardy* (1946, MGM, starring Mickey Rooney) and did a straight role in *Adventure* (1945, MGM, starring Clark Gable). Olga San Juan (born in 1927) was billed as "The Puerto Rican Pepperpot," a "triple threat" singer-dancer-actress who debuted in *Rainbow Island* (1944, Paramount), followed by *Duffy's Tavern* (1945, Paramount), *Blue Skies* (1946, Paramount), *Variety Girl* (1947, Paramount), and *One Touch of Venus* (1948, Universal).

Carmen Miranda was the acknowledged Latina star of the Latina musical, and many of the other Latinas got their opportunities because of the mad rush by the other studios to copy Miranda's success. The other studios quickly put up their own Latina stars against Fox and Miranda. Lina Romay worked for MGM; Margo for RKO, Olga San Juan for Paramount, and the two stars who were featured mostly in jungle and exotic films rather than Latina musicals, María Montez and Acquanetta worked for Universal.

In the years from 1939 to 1944, just prior to and during U.S. involvement in World War II, Miranda, known as the "Brazilian Bombshell," appeared in eight Hollywood musicals as well as two Broadway musical reviews. She became an extraordinary wartime phenomenon. According to Roberts (1993), when Miranda's *Weekend in Havana* (1941) opened it received top box office receipts that week ($25,000), over twice the amount realized by *Citizen Kane* ($9,000) which was in its second week. Standard practice for Fox was to pair her against blondes, who during the war had become to be perceived as incarnating Americanness. Miranda's studio, Fox, featured Betty Grable, Alice Faye, and Vivian Blaine, all blondes. Miranda was paired against Grable. Although her screen persona increasingly parodied itself, minus the erotic element, over the years, the initial impression that audiences had of her involved the exotic, sensual, primitive, and wild. *Time* described her in 1939 as an exotic and somewhat wild animal, "enveloped in beads, swaying and wriggling, chattering macaw-like, skewering the audience with a merry, mischievous eye" ("New Shows in Manhattan," *Time*, 3 July 1939, 42). According to a fan magazine, she was "a princess out of an Aztec frieze with a panther's grace, the plumage of a bird of paradise and the wiles of Eve and Lileth combined" (Ida Zeitlin, "Sous American Sizzler," *Motion Picture,* September 1941).

She was also a cross-cultural Good Neighbor phenomenon, both Brazilian (latter Pan-American) and a Hollywood artifact.

> If Grable was the norm, Miranda was the allowable cultural Other for wartime Hollywood, playing the dark but comic and, therefore unthreatening foil to all the gilded wartime female musical stars. The press and her North American fans saw Miranda as the "Ambassadress of goodwill from Latin America," "an unofficial envoy from a carefree country. . . ." Through an exchange of good will orchestrated by Gable and Miranda, Fox films achieved the illusion of international, economic, and personal harmony. . . . In the opening shots of *The Gang's All Here* (1943, Fox), the *SS Brazil* unloads the major exports of Latin America including sugar, coffee, fruit, and finally Carmen Miranda, Brazil's most significant export. At this point the nightclub host [in the film] comments, "Well, there's your Good Neighbor policy!" and Miranda goes on to teach the audience the "Uncle Sam-ba." (Roberts, 1993, 4-5).

The lyrics of the Latin musical were notable for their code-switching, but here the alternation between English and Spanish that operated according to an extraordinarily different ideology than subsequent Chicano film or literature, or even from contemporaneous work such as Hemingway's fiction (e.g., *For Whom the Bell Tolls, The Old Man and the Sea).* The Latin musicals promoted the concept of alliance between the United States and Latin America in part through an exchange of culture communicated by the universal language of music and dance. As Roberts points out, many of the songs in the Latin musicals involved a "getting to know you" theme in which the main characters who are representatives of either Latin America or the United States "demonstrate the ease with which one can *learn* another country's songs, dances, and language—can *acquire* another country's culture" (1993, 6). In *Down Argentine Way* (1940), Don Ameche first sings the title song in Spanish, then Betty Grable provides an English rendition, and the performance ends with the couple's bilingual duet:

> You'll be as gay as can be
> If you can learn to "sí, sí" like Aladdin
> For just as soon as you learn then you'll never return to Manhattan
> When you hear, "Yo te amo," you'll steal a kiss and then,
> If she should say, "Mañana," it's just to let you know that you're gonna meet again.

With saccharine songs like the above, a mélange of dancing styles and tempos, and a skin-deep promise of Pan-American romance or harmony, it is no wonder Carmen Miranda had her star status in Brazil undercut by Hollywood. She had made at least 136 records and appeared in five full-length Brazilian films before arriving in the United States in 1939. However, she was typecast as a Latina ingenue, awed by North American culture, who mangled the English language and who would say things like, "Best I know ten English werds. Men, Men, Men, Men, Men and Monnee, Monnee, Monnee, Monnee, Monnee." In the same homogenizing spirit, Fox cast Miranda in any number of Latin American nationalities. She traveled Argentine way, spent a night in Rio, a weekend in Havana and appeared either as herself or as an equally stereotypical Latina: Querida, Chiquita, Chita, Marina, Carmelita, and, in four films, Rosita. In later years, she was even further distanced from her extravagant but sensual Brazilian origin and she was increasingly depicted in a grotesquely comic rather than erotically comic fashion. In *Greenwich Village* (1944, Fox, also starring Don Ameche and William Bendix), she was removed from her Latin setting and appeared in a candy-cane costume. Similarly, in *Doll Face* (1945, Fox, also starring Vivian Blaine and Perry Como), she appeared in a battery-operated lighthouse costume.

The homogenization of Miranda's ethnicity and the "improvisation of cultural details for whatever Latin American country was highlighted in each film" (Roberts, 1993, 8) failed to impress audiences or reviewers in Latin America who were often offended by the Tin Pan Alley rumbas and other dances that seemed neither Latin nor Hawaiian but something of both. Contemporary accounts of Miranda's return to Brazil in 1940 reveal the split between Brazilian and U.S. perceptions of the star. Brazilian news reports described her reception as quite hostile with the crowd booing and whistling. It was claimed that Miranda had lost her voice and had changed her style and her soul. Miranda had become Americanized. Miranda cleverly incorporated this negative reaction into subsequent Rio performances by adding new songs such as "Disseram Que Voltei Americanisada" ("They Say I Came Back Americanized") and "Voltei P'ro Morro" ("I'm Back in the Morro"). On the other hand, in the United States, most articles reported that the "South American Bombshell" returned to loving crowds, "making Brazil and Brazilian people complicit with how North American imagined and distorted South America" (Roberts, 1993, 13).

Carmen Miranda, for better or for worse, continues to have an impact not only on the United States but Brazil. In Brazil, she became the symbol of tropicalism, one of the developments of Cinema Novo, which parodied myths that represented Brazil as a tropical paradise.[4] In the United States, as Roberts (1993, 16) observes, she "was and continues to be imitated by both women and men in drag, from Mickey Rooney in *Babes on Broadway* (1941, MGM), to Bugs Bunny in *What's Cookin', Doc* (1944, Warner) to Ted Danson in *Three Men and a Little Lady*" (1990, Touchstone)."

Utilizing the work of feminist scholars (see V. Burgin, J. Donald, and C. Kaplan, 1988; M.A. Doane, 1982, 1988-89; and C. Johnston, 1990), Roberts has theorized that Carmen Miranda's continued influence is in part explicable because in contrast to many other entertainers who simply became the unsupervised objects of parody, she consciously conjured a screen persona that was self-parodic and simultaneously she spoofed through extreme exaggeration the stereotypes of ethnicity and femininity. Miranda became "famous *as* spectacle, as excess, as parody or masquerade" (Roberts, 1993, 15) and this masquerade had an element that not only supported racist and sexist conceptions of the dominant ideology during the period, but also allowed "for negotiated or subversive readings. . . . Miranda's text could, in this way, be used to speak for particular marginalized minority audiences, including ethnic and female viewers" (Roberts, 1993, 19).

Postwar continuation of the Latin musical along the usual lines was provided by *Cuban Pete* (1946, Universal) starring Desi Arnaz as a Cuban orchestra leader who comes to New York, *Carnival in Costa Rica* (1947, Twentieth-Century Fox, starring César Romero), and another film with the title *Fiesta* (1947, MGM) featuring Ricardo Montalbán, Esther Williams, and Cyd Charisse and incorporating into the production, the "Salón México" suite of Aaron Copeland. *Road to Rio* (1947, Paramount, featuring Bing Crosby, Bob Hope, and Dorothy Lamour) was part of the well-known "Road" series. *The Kissing Bandit* (1948, MGM) starred Frank Sinatra as a young businessman in Old California who finds that he is expected to keep up his bandit father's criminal and romantic reputation; thus he becomes a singing type of gay caballero.

García Riera (1988, vol. 2, 24) has found over twenty B Westerns made in the 1940s that attempted to capitalize on the success of *Down Mexico Way* with the inclusion of typically ersatz Mexican music and usually mention of "border" or "Río Grande" in their titles. Among them: *Down Rio Grande Way* (1942, Columbia), *Below the Border* (1942, Monogram), *Hands Across the Border* (1943, Republic, starring Gene Autry), *Border Buckaroos* (1943, Producers Releasing Co., starring Roy Rogers), *The Man From Rio Grande* (1943, Republic), *Renegades of the Rio Grande* (1943, Universal), *West of the Rio Grande* (1944, Monogram), *South of the Rio Grande* (1945, Monogram), *Twilight of the Rio Grande* (1947, Republic), and many others.

The Latin musical genre quickly died out in the 1950s, probably because of its own excesses, the lack of any Pan-American or Good Neighbor support in an America concerned about the Cold War and other postwar circumstances, and because of the onset of television which offered, albeit in black and white, the same sort of musical and sometimes comical reviews that characterized the Latin musicals. Carmen Miranda, who did her last film, *Scared Stiff* in 1953 (Paramount, starring Dean Martin and Jerry Lewis), died of a sudden heart attack in 1955. She had already moved from film to television. Among the last of the Latin musicals until much later films like *Salsa* (1988) and even *The Mambo Kings* (1992) were *Sombrero* (1952, MGM, starring Ricardo Montalbán, Yvonne de Carlo, and Cyd Charisse, with José Greco), based on Josefina Niggli's novel, *A Mexican Village* and *Cha Cha Cha Boom!* (1956, Columbia). However, Latin songs continued to appear often in films as various as *Because Your Mine* (1952, MGM), *Havana Rose* (1951, Republic), *My Man and I* (1952, MGM), *Ride Clear of Diablo* (1954, Universal), *Federal Agent at Large* (1950, Republic), *Garden of Evil* (1953, Fox), *Around the World in 80 Days* (1956, United Artists), *Bandido!* (1956, United Artists), *Wetbacks* (1956, Realart), *The Left-Handed Gun* (1957, Warner Brothers), and many others.

Socially Conscious Films

The Great Depression brought with it a new genre, the "Hollywood social problem film." For the first time, U.S. Hispanics were portrayed in a somewhat different, and occasionally a radically different light in these Hollywood movies.

The economic breakdown represented by the depression, the rise of fascism and other totalitarianisms world wide, the war against these political forms of oppression, and the idealistic vigor of the post-World War II years (up to the advent of McCarthyism) all fostered a concern with social conditions, and an impulse toward political change. The theater of Clifford Odets, the novels and screenplays of John Steinbeck, and the songs of Woody Guthrie all found a large public response to their criticism of American society, government, and business during the period.

This era of social consciousness also found reflection in Hollywood social problem films, which usually were produced in accordance with the conventions of the Hollywood formula. The Hollywood conventions were that America is a series of social institutions that from time to time experience problems that, like those of an automobile, need to be tinkered with and corrected. For the most part, the films attacked such problems in order to inspire limited social change or restore the status quo to an ideal level of efficiency. While the Hollywood social problem genre places great importance on the surface mechanisms of society, there is only an indirect or covert treatment of broader social values (those of the family, sexuality, religion, etc.) that function behind and govern the mechanisms.

Certainly the depiction of minority and out-groups improved markedly in films formulated according to the conventions of the social problem film. For example, anti-Semitism was grappled with, and in 1947 in such films as *Crossfire* (RKO) and *Gentleman's Agreement* (Fox) the issue generated large box-office returns. Just as anti-Semitism was the theme of 1947, the Negro became the problem of 1949 in films such as the Stanley Kramer production *Home of the Brave* (the central character in the Arthur Laurents book was a Jew, Kramer changed the character to a black), *Lost Boundaries* (Film Classics/Louis de Rochemont), and *Pinky* (Fox, directed by Elia Kazan), where the problem centered around mulattoes who can pass for white. The most unaffected and best realized of the cycle was *Intruder in the Dust,* adapted from the William Faulkner novel (MGM). In 1950, *No Way Out* (Fox) introduced Sidney Poitier in what was to become his standard role as a noble and loyal black who endures and patiently waits for white society to recognize his rights rather than go out and demand them. To be too insistent would only threaten white society and thereby prolong racial inequality, or so the Hollywood convention went. Even so, this Cold War and McCarthy-era film raised hackles and fear. *Films in Review* said it was "A production designed solely for purposes of agitation and propaganda, unworthy of literary or cinematic consideration" (see Roffman and Purdy, 1981).

Subsequent films followed the integrationist solution to the social problem, both reflecting growing integration in some American institutions, such as sports, and emphasizing the need for blacks, with infinite tolerance and patience, to prove themselves worthy: *The Jackie Robinson Story* (1950, Eagle-Lion, director Alfred E. Green, starring Jackie Robinson as himself, and Ruby Dee), *The Joe Louis Story* (1953, United Artists), *Bright Victory* (1951, Universal), *The Well* (1951, Cardinal/Harry M. Popkin), and numerous others.

The social problem film genre was the occasion for some atonement for the earlier, mostly deplorable treatment of the American Indian by the studios. *Massacre* (1931, First National), *Broken Arrow* (1950, Fox, starring Jeff Chandler), *Jim Thorpe–All American* (1951, released in Great Britain as *Man of Bronze,* Warner Brothers, director Michael Curtiz, starring Burt Lancaster and Charles Bickford), and many others presented a more positive depiction of the American Indian. *Broken Arrow* was acclaimed at the time for presenting the American Indian's point of view, something that had scarcely happened since early silent films, and the film launched Jeff Chandler on a career playing Cochise with numerous variations; the film also spun off a Cochise TV series.

The Japanese, who during the war had been demonized, were permitted back into the human race and depicted sympathetically by means of social problem films: King Vidor's *Japanese War Bride* (1952, Fox), *Go for Broke* (1951, MGM), most importantly *Bad Day at Black Rock* (1954, MGM, director John Sturges, starring Spencer Tracy, Robert Ryan, Ernest Borgnine, Lee Marvin, and Anne Francis), which has survived as a canonical example of a suspense thriller, and *Three Stripes in the Sun* (1955, Columbia) all dramatized the Japanese as victims of American bigotry.

On behalf of the depiction of Chicanos, Mexicans, and other Hispanics, the social problem vehicle produced some noteworthy if flawed films, but the positive depiction of Hispanics was still the exception rather than the rule. Noriega (1991) has undertaken a search and analysis of social problem films that address the "place" of Mexican

Americans and between 1935 and 1962 he uncovered ten such films: *Bordertown* (1935, Warner), *A Medal for Benny* (1945, Paramount), *The Lawless* (1950, Paramount), *Right Cross* (1950, MGM), *My Man and I* (1952, MGM), *The Ring* (1952, United Artists), *Salt of the Earth* (1954, independently produced), *Trial* (1955, MGM), *Giant* (1956, Warner Brothers), and *Requiem for a Heavyweight* (1962, Columbia). There are probably a few more still fugitive films that would fall within the social problem category, including at first blush, *Daughters Courageous* (1939, Warner Brothers, director Michael Curtiz, starring John Garfield and Claude Rains) about a vagabond, prodigal father who returns to his family after twenty years to sort out their problems. Gabriel López, played by John Garfield, is the Mexican American youngster in love with one of the daughters, a typical American girl but López resonates to the Anglo father's wanderlust. Some of the smuggling films might well qualify within the social problem matrix as well. *Border Incident* (1949, MGM, director Anthony Mann, starring Ricardo Montalbán, George Murphy, and Alfonso Bedoya) took on a semidocumentary tone typical of the social problem film. The plot of this production, which has one of the nastiest murder scenes in U.S. film (of migrant workers tied up and crushed by a tractor), has the character Pablo Rodríguez and his partner overcome an ethnically mixed gang of Anglos and Hispanics (headed by an Anglo). In *Knock on Any Door* (1948, Columbia, starring Humphrey Bogart and John Derek), a Mexican confesses on the witness stand that he was forced to lie about a murder by authorities in order not to be deported. (See also García Riera, 1987-1988 for a good filmography of the period).

Noriega, actually accessing and analyzing Hollywood studio production files, has reviewed the ten target films that he identified in various important ways. From the point of view of their plots, he discerns three: romantic melodramas like *A Medal for Benny*, courtroom drama/juvenile delinquent such as *The Lawless*, and boxing films, such as *Right Cross*. In addition he analyzes the way that these films engaged relevant social-problem issues such as the citizenship status of the Mexican American figures and the quality and level of their acceptance/marginalization within American society.

Bordertown (1935, Warner Brothers, director Archie Mayo, starring Paul Muni in brownface and Bette Davis in her standard performance as a lunatic) is the first Hispanic social problem film. (*Blowing Wild* [1953, Warner Brothers, starring Gary Cooper, Barbara Stanwyck, and Anthony Quinn] was a partial, uncredited remake of *Bordertown*. The latter film involves a Mexican oil driller who becomes involved with the psychotic wife of an old friend; the triangle leads to murder and retribution.)

The central concern of *Bordertown* is not the oppression of Chicanos but rather who committed a murder. What social comment there is exists as a sedative against militancy by Hispanics. The filmic creation of Johnny Ramírez was certainly a more complex one than the standard Hollywood border type. Relative psychological complexity aside, the soothing conventions of the formula determined the finale. The film ends with Johnny, disillusioned over the corruption and meanness of success, returning to his barrio home. He says his confession to the priest, prays with his mother, and all three walk down the church aisle. The padre asks, "Well, Johnny, what are you going to do now?" and Johnny gives the expected reply, "Come back and live among my own people where I belong." *Bordertown* hypothesizes that for a Chicano, success is fruitless and undesirable, that true virtue lies in accepting life as it is. Johnny has learned the padre's lesson of patience and no longer holds impractical ambitions. *Bordertown* celebrates stoic acquiescence to the status quo and denigrates the aspiration for social change.

Ramírez Berg, in his valuable analysis of *Bordertown* has judged it to be "the first Hollywood sound film to deal with a Mexican American's attempt to enter the mainstream and participate in the American Dream," and consequently "the prototypical Chicano social problem film" (1992, 35). Ramírez Berg analyzes the film from two separate but related points of view. One concept is the normality-monster conflict generally developed by Robin Wood (1986). The formula for the basic horror film is "normality threatened by the monster." The minority social melodrama has as its analog: the mainstream threatened by the margin. The problem for society presented by monsters and by marginalized individuals are analogous:

> . . . the "problem" of the ethnic/racial problem films is the perceived threat the margin's very existence poses to the dominant. The dilemma ethnic/racial Others raise for the American mainstream is how to combine two essentially incompatible ideas: the dominant's desire to preserve and protect its identity as a superior, racially pure in-group by exclusionary practices, and the imple- mentation of the democratic ideal that guarantees freedom, equality and op- portunity for all American citizens. (199, 39)

Analyzing *Bordertown* and other analogous films as "assimilation narratives," Ramírez Berg concludes that in these films what the marginal subjects "are supposed to learn is not how to assimilate, but rather, how to become the 'right' kind of marginalized subjects" (1992, 39). *Bordertown* and others depict the compromise between success and loss of ethnic and cultural identity. "Trying to have it both ways exacts a high price, resulting in a tragedy of some kind." The conclusion for *Bordertown* and others of its ilk is "to go home to their old ethnic neighborhood, the locus of all that is good and true. Abandoning their aspirations of mainstream integration and success, these characters can remain content in the knowledge that they have gained morality, a prize far greater than fame or fortune" (1992, 36-37). Ramírez Berg uses examples from many other social problem films that depict Chicanos to develop his analysis including *Trial, Giant, The Lawless, My Man and I, A Medal for Benny, Right Cross, Salt of the Earth,* and *The Ring.*

Despite the limitations of the social problem film, it is true that psychologically complex and, occasionally, resolute and strong characters emerged from this genre. Among them were several Chicano protagonists in *Giant* (1956, Warner Brothers, starring Rock Hudson, Elizabeth Taylor, and James Dean, and featuring various Hispanic characters played by Sal Mineo and other non-Hispanic actors), including the proud and dedicated nurse María Ramírez who experiences the racism of Texans. This epic struggle between cattle men and oil men and between Hispanics and Anglos depicts ethnic intermarriage implying that the future of Texas will have to be shared by both Anglos and Hispanics alike.[5]

Other powerful, resolute, or dignified Hispanics included the family of Leo Mimosa, who is buried alive in a New Mexico cave in Billy Wilder's notable *The Big Carnival* (1951, Paramount, starring Kirk Douglas; later this film was distributed as *Ace in the Hole*), which depicts a tragic act of God turned into a public relations event; and the women Katy Jurado and Pina Pellicer in *One-Eyed Jacks* (1961, Paramount, starring Marlon Brando).

From time to time a Hispanic shows up in a boxing film. In *The Ring* (1952, United Artists), a sequel to *The Lawless,* the main protagonist, Lalo Ríos, under the guidance of an Anglo manager is renamed "Tommy Kansas." As a denatured Hispanic, things go pretty well at first. The manager eventually realizes that Ríos is not champion material, however, and ultimately that judgment is borne out. Ríos is defeated and resolves to leave the ring forever. *Right Cross* (1950, MGM, starring Ricardo Montalbán and June Allyson, with Marilyn Monroe in a bit part) is excellent material for Ramírez Berg's analysis (1992) since it evokes a Mexican who is not "really" treated as inferior, he only thinks so. This Mexican with an inferiority complex learns to control his anger and accept American life and love, although at the cost of his punching hand. *Requiem for a Heavyweight* takes the Mexican fighter into the early 1960s (1962, Columbia, starring Anthony Quinn, Jackie Gleason, Mickey Rooney, and Julie Harris, with Jack Dempsey and Cassius Clay in secondary parts). Adapted from a Rod Sterling television play to which footage was added, the film is a potboiler about Mountain Rivera, a declining New Mexican prizefighter who doesn't realize that his time in the ring is up. Mountain (Anthony Quinn) is forced into corruption and degradation as a result.

The courtroom trial genre can boast of the 1955 anti-communist potboiler, *Trial* (1955, MGM) starring Glenn Ford as a law professor who successfully defends an innocent teenage Chicano accused of killing a white girl at a beach party. The absurd and highly insulting point of this film is to show how the communists can score points with gullible people (in this case, the Chicano community) in order to spread their nefarious designs. It takes an Anglo hero to see that the ingenuous Chicanos are being misused and to set things straight. Another communist potboiler is *I Married a Communist* (1949, RKO), where Thomas Gómez plays a communist chieftain almost indistinguishable from a mobster who blackmails shipping executive Robert Ryan into doing his bidding.

The socially conscious era of the Great Depression and its aftermath brought in a new wave of Westerns and border films featuring Anglo Good Samaritans who acted on behalf of innocent and defenseless Mexicans. To a certain extent this represented a continuation of character and plot types of the silent era: *A Mexican's Gratitude* (1909, Essanay), *The American Insurrecto* (1911, Kalem), *The Americano* (1915, Komic), and *The Gringo* (1916, Overland Feature Film Corp.) In films such as *Border G-Man* (1938, RKO), *Durango Valley Raiders* (1938, Republic), *Rose of the Rancho* (1935, Paramount), or for that matter in the pertinent films of Hopalong Cassidy, Gene Autry, The Lone Ranger, Roy Rogers, and Tex Ritter (*In Old Mexico,* 1938, Paramount, *Song of Gringo,* 1936, Grand National, *South of the Border,* 1939, Republic and numerous others), the emphasis changes during this period from the hero as implacable and brutal conqueror of greasers. Now he is the hero, often a singing one, who is an implacable and devoted defender of Mexican rights, typically as he tramps tourist-like through the exotic local Hispanic community, whether it be north or south of the border. Often the Anglo is fighting bad Mexicans on behalf of good, defenseless, passive Mexicans. The depictions of these Good Samaritans strongly reinforced the stereotype of Mexicans as people who were incapable of helping themselves.

A number of more complex productions featuring the Good Samaritan have been identified by García Riera (1988, vol. 2, 74) including: *The Mysterious Desperado* (1949, RKO) where an Anglo Good Samaritan and his half-breed partner Chito protect some Hispanics from crime; *Apache War Smoke* (1952, MGM, starring Gilbert Roland) where a generous, Cisco Kid type bandit is falsely accused of killing Indians; *San Antone* (1953, Republic) where a Juarista is falsely accused of rape but saved; *Make Haste to Live* (1953, Republic) where the same plot of false accusation is played out; *Headline Hunters* (1955, Republic) with the same plot line except that the falsely accused Mexican is a "wetback";

Strange Lady in Town (1955, Warner Brothers) where Greer Garson plays a doctor who confronts anti-Mexican prejudice in the 1880s; and *Man in the Shadow* (1957, Universal) where Jeff Chandler, an Anglo sheriff investigates the death of a young Mexican ranch hand killed because he had allegedly courted the daughter of the Anglo owner (Orson Welles).

A variation of the white Good Samaritan acting on behalf of the Hispanic is developed in *Right Cross* (1950, MGM), a Ricardo Montalbán B-picture notable in that it depicts a love relationship between a Chicano male and a white female that is set in the contemporary time frame. Montalbán plays a "neurotic" boxer named Johnny, bitter with Anglos, who resentfully spurns society, assuming that he is accepted only because he is a boxing champ and will be rejected as soon as he loses his crown. Johnny is cured of these so-called "neurotic" assumptions which most Hispanics would view as highly accurate and normal by his manager's all-American, girl-next-door blonde daughter (June Allyson) who convinces him through her love and loyalty (she herself is a female stereotype in deep need of the women's movement) that the Gringos really like him for himself. Two years later, Montalbán did another B-picture for MGM, *My Man and I,* which is vintage social problem formula, promoting the social cliché that if the oppressed are forbearing enough, the good that exists in American society will ultimately come to the rescue and overturn the bad. Here he depicts a fruit picker exploited by a nasty white boss who cheats him out of his wages and then has him arrested. Yet throughout his ordeal, this upstanding Citizen Chicano (Chon Noriega, 1991) with the name of Chu Chu maintains his patriotic optimism (he even becomes a naturalized citizen), confident that everything will work out, which is precisely the case. Montalbán in this film is the standard friendly, happy Mexican whose faith in America is upheld when the injustice is rectified.

The most daring and best realized of the Hispanic-focused social problem films are *The Lawless* (1950, Paramount, starring Macdonald Carey and Lalo Ríos) and *Salt of the Earth* (1954, independently produced, starring Rosaura Revueltas and Juan Chacón), and it is precisely because neither was made within the confines of the studios (the former was a low-budget independent released through Paramount, while the latter was made outside the studio system altogether by blacklisted artists including writer Michael Wilson, producer Paul Jarrico, and director Herbert J. Biberman) that a deeper and more artistically elaborated interpretation of racial oppression is realized. (Earlier Michael Wilson had written the script for a Hopalong Cassidy film, *Border Patrol,* 1942, United Artists, with Duncan Renaldo where Mexicans were used as slave labor in silver mining.)

In contrast to the usual treatment that viewed racial prejudice against minorities as the product of a white sociopath or other such deranged troublemaker who is then blamed for inciting a mostly ingenuous but somewhat blameless populace, the lynch mob violence in *The Lawless* and the vicious labor strife in *Salt of the Earth* are deemed to be typically middle American. In these films by stereotyping "spics" as lazy and no good, Anglos find a scapegoat for their hatreds and a rationale for injustice.

Both *The Lawless* and *Salt of the Earth* expose the deplorable working and living conditions of the Chicano community. The only employment opportunities open to Chicanos in *The Lawless,* directed by Joseph Losey and scripted by blacklisted Daniel Mainwaring using a pseudonym, are as fruit pickers earning subsistence wages. Because of their meager, unstable income the only houses the workers can afford are flimsy shacks lacking indoor plumbing and located "on the other side of the tracks."

Salt of the Earth goes further and provides historical background on how the Chicanos' rights were violated by Anglo industrial interests. The community once owned the land but the zinc company moved in, took over the property, and offered the Chicanos the choice of moving or accepting employment at low wages. They are forced to live in management-owned houses and buy at management-owned stores. The houses are shacks with poor sanitation and plumbing; the stores sell goods at inflated prices and entrap the workers into a state of continual debt. Safety provisions for the Chicano miners are lax, especially when compared to those in neighboring mines operated by whites. Whereas Anglo miners are allowed to work in pairs, the Chicanos must perform dangerous chores individually. When the Chicano workers protest to the company, the manager warns them that he will find others to replace them. "Who? A Scab?" asks a Chicano. "An American," retorts the manager.

In both films racism is clearly linked to social authority. In *The Lawless,* a peaceful dance in the Chicano community is invaded by white hoodlums and a rumble erupts. When the police arrive, eleven Mexicans and only one white are arrested. White business leaders unofficially intervene and the Chicanos are forced to accept full responsibility for the violence. The newspapers then report that the incident was a battle between two gangs of "fruit tramps." In *Salt of the Earth,* the police conspire with the mine owners to defeat the strike, disrupting the picket line and arresting one of the spokesmen. Snarling racial epithets, two deputies viciously assault the Chicano and then charge him with resisting arrest. Later, as the strike continues, the police evict the miners from their homes, carelessly damaging their possessions in the process.

The films' portrait of the Chicano personality does not conform to the conventional Hollywood social problem film stereotype of the noble victim seeking only to gain acceptance from the white man. For example, in *Salt of the Earth* the strikers are militant and articulate. They debate the issues at union meetings, thoroughly defining their goals and examining the nature of their enemies. Every tactic the company uses against the Chicanos they ultimately are able to thwart, and every cunning argument for a return to work they refute with solid reasoning. (See Miller, 1984, for an interesting update on the impact *Salt of the Earth* has had over the years as an underground classic and the books and documentary that it has spawned.)

The Lawless is a social problem film that deserves recognition in the history of Hispanic-focused cinema for its artistry, its ability to transcend the social cant of the genre, and for the depth of its psychological analysis. *The Lawless* presents us with characters whose attitudes and behavior are as diversified as human experience. The characters range from the idealistic to the confused and fearful, the destructively embittered to the resigned and defeated. The Anglos are similarly varied. For example, some cops are blatant racists but others offer genuine sympathy even while they follow orders and arrest the Chicanos. The character of Prentiss, a well-meaning, guilt-ridden "liberal" businessman whose actions compromise Chicano youths, is an excellent depiction of the type. The film well evokes the effects of such double-edged benevolence.

Salt of the Earth, of course, has won a place in the international history of film not only as one of the best works on Chicano subjects but also as one of the most significant feminist films. Just as importantly, *Salt of the Earth* is notable because of the historical circumstances of its production. As Paul Jarrico puts it, it was "the first feature film ever made in this country of labor, by labor, and for labor" (Rosenfelt, 1978, 93). The film only had the most limited theatrical distribution because of virulent attacks on it by Howard Hughes, the American Legion, and others, but it has become a classic on university campuses and seems to grow yearly in importance. Linda Williams (1985) points out that *Salt of the Earth* as well as the Chicano film, *Alambrista!* are artistically successful as depictions not of Hollywood "heroes" or stereotypes, but true Chicano types. Rather than the individual triumphs of particular heroes, a genuine sense of Chicano reality is evoked through a documentary-style presentation of the social and historical context. Moreover, the vexed history of *Salt of the Earth* is instructive, for this film serves to define the limits of the Hollywood social problem film and the consequences for filmmakers who would seek to overreach the boundaries of the Hollywood formula. Film in the United States has not been a medium noted for its respect of artistic freedom.

Closely aligned to the social problem films were the historical "message" pictures such as Warners' Paul Muni biography cycle initiated with *the Life of Emile Zola* (1937, Warner Brothers), which devoted considerable attention to the Alfred Dreyfus (1859-1935) affair. (The anti-Semitic element is only fleetingly alluded to, however.) Two major films focused on Mexico emerged from this cycle, *Juárez* (1939, Warner Brothers, starring Paul Muni, Bette Davis, John Garfield, and Pedro de Córdoba) and the renowned *Viva Zapata!* (1952, Twentieth-Century Fox, director Elia Kazan, writer, John Steinbeck, starring Marlon Brando, Jean Peters, Joseph Wiseman, Anthony Quinn, and Margo)

Juárez has Paul Muni in the title role, Bette Davis as Carlota, and John Garfield as a youthful Porfirio Díaz learning Lincolnesque democracy at the master's feet. John Huston also worked on this film as one of various secondary scriptwriters. This was another film marked by renewed efforts on the eve of the war by Franklin Roosevelt's administration to enhance the Good Neighbor policy. The film itself is not only a tribute to Juárez, but as Pettit (1980, 147) observes, "also stars Abraham Lincoln. His spirit haunts the film from start to finish. Juárez rarely appears in his office without a portrait of the Great Emancipator peering over his shoulder." The passage of the years has not been good to *Juárez*, but despite its faults, which include the cultural chauvinism of an omnipresent Lincoln, the film rises way above the standard degrading stereotypes of Hollywood. *Juárez* reflects relatively accurate documentation of Mexican history and society. It was a box office success and mostly a critical one in the United States and it received an impassioned, mixed reception among opinion makers in Mexico (see Vanderwood, 1983 and García Riera, 1987, vol. 1, 235-243).

The clear masterpiece of the message biographies is also one of the best Hollywood Hispanic-focused films, *Viva Zapata!* (1952, Twentieth-Century Fox, screenplay by John Steinbeck, direction by Elia Kazan, and starring Marlon Brando and Anthony Quinn). The Mexican Revolution had been quiescent until the production of this film for many years, particularly during World War II when such productions could have been politically problematic for the Allied efforts. Nevertheless, two Mexican films in English language versions were released in the United States. One was *The Torch* (released in 1950), an English language version of *Enamorada* (1946). The film, directed by Emilio "El Indio" Fernández, starred Paulette Goddard (instead of the original María Félix), Pedro Armendáriz, and Gilbert Roland. In it a Mexican revolutionary captures a town and falls for the daughter of nobility. Miguel Contreras Torres directed *Pancho Villa Returns/Pancho Villa vuelve* (1949) with Pedro Armendáriz in the Spanish version and Leo Carrillo starring in the English version. Neither film was successful in the United States.

Viva Zapata! is not free of problems and stereotypes, many of which relate to turning Zapata into a Hollywood-style hero at the expense of historical veracity; nevertheless, it is the most comprehensive and attentive Hollywood film ever produced about the Mexican Revolution (with the possible exception of *Old Gringo* [1988] which is not accurately a Hollywood film, but an independent one). One of the reasons for the enduring popularity of the film is precisely the nature and complexity of the message. *Viva Zapata!* is not only about power and rebellion but also about the ways of corruption and how easy it is for a social movement to be debased. Zapata resists the corruption of his brother Eufemio, of the power hungry Fernando who betrays the revolution and goes to the side of Huerta and he even resists the tendency of the *campesinos* to look for heroes or leaders to whom they can abdicate their own responsibilities. As Zapata says to his people shortly before he goes to his death in the film: "You've looked for leaders. For strong men without faults. There aren't any. . . . There's no leader but yourselves . . . a strong people is the only lasting strength" (Morsberger, 1975, 104-5). (See Keller, 1985, 35-37 for additional commentary on this film. Also, García Riera, 1988, vol. 2, 116-122, develops a cogent, gripping, unconventional, critical view of the film. His is a very different understanding, shaped by a Mexican perspective. García Riera also brings much interesting and unusual information about Elia Kazan's ideas, the production of the film, and its reception in Mexico where it was a box office failure.)

In addition to *Viva Zapata!,* Steinbeck did several other treatments of Hispanic material. His other contributions make for a mixed, but on balance, positive record. In 1941, he wrote the screenplay and collaborated with director/producer Herbert Kline to film *The Forgotten Village* (Mayer-Burstyn), an artistic semidocumentary about science versus superstition in a small Mexican mountain village. This film, which was done outside the studio system, won numerous prizes as a feature documentary but played only in small independent art theaters because it did not benefit from studio distribution. In 1945, Steinbeck helped write the screenplay for *A Medal for Benny* (1945, Paramount) adapted from one of his paisano (rustic Hispanic) short stories. Starring Arturo de Córdova and Dorothy Lamour, this comedy treats the hypocrisy of town officials who exploit the posthumous awarding of the Congressional Medal of Honor to a brawling paisano. It contains many of the stereotypes of Hispanics that mark the novel *Tortilla Flat* (drunkenness, immaturity, brawling, but also a chivalric sense of honor) which was also adapted into a film (1942, starring Spencer Tracy, John Garfield, Hedy Lamarr, Akim Tamiroff, and Academy Award nominee for supporting actor, Frank Morgan), but without Steinbeck's participation. *A Medal for Benny* was a critical and box office success and Steinbeck and his cowriter Jack Wagner received Academy Award nominations. This film, however, is hardly his best effort in depicting Hispanics, although the Chicano actually wins the hand of an Anglo girl.

The 1948 release *The Pearl* (RKO/Oscar Dancigers) was coauthored by Steinbeck, Emilio "El Indio" Fernández, and Jack Wagner. In addition, Fernández directed the film, which starred Pedro Armendáriz, María Elena Marqués, and Alfonso Bedoya. *The Pearl* was in fact a 1946 Mexican movie widely distributed by RKO in the United States in 1948. The film, an adaptation of the Steinbeck novella, is a well-made, sensitive, and genuine treatment of Mexican fishermen, as might be expected of the Mexican director and crew. The plot itself is a parable of a poor Mexican fisherman who learns that wealth brings corruption and death. The critical response and the box office receipts on this film were respectable, but it has not endured.

The Continuation of Earlier Genres

Even as significant numbers of Hispanic-themed films of the Latin musical, social problem and historical message varieties were being produced, in parallel fashion production of the Western continued unabated and the Hispanic-focused jungle and other exotic films increased. Many of the other genres of the first decades continued to be produced as well, although in reduced numbers.

Westerns

Large numbers of Westerns were produced in the period between the Great Depression and the Civil Rights movement. In addition to the Westerns referred to earlier in this chapter, because they included features of the Latin musical or the social problem film, other Westerns containing significant Hispanic elements included: *Billy the Kid* (1930, MGM, director King Vidor, starring Wallace Beery), remade in 1941 (MGM, starring Robert Taylor); *The Ox-Bow Incident* (1943, Twentieth-Century Fox, director William Wellman, starring Anthony Quinn and Henry Fonda); *The Outlaw* (independent production, 1943, director Howard Hughes, starring Jane Russell), a film notable for its struggle with and challenge of censorship imposed by the Production Code; *My Darling Clementine* (1946, Twentieth-Century Fox, director John Ford, starring Linda Darnell and Victor Mature); *Treasure of the Sierra Madre* (1947, Warner Brothers, director John Huston, starring Humphrey Bogart, Walter Huston, and Alfonso Bedoya); *The Furies* (1950, Paramount, director Anthony Mann, starring Walter Huston, Barbara Stanwyck, and Gilbert Roland); *Branded* (1951, Paramount, starring Alan Ladd); *High Noon* (1952, Stanley Kramer Production, director Fred Zimmerman, starring Gary Cooper, Katy Jurado, and Grace Kelly); *Rancho Notorious* (1952, RKO, director Fritz Lang, starring Marlene Dietrich, and Mel Ferrer); *Ride, Vaquero* (1953, MGM, starring Ava Gardner, Robert Taylor, and Anthony Quinn); *Vera Cruz* (1954, United Artists, director Robert Aldrich, starring Gary Cooper, Sarita Montiel, Burt Lancaster, and César Romero); *The Burning Hills* (1956, Warner Brothers, starring Tab Hunter and Natalie Wood); *The Sheepman* (1958, MGM, starring Glenn Ford and Shirley MacLaine); *The Left Handed Gun* (1958, Warner Brothers, director Arthur Penn, script by Gore Vidal, starring Paul Newman); and *Río Bravo* (1959, Warner Brothers, director Howard Hawks, starring John Wayne, Dean Martin, and Ricky Nelson).

Billy the Kid (both versions), *The Outlaw, The Left-Handed Gun, Chisum* (1970, Warner, starring John Wayne), and *Pat Garrett and Billy the Kid* (1973, MGM, director Sam Peckinpah, starring Kris Kristofferson, James Coburn, and Katy Jurado) form part of the cycle on that folk hero; each of these films perpetuate the legend of the Kid as the friend of oppressed Hispanos and the foe of the Anglo cattle barons.

Most of these films perpetuate the major Hispanic stereotypes of the Western: the seductress or loose woman or the badman or bandido, either effective or buffoon-like. However, *The Ox-Bow Incident* in 1943 returns to a type rarely seen after the silent films, and even there only occasionally. The Mexican avenger is played by Anthony Quinn, who is hanged along with two Anglos for murdering a Nevada cowboy. Of the three, he is the only one to die with his dignity and honor intact, subverting the stereotypical role of the cowardly and inept greaser. Similarly, *The Man from Del Rio* (1956, United Artists) starred Anthony Quinn as a Dave Robles, a Mexican gunman whose quick-draw earns him the job of sheriff in the frightened border town of Mesa. It doesn't earn him the respect of the bigoted Anglo Texans, however; in non-law enforcement roles he is shunned by the town Anglos. Even Estella (Katy Jurado) rebuffs him for Anglo lovers. Reportedly (Hadley-García, 145), Quinn referred to Robles as one of his favorite roles: "The man has a tenacity and spirit that can't be broken, by other people or his own, and in the end he proves himself braver and more stubborn than any of his oppressors." Beginning in the 1960s, more examples of this strong Hispanic type emerge in the Western: *The Outrage* (1964, MGM) and *Death of a Gunfighter* (1969, Universal).

The more substantial Hispanic "loose woman" roles of the Westerns of the 1930s through the 1950s were assigned to mistresses of white gunmen. This was the case of such films as *My Darling Clementine, Vera Cruz*, and of course, above all, the classic *High Noon*, which is undoubtedly the best of these films. Katy Jurado, playing the role of Helen Ramírez, the former mistress of both the murderer and the marshall who sent the villain to prison, is memorable for her sensitive and original treatment of a Chicana. Unlike the shallow, stereotyped Hispanic seductress who flits from man to man with no qualms, Helen Ramírez articulates the essential moral posture of the film: the "respectable" townspeople are hypocrites acting in bad faith and self-delusion; Marshall Kane must confront the murderer even if he does it on his own in order to preserve his integrity.

One of a handful of Westerns that has survived its time and attained canonical status, *Treasure of the Sierra Madre*, depicted the stereotypical Mexican bandit in the figure of "Gold Tooth" played by Alfonso Bedoya. John Huston, through his use of neorealistic cinematic techniques, then in vogue in the Italian cinema, was able to squeeze a sort of sordid culmination out of the faithful, old stereotype. The director, veteran of *The Maltese Falcon* (1941) and several wartime documentaries including *Report From the Aleutians* (1943) and *The Battle of San Pietro* (1944), in this, his sixth film, adapted B. Traven's Marxist-leaning novel, with its evocation of the long history of colonial, Catholic, and capitalist exploitation of Mexico, into a neorealistic depiction of greed's impact on the human psyche. In this essentially all-male-cast story of psychological disintegration, few figures stand out as noble (Walter Huston, the old prospector and the noble savage Indians), and the main villain is an Anglo played by Humphrey Bogart. Amorous intrigues and a total lack of glamour gave a stark and more cinematically fitting quality to the Mexican bandits and corrupt Mexican officials as well. In this film, the Mexicans may be bad but they do not function as foils to good Anglos.

In *Ride Vaquero* (1953, MGM, director John Farrow, starring Robert Taylor, Ava Gardner, Howard Keel, and Anthony Quinn), Quinn plays the stereotypical bandit to a new extreme for the period (prior to the amoral spaghetti Westerns) as Esqueda, a cutthroat and braggart who connives to keep God-fearing Anglo settlers out of the Brownsville, Texas area by killing the men and raping their women.

During this period, a series of Westerns was established, "The Three Mesquiteers" (punning on musketeers and the mesquite tree) that gave work opportunities for several Hispanic actors, either in major or minor parts, including Duncan Renaldo and Rita Cansino (who subsequently changed her name to Rita Hayworth). The series featured a three-man cowboy team the make up of which varied. The most utilized actors were John Wayne, Max Terhune, Bob Livingston, Ray Corrigan, Bob Steele, Rufe Davis, Tom Tyler, Raymond Hatton, Duncan Renaldo, and Jimmy Dodd. The first film was made for RKO and all the rest for Republic. The most frequent directors were George Sherman, Mack V. Wright, Joseph Kane, John English, and Lester Orlebeck. Between 1935 and 1943, over fifty films were made in this series including *The Three*

Mesquiteers (1935), *Ghost Town* (1936), *Hit The Saddle* (1937, which depicted Rita Cansino dancing "La Cucaracha" in a bar), and the following in which Duncan Renaldo appeared: *The Kansas Terrors, Cowboys from Texas* (1939); and *Heroes of the Saddle, Pioneers of the West,* and *Covered Wagon Days* (1940).

Border Films

Undocumented immigration from Mexico, as we have reviewed in the preceding chapter, (see section, *The Border)* dates at least as early as the 1930 film, *On the Border.* In this film and in the 1932 *I Cover the Waterfront* (see Greenfield and Cortés, 1991, 51), the undocumenteds were Chinese being smuggled into the United States from Mexico. The plot characteristic of Chinese illegals continued into the 1940s. The 1941 *Hold Back the Dawn* (Paramount) was a well-received film that dramatized the desperate efforts of European refugees living temporarily in Tijuana to enter the United States. Based on the research to date, apparently not until the post-World War II era did films like *Border Incident* (1949), *Borderline* (1950), *The Lawless* (1950), and *Wetbacks* (1956, Realart, starring Lloyd Bridges) begin to deal with Mexican immigrants even though they often functioned as passive pawns to incite Anglo crime and Anglo crime-fighting. We have described *Border Incident* and *The Lawless* earlier. *Borderline* (1950, Universal, starring Fred MacMurray, Claire Trevor, and José Torvay) has an unlikely plot featuring separate law enforcers each tracking down dope smugglers on the Mexican border, neither knowing the other isn't a crook. *The Wetbacks* was an uninspired depiction of the immigration service's capture of a band of Mexicans smuggling "wetbacks" into San Diego by sea.

Bullfighting Films

A number of bullfighting films were made in this period along lines comparable to the first decades. *The Brave Bulls* (1951, Columbia, director Robert Rossen, starring Mel Ferrer, Miroslava [a Mexican film actress of Czech descent], and Anthony Quinn) was based on the book of the same title by Tom Lea. This film, directed by Rossen just after having won Oscars and critical accolades for *All the King's Men* (1949, Columbia), was a sincere attempt to produce a realistic depiction of the bullfight and its psychology. The film was praised for its honesty and authenticity (see, however, García Riera, vol. 2, 99-100 for a somewhat different perspective and an account of the Mexican reaction to the film). The *Bullfighter and the Lady* (1951, director Budd Boetticher, starring John Wayne) was a different breed of film, however, pure convention, featuring an Anglo bullfighter whose ineptitude causes the death of his Mexican teacher (Gilbert Roland), the most beloved fighter in the ring. However, the Gringo eventually prevails with the public, through his artistry in the ring. *The Magnificent Matador* (1954, Fox, director Budd Boetticher, starring Anthony Quinn) is Boetticher's second bullfighting film, but one equally tawdry, with Quinn as the most beloved bullfighter in Mexico and Maureen O'Hara, a rich American, making him suffer love pangs. Mario Moreno, "Cantinflas" also did a buffoon bullfighting scene in *Around the World in 80 Days* (1956, United Artists). The Three Stooges weighed in with bullfighting films: *What's the Matador* (1942, Columbia) and *Sappy Bullfighters* (1959, Columbia), a short. Two cartoons were built about the corrida: a Heckle and Jeckel *Bulldozing the Bull* (1951) and *Matador Magoo* (1957, Columbia). Jerry Lewis did a supermacho buffoon bullfighting number in *Rock-a-bye Baby* (1958, Paramount). (See also García Riera, vol. 2, 102-103 for related films including children who save bulls and bulls in Westerns).

Jungle and Other Exotic Films

Second only to the Latin musical, the increase of jungle and other exotic films provided vehicles for Hispanic actors as well as other exotic types generally. The jungle and exotic films proliferated beginning in the 1940s with technological improvements in color film. Dominican actress María Montez particularly benefitted from the development, and during the heyday of her career (which ended in 1951 due to her untimely death) she was affectionately known as "The Queen of Technicolor." Montez, not noted for her acting (nor for that matter, singing or dancing) ability, nevertheless became immensely popular in a string of color adventure films often costarring fellow camel riders John Hall, Sabu, or Turhan Bey. Among these films were *Cobra Woman* (1944, Universal, also starring John Hall, Sabu, and Lon Chaney), a technicolor fantasy-escape taking place on a jungle island in the Indian Ocean. Montez plays a good twin, evil twin in this romance containing temple rituals, chases, and fights. *Arabian Nights* (1942, Universal, also starring Jon Hall, Sabu, Thomas Gómez, and Turhan Bey) had dancer Montez help the deposed Caliph of Baghdad win back his throne. *White Savage* (1943, Universal, also starring Jon Hall, Sabu, Thomas Gómez, and Turhan Bey) featured Montez as the queen of a beautiful South Sea island in trouble with shark hunters and crooks after her mineral deposits. In *Sudan* (1945, Universal, also starring Jon Hall, Turhan Bey, and Andy Devine), Queen Montez escapes her evil prime minister. In *Tangier* (1946, Universal, also starring Robert Paige and Sabu; this was a black-and-white film clearly derivative of *Casablanca*), Montez is a dancer hunting for the Nazi war criminal responsible for her father's death. *Pirates of Monterey* (1947, Universal, also starring Rod Cameron and Gilbert Roland) was a romance set in California in the early 1800s during which the young Republic of Mexico protected the faraway land from brigands with the help of Anglo mercenary adventurers. Montez and her films enjoyed a second wave of popularity, particularly during the 1970s as the object of an extensive fan cult characterized either by nostalgia or the quest for high camp.

Burnu Acquanetta was another Hispanic actor whose career was based on her appearance in jungle or exotic films. The American-born Acquanetta was discovered by Charles Boyer and billed as the "Venezuelan Volcano." She first appeared in *Arabian Nights* (1942) starring María Montez. She also appeared in *Dead Man's Eyes* (1944, Universal, starring Lon Chaney, Jr.), *Captive Wild Woman* (1943, Universal) and its sequel, *Jungle Woman* (1944, Universal), and *Tarzan and the Leopard Woman* (1946, RKO, starring Johnny Weissmuller). She was in *The Lost Continent* (1951, starring César Romero) where scientists looking for a lost rocket ship on an unknown island find death and dinosaurs instead.

The genre gave work to a number of other Hispanic actors including the following: Pedro de Córdoba appeared in *South of Pago Pago* (1940, United Artists), Rodolfo "Rudy" Acosta appeared in *Destination Gobi* (1953, Twentieth-Century Fox, starring Richard Widmark) a combination camel opera/war adventure where American soldiers get help from Mongols against the Japanese, Armida was in *Jungle Goddess* (1948), Julián Rivero appeared in *Green Hell* (1940, Universal), Gilbert Roland was in *Malaya* (1949, MGM), César Romero did *The Jungle* (1952), Adele Mara and Duncan Renaldo were in *The Tiger Woman* (1944, Republic), Chris-Pin Martin appeared in *Ali Baba and the Forty Thieves* (1943, Universal, starring María Montez), Ricardo Montalbán did *The Saracen Blade* (1954, Columbia), Thomas Gómez was in *Macao* (1952, RKO, director Josef von Sternberg, starring Robert Mitchum and Jane Russell), and Pedro

Armendáriz was in *The Conqueror* (1956, Howard Hughes Production, starring John Wayne and Susan Hayward). (Several members of the cast died of cancer including Armendáriz, and it has been speculated that the site, the Escalante Desert in Utah, which had been used for atomic bomb tests, might have been a contributing factor.)

Latin Lover Films

Latin Lover films, both within the confines of the Latin musical and outside of it were the basis of the careers of Fernando Lamas, César Romero (in addition to his roles as Cisco Kid), and at the beginning of his career, Ricardo Montalbán.

We have already reviewed the Latin musical. Some of the other Latin Lover films included *Tall, Dark and Handsome* (1941, Fox, starring César Romero), a crime comedy where a gangster aspires to be a gentleman. *Wife, Husband and Friend* (1939, Fox, starring Loretta Young and Warner Baxter, with César Romero) was about a man sabotaging his wife's efforts to become a professional singer. *A Gentleman at Heart* (1942, Fox, starring César Romero) was about a racetrack bookie with aspirations to the art business and classier women. *Julia Misbehaves* (1948, MGM, starring Greer Garson and Walter Pidgeon, with Elizabeth Taylor and César Romero) is about an actress who eventually returns to her stuffy husband when her daughter is about to marry. In *Dangerous When Wet* (1953, MGM, starring Esther Williams), a film about swimming across the English Channel, Fernando Lamas does the honors. *The Girl Who Had Everything* (1953, MGM), depicted Elizabeth Taylor falling in love with crooked Fernando Lamas. *The Merry Widow* (1952, MGM, a remake of a stronger 1934 production) had Fernando Lamas paired against Lana Turner. Thomas Gómez also appeared in this film. *The Furies* (1950, Paramount) was a psychological thriller with Gilbert Roland playing Barbara Stanwyck's secret lover. *Latin Lovers* (1953, MGM) featured Ricardo Montalbán squiring Lana Turner as an heiress on holiday in Brazil looking for a man who will love her for herself alone. Arturo de Córdova did *Adventures of Casanova* (1948, Eagle-Lion).

Mexican Revolution Films

During this period, the number of Mexican Revolution films was much reduced. Some significant productions were made, nevertheless, including *Viva Villa!* and a few others we have referred to earlier in this chapter. *The Fighter* (1952, United Artists, director Herbert Kline, based on the short story "The Mexican" by Jack London, starring Richard Conte, Lee J. Cobb, Martin Garralaga, and Rodolfo Hoyos) was a cross between a boxing and a revolution film. In 1910, Felipe, a Mexican, leaves his town which has been destroyed in a massacre (killing his family and girlfriend) and goes to El Paso to become a guerrilla under the leadership of one, Durango, fighting against Porfirio Díaz. Felipe becomes a boxer and uses his earnings to support the guerrilla movement.

The Treasure of Pancho Villa (1955, RKO) had an Anglo mercenary get into trouble because he brought gold belonging to the U.S. government to Pancho Villa that Castro, a Villista bandit had stolen from an American train. In *Bandido* (1956, United Artists), Robert Mitchum played the Gringo mercenary, for whom the revolution was an adventure and a money-making activity, opposite Gilbert Roland, the Mexican who had true revolutionary zeal.

Villa! (1958, Fox) starred Gilbert Roland with Rodolfo Hoyos in the role of Pancho Villa and César Romero as Rodolfo Fierro, his fearsome aide. The film was shallow and unconventional and has fallen into obscurity. *They Came to Cordura* (1959, starring Gary Cooper, Rita Hayworth, and Van Heflin) was an adventure film set in Mexico in 1916 against the backdrop of the punitive expedition against Villa. The film features Cooper as an army officer accused of cowardice who is sent to find five men worthy of the Medal of Honor and meets a shady, non-Hispanic lady played by Hayworth.

Other Notable Films

A number of films during the period worth mentioning either don't fit well into any of the standard genres or formulas or transcend genre film. *The Fugitive* (1947, Argosy, director John Ford, photography by Gabriel Figueroa, starring Henry Fonda, Pedro Armendáriz, Dolores del Río, and Leo Carrillo), based on the Graham Greene novel, *The Power and the Glory,* featured a priest on the run during Mexico's strongly anticlerical period. The film had a mixed reception but it has survived the decades, partially because of Figueroa's superb photography.

For Whom the Bell Tolls (1943, Paramount, director Sam Wood, starring Gary Cooper, Ingrid Bergman, Akim Tamiroff, Arturo de Córdova, and Katina Paxinou) was a wartime super production, following the Hemingway novel rather closely. The film, a combination of adventure and romance, had excellent acting and innovative casting, but suffered somewhat of portentousness and solemnity. Everyone appeared to have thought that they were making a classic. *Variety* reviewed it as "one of the important pictures of all time although almost three hours of running time can overdo a good thing." The film has well survived the decades, and deservedly so. Other Hispanic-focused productions based on Hemingway's work during the period included *The Sun Also Rises* (1957, starring Tyrone Power, Ava Gardner, and Mel Ferrer), and Hemingway himself narrated the war documentary, *The Spanish Earth* (1937, story adaptation Archibald MacLeish and Lillian Hellman). In 1958 appeared *The Old Man and the Sea* (Warner) starring Spencer Tracy with Felipe Pazos in the role of the sympathetic boy.

A Touch of Evil (1958, director Orson Welles, starring Charlton Heston, Janet Leigh, Orson Welles, and Marlene Dietrich), filled with Wellesian touches, has transcended the border genre and become a cult classic. Nericcio (1992) has written an interesting paper on the ideological and sociocultural dimensions of this film. From the point of view of performance however, wooden Charlton Heston has been seen to make a better Moses than a mexicano.

Seven Cities of Gold (1955, Fox, starring Michael Rennie, Anthony Quinn, and Rita Moreno) was a semihistorical, semireligious film about explorer Gaspar de Portola and Father Junípero Serra exploring California. Rita Moreno played an Indian noble savage who was seduced by a Spanish soldier and subsequently leaped from a cliff to her death in shame.

Also during the period, United States audiences watched work by Eisenstein on Mexico, inasmuch as *Thunder Over Mexico* (1933, Upton Sinclair/Principal Pictures) was released in the United States; this was not the final Eisenstein work but consisted of 7,000 feet cut from 280,000 feet of film shot by the Russian master. The film caused a controversy that lasted years in the United States. One of the scenes included a young man's lady being raped by a vicious hacendado's men. Another had a poor peon buried up to his neck and trampled by the hacendado's cows for protesting. The oppression provokes the rebellion of the masses and the promise of revolutionary happiness thereafter. (For further information on Eisenstein in the United States and in Mexico, see Richard, 1992, 473, and García Riera, 1987, vol. 1, pp. 184 ff).

Hispanics Who Figured in the Movies between 1937 and 1959

The most productive genres in terms of work for Hispanic actors during this period were the Latin musicals and the jungle and other exotic films. New participants in the industry through these genres of films included: Acquanetta, Desi Arnaz, Xavier Cugat, Adele Mara, Carmen Miranda, Ricardo Montalbán, María Montez, Lina Romay, and César Romero. Outside of these genres few new Hispanic actors were introduced to the American screen. Nevertheless, some Hispanic actors during the period did successfully transfer from the stage to the silver screen, notably José Ferrer, Mel Ferrer, and Thomas Gómez. The other conduit into Hollywood for Hispanics was via either the Mexican or Argentine film industry. The following were brought to Hollywood from Mexico: Rodolfo "Rudy" Acosta, Pedro Armendáriz, Alfonso Bedoya, Arturo de Córdova, Gabriel Figueroa, Emilio "El Indio" Fernández, and Katy Jurado. Fernando Lamas was imported from Argentine cinema.

Some opportunities for Hispanics to work in the film industry remained in the Western genre, although even here many of the parts were played by Anglos. Richard "Chito" Martin entered Hollywood during this period and Rita Hayworth (Cansino) got her start as a cantina dancer. In other genres the Hispanic presence in fact was greatly diminished, and the roles that were made available to Hispanics went to established actors such as Armida, Anthony Quinn, Leo Carrillo, Chris-Pin Martin, Don Alvarado, Margo, and perhaps a dozen others. Even the socially conscious films more often than not featured Anglo (actually often Jewish or Italian) actors such as John Garfield, Paul Muni, and Sal Mineo. Some World War II movies would contain a bit part for a Hispanic character, presumably to promote patriotism, a sense of unity, and the brotherhood (not yet sisterhood in these self-satisfied times) of races against the fascist menace. In *Bataan* (1943), Desi Arnaz was cast as Félix Ramírez, a "jitterbug kid" from California who promptly dies of malaria before anything significantly heroic transpires. Outside of major figures, Hispanics would appear in secondary or minor roles as seductresses, "other" women, Latin Lovers, gangsters, communists, revolutionaries, bandits, half-breeds, Indians or other "savages" both noble and not, bullfighters or participants in bullfighting (e.g., corrupt, small-time impresarios), and other such roles that were either villainous, inconsequential, or in support of local color.

Rodolfo "Rudy" Acosta, having worked in Mexican films, went to Hollywood in the late 1940s and had a secondary role in John Ford's *The Fugitive* (1947) which was shot in Mexico. He played character roles, specializing in Mexican and Indian villains including *One Way Street, Pancho Villa Returns* (1950), *The Bullfighter and the Lady* (1951), *Horizons West* (1952), *Destination Gobi* (1953), *Hondo, Night People* (1954), *Bandido* (1956), and *The Tijuana Story* (leading role, 1957).

Burnu Acquanetta, the "Venezuelan Volcano," was discovered by Charles Boyer and first appeared in *Arabian Nights* (1942) starring María Montez. She appeared in *Captive Wild Woman* (1943, Universal) and its sequel, *Jungle Woman* (1944, Universal), *Dead Man's Eyes* (1944, Universal, starring Lon Chaney, Jr.), and *Tarzan and the Leopard Woman* (1946, RKO, starring Johnny Weismuller).

Don Alvarado appeared in *The Lady Escapes, Love Under Fire, Nobody's Baby* (1937), *Rose of the Río Grande, A Trip to Paris* (1938), *Cafe Society, Invisible Stripes* (1939), *Knute Rockne–All American, One Night in the Tropics* (1940), and *The Big Steal* (1949).

Pedro Armendáriz, the famous Mexican actor began working in the Mexican film industry in 1935, becoming one of the top stars and appearing in some forty-five films, many directed by Emilio "El Indio" Fernández. In American or coproductions during this period, he appeared in *La perla/The Pearl* (1946, released in the United States in 1948), *The Fugitive* (1947), *Fort Apache* (1948), *Three Godfathers* (1948), *We Were Strangers, Tulsa* (1949), *Border River* (1954), *The Littlest Outlaw* (1955), *Diane, The Conqueror* (1956), and *The Wonderful Country* (1959).

Armida (Armida Vendrell) appeared in *Border Cafe, Rootin' Tootin' Rhythm* (1937), *La Conga Nights* (1940), *Fiesta, South of Tahiti* (1941), *Always in My Heart* (1942), *The Girl From Monterey*

(1943), *Machine Gun Mama* (1944), *South of the Río Grande* (1945), *Bad Men of the Border* (1945), *Jungle Goddess* (1948), and *Rhythm Inn* (1951).

Desi Arnaz debuted on the screen in 1940 in *Too Many Girls*, starring Lucille Ball. He was in *Four Jacks and a Jill, Father Takes a Wife* (1941), *The Navy Comes Through* (1942), *Bataan* (1943, MGM), *Cuban Pete* (1946), *Holiday in Havana* (1949), *The Long Long Trailer* (1954), and *Forever Darling* (1956). He propagated the Latin sound until long after it had waned on the silver screen via 1950s television as Ricky Ricardo. He was costar of the *I Love Lucy Show* opposite Lucille Ball, among the most popular television series of all times, which ran between 1951 and 1956.

Alfonso Bedoya, who had developed a significant career in Mexico as a character actor, debuted in the United States in 1948 in *Treasure of the Sierra Madre* as the Mexican bandit, Gold Hat. He starred in *La perla/The Pearl* (1946, Mexican production, released in the United States in 1948) and appeared in *Streets of Laredo, Border Incident* (1949), *Man in the Saddle* (1951), *California Conquest* (1952), *Sombrero, The Stranger Wore a Gun* (1953), *Border River* (1954), *Ten Wanted Men* (1955), and *The Big Country* (1958). Bedoya died in December of 1957.

During this period, Leo Carrillo appeared in numerous films including *History is Made at Night*, *The Barrier*, *52nd Street*, *Hotel Haywire*, *Manhattan Merry-Go-Round* (Republic, as an Italian mobster), *I Promise to Pay* (1937), *The Girl of the Golden West, Blockade, Flirting with Fate, Little Miss Roughneck*, *City Streets*, *Too Hot to Handle* (1938), *Society Lawyer, The Arizona Wildcat, The Girl and the Gambler, Rio, Fisherman's Wharf, Chicken Wagon Family* (1939), *Twenty-Mule Team, Lillian Russell, Wyoming, Captain Caution* (1940), *Horror Island, Barnacle Bill* (1941), *Sin Town, American Empire* (1942), *Crazy House* (1943), *Ghost Catchers, Gypsy Wildcat, Bowery to Broadway* (1944), *Crime Incorporated*, Mexicana (1945), *The Fugitive* (1947), and *The Girl From San Lorenzo* (1950). In the early 1950s, Carrillo retired from the screen to play Pancho, Duncan Renaldo's sidekick in The Cisco Kid television series.

Xavier Cugat introduced his first band at Hollywood's Coconut Grove in 1928. In the 1930s and 1940s, he became known as the "Rumba King" and was most influential in introducing and popularizing Latin rhythms in the United States. He appeared in occasional films during this period, usually playing himself, and he led his orchestra memorably in MGM musicals of the 1940s. He appeared with his band in *Go West, Young Man* (1936) and *The Heat's On* (1943), both starring Mae West. He also appeared in *You Were Never Lovelier* (1942), *Stage Door Canteen* (1943), *Two Girls and a Soldier, Bathing Beauty* (1944), *Weekend at the Waldorf* (1945), *Holiday in Mexico, No Leave No Love* (1946), *This Time for Keeps* (1947), *Luxury Liner, On an Island With You* (1948), and *Chicago Syndicate* (1955).

Pedro de Córdoba appeared in many films including *The Firefly, Girl Loves Boy, Maid of Salem, Marriage Forbidden* (1937), *Dramatic School, Gold Diggers in Paris, Heart of the North, International Settlement, Keep Smiling, Storm over Bengal* (1938), *Chasing Danger, City in Darkness, Devil's Island, Escape to Paradise, Juárez, Law of the Pampas, Man of Conquest, Range War, Winner Take All* (1939), *Before I Hang, Earthbound, The Ghost Breakers, The Light That Failed, The Mark of Zorro, My Favorite Wife, Phantom Submarine, The Sea Hawk, South of Pago Pago* (1940), *Blood and Sand, Romance of the Rio Grande* (1941), *For Whom the Bell Tolls* (1943), *The Keys of the Kingdom* (1945), *Samson and Delilah* (1949), *Comanche Territory, and Crisis* (1950).

Arturo de Córdova, the Mexican actor, appeared in some Hollywood films including *Los hijos mandan, Miracle on Main Street* (foreign version) (1939), *For Whom the Bell Tolls* (1943), *Masquerade in Mexico, A Medal for Benny* (1945), *New Orleans* (1947), and *Adventures of Casanova* (1948).

Juan de la Cruz appeared in *Magnificent Obsession, Suzy* (1936), and *Meet the Wildcat* (1937).

Dolores del Río did only a few Hollywood films during this period. She became dissatisfied with the roles she was obtaining and returned to Mexico in 1943 to do a number of important films in that country. Her Hollywood films included *Ali Baba Goes to Town, The Devil's Playground, Lancer Spy* (1937), *International Settlement* (1938), and *The Man from Dakota* (1940).

Andrés de Segurola did *One Hundred Men and a Girl* (1937), *Castillos en el aire* (1938), *First Love, Three Smart Girls Grow Up* (1939), and *Spring Parade* (1940).

Emilio "El Indio" Fernández directed *María Candelaria* (1943, Mexico) which won the Grand Prize at Cannes and *La perla/The Pearl* (1946, released in the United States in 1948) which won the International Prize at San Sebastian, Spain. He had a bit part in *Flying Down to Rio* (1933).

José Ferrer, Puerto Rican actor and director, had established a solid reputation for himself on the stage (e.g., he did Iago opposite Paul Robeson's *Othello* in 1942) before he debuted in 1948 in film. He won the Oscar for best actor as *Cyrano de Bergerac* (1950). Ferrer had his greatest success playing Frenchmen; in addition to Cyrano he was in *Joan of Arc* (1948) as the Dauphin, and played Toulouse-Lautrec in *Moulin Rouge* (1952). Beginning in the late 1950s, he also directed. During this period he was also in *Whirlpool, Crisis* (1950), *Anything Can Happen* (1952), *Miss Sadie Thompson* (1953), *The Caine Mutiny, Deep in My Heart* (1954), *The Shrike* (also director, 1955), *The Great Man* (also director 1957), *I Accuse* (as Dreyfus, also director) and *The High Cost of Living* (also director), both in 1958.

Mel Ferrer costarred with his then wife, Audrey Hepburn in *War and Peace* (1956) and directed her in *Green Mansions* (1959). As an actor he was also in *Lost Boundaries* (1949), *The Brave Bulls* (1951), *Rancho Notorious, Scaramouche* (1952), *Lili* (1953), *The Sun Also Rises* (1957), and *The World, the Flesh and the Devil* (1959).

Gabriel Figueroa went to Hollywood from Mexico to study motion picture photography and returned to Mexico the following year to begin a prolific career as a cameraman. He worked for Luis Buñuel, John Ford, and Emilio Fernández. Among the notable Mexican productions he did during this period were *La perla/The Pearl* (1946), *Los olvidados (The Forgotten,* 1952), and *Nazarín* (1959).

Martin (also spelled Martín) Garralaga appeared in many films including *Anthony Adverse, The Border, The Charge of the Light Brigade, A Message to Garcia, Song of the Gringo* (1936), *Another Dawn, Boots of Destiny, Love Under Fire, Riders of the Rockies, The Sheik Steps Out* (1937), *Four Men and a Prayer, Outlaw Express, Rose of the Rio Grande, Starlight over Texas* (1938), *Another Thin Man, Code of the Secret Service, The Fighting Gringo, Juárez, Mutiny on the Blackhawk* (1939), *Legion of the Lawless, Meet the Wildcat, Rangers of Fortune, Rhythm of the Rio Grande, Stage to Chino,* and *Wagon Train* (1940). He also did numerous Spanish-language productions.

Thomas Gómez (Sabino Tomás Gómez), following considerable stage experience, began his film career in the 1940s. This heavyset character actor appeared typically as a crafty villain. He was nominated for a best supporting actor Academy Award for his role in *Ride a Pink Horse* (1947). During this period he appeared in *Sherlock Holmes and the Voice of Terror, Arabian Nights* (starring Acquanetta), *Pittsburgh* (1942), *White Savage, Corvette K-225, Crazy House* (1943), *Phantom Lady, Dead Man's Eyes* (starring Acquanetta), *The Climax* (1944), *Frisco Sal* (1945), *Night in Paradise* (1946), *Johnny O'Clock, Singapore, Ride a Pink Horse, Captain From Castile* (1947), *Casbah, Key Largo, Force of Evil* (1948), *Sorrowful Jones, That Midnight Kiss* (1949), *The Woman on Pier 13* (originally released as *I Married A Communist;* he plays a murderous communist who blackmails shipping executive Robert Ryan), *The Eagle and the Hawk, The Furies, Kim* (1950), *Anne of the Indies* (1951), *Macao, The Merry Widow, Pony Soldier* (1952), *Sombrero* (1953), *The Adventures of Haji Baba* (1954), *The Magnificent Matador* (1955), *The Conqueror, Trapeze* (1956), *John Paul Jones,* and *But Not for Me* (1959).

Rita Hayworth, who got her start as a cantina dancer and seductress repositioned herself during this period with great success. Her early movies, under the name Rita Cansino, included work in the "Three Mesquiteers" series (a take-off on both the *Three Musketeers* and the mesquite plant), a seemingly unending cycle of movies featuring trios of cowboys. Rita played the seductive cantina dancer, doing the song, "La Cucaracha" in *Hit the Saddle* (1937). It was precisely in that year that she married the shrewd businessman Edward Judson, who convinced her that being a Hispanic limited her to work as a cinematic loose woman. Under his guidance, she changed her name to Rita Hayworth and was transformed from a raven-haired Hispanic dark lady into an auburn-haired sophisticate. By the early 1940s, she attained Anglo recognition as the hottest of Hollywood's "Love Goddesses." Her picture in *Life* magazine was so much in demand that it was reproduced in the millions and adorned the atomic bomb that was dropped on Bimini. She appeared in *Trouble in Texas, Old Louisiana* (1937) as Rita Cansino. As Rita Hayworth, she was in *The Shadow* (1937), *Angels Over Broadway* (1940), *The Strawberry Blonde, Blood and Sand* (1941), *Cover Girl* (1944), *Gilda* (1946), *The Lady from Shanghai, The Loves of Carmen* (1948), *Salome, Miss Sadie Thompson* (1953), *Pal Joey* (1957), *Separate Tables* (1958), and *They Came to Cordura* (1959).

Katy Jurado was brought to Hollywood from Mexico in 1951 for *The Bullfighter and the Lady.* She hit her Hollywood peak in 1952 as Helen Ramírez in *High Noon.* She was nominated for an Oscar for her supporting role in *Broken Lance* (1954). She appeared in *Arrowhead* (1953), and *Trapeze* and *The Man from Del Rio* (1956).

Soledad Jiménez (a Spaniard according to the Mexican magazine, *Filmografía,* June, 1935) may have the dubious distinction of the most Hollywood-misspelled Hispanic name of all times. She has been listed, in addition to accurately, as Saladad Jeminez, Solidad Jimines, and Soledad Jiminez. Disgraceful! She worked during this period in *Kid Galahad, Law and Lead, Live, Love and Learn* (1937), *California Frontier, Forbidden Valley* (1938), *Girl from Rio, The Real Glory, Rough Riders Round-Up, The Return of the Cisco Kid* (1939), and *Seven Sinners* (1940).

Fernando Lamas debuted in 1942 in Argentine cinema and came to Hollywood at the age of 35. He did frivolous pictures featuring him as a caddish Latin playboy such as *Rich, Young and Pretty* (1951) and partnered top actresses in the *Merry Widow* (1952, starring Lana Turner), *The Girl Who Had Everything* (1953, starring Elizabeth Taylor), *Dangerous When Wet* (1953, starring Esther Williams, his fourth wife), and *The Girl Rush* (1955, starring Rosalind Russell). He also appeared in *The Avengers* (1950), *The Law and the Lady* (1951), *Sangaree, The Diamond Queen* (1953), *Jivaro* (1954), and *Rose Marie* (1954).

Adele Mara got her start as a singer-dancer with Xavier Cugat's band. She did seductresses or "other woman" parts in *Navy Blues* (1942), *You Were Never Lovelier, Alias Boston Blackie* (1942), *Atlantic City* (1944), *The Tiger Woman, Song of Mexico* (1945), *The Catman of Paris, I've Always Loved You* (1946), *Twilight on the Rio Grande, Robin Hood of Texas, Blackmail, Exposed* (1947), *Campus Honeymoon, Wake of the Red Witch, Angel in Exile* (1948), *Sands of Iwo Jima, The Avengers, California Passage* (1950), *The Sea Hornet* (1952), *Count the Hours* (1953), *Back from Eternity* (1956), and *The Big Circus* (1959).

Margo was best known in this period for her nondancing role in *Lost Horizon* (1937), for her role as the mother in *Viva Zapata!* (1952), and for *The Leopard Man* (1943) in which she played Clo-Clo, an ill-fated "Spanish" dancer in a New Mexico town. She also appeared in *Behind the Rising Sun* (1943), *The Falcon in Mexico* (1944), *I'll Cry Tomorrow* (1955), and *From Hell to Texas* (1958).

Mona Maris during these years appeared in *Flight From Destiny, Law of the Tropics* (1941), *My Gal Sal, Pacific Rendezvous, I Married an Angel, Berlin Correspondent* (1942), *The Falcon in Mexico* (1944), *Heartbeat* (1946), and *The Avengers* (1950).

Chris-Pin Martin appeared in a large number of movies including *Boots and Saddles, A Star is Born* (1937), *Billy the Kid Returns, Four Men and a Prayer, The Texans, Too Hot to Handle* (1938), *The Arizona Wildcat, The Cisco Kid and the Lady, Espionage Agent, The Fighting Gringo, The Girl and the Gambler, The Llano Kid, The Return of the Cisco Kid, Rio, Stagecoach* (1939), *Charlie Chan in Panama, Down Argentine Way, The Gay Caballero, Lucky Cisco Kid, The Mark of Zorro, Viva Cisco Kid* (1940), *Romance of the Rio Grande, Weekend in Havana* (1941), *Tombstone* (1942), *The Ox-Bow Incident* (1943), *Ali Baba and the Forty Thieves* (1944), *San Antonio* (1945), *The Fugitive* (1947), *Mexican Hayride* (1948), *The Beautiful Blonde from Bashful Bend* (1949), and *Ride the Man Down* (1952). He died in 1953.

Richard "Chito" Martin (born in 1918) appeared in more than thirty RKO Westerns through the 1940s and early 1950s, most often paired with Tim Holt, as well as Robert

Mitchum and James Warren. Unlike typical cowboy sidekicks who were shorter, heavier, and funnier than the star, Chito was handsomer than his partners. Chito usually provided comic relief via his difficulty with English, although in real life he had no accent. Among his films were *The Tonto Rim* (1947), *Brothers in the Saddle* (1949), *Dynamite Pass* (1950), and *Gunplay* (1951).

Carmen Miranda had worked in Brazilian films before coming to Hollywood in 1939. These films included *A Voz do Carnaval* (1933), *Alo Alo Brasil, Estudantes* (1935), *Alo Alo Carnaval* (1936), and *Banana de Terra* (1939). Her Hollywood films included *Down Argentine Way* (1940), *That Night in Rio, Week-End in Havana* (1941), *Springtime in the Rockies* (1942), *The Gang's All Here* (1943), *Four Jills in a Jeep, Greenwich Village, Something for the Boys* (1944), *Doll Face, If I'm Lucky* (1946), *Copacabana* (1947), *A Date with Judy* (1948), and *Nancy Goes to Rio* (1950). Her last film was a parody of her earlier work. She appeared in the Dean Martin and Jerry Lewis film *Scared Stiff* (1953) in which Lewis impersonated the lady with the platform wedgies and the edible headdresses. Miranda died in 1955.

Ricardo Montalbán, after five years of film work in Mexico, spent seven years with MGM beginning in 1947, usually playing a sophisticated but jealous Latin Lover often opposite swimming star Esther Williams or dancing with Cyd Charisse. Due to his accent he was always cast as a Latin or other alien, including Japanese in *Sayonara* (1957). He was also in *Fiesta* (1947), *The Kissing Bandit* (1948), *Neptune's Daughter, Border Incident* (1949), *Two Weeks with Love* (1950), *Across the Wide Missouri, Mark of the Renegade* (1951), *Latin Lovers, Sombrero* (1953), *The Saracen Blade* (1954), and *A Life in the Balance* (1957). In *Mystery Street* (1950), he played a Hispanic police officer on Cape Cod. He starred in two Hispanic social problem films: *Right Cross* (1950) and *My Man and I* (1952).

María Montez debuted in 1940 and made her last films in 1951. She specialized in playing sexually alluring, exotic roles, often with costars Jon Hall, Turhan Bey, and Sabu (Sabu Dastagir, 1924-1963). Her films included *Lucky Devils, The Invisible Woman, Boss of Bullion City, That Night in Rio, Raiders of the Desert, Moonlight in Hawaii, South of Tahiti* (1941), *The Mystery of Marie Roget, Arabian Nights* (as Scheherazade), *Bombay Clipper* (1942), *White Savage* (1943), *Cobra Woman* (her most famous film), *Ali Baba and the Forty Thieves, Follow the Boys, Gypsy Wildcat, Bowery to Broadway* (1944), *Sudan* (1945), *Tangier* (1946), *The Exile, Pirates of Monterey* (1947), *Siren of Atlantis* (1949), and a number of European productions. She died in 1951 at the age of 33, drowned in her bath after a possible heart attack.

Antonio Moreno, in his fifties by the late 1930s, was on the wane. He did *Rose of the Rio Grande* (1938), *Ambush* (1939), *Seven Sinners* (1940), and had secondary roles in such films as *They Met in Argentina* (1941, RKO), *Fiesta* (1947, MGM), and *Tampico* (1944, Fox). He also appeared in *Dallas, Crisis, Saddle Tramp* (all 1950) and *The Creature from the Black Lagoon* (1954).

Mario Moreno "Cantinflas," the premier Mexican comic star, appeared in *Around the World in 80 Days* (1956).

Rita Moreno, debuted in a women-in-prison film, *So Young, So Bad* (1950), was in *The Toast of New Orleans* (1950, starring Mario Lanza), and got bit roles in 1952 in various films including *Ma and Pa Kettle on Vacation, The Fabulous Señorita*, and *Singin' in the Rain*. She did a number of tempestuous Latinas, Native Americans, and half-breeds in films starring Gary Cooper, Tyrone Power, and others in the 1950s where she seldom did much more than wear off-the-shoulder peasant blouses and smoulder. However, in 1956 she made a serious impact in her role of the Burmese Princess Tuptim in *The King and I*. The better part of her career was to come.

Barry Norton continued to do a number of films including *Captain Calamity, Murder at Glen Athol* (1936), *History is Made at Night, I'll Take Romance, Rich Relations, She's Dangerous* (1937), *The Buccaneer* (1938), *Papá soltero, Should Husbands Work?, El trovador de la radio* (1939), *Devil Monster* (1946), and *Around the World in 80 Days* (cameo role, 1956). He died in 1956.

Ramón Novarro's career was largely cut short because he refused Louis B. Mayer's ultimatum that he marry in order to conceal his homosexuality. He appeared in the *Sheik Steps Out* (1937), *A Desperate Adventure* (1938), *The Big Steal* (1949), *The Outriders*, and *Crisis* (1950).

Nena Quartaro (same as Nena Quartero and Nina Quartero) appeared in *The Phantom of Santa Fe*, *The Three Mesquiteers*, *Two in a Crowd*, *Wife Vs. Secretary* (1936), *Left-Handed Law*, *Submarine D-1* (1937), *Torchy Blane in Panama* (1938), and *Green Hell* (1940).

Anthony Quinn did dozens of films during this period. He appeared in *Guadalcanal Diary* (1943) as Soose, a Mexican American marine private who was the sole survivor of a patrol. Also in 1943, Quinn played a Mexican in *The Oxbow Incident*, starring Henry Fonda, and in *California* (1946) he was a dignified Spanish marquis. He won an Oscar for his role as Emiliano Zapata's brother, Eufemio in *Viva Zapata!* (1952), and a second Academy Award for *Lust for Life* (1956), in the role of Gauguin. Some of the other films he appeared in included *The Last Train From Madrid*, *Partners in Crime*, *The Plainsman*, *Swing High, Swing Low*, *Waikiki Wedding* (1937), *The Buccaneer*, *Bulldog Drummond in Africa*, *Dangerous to Know*, *Daughter of Shanghai*, *Hunted Men*, *King of Alcatraz*, *Tip-Off Girls* (1938), *Island of Lost Men*, *King of Chinatown*, *Television Spy* (about an invention called the television), *Union Pacific* (1939), *City for Conquest*, *Emergency Squad*, *The Ghost Breakers*, *Parole Fixer*, *Road to Singapore*, *Texas Rangers Ride Again* (1940), *Blood and Sand*, *Knockout*, *Thieves Fall Out*, *Bullets for O'Hara*, *They Died with Their Boots On* (as Chief Crazy Horse), *The Perfect Snob* (1941), *Larceny, Inc.*, *Road to Morocco*, *The Black Swan* (1942), *Buffalo Bill*, *Roger Touhy–Gangster*, *Ladies of Washington*, *Irish Eyes Are Smiling* (1944), *China Sky*, *Where Do We Go From Here?* *Back to Bataan* (1945, a sequel to the 1943 *Bataan* that had Desi Arnaz in a minor role), *California*, *Sinbad the Sailor*, *Black Gold*, *The Imperfect Lady*, *Tycoon* (1947), *The Brave Bulls*, *Mask of the Avenger* (1951), *Against All Flags*, *The Brigand*, *The World in His Arms* (1952), *Ride Vaquero*, *City Beneath the Sea*, *Seminole* (as Chief Osceola), *East of Sumatra*, *Blowing Wild* (1953), *The Long Wait* (1954), *The Magnificent Matador*, *The Naked Street*, *Seven Cities of Gold* (1955), *The Wild Party*, *Man from Del Rio* (1956), *The River's Edge*, *The Ride Back*, *Wild is the Wind* (1957), *Hot Spell*, *The Black Orchid* (1958), *Warlock*, and *Last Train from Gun Hill* (1959).

In the early 1930s, Duncan Renaldo experienced serious problems with the U.S. Immigration Service. He was arrested and charged in 1931 with being an illegal immigrant and making false statements about his place of birth in order to obtain a passport. In the next six years, Renaldo was indicted by a Grand Jury, taken to trial, convicted of perjury and making false statements, sentenced to two years in a federal jail, served eighteen months on McNeil Island, and was chased out of the United States by immigration authorities. Finally, in 1936, the actor, who had been on the verge of stardom at the beginning of the decade, was granted an unconditional presidential pardon by Franklin D. Roosevelt. Despite his problems, he appeared in numerous films including *Lady Luck*, *Moonlight Murder*, *Rebellion*, *Two Minutes to Play* (1936), *Mile-a-Minute-Love*, *Special Agent K-7* (1937), *Rose of the Rio Grande*, *Spawn of the North*, *Ten Laps to Go*, *Tropic Holiday* (1938), *Cowboys from Texas*, *The Kansas Terrors*, *Rough Riders Round-Up*, *South of the Border*, *Zaza* (1939), *Covered Wagon Days*, *Gaucho Serenade*, *Heroes of the Saddle*, *Oklahoma Renegades*, *Pioneers of the West*, *Rocky Mountain Rangers* (1940), *Outlaws of the Desert*, *Down Mexico Way* (1941), *For Whom the Bell Tolls* (1943), *The Fighting Seabees* (1944), *The Cisco Kid Returns* (1945), *Jungle Flight* (1947), *Sword of the Avenger* (1948), *The Gay Amigo*, *The Daring Caballero*, *Satan's Cradle*, *We Were Strangers* (1949), *The Capture* (1950), and *Zorro Rides Again* (1959).

Julián Rivero played in *Heroes of the Alamo*, *Love Under Fire*, *The Mighty Treve*, *Ridin' the Lone Trail*, *Wells Fargo* (1937), *Flight into Nowhere*, *Outlaw Express* (1938), *The Arizona Wildcat*, *Code of the Secret Service*, *Drifting Westward*, *The Girl and the Gambler* (1939), *Arizona Gang Busters*, *Billy the Kid's Gun Justice*, *Death Rides the Range*, *Down Argentine Way*, *Green Hell*, *Meet the Wildcat*, *Riders of Black Mountain*, *The Westerner*, and *Young Buffalo Bill* (1940).

Gilbert Roland during this period appeared in *Juárez* (as Col. Miguel López), *The Furies* (1950, as Barbara Stanwyck's clandestine Latin Lover), *The Bullfighter and the Lady* (1951), *The Bad and the Beautiful* (1952), and *The French Line* (1954). Additionally, he was in *The Last Train*

From Madrid, Thunder Trail (1938), *The Sea Hawk* (1940), *Isle of Missing Men* (1942), *Captain Kidd* (1945), *The Gay Cavalier, Beauty and the Bandit, South of Monterey* (1946), *King of the Bandits, Robin Hood of Monterey* (1947), *We Were Strangers* (1949), *Malaya, The Torch, Crisis* (1950), *Ten Tall Men, Mark of the Renegade* (1952), *My Six Convicts, Glory Alley, The Miracle of Our Lady of Fatima, Apache War Smoke* (1952), *Thunder Bay, Beneath the 12-Mile Reef* (1953), *Underwater!, The Racers, That Lady* (1955), *Bandido* (1956), *Three Violent People, The Midnight Story* (1957), and *The Big Circus* (1959).

Lina Romay (Elena Romay), the Brooklyn-born daughter of a Mexican diplomat, obtained a screen career through her affiliation with Xavier Cugat's band. After the success of Carmen Miranda, Romay was billed as "Cugie's Latin Doll" and sang with the bandleader for a few years, making a screen debut as part of Cugat's act in *You Were Never Lovelier* (1942, Columbia, starring Rita Hayworth). She emerged as a singing star in *Weekend at the Waldorf* (1945, MGM) and *Love Laughs at Andy Hardy* (1946, MGM, starring Mickey Rooney), *Honeymoon* (1947, RKO) and did a straight role in *Adventure* (1945, MGM, starring Clark Gable).

César Romero alternated in American and ethnic roles in films such as *Public Enemy's Wife* (1936), *Wee Willie Winkie* (1937, starring Shirley Temple), and *Charlie Chan at Treasure Island* (1939). Romero's heyday arrived in the 1940s when he appeared in numerous Latin musicals produced by Fox including *Weekend in Havana* (1941), *Springtime in the Rockies* (1942), and *Carnival in Costa Rica* (1947). In 1939, Romero had a supporting role in *Return of the Cisco Kid* and he assumed the title role the following year. Additionally he appeared, in among other films, *Happy Landing, Always Goodbye, My Lucky Star, Five of a Kind* (1938), *Wife, Husband and Friend, The Little Princess, Frontier Marshal* (as Doc Holiday), *The Cisco Kid and the Lady* (his first as the Cisco Kid) (1939), *He Married His Wife, Lucky Cisco Kid, The Gay Caballero* (as the Cisco Kid), *Romance of the Rio Grande* (as the Cisco Kid),*Viva Cisco Kid* (1940), *Tall Dark and Handsome, Ride on Vaquero* (as the Cisco Kid), *The Great American Broadcast, Dance Hall* (1941), *A Gentleman at Heart, Orchestra Wives, Tales of Manhattan* (1942), *Coney Island, Wintertime* (1943), *Captain From Castile* (as Cortez), *Deep Waters, That Lady in Ermine, Julia Misbehaves* (1948), *The Beautiful Blonde from Bashful Bend* (1949), *Love that Brute, Once a Thief* (1950), *Lost Continent, FBI Girl* (1951), *The Jungle* (1952), *Vera Cruz* (1954), *The Americano, The Racers* (1955), *The Leather Saint, Around the World in 80 Days* (1956), *The Story of Mankind* (1957), and *Villa!* (1958).

Olga San Juan was another actress who got her start as a copycat of Carmen Miranda. She was billed as "The Puerto Rican Pepperpot," a "triple threat" singer-dancer-actress who debuted in *Rainbow Island* (1944), followed by *Duffy's Tavern* (1945), *Blue Skies* (1946), *Variety Girl* (1947), *One Touch of Venus* (1948), and *The Beautiful Blonde from Bashful Bend* (1949, Fox, director Preston Sturges, starring Betty Grable and César Romero). She was also in *The Third Voice* (1959, Fox).

Lupita Tovar appeared in Captain Calamity (foreign version) (1936), *Blockade* (1938), *The Fighting Gringo, South of the Border, Tropic Fury* (1939), *Green Hell*, and *The Westerner* (1940).

During this period, while Rita Cansino repositioned herself as Rita Hayworth, Lupe Vélez went the other way and was dead at 36. By the late 1930s, Hollywood had seemed to run out of ideas to showcase Lupe Vélez's talent, but her career skyrocketed with her film, *The Girl from Mexico* (1939, RKO). The film subsequently initiated a whole series of second feature comedies all produced by RKO and all directed by Leslie Goodwins known as the Mexican Spitfire films. The series had Vélez as a yelling, kicking, punching, and English-mangling comedienne as the temperamental Mexican wife of a young businessman played by Donald Woods and also included Ziegfield comic Leon Errol in the double role as the businessman's aristocratic boss Lord Epping and as the young man's accident-prone uncle. The plots were exceedingly shallow but the hectic situations provoked gales of laughter. The series consisted of: *The Girl From Mexico, Mexican Spitfire* (1939), *Mexican Spitfire Out West* (1940), *Mexican Spitfire's Baby, Mexican Spitfire at Sea* (1941), *Mexican Spitfire Sees a Ghost, Mexican Spitfire's Elephant* (1942), and *Mexican Spitfire's Blessed Event* (1943). Other films that Vélez did during the period included *High Flyers* (1937), *Six Lessons from Madame La Zonga, Playmates, Honolulu Lu* (1941), *Ladies Day, Redhead*

From Manhattan (1943), and *Nana* (Mexican production, 1944). Lupe Vélez committed suicide in 1944.

Among the films that Raoul Walsh directed during this period were: *Artists and Models*, *Hitting a New High* (1937), *St. Louis Blues*, *The Roaring Twenties* (1939), *Dark Command*, *They Drive by Night* (1940), *High Sierra*, *Strawberry Blonde* (1941), *Desperate Journey*, *Gentleman Jim* (1942), *Background to Danger*, *Northern Pursuit* (1943), *Uncertain Glory* (1944), *Objective Burma!*, *The Horn Blows at Midnight* (1945), *The Man I Love*, *Pursued* (1947), *Silver River*, *Fighter Squadron* (1948), *Colorado Territory*, *White Heat* (1949), *Along the Great Divide*, *Captain Horatio Hornblower*, *Distant Drums* (1951), *Glory Alley*, *The World in his Arms*, *Blackbeard the Pirate* (1952), *The Lawless Breed*, Sea *Devils*, *A Lion Is in the Streets* (1953), *Saskatchewan* (1954), *Battle Cry*, *The Tall Men* (1955), *The Revolt of Mamie Stover*, *The King and Four Queens* (1956), *Band of Angels* (1957), *The Naked and the Dead* (1958), and *A Private's Affair* (1959).

Notes

[1]Ruritania was the imaginary setting of Anthony Hope's novel, *The Prisoner of Zenda* (1894), subsequently made into several films.

[2]Considerable information about Mexican and other Hispanic countries's history of protest appears in García Riera (1987-88), Richard (1992), Aurelio de los Reyes, *Cine y sociedad en México, 1896-1930*, Woll, "Hollywood's Good Neighbor Policy: The Latin American Image in American Film, 1939-1946," Woll, "Latin Images in American Films," and Woll, *The Latin Image in American Film*. While the information from these sources are in general agreement, there is some variation with respect to specific films and the nature and tenor of the protests. A broad history of the difficulties with and protests about United States film among the Spanish-speaking countries still awaits a focused and concerted analysis.

[3]See "Caja de sorpresas," *Tiempo*, March 30, 1945, p. 39 and Christopher Finch, *The Art of Walt Disney: From Mickey Mouse to the Magic Kingdom*, 113-14.

[4]Concerning both tropicalism and Carmen Miranda's subsequent influence in Brazil or by Brazilians in the United States, see Roberts (1993), Randal Johnson and Robert Stam (1982), Caetano Veloso (1991), and Julian Dibbell (1991).

[5]I saw the version of this film that was exported to Mexico (as well as the uncut U.S. version); the Mexican version cut out the entire end of the film, beginning with the notable scene where Rock Hudson gets into a no-holds barred fight with a redneck owner of a greasy spoon diner because the latter refuses to serve his Mexican daughter-in-law.

6

Films Since 1960

The 1960s witnessed two important social developments that had significant impacts on filmmaking: a liberalizing or loosening of social values, often referred to as the sexual revolution, and the emergence of the civil rights movements. The first phenomenon was a factor in the decline of the production code. Beginning in the 1960s, films became much bolder in their depiction of both sex, including interracial sex, and violence. However, this was a double-edged sword for Hispanics and other minorities because often they were cast in roles where their villainy was far more graphic and horrifying than the snarling but ineffective criminal or would-be rapist of blander times. In this sense, the stereotyped depictions of violence and loose morals of many Hispanic characters were much intensified by the relaxation of Hollywood moral codes. Thus, the 1960s and 1970s were marked by far more diversity in films but also by a group of films that featured even more serious, racially damaging put-downs of U.S. Hispanics. For example, the bandidos, federales or revolutionaries, gang members, juvenile delinquents or drug runners were now often engaged in visually explicit and gory violence. The torrid vamp *hispanas* were now engaged in R-rated loose sex with Anglo heroes or an occasional black superstud. The *hispano* became the toy of Anglo producers, directors, and audiences, all competing in the effort to create for Anglos ever more titillating and vicariously experienced films. As a result new subgenres of film emerged, such as the fiendish group of plotters (particularly the group Western or gang film) featuring casual brutality and other actions that Anglos stereotypically and inaccurately identify under the rubric of "macho." Macho entered the Anglo lexicon and films (one film was even titled *Macho Callahan)* in a way that is ungrammatical in Spanish as an abstract quality ("mucho macho" could be heard from time to time in bars or seen on T-shirts around the nation).

Beginning in the late 1960s and 1970s, the Civil Rights movement took hold in the film industry in two separate ways. One was the ethnic exploitation film. The other was the training of a number of Hispanic professionals in the industry who would go on to both figure in the so-called "Hispanic Hollywood" phenomenon, working within the industry to do more pertinent Hispanic films or, working primarily outside of the mainstream, to create independently produced Chicano and occasionally Puerto Rican or Cuban American films.

The period from 1980 to the present has been a relatively exhilarating one for Hispanics in the film industry, and especially since 1987, the year that *La Bamba, Born in East L.A.,* and *The Milagro Beanfield War* were distributed. This has been due primarily to three sets of closely interrelated events or trends. The first has been the increased appreciation of the importance of Hispanic culture and of the Hispanic population in the United States. Demographics projected that Hispanics would become the largest minority group in the United States some time early in the twenty-first century. This underlying fact of population power and consequently political, economic, and cultural importance spurred all sorts of film, television, and video initiatives for and by U.S. Hispanics and even underlay their national promotion, such as an extended article in *Time* magazine which featured James Edward Olmos on its cover, the first time in memory that any U.S. Hispanic had achieved such recognition, much less a U.S. Hispanic actor and filmmaker. A second factor, somewhat encouraged by the Hollywood appreciation of U.S. Hispanic box office potential, was the emergence of a considerable number of actors and filmmakers who attained star status or national recognition during the contemporary period. These included María Conchita Alonso, Rubén Blades, Julie Carmen, Héctor Elizondo, Emilio Estévez, Erik Estrada, Andy García, Raúl Julia, Esai Morales, Edward James Olmos, Elizabeth Peña, Rosie Pérez, Lou Diamond Phillips, Charlie Sheen, Jimmy Smits, Madeleine Stowe, Rachel Ticotin, and Daphne Zúñiga.

Similarly, film figures who had labored under less-recognized conditions in the 1970s also made quantum leaps with respect to their weight in the film industry as producers, directors, or production/financial executives, including Moctesuma Esparza, Luis Valdez, Ricardo Mestre, Richard "Cheech" Marín, Paul Rodríguez, and Martin Sheen. Finally, together with both the factors of more interest in U.S. Hispanic themes and market penetration and more power and recognition by U.S. Hispanic filmmakers and actors, came more control of product within Hollywood. (The emergence of U.S. Hispanic films independent or semi-autonomous of Hollywood is reviewed in the next chapter of this book.) For the first time a Hispanic ran a major studio, Ricardo Mestre of Disney. Similarly, Moctesuma Esparza co-established Esparza/Katz productions, raising tens of millions of dollars for a variety of projects, some but not all Hispanic-focused, and Edward James Olmos, Andy García, Joseph P. Vásquez, and comedian Paul Rodríguez all entered the film production business with considerable diversity in their level of affiliations with or independence from traditional Hollywood sources of backing. Both the number of production outlets and either realized or pending film deals and the number of actors and other filmmakers with national recognition has never been greater, surpassing even a few "silver" years of the silent period when Latin Lovers and hot-blooded Latinas were in great demand, albeit with virtually no control over their acting roles. On the other hand, it should be noted that African-American filmmakers made even greater strides during the current period, led by Spike Lee, John Singleton, and several others.

The Relaxation of Morality Codes and The Western

The most notable development in Westerns during the 1960s and early 1970s was the Spaghetti Western. Hollywood productions of Westerns had waned by 1959. The termination of the studio and other production facilities for B Westerns (and other B films) greatly reduced production and eliminated the careers of various (mostly aged) actors or screenwriters like Oliver Drake who between 1927 and 1949, according to García Riera (1987, Vol. 3, 145) produced over thirty Mexican-themed Westerns. However, the Spaghetti Western emerged to fill this gap in a somewhat new and different way. The Spaghetti Western was partially a creation that reflected on the one hand the artistic trend toward "realism" of the 1960s, particularly in Europe, and on the other hand, the worldwide filmmaking efforts to break down strict censorship and taboos. These initiatives themselves were underpinned by the radical changes in social, sexual, and cultural values and mores in many countries. One effect of these trends, well-represented by the Spaghetti Western, was the increasing prominence of nudity (both with respect to the number of films and the extremity of the phenomenon), interracial sex, rape, and other sexually related crimes and acts of violence, extreme acts of cruelty or sadism, offensive or "dirty" language, and so on.

In Italy, the Spaghetti Western took over among the *grueso público*, the role which in the 1950s had been occupied by shallow films based on classical or mythological subjects (Hercules, Samson, and so on), which have had a long tradition in Italian cinema. Moreover, the Spaghetti Western (often coproduced by Spanish or German interests and set in Spain) had a great international impact, including in the United States and Mexico where they were widely screened.[1] García Riera has found that between the years of 1965 and 1968, the Italian production of Westerns actually exceeded United States production:

	1965	1966	1967	1968
Italian Westerns	25	51	62	68
Hollywood Westerns	24	20	20	19

Nevertheless, the Spaghetti Western was relatively short lived as a major production phenomenon; by 1969 only fifteen Italian Westerns were produced and the genre declined even more rapidly in the 1970s.

While the first major Spaghetti Western, *Per un pugno de dollari/A Fistful of Dollars* was released in 1964 (Italian, West German, Spanish coproduction, released in the United States through United Artists), the concept had already been realized a few years before. One such notable film was *The Savage Innocents*, a Spanish-United States coproduction distributed through MGM a full two years earlier (released in Spain as *Tierra brutal)*, which had the characteristics of the forthcoming Spaghetti Western. The evil bandit leader, Ortega (played by José Nieto) establishes a reign of terror in Mexico with the help of gunman Danny Post (played by Alex Nicol). He is stopped by a good Anglo but not before the latter suffers mutilation of his hands.

However, films like *The Savage Innocents* were not notable productions. At the onset, the Spaghetti Western derived its notoriety and *Per un pugno de dollari/A Fistful of Dollars* its stature in film history primarily because of the technical expertise of director Sergio Leone and acting skill of Clint Eastwood; in turn, the film greatly promoted both of their careers. Like the American productions *The Magnificent Seven* (1960, United Artists) and *The Outrage* (1964, MGM), the movie adapted the plot of a Japanese film (Akira Kurosawa's 1961 *Yojimbo*) and transposed it to the West. The film, set on the border, allegedly in the "lawless" times following the death of president Benito Juárez, features murder, torture, arson, and the kidnapping of a beautiful woman, Marisol, set against an interracial feud between rival clans of contrabanders, the Rojos and the Baxters. *Dollars* is a prominent example of the amoral Western and with it the return of the bad Mexican and the bandido in a more brutal guise reflective of the relaxation of film censorship policies and practices. The enormously successful film quickly generated a sequel, *Per qualche dollari in più/For A Few Dollars More* (1965, Italian,

Spanish, West German coproduction, released in the United States through United Artists) with Clint Eastwood again in the the role of "the man with no name" as a bounty hunter searching for the sadistic rapist/outlaw, Indio. By the time of this second film, the United States market had already dominated box office considerations and the film was not released in Italy, Germany, and Spain until 1966.

The *Dollari* box office successes spawned a host of Spaghetti Westerns simplistically featuring "dollars" in their titles: *Un dollaro tra i denti* (1966), *100,000 dollari per Ringo* (1966), *Sette dollar sul rosso* (1966), *Un fiume di dollari* (1966), *Per mile dollari all giorno* (1966), *Un dollaro a testa* (1966), *Diecimila dollar per un massacro* (1967), *200,000 dollar sul nero* (1967) and the parody of the above, *Per qualche dollari in meno* (1966). And if *dollari* were not suitable in the titles of these copycat films, firearms were used: *Una pistola per Ringo* (1965), *All'omba de una Colt* (1965), *Sette pistole per i MacGregor* (1965), *Trenta Winchester per El Diablo* (1965), and *Le Colt cantarono la morete e fu tempo di massacro* (1966). These films featured "mucho macho" scenes by Bad Mexicans against Anglos, including sadistic bandits whipping pretty women, horse hooves running over the hero's hands, burying heroes in the sand up to their neck, and branding heroes like cattle, in addition to the more conventional varieties of murder, rape, kidnapping, robbery and general villainy. The genre became so widely recognized that it even produced its own film on the paradigm itself, *Spaghetti Western* (1969, [see Martin and Porter, 1992, 1131] starring Martin Balsam and Sterling Hayden) about big-name actors who trek to Italy for dollars to do a Clint Eastwood type film. The film slightly parodied the genre but primarily imitated it, featuring Spaghetti Western style carnage.

In 1966, Leone directed the third of the series: *Il buono, il brutto, il cattivo/The Good, The Bad and The Ugly* (1967, distributed in the United States through United Artists) starring Clint Eastwood, Eli Wallach as the Mexican bandit Tuco the Terrible who liked to cross himself before doing evil (one surmises a certain Italian touch to this feature), and Lee Van Cleef as an even more terrible Setenza. Pettit holds this film as an example of work that closes "the once unbridgeable gap between the heroic Saxon and the wicked greaser" (1980, 214). In this film, typical of the new, amoral Western, both Anglos and Mexicans are equally evil from the moral perspective and good becomes merely identified with technical skills such as a quick draw or creative thievery. When productions were closely monitored and censored, the evil Hispanic was usually a tame utterer of incomplete curses or hisses who was incapable of really delivering the deeds, at least on screen. He might tie the girl to the railroad track or inside a house he would set on fire, but the deed was never consummated. With the relaxation of the Hollywood morality codes this character suddenly became "competent".

Two film critics, the Frenchman Pierre Baudry and the Mexican Tomás Pérez Turrent (see García Riera, 1988, III, 160-61) have made interesting analyses of some Italian contributions to the Spaghetti Western. Baudry finds that some of the basic concepts of the American Western are displaced in the Italian counterpart. The traditional Hollywood outlaw becomes an Italian *forestiero* (stranger), traditional violence is turned into brutality, the adventurer or wanderer of the American Western becomes in the Italian counterpart the "gringo," and the traditional gunfight becomes a final showdown, a *resa dei conti* or *arreglo de cuentas*. Moreover, in contrast to the typical American Western where the Anglo hero needs to construct his own morality and law and order in a place without bounds or civilization, Baudry observes that in the Spaghetti Western the conflict is usually between two civilizations. Mexicans are representatives of Latinness. For his part, Pérez Turrent reviews how Italian scriptwriters introduced the left-leaning conventions of Italy in the 1960s into the plots particularly once the Spaghetti Western had taken off: "The evildoers become good and vice versa. Mexicans are now victims of the rapacity of gringos, fight for their rights and the films display a sort of anti-gringo progressivism. An hour and more of torture and gratuitous sadism, characteristic of almost all of the Spaghetti Westerns, is justified by a democratic subtext filled with edifying leftist maxims (translation mine)."

The financial success of the Spaghetti Western gave new impetus to Hollywood productions in the genre,[2] which in any event had never ceased but only declined in number. While Anglo morality or values descend to the level of the stereotypical bandits in *The Good, the Bad, and the Ugly,* the converse was true in the extremely popular United States produced team-Western, *The Magnificent Seven* (1960, United Artists), (which spawned United Artists sequels: *The Return of the Seven,* 1966, *Guns of the Magnificent Seven,* 1969, *The Magnificent Seven Ride,* 1972, United Artists) where two Mexican characters on the good-Samaritan team are uplifted along with the Anglos in their battle against Calavera, the bad bandido. Unfortunately for Hispanic actors in this film about the defense of a Mexican village against a Mexican bandit, the stereotypical "bandido" role is not even played by a Hispanic but by Eli Wallach, who became the new Leo Carrillo, replaying the greaser-style performance of numerous Spaghetti Westerns. Moreover, Hollywood was perfectly capable of doing its own versions of the Spaghetti-style Western as evidenced by *Bandolero!* (1968, Fox) with Dean Martin, Raquel Welch, and James Stewart, enacting rape, hanging, and much other carnage a la italiano.

Bandolero! was not an isolated example of a film with Spanish in the title. *Hombre* (1967, Fox) was advertised with the slogan, "Hombre means man! . . . and Paul Newman is HOMBRE!" No matter that Paul Newman is not a Hispanic but a supposed Apache who is actually a white boy raised by Apaches. Other Spanish-titled Westerns of the 1960s and early 1970s were *Charro!* (1969, National General), a failed attempt to introduce Elvis Presley as a serious actor; *Chino* (1973, Dino de Laurentis) starring Charles Bronson as a horse breeder trying to lead a peaceful life; *The Comancheros* (1961, Fox, starring John Wayne), *Duel at Diablo* (1966, United Artists, starring James Garner and Sidney Poitier), *El Condor* (1970, National General, starring Jim Brown), *El Dorado* (1967, Paramount, starring John Wayne), *Rio Conchos* (1964, Fox, starring Richard Boone), and *Rio Lobo* (1970, Cinema Center/Howard Hawks, starring John Wayne). *Adios Amigo* (1975, Atlas Productions, starring Richard Pryor) was a parody on the Hollywood Western. Films with Spanish proper names included *Elfego Baca: Six Gun Law* (1962, Disney, starring Robert Loggia) about a Hispanic legendary hero fighting to help an Englishman in Tombstone, Arizona, *Macho Callahan* (1970, Avco/Felicidad, starring David Janssen and Jean Seberg) about a hardened killer, and *Alvarez Kelly* (1966, Columbia, starring William Holden).

Not all Hispanics of the period were competent, macho killers, however. The film industry continued to produce Westerns with some buffoons. *The Sheepman* (1958, MGM, supporting role by Pedro González González) provided a comic sidekick to the Anglo played by Glenn Ford, and in *Río Bravo* (1959, Warner) we view the antics of Carlos and Consuela, a comedy couple. In *The Train Robbers* (1973, Warner), John Wayne's gun quickly turns a Mexican railroad engineer from a "¡No! ¡No!" stance to a "¡Sí! ¡Sí!"

The revival of the Western was the occasion of a number of new productions devoted to legendary or mythical aspects of the West, including Billy the Kid, Joaquín

Murrieta, or the Alamo (see chapter 4). This phenomenon has continued into the present. *Chisum* (1970, Warner Brothers), while it depicted Billy the Kid as an erratic and violent character, is true to the folk concept that he got along well with Mexicans. Sam Peckinpah's excellent film (in the "Restored Director's Cut" version) *Pat Garrett and Billy the Kid* (1973, MGM) continued and reinforced that notion, having the Kid actively aid helpless Hispanics who have been victimized by Anglos. The Kid continued to live into the 1980s and beyond via *Young Guns* (1988, Vestron, starring Emilio Estévez, Lou Diamond Phillips, and Charlie Sheen), which updates the cycle, having us believe that the Kid whips up the inherent violence of six young punks, including Hispanic members. The first film was popular enough to spawn *Young Guns II* (1990, Fox). The two *Young Guns* films serve as "teen fave" vehicles with scripts that are inferior but do contain strong acting performances. Interestingly Estévez plays not a Hispanic but Billy the Kid. The first of the two had Lou Diamond Phillips and Charlie Sheen in it as well. Only Lou Diamond Phillips survived into the second film in which the score and main theme song, "Blaze of Glory" written by Jon Bon Jovi outshine the script. *Gore Vidal's Billy the Kid* (1989, TV film) was a failed attempt to recreate the last years of the Kid. This film, as well as *The Left-Handed Gun* (1958, Warner, starring Paul Newman), both had their roots in a 1955 *Philco Playhouse* TV play that Gore Vidal wrote and in which Newman starred.

The legendary hero Joaquín Murrieta was depicted in the gory mode of the mid-1960s through a Spanish production, *Murieta* (1965, released through Warner Brothers, original title, *Joaquín Murrieta*, starring Jeffrey Hunter and Arthur Kennedy). The film follows the traditional story: Murrieta and his wife, Rosita, emigrate from Mexico to seek their fortune in the California Gold Rush of 1849. They encounter fierce anti-Mexican bigotry and several local toughs rape and murder his wife. Murrieta takes over the leadership of a gang and trains the outlaws as a disciplined army to chastise the gringos. Eventually he is killed by his former friend, the Anglo Captain Love. Another Murrieta film was *The Firebrand* (1962, Fox) starring Valentín de Vargas as Joaquín Murrieta and Kent Taylor as the Major Bancroft who pursues him.

The revival of the Western also affected the careers of actors not earlier associated with roles in that genre. Marlon Brando was cast in several movies during the 1960s after his role as Emiliano Zapata in *Viva Zapata!* (1952, Fox) including *One-Eyed Jacks* (1960, Paramount) where he did a Mexicanized gringo bandit and *The Appaloosa* (1966, Universal) where he dressed like a Mexican in order to recover his stolen horse from a Mexican bandit. He did other Westerns as well, but not in the role of a Hispanic. Emilio "El Indio" Fernández, who had done Mexican bandits many years earlier, reprised this character, playing an evil Mexican official, Sargento López, in the twentieth-century Western *The Reward* (1965, Twentieth Century Fox) starring Max von Sydow (imported from Ingemar Bergman's Sweden) and Yvette Mimieux.

Because of the trend toward amorality, the films produced in the 1960s and 1970s that treated the Mexican Revolution of 1910 or the struggle of the *juaristas* seriously distorted history, taking the image of Hispanics and the understanding of those events a giant step backward from the peak that was established by the 1952 *Viva Zapata!* In the amoral Westerns of director Sergio Leone which were also set in war period, *A Fistful of Dollars*, its sequel *For A Few Dollars More*, and *Duck, You Sucker* (1972, United Artists, also *A Fistful of Dynamite*), the viewer is given no moral guidelines to measure or judge history. Both the *federales* and the rebels are repulsive. If the former are sadistic, pretentious, class-conscious, and stupid, the latter are sadistic, filthy, promiscuous, contemptuous, and stupid.

The cycle of Pancho Villa movies displays the same sort of denigration. The first Villa film of the sound era, *Viva Villa!* (1934) presented the revolutionary hero "as a cross between Robin Hood and the Marquis de Sade" (Pettit, 1980, 220). Subsequent films, *Villa!* (1958, Fox), *Villa Rides* (1968, Paramount), and *Pancho Villa* (1972, Spanish production starring Telly Savalas) stray little from this general depiction. Only the latest film to depict Villa, *Old Gringo* (1989, Columbia), based on a novel by Mexican Carlos Fuentes and produced by Jane Fonda with the avowed intention of injecting realism into the relationship between the United States and Mexico, stands in marked positive contrast to the rest of the cycle.

Set against the simplistic, amoral standard of most of the Spaghetti Westerns and other Hollywood Westerns of these years, the work of Sam Peckinpah, particularly *The Wild Bunch* (1969, Warner Seven Arts), *Pat Garrett and Billy the Kid* (1973, MGM), and *Bring Me the Head of Alfredo García* (1974, United Artists), developed a more sophisticated view of Hispanics, particularly in the context of the Mexican Revolution in the case of the first film. In *The Wild Bunch*, the two Mexicos of the Revolution are contrasted through Angel, the morally pure *Villista* who represents Mexican village life, and Mapache, the degenerated revolutionary. In a film that is, ironically, one of the most violent on record, Angel occupies a pivotal role in that by his Christ-like example he turns the drifting, amoral Anglo mercenaries to good purpose and sacrifice, thus redeeming them. *The Wild Bunch* is one of the most memorable films of the period, combining outsized violence and explicit sex together with a certain sense of high moral purpose and interethnic camaraderie. In its own way, it is a distinctively realized combination of the decline of the moral code and the rise of civil rights.

The emergence of the civil rights movement could have subtle effects even on the Western of the period. For example, a Chicano flavor or sensibility appears in *Land Raiders* (1969, Columbia), an otherwise forgettable film about the rivalry between two Mexican American brothers in Arizona. Telly Savalas plays the evil brother who rejects his Mexican origin and George Maharis the good brother who accepts it. Even film titles became different and strange when compared to earlier decades: *Alvarez Kelly* (1966, Columbia) had William Holden play an Irish-Mexican, good-bad opportunist during the Civil War.

A more significant film was *The Professionals* (1966, Colombia) directed by Richard Brooks, who was noted for other "fair play" films including *The Blackboard Jungle* (1955, MGM), *The Last Hunt* (1956, MGM), *Something of Value* (1957, MGM), and *Elmer Gantry* (1960, United Artists). In this Western, tenuously related to the Mexican Revolution, four soldiers-of-fortune attempt to rescue the kidnapped Mexican wife from the guerrilla-bandit captain with a name no less than Jesús Raza (Jack Palance) but ultimately learn that she is not kidnapped and the two are lovers. The professionals help the Mexicans escape at the end of the film. Evocative of the early civil rights climate, one of the professionals, played by Burt Lancaster, talks about how from the beginning of time there has only been one revolution, that of the exploited against the exploiters.

The Hispanic Avenger and Hispanic Exploitation Films

The milieu of loosened production censorship and subsequently increased sensitivity to civil rights not only affected the Western, it led to the figure of the Hispanic avenger, a character who appeared in Westerns almost exclusively. This figure was modeled on the example of the black avenger who appeared primarily in urban crime films. Both the black and Hispanic aggressive, superstud types reflected growing Hollywood awareness of the changing population distribution of its market, namely that ever-increasing percentages of blacks and Hispanics attend the movies. Although this demographic fact provided the underpinning for the superstud phenomenon it doesn't explain the inciting reason for the sudden creation of the genre nor its content. For an explanation of the mechanisms that triggered the black and Hispanic superstud characters we need to turn to the climate of civil rights legislation and to the changes in prevailing cultural attitudes in the 1960s and 1970s.

Periodically in the late 1950s and early 1960s, *Variety* and other trade journals took note of the "growing Negro audience" which was "now a sizable segment of film patronage as a whole" (*Variety*, May 9, 1956, 5 and May 8, 1957, 3). These observations made little difference at the time. In 1963, however, in the midst of the civil rights movement, after the National Association for the Advancement of Colored People (NAACP) abandoned mere persuasion and threatened to take legal and economic action against the industry, blacks began to play police officers, civil servants, students, and workers both in features and in movies and shows filmed and taped for television. Chicano scholar Carlos Cortés (1983, 1984) has documented a similar practice of giving bit parts to *hispanos*.

Goaded by the civil rights movement and sensing that the mood of black militancy could be used to its advantage in the creation of a new film type, Hollywood responded with the "superspade" formula (Leab, 1975), and thus was born a new form, the "blaxploitation" film. An NAACP official condemned the transformation "to supernigger as just another form of cultural genocide" but black moviegoers, finding the superspade an emotionally satisfying tonic to the patient black represented by Sidney Poitier features, turned out in mass and "produced the first gold mine in years for the struggling industry" (*Newsweek*, Oct. 23, 1972, 74).

It was Sidney Poitier's success that had brought home to filmmakers just how significant a percentage of the moviegoing public was black: in 1967 Poitier was one of the top five box office draws in the United States. According to a 1967 estimate, although blacks represented only about 15 percent of the American population, they accounted for roughly 30 percent of the moviegoing audience in the nation's cities, where the biggest movie theaters were located. As one industry executive summed up the situation, "the black population of this country comprises a much larger proportion of the movie picture audience than its proportion of our total population would indicate" (*Variety*, August 26, 1970, 5). Once the industry grasped this fact, filmmakers began to reappraise and revise their product.

The new, aggressive, and hip black audience found its first star in Jim Brown, the football star, who ironically but not surprisingly often scored macho coups at the expense of Hispanics and American Indians. In *Río Conchos* (1964), Brown refuses to repay Indian brutality in kind with the terse comment that "doing like they do, don't make it right," and in *100 Rifles* (1969, Fox) he beds Raquel Welch, who in this early example of explicit interracial sex is treated as white in the movie's promotion, but who turns out to be a half-caste Mexican in the actual production itself.

When Brown's career declined, partly due to personal problems, other black superstuds emerged, including Ossie Davis in *The Scalphunters* (1968, United Artists), Roscoe Lee Browne in *The Liberation of L.B. Jones* (1969, Columbia), Raymond St.

Jacques in *If He Hollers Let Him Go* (1968, Forward Films), Godfrey Cambridge in *Cotton Comes to Harlem* (1970, United Artists) and *Come Back, Charleston Blue* (1972, Warner, a sequel to *Cotton*), Melvin Van Peebles in *Sweet Sweetback's Baadasss Song* (1971, Cinemation Industries, a film which transcends the blaxploitation formula both in pretension and achievement), Richard Roundtree in *Shaft* (1971, MGM) and its MGM sequels, *Shaft's Big Score* (1972) and *Shaft in Africa* (1973), the Gordon Parks, Jr.-directed *Super Fly* (1972, Warner, the most financially profitable of the genre), Calvin Lockhart in *Melinda* (1972, MGM), Fred Williamson in *Black Caesar* (1973, American International), and many others.

The black superstud films, despite the early Jim Brown vehicles that included Westerns and war roles such as *The Dirty Dozen* (1967, MGM), were mostly set in the black urban milieu. The same market considerations (drawing a new ethnic group to the box office in a more substantive way), civil rights prodding, and increased Hispanic militancy in the United States affected the creation of the Hispanic macho, whose films were set in the Western genre. An early, transitional example of the type, still displaying the qualities of the Spaghetti Western and its Hollywood clones was *The Violent Ones* (1967, Feature Film Corp. of America), starring Fernando Lamas, in which a local manita is raped and beaten in a small New Mexico town. Before she dies she identifies her assailant merely as a "gringo." Three suspects are brought in and become the objects of a Chicano lynch mob. Lamas, the deputy sheriff, saves the suspects and extracts a confession from one of them. In *Río Lobo* (1970, Twentieth Century Fox), Jorge Rivero helps John Wayne bring Arizona landgrabbers to justice with a dazzling combination of gunplay and oriental martial arts. The Mexican American deputy sheriff played by Burt Lancaster in *Valdez is Coming* (1971, United Artists) single-handedly defeats a brutal cattle baron and his army. The bizarre plot of *Mr. Majestyk* (1974, United Artists) carries the super-Mex formula to absurd lengths. The hero, half-Mexican, half-Slavic (why not two ethnicities for the price of one?) Vincent Majestyk (Charles Bronson) keeps the Mafia out of his melon patch by hiring Mexican migrants instead of the American winos who are thrust upon him by labor racketeers.

Sporadic examples of Hispanic avenger types emerged during the silent period (see chapters 3 and 4), although not usually directed to Anglos but rather against *federales* of the Mexican government. Also, in the Western *The Ox-Bow Incident* (1943, Fox) Anthony Quinn plays a Mexican who is hanged along with two Anglos for murdering a Nevada cowboy. Of the three outlaws, he is the only one to die with his dignity and honor intact, subverting the stereotypical role of the cowardly and inept "greaser." These pre-civil rights examples, however, have a quite different tone about them, primarily because they were pitched to a non-Hispanic audience. This is the case as well of the films *Death of a Gunfighter* (1969, Universal) and *The Outrage* (1964) which also depict assertive Hispanics even though they are not part of the Hispanic exploitation model. In *Death of a Gunfighter*, the aging white marshall (Richard Widmark) has become an embarrassment to a prospering Kansas town that no longer needs him. In the final, shocking scene, the shopkeepers and bankers gun him down, leaving his Chicana mistress without a husband after a last-minute wedding ceremony. However, in the figure of Lou Trinidad (played by John Saxon) we are confronted with a different sort, a Chicano survivor, a Mexican sheriff who knows his "place" and adopts the necessary public servility to make his way. He publicly tolerates epithets like "greaseball" and "Mex" but exacts his private physical revenge on the name-callers. Trinidad is a cautious but brave loner caught between the Anglo power structure and the oppressed

Mexican populace. *The Outrage* is a remake of the classic Japanese film, *Rashomon*, and features Paul Newman as a Mexican who murders the husband and rapes the wife. Newman's character observes that if he were freed he would wreak revenge on his oppressors; this is a direct threat to the Anglo social order that was not often tolerated in earlier films. The film reflects the morality of the genre in the Spaghetti Western period but its radicalism is merely an artifact of attempting to transplant a samurai story to the U.S. Southwest.

It should be noted that the Hispanic avenger type appears far less frequently than his black counterpart. One of the reasons is that the genre diminished greatly beginning in 1974, which was a bust year, and the Hispanic version got off to a much later start. Also, the Hispanic market, particularly in the late 1960s, was much smaller than the black market. An additional reason is that neither the black nor brown versions of the genre attracted white audiences, making for a limited run of this type of film, Finally, the genre itself was initially successful for its novelty value but soon became boring and wearing even for the black or Hispanic moviegoers to whom the films were directed.

Interplay in Other Film Genres between Relaxation of Censorship and Rise of Civil Rights

The crosscurrents and interplay of two major factors of the 1960s and 1970s, the relaxation of censorship and the rise of civil rights, not only affected the Western and the rise of the Hispanic avenger within the Western. Ironically, these trends served to reduce the number of roles for Hispanic actresses and actors because they reduced the casting of "dark ladies" (we have usually separated this category into more specific roles such as cantina dancer and vamp; see chapter 3) and "Latin Lovers." Beginning in the 1960s and intensifying in the 1970s, changes in American society and consequently American film and television made the roles of "dark lady" and "Latin Lover" considerably less important. One of these changes related to ethnicity. Particularly in the 1970s, Hollywood and other media centers rediscovered the significance of ethnicity, both from the point of view of plot and of box office. However, the ethnicities that were cultivated were primarily the Italian/Italian American, and secondarily Jewish American, Slavic, and through the blaxploitation model, African American. This period witnessed the rise to stardom of such actors as Robert De Niro, Sylvester Stallone, Al Pacino, Barbra Streisand, and others. However, the cultivation of various U.S. cultures and ethnicities primarily reflected English-speaking groups, not Spanish or other non-English speakers. In the increased attention to multiethnicity, the Hispanic variety played a limited role. The phenomenon of increased multiculturalism in plots and acting styles combined with yet another factor to the detriment of *hispanidad* in film, namely the expectation of increased sexuality on the part of actors and actresses, irrespective of their culture. In earlier decades the "carnal" tended to be the province of Hispanic Latin Lovers and dark ladies. Or as Freddy Prinze once joked, "If you're Hispanic, man, they think you really *got* something downstairs" (Hadley-García, 1990, 201). While this expectation produced degrading stereotypes, it also provided considerable work for Hispanic actors and actresses who consistently had roles exposing their "hot-blooded" nature. In contrast to the earlier traditions of WASPs and some of the other ethnicities who were expected to be aloof, glacial, dispassionate, and so on, the film expectations of the 1960s and onward cultivated unabashed carnality and hot bloodedness on the part of all actors and actresses, whatever their national origin. Thus, essentially as a result of the fall of censorship and the rise of many ethnicities, few of the traditional dark lady or Latin Lover films were made. Or if they were, they were minor productions such as *Fun in Acapulco* (1963, Paramount) where the character played by Elsa Cárdenas goes down to defeat for the affections of Elvis Presley at the hands of the blonde played by Ursula Andress.

On the other hand, Hispanics continued to obtain roles not only as hot-blooded and sexual but immoral or evil as well. Hispanics still functioned in their traditional role as one of the out-groups capable of radically bad deeds. In fact, precisely because of the relaxation of censorship, a number of films tilted toward the salacious. *The Devil's Sisters* (1966, Thunderbird International Pictures) depicted evil Mexican sisters based in Tijuana who ran a white slavery ring and tortured their female victims. In *Walk on the Wild Side* (1962, Columbia, an early Jane Fonda film), Anne Baxter played Teresina Vidaverri, a sex-starved Mexican widow who operates a café in New Orleans.

Also attributable to a franker, less censored film climate, the use of "bean," a more chic variety of the older dysphemism, "beaner," came back into vogue. The World War II film *Midway* (1976) included a Hispanic character nicknamed Chili Bean. Similarly, *Freebie and the Bean* (1974, Warner) provided Alan Arkin work as the Bean; this film led to a television series with the same title except that an actual Hispanic, Héctor Elizondo, got the opportunity to play the Bean.

Other films tilted more on the exploitation avenger model, depicting Hispanics either successfully thwarting evil Anglos or obtaining their just revenge. *Big Enough N' Old Enough* (1968, Trans-International Films) had the leader of "The Black Angels" motorcycle gang attempt to rape Teresa, the teenage daughter of a Mexican American migrant laborer. Teresa kills the gang leader and is rescued by her brother, Marco. *The Young Animals* (1968, American International Films) is a modest production starring Tom Nardini as a Mexican American teenager who attempts to help other Chicano students at a border high school. The film emphasizes interracial rape and violence (Anglo gang members rape a Mexican girl; a Mexican teenager kidnaps one of the gang members in retaliation). The final scene has the entire student body picketing the school on behalf of the Mexican Americans and forcing the principal to give a hearing to student demands.

The Hispanic community, following the lead (although with fewer concrete results) of the African American community were also able to eliminate some of the more egregious visual stereotypes. The protests of Hispanic community-based and professional organizations put to rest company stereotype characters such as Frito-Lay's Frito Bandito, a version of the Mexican bandit, and Chiquita Banana, loosely based on the persona of Carmen Miranda. Also Bill Dana, the creator of the comic bellhop, dim-witted speaker of fractured English, José Jiménez (who was the most popular Hispanic TV character of the 1960s among the general public, surpassing Desi Arnaz and Duncan Renaldo's *Cisco Kid)*, agreed at the 1970 meeting of the Congress of Mexican American Unity to shelve this persona. In addition to eliminating stereotypes, some progress was made on television on behalf of more positive characters, notably Linda Cristal, who debuted on the television series, *High Chaparral* (1967). Observing in 1982 about her role in the series as a powerful *hispana,* Cristal remarked: "I was very conscious of being a role model. I received countless letters from the Spanish-speaking fans. . . ." (Hadley-García, p. 199). However, holding out for better roles also had the consequence of reduced work opportunities for Rita Moreno, the first Hispanic to win an Academy Award. While Moreno courageously turned her back on the opportunity to do "looney Latina" roles, between 1964 and 1968 she rarely appeared on screen, observing:

> It's really demeaning after you've won the Oscar to be offered the same role over and over again. They only wanted me to drag out my accent-and-dance show over and over again. And boy, I was offered them all—gypsy fortune tellers, Mexican spitfires, Puerto Ricans. . . . (Hadley-García, 174)

Other actresses were less finicky. In the comic mode, the period marked the rise of Charo taking up where Lupe Vélez had left off in a familiar role of flake and spouter of malaprops.

The Proliferation of Gang Films

Gang films, focusing on juveniles, date back in the U.S. film industry to the earliest days of the silent period, before the move to Hollywood, with the bad boy films. The genre was not associated particularly with Hispanics, however, until the 1960s. In the 1950s, a few films of the social problem type such as *The Lawless* and *Trial* (see chapter 5) had adults defending Hispanic boys and in these films there was a secondary element related to groups of youths. Nevertheless, youth gang films focusing on Hispanics were a product originating in the 1960s and they have abounded ever since. The Hispanic gang films are another genre that reflect the relaxation of censorship in film productions, and generally, like the amoral Westerns, the urban violence, primarily juvenile gang films have been exploitative of Anglo willingness to pay for explicit sex and brutality—both premeditated and mindless—and the pleasures of vicariously induced but movie-house controlled fear of the alien, as in the horror movie. These films play upon the baser assumptions about Hispanic youth and mostly do damage to racial relations in our society. To add insult to injury, most of the time Hispanic actors did not even get the top parts in these films.

West Side Story (1961, United Artists, director Robert Wise, starring Natalie Wood, Richard Beymer, George Chakiris, and Rita Moreno), the cinematic adaptation of the Broadway musical, was a major achievement of the period and of course a film that transcends the gang film genre. Unfortunately, only one Hispanic, Rita Moreno, had a major role in the film. This update of Romeo and Juliet had a major influence on the Broadway musical, but in drawing attention to Hispanic gangs, its greatest impact on Hispanic-focused material appears to have been to help turn the juvenile gang or delinquent film away from blacks primarily (e.g., *The Blackboard Jungle*, MGM, 1955, starring Glenn Ford and Sidney Poitier) to the direction of Hispanics. It was probably a factor in a spate of either Hispanic-focused, exploitation, juvenile delinquent/gang films or films with other premises that brought in Hispanic gang members for their recognition value in films such as *The Pawnbroker* (1965, Allied Artists, starring Rod Steiger with Jaime Sánchez and Juano Hernández in supporting roles), and *Change of Habit* (1969, Universal, starring Elvis Presley).

In any event, the genre began to focus on Hispanics in the 1960s. *The Young Savages* (1961, United Artists) starred Burt Lancaster with Pilar Seurat as the Puerto Rican mother who demands justice for her dead blind son (who is also a pimp for his sister, a prostitute). *The Wild Angels* (1966, American International Pictures, starring Peter Fonda, Bruce Dern, and Nancy Sinatra) was about the Hell's Angels, with a Mexican

American motorcycle doing counterpart as the rival group. *The Young Animals* (see preceding section) is another example of this type of film.

In the 1970s, the Hispanic-focused or multiethnic versions of the genre really took off with *Badge 373* (1973, Paramount), *Assault on Precinct Thirteen* (1976, CKK/Joseph Kaufman, director John Carpenter), *Boardwalk* (1979, ITC/Stratford), *Boulevard Nights* (1979, starring Richard Yniguez and Danny de la Paz), *Walk Proud* (1979, featuring blue-eyed Robby Benson in contact lenses as a Hispanic), *The Warriors* (1979, Paramount), and many others. Other films of the same general stripe didn't single out Hispanics but merely included them among other various and sundry riffraff: *Dirty Harry* (1971, Warner), *The French Connection* (1971, Fox), *The New Centurions* (1972, Columbia), *The Seven-Ups* (1973, Fox), *Magnum Force* (1974, Warner), *Death Wish* (1974, Paramount), and *Fort Apache-The Bronx* (1981, Time Life/Producer Circle). Puerto Rican gang members appeared in *Night of the Juggler* (1980, Columbia, with Julie Carmen in a supporting role), which was primarily about a psychopath's kidnapping of the daughter of an ex-cop who leads a city-wide rampage to get her back.

In *Badge 373*, a minor follow-up to *The French Connection*, Robert Duvall plays a cop who single-handedly fights the mafia as well as Puerto Ricans, who are blamed for all sorts of evil and wrongdoing. *Boulevard Nights* rose above the pap; this sincere but conventionalized story about a Chicano youth who yearns to move away from street-gang life can point to an all Latino cast, reasonably successful use of Chicano and pachuco dialect, and a serious theme and plot development that includes Hispanic violence against Hispanics—an all too real phenomenon of gang life. It deserves recognition, within B-movie limitations, as one of the better Hollywood achievements in Chicano-focused film. *The Warriors*, although its artistry demands more respect than most of the others, primarily perpetuates the usual stereotypes.

With the aid of feverish media attention dedicated to gangs, the cycle has been running strong to the present day. *The Exterminator* (1980, Interstar) and *The Exterminator II* (1984, Cannon) copycat the plot of *Death Wish*. Esai Morales, an excellent actor who made a name for himself in *La Bamba* but who has been typecast merely as a Hispanic gang member, got to do his repartee also in *The Principal* (1987), featuring Jim Belushi as a principal fighting to keep his students safe from school thugs, another example of the heroic school authority versus gang film. The principal overpowers the Hispanic youth warlord in a fashion reminiscent of the way honest Anglo do-gooders used to bring down Hispanic and other alien power brokers in the 1940s films about Washington, DC. In *Stand Alone* (1985), a similar, but more vigilantist film, Charles Durning plays a war vet who goes after Latino thugs who are preying on the neighborhood. On the other hand, *Colors* (1988, director Dennis Hopper, starring Sean Penn and Robert Duvall with María Conchita Alonso, Rudy Ramos, and Trinidad Silva in supporting roles) was a superior version of the genre, representing an advance in the Hollywood understanding of gang psychology. Unfortunately, the film misused Alonso in a silly romantic subplot. Trinidad Silva was as excellent in this film as he was in *The Night Before* (1988), an offbeat comedy about a young man on a senior prom who wakes up in an East Los Angeles alley. *Bound by Honor* (1993, also released as *Blood In, Blood Out*, Hollywood Pictures, director Taylor Hackford with Jimmy Santiago Baca receiving partial credit as scriptwriter), starring Jesse Borrego, Damian Chapa, and Benjamin Bratt, is a superior version of the genre. Taking the old convention of family members or friends growing up together and emerging on different sides of the law, this film, which has a script emerging from the same roots as *American Me* (see chapter 7) sometimes goes overboard but it makes use of credible Chicano speech and characterizations to evoke gang, family, and prison life.

John Singleton's *Boyz N the Hood* (1991, Columbia) about black gangs and Vásquez's *Hangin' with the Homeboys*, (1991, New Line Cinema) are in a class by themselves but essentially were created outside of the Hollywood system (see chapter 7).

The "Hispanic Hollywood" Phenomenon

Between the summer of 1987 and spring 1988, Hollywood released four films that depicted the Chicano experience: *La Bamba* (1987, Columbia), *Born in East L.A.* (1987, Universal), *The Milagro Beanfield War* (1987, Universal), and *Stand and Deliver* (1988, Warner/American Playhouse). As Chon Noriega (1991, 55) points out, these films were seen as part of a new phenomenon, a hybrid called "Hispanic Hollywood" by the mass media such as *Time* magazine which depicted actor (and subsequently director) Edward James Olmos on the cover of its July 11, 1988, issue (Vol 132, No. 2). The term Hispanic Hollywood has significantly entered the discourse of general interest, business, and industry magazines (see Noriega, 1990-91, p. 55ff; Noriega, 1988-90) such as *Newsweek, Time, Advertising Age, Variety,* and other publications, focusing not only on film products but on the potential of the Hispanic market. For example, market studies done for the film industry estimate that the Hispanic population, estimated at about 25 million, approximates in its movie-going behavior the peak audiences during the 1930s and 1940s who went to the theaters on a regular basis rather than to see a specific film.

As we have seen in previous chapters, even from the beginning of film production in every period there have been a few films sympathetic to Hispanics or which were controlled to a greater degree by Hispanic industry figures. In the silent period there were the faithful señoritas and the faithful male Mexicans and even the Hispanic avengers. From time to time, as in the case of *The Pearl* (1948, RKO), a Hispanic-produced film was released in the market, usually by Mexican interests. However, the Hispanic Hollywood phenomenon was something new, albeit a phenomenon that was a long time in the making until it broke open with a vengeance and became readily apparent. Hispanic Hollywood could not have occurred without the Civil Rights movement which provided in the 1960s and 1970s two essential preconditions. One was the training of U.S. Hispanic filmmakers who would take positions of authority and leadership in the creation of a few but highly significant U.S. Hispanic films in the 1980s. The second was the sensitivity toward and acceptance of U.S. Hispanic story lines, character depictions, and plot conflicts from a Hispanic point of view, which the Civil Rights movement gradually facilitated.

Another significant, albeit complex factor, was the heterogenization and globalization to some degree of the U.S. film industry itself. This trend can be traced at least to the 1950s and 1960s phenomenon of film production (primarily of Westerns) in Mexico and soon after the rise of the Spaghetti Western as a vehicle for international coproduction. As a result of a considerable number of productions in Mexico in the 1950s, many Mexicans and some Spaniards entered the U.S. film industry. While they did not gain control over film productions, the pump was primed for more Hispanic participation in U.S. films. Moreover, with the emergence of the Spaghetti Western, film in the 1960s became more globalized. Films released in the United States could be funded in part by West Germany, shot in Spain, and feature Mexican, U.S. Hispanic, Spanish, or Italian actors in some of the Hispanic roles. The model of coproduction also fit the marketing economics of U.S. film beginning in the 1960s. The foreign market became an ever more important consideration in putting together a film, and in the case of Hispanic-focused productions, the Spanish-speaking countries of Latin America and in Europe, Spain, were given special marketing attention. While the globalization of U.S. film was a secondary factor in the creation of Hispanic Hollywood it was significant and it also helps explain the parallel importation of Latin American and Spanish directors and actors (e.g., Norma Aleandro, Néstor Almendros, Hector Babenco, Antonio Banderas, Barbara Carrera, Luis Puenzo, and others) parallel to but also spurred by the Hollywood-authorized rise of U.S. Hispanic figures, such as Edward James Olmos, Moctesuma Esparza, "Cheech" (Richard) Marín, and Raúl Julia.

Although Chicano films such as *Zoot Suit* (1981, Universal, however, the film was essentially a filmic rendition of the play rather than a wholly independent production) had been released by the mainstream industry before, the phenomenon achieved major status in the mid-1980s. The Hispanic directors, producers, and writers who made these films had typically been given junior roles by the film and television industry in the 1960s and then began to work as principals in the conceptualization, development, and execution of alternative, independent U.S. Hispanic films, such as *Los vendidos, Seguín, Alambrista!, The Ballad of Gregorio Cortez,* or *Once in a Lifetime* in the 1970s and early 1980s (see chapter 7). They reentered the mainstream (although not necessarily giving up their commitments to independent, alternative films or in the case of *Raíces de sangre*, a Mexican production) bringing Hollywood production values to the creation of strong Hispanic images that also had (or at least were intended to have) box office appeal and establishing distribution through mainstream outlets. The cross-pollination and collaboration inherent in the Hispanic Hollywood phenomenon ran the gamut. At one pole is *The Milagro Beanfield War* where Anglos like Robert Redford carried most of the picture (the script itself being based on the novel by Anglo connoisseur of New Mexican culture, John Nichols) and consequently Hispanics like Moctesuma Esparza had highly significant but less than primary roles. At the other pole are *Stand and Deliver* and *El mariachi* where essentially the entire film including scripting, producing, financing, directing, and acting was controlled by Hispanics up to the point of distribution, when the appeal of the film earned its release through the industry mainstream. Somewhere between those two extremes is *La Bamba*. It was created more on the model of a coproduction between Taylor Hackford's production company New Visions, Columbia, the studio which distributed the film, and Luis Valdez, the director and writer of the film, with Valdez entrusted with most but not all of the artistic control and the New Visions and Columbia providing technical support, financing, and marketing/distribution.

La Bamba reprises the career of 1950s teenage rock-n-roll singer Ritchie Valens (Valenzuela), whose emerging career was cut short by a plane crash in 1959 that also killed Buddy Holly and The Big Bopper. The film had strong appeal in diverse markets. Hispanic viewers liked it for its stirring plot and authenticity of character, languages (bilingualism), and locale, and for its theme of identity formation and family rivalry and cooperation. In critical ways the film is eminently Chicano: the intensive use of bilingualism, the focus on Chicano characters, the evocation of the Chicano lifestyle, the connections it makes between Mexico and U.S. Hispanic border culture, epitomized by the song "La bamba" itself which became emblematic of a Hispanic binationalism that binds those who live *aquí* and those who live *allá*. Although the film has also been criticized in the Chicano community and by Anglo critics as an American success film that supports an assimilationist ideology, those elements appear mostly to derive from the biography of Valens himself and are not imposed on the film as was the case of the social problem examples made by Anglos in the 1930s through the 1950s. *La Bamba* was also a significant "crossover" success, appealing to teenagers of all cultures both in the United States and internationally. It featured stirring music that could be related to universally even though much of it was genuinely Hispanic, nostalgia for the early rock-n-roll period, a teenage love and tragedy story that viewers around the globe could easily empathize with, and psychological themes that could be readily identified with irrespective of culture. A film that rarely compromised on its Hispanicity, it also had that universal appeal that makes for an enduring work of art.

La Bamba was important not only for its artistic qualities but because it also proved itself financially successful in the United States not only in the English-language release, but the Spanish one as well. A record seventy-seven Spanish-language prints were released and the Hispanic market provided a two-to-one return over mainstream audiences on costs. (Columbia allocated 5 percent of its distribution and advertising budget to the Hispanic market which in turn accounted for 10 percent of the viewers and the box office receipts.) Yet despite the success of *La Bamba* and the predictions that both the Hispanic Hollywood phenomenon and the film career of Luis Valdez would take off, the situation has been quite to the contrary. The Hispanic Hollywood phenomenon has been characterized by a slow and erratic course; a small accretion of films with U.S. Hispanic plots or themes have been added to the corpus. The rate of Hollywood productions of U.S. Hispanic-focused films has paled beside the the opportunities Hollywood has recently afforded Hispanic actors to do roles of various sorts, as Hispanics (in Latin America, or as drug dealers, vamps, gang members, or detectives) or in non-Hispanic character parts.

If the peculiarities of *La Bamba* precluded it from having a conflict predicated on cultural thems versus us, the other three initial Hispanic Hollywood films were premised on a conflict between Hispanics and Anglos. *Born in East L.A.* (1987, Universal) marked Richard "Cheech" Marín's debut as director and also his first film without former partner Tommy Chong. The film, based on a video parody of Bruce Springsteen's song "Born in the U.S.A." also parodies past U.S. policies toward immigrants, including the deportation of Chicanos, most of whom were either born in the United States or are legal residents. *Stand and Deliver* (1988, director Ramón Menéndez) has been both an artistic and critical triumph and a box office success. Although released theatrically by Warner Brothers, it is essentially a Hispanic film and will be discussed in the following chapter. *The Milagro Beanfield War* (1988, director Robert Redford) was the least artistically realized of this group; it also was a financial failure. As Noriega (1991, 64) has pointed out, this beautiful film was variously seen as a "progressive fairy tale" by most Anglo reviewers, but as an example of "magic realism" (associated with Latin American authors including Nobel Prize winner Gabriel García Márquez) by some Hispanic reviewers, thus giving compelling documentation to the fact that films are criticized not in a vacuum but from definite and often divergent cultural, political, or racial/ethnic perspectives. However, with respect to character development and depth of plot the film does not succeed.

Not only U.S. Hispanics got an opportunity to create Hispanic Hollywood. Luis Puenzo, director of the remarkable, Academy Award-winning Argentine film *The Official Story* (1985), was able to break into Hollywood as the director of *Old Gringo* (1989, Columbia), an intense, beautifully filmed epic about a young revolutionary

Mexican general (Jimmy Smits), Ambrose Bierce (Gregory Peck), and a spinster (Jane Fonda) set against the background of the Mexican Revolution of 1910. The film, based on a screenplay by Carlos Fuentes, was not financially successful but it provides a much more realistic view of Mexico and the border area than most Hollywood films. Its depiction of Pancho Villa is probably the most sophisticated that has been achieved to date by American film. Norma Aleandro, who was named best actress at Cannes for her wonderful performance in *The Official Story* (1985), crossed over into American (but not U.S. Hispanic-focused) films, *Cousins* (1989, Paramount), *Vital Signs* (1990, Twentieth Century Fox), and others, even as she continued to do Spanish-language films. Leon Ichaso, who first directed *El Super* (1979), a Spanish-language film billed as the first Cuban American comedy film about the trials of a homesick Cuban exile who labors as a "super" in a Manhattan apartment building, represents another example of Hispanic Hollywood. He went on to direct *Crossover Dreams* (1985, independent production), starring Panamanian Rubén Blades, which did in fact cross over to Anglo audiences. The film evokes the life of a salsa performer hoping to become a mainstream performer but whose record flops. He then finds solace in his own roots and culture.

Hector Babenco, noted for his direction of *Pixote* (1981), was able to leverage that Brazilian film about a child street criminal. He directed the United States/Brazilian co-adaptation of Manuel Puig's novel, *Kiss of the Spider Woman* (1985), an extraordinary movie about an apolitical homosexual (William Hurt) and a political activist (Raúl Julia) thrown in the same prison cell. (Hurt won the Oscar as best actor for his portrayal.) Babenco went on to do a film without Hispanic content, *Ironweed* (1987, Taft Entertainment/Home Box Office, starring Jack Nicholson and Meryl Streep) about street people in Albany, New York during the Great Depression.

It is instructive to note that the Hispanic Hollywood juxtaposition has permitted novel sorts of interactions. For example, it is now documentably possible to put additional pressure on Hollywood through the intermediary of the Hispanic representative working with the major studios. We now see instances where the Hispanic professional film community accuses the Hispanic filmmaker of selling out to Hollywood. Moreover, the relationship between Hispanic filmmaker and Hollywood studios is such that the filmmaker can often pass the blame to the supposed higher-ups. One example of this flip side, as it were, of Hispanic Hollywood was the ability of Hispanic actors and other film industry professionals to stymie Chicano filmmaker Luis Valdez in his efforts to put together a film on Mexican painter Frida Kahlo. Because of the Hollywood studio affiliation, the film stakes were heightened by the fact that Valdez was seen to be casting a non-Hispanic, Laura San Giacomo, as Frida Kahlo even though Raúl Julia had been cast as Diego Rivera, Edward James Olmos as Leon Trotsky, and Mexican actor Claudio Brook as Henry Ford. The furor that ensued is generally credited to have been a major factor in the initial derailment of the project. For his part, leaning on the Hollywood studio part of the Hispanic Hollywood calculus, ironically Valdez the original creator of *Los vendidos,* appeared in the eyes of some infuriated activists to have reprised one of the parts in that film about selling out to Anglo interests, because he protested his lack of total control over the matter of casting and blamed the casting of the Frida Kahlo role the insistence of Hollywood executives on someone with bankable, box office recognition.

Hispanic Hollywood is also characterized by the creation for the first time in the U.S. film industry of a small cadre of U.S. Hispanic directors, supplemented by other Hispanic directors from Latin America. This has been a very slow, painful, and erratic process. Nevertheless, the ranks of Hollywood now include as directors Luis Valdez, Edward James Olmos, Richard "Cheech" Marín, León Ichaso, Robert Rodríguez, Jesús Salvador Treviño, Marcus de León, Joseph B. Vásquez, Camilo Vila, and Latin Americans Hector Babenco and Luis Puenzo. We have already discussed the first four and the two Latin Americans. Robert Rodríguez is the director of the phenomenal *El mariachi* (see following chapter). Jesús Salvador Treviño, primarily a director of independent Chicano films (see following chapter) has also done considerable directing for television, particularly CBS. He won a Directors Guild of America Award (1989) for his CBS *Schoolbreak* special, *Gangs*. Marcus de León directed a Hispanic analog of *The Postman Always Rings Twice, Kiss Me a Killer* (1991, starring Julie Carmen and Robert Beltrán) which was produced for half a million dollars. Joseph B. Vásquez has directed two low-budget independent films, *Street Story* and *The Bronx War* (1989) which helped him obtain the funding for the $2 million, well-received feature, *Hangin' with the Homeboys* (1991, New Line Cinema). Camilo Vila, born in Cuba and now living in New York, has directed the independent political thriller, *The Worms, Unholy* (1988, Vestron Pictures) and a comedy, *Options* (1988, TV film).

While some filmmakers may have advanced to the rank of director, the total amount of directorial work (including the roles of assistant director and other titles) has barely budged. When serving as the chair of the Directors Guild of America's Latino Committee, Jesús Salvador Treviño (1992, 76) reported that a study by the Directors Guild of America (DGA), released April 20, 1992, reported that the number of days worked by Hispanic directors increased from 1 percent of all TV and film work done in 1983 to 1.3 percent in 1991, an increase of a mere one-third of 1 percent in almost a decade! Similar conditions prevail in the other two major Hollywood guilds. Over the same period as the DGA study, the number of days worked by Hispanic members of the Screen Actors Guild (SAG) varied from 3 to 4 percent over any given year. For Hispanics in the Writers Guild of America (WGA), the percentage employed as writers from 1982 to 1987 in any given year was less than one-half of 1 percent. Treviño pointed out that the African American community has made more strides than the Hispanic community because of the effectiveness of the NAACP. Treviño has judged "As long as a protest or complaint comes from someone within the industry, the person can be bought off or blacklisted" (1992, 76). This has been the situation with Hispanic protests; in contrast, the NAACP has functioned as an independent industry watchdog challenging the industry on the issues of employment and portrayals but not dependent on the industry for employment. In sum, the Hispanic Hollywood phenomenon, while it has fostered the production of a few important U.S. Hispanic-focused films (and others that are less significant) and helped the careers of a handful of directors, actors, and other film professionals, it has made no significant difference in the goal of increasing the overall number of U.S. Hispanic professionals in the industry.

In 1988, the Hispanic Film Project (HFP) was created as a nonprofit, joint program between Universal Television and the National Hispanic Media Coalition. Each year the HFP selects two filmmakers to direct and produce an original 22-minute short with the supervision and support of industry professionals. Upon completion, each film is presented at an industry showcase and entered into international film exhibitions and festivals. Given the lack of progress in expanding the career lines of U.S. Hispanics into the film industry much more needs to be done.

Other Film Genres since 1960

The most notable phenomenon of the 1960s was the emergence of violent and sala-cious Westerns. In the 1970s, we witnessed the proliferation of Hispanic-focused or multiethnic gang pictures. In the 1980s, it was the establishment of the Hispanic Hollywood phenomenon. Concurrently, numerous other Hispanic-focused films were produced during the period, and many of these are described and categorized below.

Acapulco Films

The Acapulco cycle of films were short-lived but their nature was such that they are best categorized separately from the Latin American films. Acapulco caught the atten-tion of the world's media in the early and mid-1960s as a chic place for jetsetters and as a desirable vacation spot for everyone, including fans of Elvis Presley. The Acapulco films exploited that image for everything it was worth. *Fun in Acapulco* (1963, Paramount) featured Elvis Presley working as a lifeguard and entertainer with Ursula Andress as the costar. Alejandro Rey had a supporting role in this piece of fluff. *Of Love and Desire* (1963, New World, starring Merle Oberon) depicted a neurotic woman who toys with the affections of several men against the backdrop of magnificent Acapulco settings. *Love Has Many Faces* (1964, starring Lana Turner) was of the same ilk only more lurid, having the woman marry a beach boy and have an affair with an-other, who is murdered. Matt Helm, (a rival of James Bond) played by Dean Martin, appeared in two films of the Matt Helm series that were set in part in Acapulco: *The Silencers* (1965, Columbia) and *The Ambushers* (1966, Columbia). Also see *Drug Films*.

Boxing Films

In the early 1980s, a pair of Hispanic-focused boxing films appeared. *Honeyboy* (1982, TV film, starring Erik Estrada and Morgan Fairchild with a supporting role by Héctor Elizondo) was totally cliché ridden, depicting a barrio boy trying to fight his way out of the barrio and into the arms of the blonde honey. An even worse film launched the film career of Rubén Blades, *The Last Fight* (1983, Best Film and Video Corp.) where he plays a singer-turned boxer vying for the world championship.

Classics, Historical Films, and Spectacle Epics

In 1961, Hollywood produced *El Cid* (United States-Spain coproduction) starring Charlton Heston as the medieval Spanish hero and conqueror of the Moors in Valencia. Sophia Loren co-starred in this somewhat better than customary spectacle epic that has found a place in high school Spanish classrooms. *Kings of the Sun* (1963, United Artists, starring George Chakiris who had won an Oscar for best-supporting ac-tor in *West Side Story*, and Yul Brynner) was another spectacle film about a Mayan leader who encounters savage Indians, managing to turn the Maya into a mishmash of soap opera with loin cloths.

Man of la Mancha (1972, United Artists), starring Peter O'Toole and Sophia Loren, was a failed effort to bring the well-known musical to the screen. On the other hand, *The Mission* (1986, British production, screenplay by Robert Bolt) was a superior film about the Jesuits in the Amazon rain forest and how their work was destroyed by greedy merchants and factions within the church itself in the late eighteenth century. Featuring Robert De Niro and Jeremy Irons in leading roles (with Jesuit activist Daniel Berrigan in a bit part), the film won an Oscar for Chris Menges's spectacular cine-matography.

Recently Christopher Columbus has been on the silver screen. *Christopher Columbus* (1992, Warner, starring Marlon Brando and Tom Selleck) was an artistic and box office failure as was *1492: Conquest of Paradise* (1992, Paramount, starring Gerard Depardieu, Sigourney Weaver as Queen Isabela la Católica, and Armand Assante). Depardieu won "runner up" for the worst Hispanic accent award of *Hispanic* magazine (December 1992), making Columbus sound like Inspector Clouseau. "Ze land iz zo cloze!" (Armand Assante, the Italian American actor, won first place for sounding "like a stand-in for Don Corleone" in *The Mambo Kings*).

Drug Films

Films where the use of drugs or its smuggling is at the center of the plot were of two sorts (see also *Latin America in Films*). One type of film simply continued the long-standing conventions of the cycle that we have seen in previous chapters. New to the genre, however, were films, particularly by Cheech and Chong, which promoted the use of drugs for its good feelings (including camaraderie) and which depicted the total incompetence of narcotics officers. The slapstick comedy *Up in Smoke* (1978, Paramount), the first of this kind, marked a major volte-face in drug films; the film was enormously popular.

The period opened with the usual sorts of films. *Dangerous Charter* (1962, Crown International Pictures) was about foiling dope smuggling emanating from La Paz, Mexico. *Sol Madrid* (1965, MGM, starring David McCallum and Telly Savalas) has Mexican agent "Jalisco" (Ricardo Montalbán) helping U.S. narcotics agents foil drug smuggling by the Mafia originating in Mexico, particularly Acapulco. Similarly, *Acapulco Uncensored* (1968, Crest Film Distributors), a documentary with "hidden cameras," among its other revelations, supposedly depicted young women staging perverted shows to obtain money to support their marijuana habits. *The Candy Man* (1969, Allied Artists) has Mexican actor Manolo Fábregas foil drug dealers and kidnappers in his role as Mexican Lieutenant García. *Free Grass* (1969, Hollywood Star Pictures, later changed to *Scream Free*) depicts murder, abduction, spiking drinks with LSD, and motorcycle gangs against the backdrop or marijuana smuggling across the Mexican border.

Extreme Prejudice (1987, Carolco/Tri-Star, starring Nick Nolte and María Conchita Alonso) focuses on boyhood friends who are now on opposite sides of the law, as Texas Ranger and drug kingpin on the Texas/Mexico border. The trophy for Nolte is María Conchita Alonso. A film which is a cut above is *Q & A* (1990, Virgin/ Regency/Odyssey, director Sidney Lumet), featuring Timothy Hutton as the novice assistant district attorney investigating the brutal killing of a Puerto Rican drug dealer by a much-decorated police detective played by Nick Nolte. The poorly done but financially successful *Scarface* (1983, Universal, directed by Brian de Palma), starring Al Pacino and launching Michelle Pfeiffer's career, plays Hollywood's oldest and eminently successful box office game, building up a fabulous fable around the illicit, in this case promoting drug running as profitable, glamorous, sexy, immoral, and doomed at the same time.

Hispanic drug lords have appeared in *Code of Silence* (1985, Rank/Orion), a Chuck Norris vehicle, *Stick* (1985, Universal, starring Burt Reynolds and Candice Bergen with a supporting role by José Pérez), *Running Scared* (1986, Paramount, starring Gregory Hines and Billy Crystal with Jimmy Smits in a supporting role) and *8 Million Ways to Die* (1986, Tri-Star Pictures, director Hal Ashby, script cowritten by Oliver Stone).

The flip side of drug use is apparent in *Easy Rider* (1969, Columbia/Pando/Raybert, starring Peter Fonda and Dennis Hopper) and *Bob & Carol & Ted & Alice* (1969, Columbia). Neither film is centrally about drug use, but in the first it is treated with casual acceptance and in the second marijuana appears in one of its socially accepted roles of the 1960s as an inhibition-breaker or possible aphrodisiac.

The Cheech and Chong films took drug films into a new direction, one notable not only for their promotion of drug use but for their standing on its head the convention of Hispanics and Orientals as the primary smugglers and demons of drug smuggling, victimizing "good" Americans. The value system of traditional drug films, which meant essentially law enforcement, interdiction of drugs, and capture of villains, including outcasts such as Hispanics and Orientals, was radically subverted. Everything was turned topsy-turvy.

Cheech Marín and Thomas Chong began by adapting their nightclub act to film in *Up in Smoke* (1978, Paramount). The film featured two calabaza heads in search of "good grass," and included slapstick routines such as smoking a reefer the size of a baseball bat, crossing the border from Mexico in a van entirely made of marijuana, and seeing incompetent narcotics agents go through their silly routines. The film became the highest grossing film of the year and spurred a number of 1980s sequels including: *Cheech and Chong's Next Movie* (1980, Universal), *Cheech and Chong's Nice Dreams* (1981, Columbia), *Things are Tough All Over* (1982, Columbia), *Yellowbeard* (1983, Orion), *Cheech and Chong: Still Smokin'* (1983, Paramount), and *Cheech and Chong's the Corsican Brothers* (1984, Orion). The Cheech and Chong films brought the marijuana smoking, hippy and stoned counterculture into the Hollywood fold as paying customers.

Foreign Films

While foreign films are mostly beyond the scope of this overview, it should be noted that beginning in the 1950s, the United States became somewhat more receptive to the introduction of foreign films produced in the Spanish language with English subtitles.

This phenomenon was primarily due to the appreciation for the work of Luis Buñuel whose work in Spanish has became accessible to the United States viewing audience, first through limited theatrical distribution and more recently in home videotape. These films from the 1950s through 1970 in Spanish (but not French) include: *Los Olvidados* (1950) about Mexican youths in the slums; *Ascent to Heaven* also known as *Mexican Bus Ride* (1951); *El (This Strange Passion)* (1952, starring Arturo de Córdova); *El bruto/The Brute* (1952, starring Pedro Armendáriz and Katy Jurado); *Illusions Travel by Streetcar* (1953); *The Criminal Life of Archibaldo de la Cruz* (1955); *The Exterminating Angel* (1962, starring Silvia Pinal and Enrique Rambal); *Nazarín* (1958, starring Francisco Rabal); *Viridiana* (1961, starring Silvia Pinal, Fernando Rey, and Francisco Rabal); *Simon of the Desert* (1965, starring Claudio Brook and Silvia Pinal); and *Tristana* (1970, starring Catherine Deneuve).

Films including those by Buñuel and several others were screened in the large cities such as New York, Los Angeles, Chicago, and Washington, DC. Beginning in the 1960s, a considerable number of Spaghetti Westerns were imported, but these were usually coproductions shot simultaneously in English and other languages. Throughout the contemporary period a small but increasing number of Spanish-language films have been screened either with subtitles or dubbed into English, and some of these, including the ones referred to below, have been notable.

Macario (1960, director Roberto Gavaldón, starring Tarso Ignacio López and Pina Pellicer) is a poetic fable based on a story by B. Traven, also the author of *The Treasure of the Sierra Madre*. The film was the first Mexican production to earn an Oscar nomination. *Death of a Bureaucrat* (1966, director Tomás Gutiérrez) was a farce about a man's struggle with the red tape of bureaucracy. *Memories of Underdevelopment* (1968, director Tomás Gutiérrez Alea) is a biting satire on sex and politics, featuring a Europeanized Cuban intellectual out of kilter with Cuban society.

The Garden of Delights (1970, director Carlos Saura) is a surreal comedy about a greedy family who tries to obtain the Swiss bank account of the amnesiac patriarch. *The Green Wall* (1970, director Armando Robles Godoy) is about a young family who flees the pressures of Lima and struggles to survive in the Peruvian jungle. *The Last Supper* (1976, director Tomás Gutiérrez Alea) is about a Cuban slaveholder of the eighteenth century who decides to improve his soul by instructing his slaves in the glories of Christianity. *Mama Turns 100* (1979, director Carlos Saura) is a comic attack on Franco's Spain. *Portrait of Teresa* (1979, director Pastor Vega) is about a disenchanted housewife in Cuba who becomes involved with political and cultural groups in post-revolutionary Cuban society.

Blood Wedding (1981, director Carlos Saura) is an excellent ballet adaptation of Federico García Lorca's classic tragedy. *Demons in the Garden* (1982, director Manuel Gutiérrez Aragón) treated fratricidal rivalries and corruption in post-Civil War Spain. *Alsino and the Condor* (1983, director Miguel Littín) treated the Sandinistas in Nicaragua. *Erendira* (1983, director Ruy Guerra, starring Irene Papas and Claudia Ohana) was about a wealthy old woman who loses everything in a fire and turns her granddaughter into a prostitute. *Frida* (1984, director Paul Leduc) was an uninspired biopic of Frida Kahlo. *Camila* (1984, director María Luisa Bernberg) evoked forbidden love in Buenos Aires between an aristocrat and a Jesuit priest. *The Stilts/Los zancos* (1984, director Carlos Savrat, starring Francisco Rabal, Laura del Sol, Fernando Fernán Gómez, and Antonio Banderas) is about an aged playwright and professor who falls in love with a young actress. *Valentina* (1984, director Antonio J. Betancor, producer Anthony Quinn) is a subtle drama based on a novel by Ramón Sender about a man's love for Valentina that lasted from childhood until his death. *What Have I Done to Deserve This* (1984, director Pedro Almodóvar, starring Carmen Maura) is a comedy about a working-class housewife who struggles to maintain her sanity while keeping her crazy family afloat. *Funny Dirty Little War/No habrá más penas en el mundo* (1985, director Héctor Olivera) is about the struggle between Marxists and Peronists in Argentina in 1974. *The Official Story* (1985, director Luis Puenzo, starring Norma Aleandro) was the winner of an Oscar for best foreign-language film. It indelibly describes the destruction of a middle-class Argentinean family as the result of the "dirty war" of the 1970s.

Special recognition needs to be given to a Mexican film, *Doña Herlinda and Her Son* (1986, director Jaime Humberto Hermosillo), a comedy and homosexual homage to "mother," the first Mexican feature with a gay theme which reportedly became, at least before *Like Water for Chocolate,* "the best-selling-ever Mexican movie in the American market" (Hadley-García, p. 240).

El amor brujo (1986, director Carlos Saura) is a production of Manuel de Falla's ballet. *Half of Heaven* (1987, director Manuel Gutiérrez Aragón) portrays a woman who works her way up from poverty in Madrid. *Man Facing Southeast* (1987, director Eliseo Subiela) is about a mysterious man, perhaps an alien who appears in the midst of a Buenos Aires psychiatric hospital. *Miss Mary* (1987, director María Luisa Bamberg, starring Julie Christie and Nacha Guevara) is about a British governess brought to pre-World War II Argentina. *Matador* (1988, director Pedro Almodóvar, starring Antonio Banderas) is one of the director's best melodramas about a lame ex-bullfighter who finds sexual gratification from murder. *Debajo del mundo/Under Earth* (1988, director Beda Docampo Feijoo) is about a Polish farming community shattered by the German army. *A Very Old Man With Enormous Wings* (1988, director Fernando Birri) is a notable film that captures the magic realism of the original Gabriel García Márquez short story. *Women on the Verge of a Nervous Breakdown* (1988, director Pedro Almodóvar, starring Carmen Maura and Antonio Banderas) is a Spanish comedy featuring a pregnant soap-opera star who has just been dumped by her longtime lover.

Cabeza de Vaca (1990, Concorde, director Nicolás Echevarría) is about the famous explorer. *Tie me up! Tie me Down!* (1990, director Pedro Almodóvar, starring Victoria Abril and Antonio Banderas) is a comedy about a soft-core porno star and a recently released psychiatric patient. *High Heels* (1991, director Pedro Almodóvar) is a comedy about the neurotic daughter of a self-absorbed film and stage star. *Danzón* (1992, Sony Picture Classics) is a notable film about a working woman who is able to live a liberated lifestyle with her daughter and friends. *Como agua para chocolate/Like Water for Chocolate* (1993, Pandora Cinema, S.A., released in the United States through Miramax, made by the husband/wife, director/writer team of Alfonso Arau and Laura Esquivel) focuses on the plight of three Mexican sisters during the 1900s.

Indocumentado and Other Border Films

During this period a number of films dealt with the *indocumentado* (undocumented worker) phenomenon (see *Border Films,* chapter 5, for earlier examples). Particularly during the past two decades, as undocumented immigration has become a more widely debated public issue, a new wave of films emerged. Nevertheless, the theme of passive Mexican immigrants being saved by noble Anglos continued to dominate. None of these Hollywood treatments have ever risen above the mediocre. The films of the 1980s have scarcely improved upon the first of the lot in terms of veracity, character development, or esthetics. Hollywood *indocumentado* pictures have never surpassed the limitations of the social problem genre as originally conceived in the 1930s and 1940s. *Blood Barrier* (1979, British production, originally titled *The Border,* starring Telly Savalas and Danny de la Paz) is the usual fare of a maverick border patrolman who hates and stops the exploitation of poor Mexicans being trucked into California as day laborers. *Borderline* (1980, ITC/Martin Starger) stars Charles Bronson stalking a deranged killer, a former Vietnam veteran, on the border against the subplot of drug smuggling villains and defenseless victims who are undocumented workers. In *The Border* (1982, Universal, Jack Nicholson, Harvey Keitel, Valerie Perrine, and Elpidia Carrillo), the patrolman, spurred on by his money-hungry wife, begins taking payoffs from illegal Mexican aliens he's supposed to be arresting, eventually becoming emotionally involved with a young mother played by Carrillo.

In contrast to the stock characterizations of the Hollywood versions, two independently produced U.S. Hispanic works, *Alambrista!* (1979) and *El Norte* (1983), shine because of their strong and distinctive plot developments and intriguing characters. Similarly, Cheech Marín's *Born in East L.A.* (1987) shines as a Hispanic Hollywood exception to the bleakness of the rest, precisely because it combined Hispanic scriptwriting and acting expertise and Hollywood production values. (These films are given additional treatment in chapter 7.)

Latin America in Films

The films that were set in Latin America in the previous period were preponderantly Latin musicals and a few other Good Neighbor Policy oriented films. There were also a few that featured Latin Lovers in their natural habitat, sometimes squiring Anglo women. Beginning in 1959, the Cuban Revolution became a topic for U.S. films, and in the 1970s, revolution generally in Latin America began to be treated.

When Hollywood attempted to depict the Cuban Revolution or other Latin American revolutionary topics in a serious fashion during this period the results were often poor. *Cuban Rebel Girls* (1959, also known as *Assault of the Rebel Girls*; home video title: *Attack of the Rebel Girls*), Errol Flynn's last film, was an embarrassment. Flynn, playing himself, aids Fidel Castro in his overthrow of Batista with help from costar Beverly Aadland, Flynn's sixteen-year-old girlfriend. The pretentious comic-book treatment in *Che!* (1969, Fox, director Omar Sharif) with Jack Palance playing Fidel Castro made the film one of the biggest film jokes of the 1960s. *Cuba Crossing* (1980, known as almost everything else including, *Kill Castro, Assignment: Kill Castro, The Mercenaries,* and *Sweet Violent Tony*), starring Stuart Whitman, was an awful film. The title kept changing in an attempt to bring in more box office receipts, but that hardly saved this turkey. The most recent inferior film to weigh in is *Havana* (1990, Universal, director Sydney Pollack). The film is set on the eve of the 1959 Cuban Revolution where a high-stakes gambler with a heart of gold (Robert Redford) falls in love with the beautiful wife (Lena Olin) of a Cuban revolutionary (Raúl Julia) and single-handedly changes history (or repeats Casablanca). The only film of this ilk to rise above the dismal was *Cuba* (1979, United Artists) with Sean Connery as a disinterested mercenary who falls in love with Brooke Adams during the defeat of Batista in 1959. Héctor Elizondo had a supporting role.

Another 1960s film of the heavy kind set in Latin America is *Night of the Iguana* (1964, MGM, director John Huston, starring Richard Burton, Deborah Kerr, and Ava Gardner). While the film about a defrocked priest and an oversexed hotel proprietress is pretentious and dull, the film got enormous amounts of publicity, some of it attributable to Sue Lyon of *Lolita* (1962, MGM) fame. Puerto Vallarta became an important tourist destination as a result. From the point of view of its depictions of Hispanics, *Iguana* is particularly disappointing in its turning of the admittedly minor Mexican characters into mere cutout figures of sexuality.

While the serious treatments of the 1960s were uninspired, in the 1970s, revolution in Latin America became a common topic of film comedy with more positive results. Many of the films were screwball comedies, a long-standing Hollywood genre now attached to a new environment. In addition to Woody Allen's *Bananas* (1971, United Artists), there was *The In-Laws* (1979, Warner) starring Peter Falk. Both the Valdez brothers, Luis and Daniel, had small parts in the Richard Pryor comedy *Which Way is Up?* (1977, Universal). *The In-Laws* was a very funny film, but *Bananas* (also starring Carlos Montalbán and Louise Lasser) was in a realm by itself. Even though it embraced every imaginable banana republic stereotype, it rendered them into superb parodies, typically turning them inside out, as it did many Anglo institutions and worthies including the court system, the FBI, television news, J. Edgar Hoover, and Howard Cosell. Wyatt Cooper accurately described the film: ". . . *Bananas* would be unbelievable or offensive were it not so grounded in the ludicrous truth. . . . Its steady flow of jokes, sight-gags and parody make it one of the funniest pictures within memory" (Hadley-García, 218).

On the serious side, the 1970s produced *The Wrath of God* (1972, MGM, starring Robert Mitchum and Rita Hayworth, with Frank Langella and Gregory Sierra), another dull film about a defrocked priest in a revolution-ridden country south of the border. This was Rita Hayworth's last film. In *Sorcerer* (1977, Universal, starring Roy Scheider and Francisco Rabal), four fugitives in a seedy Latin American town try to buy freedom by driving trucks of nitroglycerine over bumpy roads to help put out an oil fire. Anthony Quinn starred in *The Children of Sánchez* (1978, United States-Mexico coproduction with supporting roles by Dolores del Río, Katy Jurado, Lucía Méndez, Ignacio López Tarso, and Duncan Quinn, son of Anthony Quinn and Katherine De Mille). The film was a poor adaptation of Oscar Lewis's notable oral history/anthropological account.

Apparently, beginning in the 1980s, revolution in Latin America didn't seem so funny. Since 1980, a number of films have focused on Latin America, reflecting the political situation of the region, human rights abuses, illegitimate American participation in Latin American affairs, or drug-running. *Evita Perón* (1981, TV film, starring Faye Dunaway, Rita Moreno, José Ferrer, and Pedro Armendáriz, Jr.) was a better than average portrayal of Evita's rise to power. *High Risk* (1982, American Cinema, with Anthony Quinn in a supporting role as a Colombian bandido) is a silly thriller about U.S. mercenaries who parachute into the jungle and rip off dope dealers only to run into bandidos. Costa-Gavras's *Missing* (1982, Universal), starring Jack Lemmon and Sissy Spacek, is a compelling drama about American collusion to overthrow Allende in Chile. It won an Academy Award for Costa-Gavras and Donald Stewart for their screenplay adaptation. *Under Fire* (1983, Orion) is a first-rate political thriller starring Nick Nolte, Gene Hackman, and Joanna Cassidy as journalists in the midst of the 1979 Sandinista revolution in Nicaragua. *Last Plane Out* (1983, starring Jan-Michael Vincent and Julie Carmen), about the final days of the Somoza regime, with Somoza appearing as Mr. Nice Guy in this propagandistically slanted film compares poorly to *Under Fire*. *Prisoner Without a Name, Cell Without a Number* (1983, TV film, starring Roy Scheider) was a compelling drama about the activist Argentine newspaper publisher who was unjustly imprisoned and tortured for several years. *Beyond the Limit* (1983, British production, starring Richard Gere, Michael Caine, with Elpidia Carrillo and A Martínez) is a muddled adaptation of Graham Greene's novel *The Honorable Consul;* it treats a British doctor who becomes involved with South American revolutionaries and sexually involved with the ex-prostitute wife of the alcoholic consul. *Under the Volcano* (1984, Twentieth Century Fox), featuring Jacqueline Bisset and Albert Finney, with supporting roles by Katy Jurado and Ignacio López Tarso, is a slow, somber, but highly literate adaptation of Malcolm Lowry's classic novel of the 1930s in rural Mexico. *Against All Odds* (1984, Columbia, director Taylor Hackford) is about a former athlete who needs cash and accepts a job from a sleazy ex-teammate to find his girlfriend who has run off to forbidding Mexico. *Latino* (1985, Cinecom International Films), directed by Haskell Wexler starring Robert Beltrán and Annette Cardona, is a left-leaning, unsuccessfully rendered film about a Chicano Green Beret "advising" U.S.-backed Contras in their war against the Sandinistas in Nicaragua. *Salvador* (1986, Hemdale/Gerald Green), cowritten and directed by Oliver Stone, featuring Jim Belushi and James Woods, with a supporting role from Elpidia Carrillo, is an uneven but compelling drama based on the real-life experiences of journalist Richard Boyle (who cowrote the screenplay) in El

Salvador in 1980-81, including his exposure of the government's use of death squads. *Two to Tango* (1988, director Héctor Olvera) is a thriller about a professional assassin sent to Buenos Aires by the "Company" but who falls for the girlfriend of his target. *Romero* (1989, Paulist Pictures, distributed through Warner Brothers, starring Raúl Julia, with supporting roles by Ana Alicia and Eddie Vélez) is a notable film that chronicled Romero's transformation from a passive cleric to an eloquent defender of his church and people. This was the first film financed by officials of the United States Roman Catholic Church.

There were a few comedies produced in the 1980s as well. *Romancing the Stone* (1984, Twentieth Century Fox) was the best of the lot, featuring Kathleen Turner as a romantic fiction writer in trouble in Colombia and hustled and eventually genuinely romanced by Michael Douglas. The usual Hispanic stereotypes were done by Alfonso Arau and Manuel Ojeda. In a *Romancing the Stone* copycat, *Miracles* (1986, Orion), bungling jewel thief Paul Rodríguez whisks away characters played by Tom Conti and Terri Garr to his South American hellhole. Adalberto Martínez had a supporting role in this film. *¡Three Amigos!* (1986, Orion starring Steve Martin, Chevy Chase, and Martin Short, with Alfonso Arau as the stereotypical bandido) is a simplistic comedy about silent-film Western heroes who think they are to do a public appearance in Mexico but have really been summoned to rid a village of its bandit chieftain. The film attempts to parody stereotypes but is only occasionally successful. *The In-Laws* did a much better job along that line. *Moon over Parador* (1988, Universal, starring Richard Dreyfuss, Sonia Braga, and Raúl Julia) made liberal use of customary stereotypes about Latin America and its dictators for uninspired humor.

In contrast to the 1980s, which produced a number of notable films set in Latin America, particularly Central America, the 1990s returned to frivolous films. *To Die Standing* (1990, starring Cliff De Young and Robert Beltrán) is a drug, sex, and power thriller about an easily irritated FBI agent who goes to Peru to extradite a drug boss. *McBain* (1991, Shapiro Glickenhaus/J. Boyce Harman Jr., starring Christopher Walken and María Conchita Alonso) is another adventure flick involving a team of mercenaries working with the rebels who are attempting to overthrow a corrupt Colombian dictator. Oscar winner Louis Gossett, Jr. starred in *Aces: Iron Eagles III* (1992, Seven Arts), yet another film about busting drug dealers in Peru. The film costarred Chicana body builder Rachel McLish.

The standout of the 1990s thus far has been *At Play in the Fields of the Lord* (1991, Universal) starring Tom Berenger, Aidan Quinn, Kathy Bates, and Daryl Hannah. Faithful to the plot of Peter Mathiessen's masterful novel, it recounts how two Protestant missionaries (one a charlatan, the other sincere) wreck havoc on the Indians of the rain forest who they are charged with helping.

Latin Musicals

A couple of Latin musicals were made during the period, one glossing the *salsa* craze and the other memorializing mambo. *Salsa* (1988, Cannon/Menahem Golan, and Yoram Globus) was inspired by *Dirty Dancing* (1987, Vestron) but had a very weak script. The film, choreographed by Kenny Ortega of *Dirty Dancing,* starred Bobby Rosa, formerly of Menudo, and Magali García, with appearances by Celia Cruz and Tito Puente. *The Mambo Kings* (1992, Warner), starring Armand Assante and Antonio Banderas as César and Néstor Castillo, is about two brothers who leave Cuba for the United States in the early 1950s to try and make it with their own band. Based on Oscar

Hijuelos Pulitzer Prize-winning novel, *The Mambo Kings Play Songs of Love,* the best part of the film is the music itself. Talisa Soto stands out in her brief appearance and Tito Puente and Celia Cruz, the real King and Queen of Mambo, make cameo appearances.

Life in the Barrio Films

In 1969, a different sort of film was released, one without drugs, gangs, or crimes, but with poverty: *Popi* (United Artists). Despite the poor Anglicized rendering of the Spanish *papi*, the film depicts in a charming and cheerful fashion Alan Arkin as a Puerto Rican widower struggling to free his two young sons (Miguel Alejandro and Rubén Figueroa), from ghetto life. Rita Moreno played in the film as well. One of his stratagems, however, having the Puerto Rican sons pass off as more prestigious Cuban refugees caused activist Richie Pérez (1990, 18) to state that "the idea of denying your identity as the only way to succeed is extremely negative." The film spawned a brief TV series in 1976, *Popi,* which starred Héctor Elizondo. *The Super* (1991, Twentieth Century Fox, starring Joe Pesci, with a supporting role by Rubén Blades) is an uneven film about a slumlord who is forced to move in with his tenants. It is not nearly as good as *El Super* (1979) about a homesick exiled Cuban in Manhattan (see chapter 7).

Prison Movies

A couple of notable prison films stand out during this period (see also *The Proliferation of Gang Films*). *Short Eyes* (1977, Film League, Inc., director Robert M. Young, retitled as *Slammer*), adapted from Miguel Piñero's play, is about the fate of a child molester in prison. José Pérez and Freddy Fender have parts as Hispanics. *Bad Boys* (1983, EMI, starring Sean Penn and Esai Morales, also was Ally Sheedy's debut) features a personal vendetta between prison worlds. Morales is superb as the sworn Hispanic enemy of the Anglo juvenile delinquent.

Television

Hispanic participation on television requires a monograph or book of its own, and only a few highlights are presented here.

Hispanic-focused material made minor inroads on television but nothing comparable to African American advances. Linda Cristal as Victoria Cannon in *The High Chaparral* (1967-71) and Elena Verdugo as nurse Consuelo in *Marcus Welby, M.D.* (1969-76) were notable as strong, self-reliant, attractive Latina characters.

Freddie Prinze's 1970 sitcom *Chico and the Man* (1974-77) was the last major comedy hit with a Hispanic in a leading role and Hispanic-focused material. Later attempts, such as Héctor Elizondo's *Popi* (1976), Carmen Zapata's *Viva Valdez* (1976), Luis Avalo's *Condo* (1983), Paul Rodríguez's *a.k.a. Pablo* (1984), and Elizabeth Peña's *I Married Dora* (1987), all met with early cancellations. Liz Torres obtained TV credits beginning with *The Melba Moore-Clifton Davis Show* (1972) and *Ben Vereen: Comin' At Ya* (1975) both variety shows, appeared in *All in the Family* as Teresa Betancourt (1976-77), and had the part of María in *The New Odd Couple* (1982-83).

Héctor Elizondo in the role of Detective Sergeant Don Delgado (Bean) was successful in the police show *Freebie and the Bean* (1980-81) and was also successful in *Foley Square* (1985-86), a comedy about District Attorney Jesse Steinberg. Erik Estrada had a long run as Officer Frank "Ponch" Poncherello in *CHiPS* (1977-83), as did René Enríquez as Lieutenant Ray Calletano in the police series *Hill Street Blues* (1981-87). Richard Yniguez played Father José Silva on the situation comedy *Mama Malone* (1984).

Edward James Olmos was Lieutenant Martin Castillo on *Miami Vice* (1984-1989); Saundra Santiago played Detective Gina Navarro Calabrese, and Martín Ferrero had occasional roles as Izzy Moreno on the same show. Jimmy Smits played Víctor Sifuentes on *L.A. Law* (1986-1992). A Martínez (Adolf Martínez III) and Henry Darrow were institutions on the soap opera *Santa Barbara*. A Martínez most recently was in the cast of *L.A. Law*. A number of Hispanics had roles in the 1980s series *Falcon Crest,* including Lorenzo Lamas, Mel Ferrer, Mario Marcelino, Carlos Romero, Ana Alicia, Victoria Racimo, César Romero, and Julie Carmen.

Other Notable Films

During this period a number of additional films that need to be mentioned either don't fit well into any of the standard genres in which Hispanic-focused material customarily appears, or which transcend genre film.

The Money Trap (1966, MGM) depicts two detectives who go bad in order to make money, the twist being, in the case of Pete Delanos, played by Ricardo Montalbán (the name "Delanos" much in the news at the time because of the farmworkers strike), that he does this because he is tired of being underprivileged. *A Covenant with Death* (1967, Warner Brothers), set in the 1920s in the Southwest, features a promiscuous Mexican American judge (played by George Maharis) who does the right thing, absolving an innocent man, Talbot, despite the fact that the latter has accused him of infidelities with his wife. *In From Nashville with Music* (1969, Craddock Films), a Chicano film director appears, played by Pedro González González. We were not aware that such a professional existed in the 1960s. In *Marlowe* (1969, MGM), Rita Moreno plays a stripper with a heart of gold who nurses the Anglo private detective back to health.

Robert Downey wrote and directed an independent production, *Greaser's Palace* (1972), set in the Wild West ruled by Seaweedhead Greaser, a vicious tyrant who keeps his mother and his mariachi band in cages. It features the arrival of Zoot Suit, a gentle song-and-dance man who descends by parachute to work miracles and bring peace and harmony to Greaser's Palace (except that the film provided no work for Hispanic actors).

That Obscure Object of Desire (1977, Spanish-French coproduction released in English) was director Luis Buñuel's last film. It is a remake of a novel by Rierre Louys, *La femme et le pantin,* which has been filmed several times, most notably as *The Devil is a Woman* (1935). The 1977 remake has a wealthy sadomasochist played by Fernando Rey falling for a young maid who is only too happy to make him "suffer." *Can You Hear the Laughter? The Story of Freddie Prinze* (1979) is a TV film that offers an affectionate account of the young comedian before his suicide in 1977. Julie Carmen had a supporting role.

Q–The Winged Serpent (1982, Larco/Larry/Cohen) is an escapist, old-fashioned rubber monster vehicle, except with better stop-motion animation, pitting the New York police against a winged serpent (Quetzalcóatl, no less) atop the Chrysler Building. *The Believers* (1987, Orion, starring Martin Sheen and Jimmy Smits) abused *santería* in the city order to make a horror/thriller. *The Penitent* (1988, New Century-Vista Film, starring Raúl Julia, Armand Assante, and Julie Carmen) did the same for the countryside; the film was a muddle that featured the eternal triangle set against the local color of New Mexican *penitentes*.

A Show of Force (1990, Paramount, director Bruno Barreto, starring Amy Irving, Erik Estrada, Andy García, Robert Duvall, and Lou Diamond Phillips), while not successful at the box office, has a significant plot. It is loosely based on the infamous Puerto Rican scandal where two pro-independence youths (one the son of renown Puerto Rican novelist, Pedro Juan Soto) were fatally shot out of political motivations. Marcus de León directed *Kiss Me a Killer* (1991), with Robert Beltrán and Julie Carmen, a Hispanic version of *The Postman Always Rings Twice*, in which a young wife and a drifter plot to eliminate her older husband and take over as co-owners of a tavern. The film was a box office and critical failure. Not about sex, which gets a different sort of treatment from Hollywood, but about interracial love, *Crazy from the Heart* (1991, a TV film, starring Rubén Blades and Christine Lahti) is a superior film about an Anglo small-town high school principal in Texas taking up with the school's Mexican janitor.

Hispanics Who Figured in the Movies since 1960

The civil rights period beginning in the 1960s also marked an important change in hiring patterns in the film industry with respect to directors, cinematographers, and other production people. For the first time an effort was made to bring Hispanics into the production process and it was this cadre of professionals who became the primary group to make U.S. Hispanic films (see the subsequent section, *The Emergence of U.S. Hispanic Films*). However, the introduction of Hispanic avenger films, group Westerns, gang exploitation, and other Hispanic-focused subgenres often did not carry with it more work for U.S. Hispanic actors. The 1960s and 1970s were not a particularly strong environment for Hispanics in acting roles since more often than not, non-Hispanic actors were awarded the roles of Hispanic characters. For example, George Chakiris and John Saxon got the Hispanic leading parts in *West Side Story* and *Death of a Gunfighter*, respectively, and Burt Lancaster, Charles Bronson, and Paul Newman were the respective leads in *Valdez is Coming, Mr. Majestyk*, and *The Outrage*. *The Young Savages* (1961), starring Burt Lancaster, about gang war between Italians and Puerto Ricans, played by non-Hispanic actors. *The Professionals* (1966) featured Claudia Cardinale as a "María" and Jack Palance as Jesús Raza who kidnaps her and sweeps her off her feet. *Villa Rides* (1968) featured Yul Brynner as Pancho Villa and Charles Bronson and Herbert Lom in the other significant Hispanic roles. *Che!* (1969), starred Omar Sharif and Jack Palance in the incongruous roles of Che Guevara and Fidel Castro, respectively. Robby Benson with contact lenses played a Chicano gang member in *Walk Proud* (1979). *Night of the Iguana* (1964), starring Richard Burton, Deborah Kerr, and Ava Gardner all in Anglo roles, exemplified the Hollywood trend of filming on Latin location but mostly for the purpose of local color, preferring stories reflecting non-Hispanic characters. What did occur was an expansion of opportunities for Hispanic actors (not often actresses, however) with talent and who did not look overly ethnic. These actors, such as Martin Sheen, Charlie Sheen, Emilio Estévez, were able to secure parts as non-Hispanics.

Other actresses who achieved considerable status but were not generally known to be partially Hispanic until they appeared "as presenters or recipients on the nationally televised Golden Eagle Awards show devised by the pro-Hispanic Hollywood organization NOSOTROS" (Hadley-García, p. 201) were television series stars Lynda Carter of *Wonder Woman*, Catherine Bach of *The Dukes of Hazzard*, and Victoria Principal of *Dallas*.

Norma Aleandro, the distinguished South American actress, playwright, director, and TV performer gained international recognition, including being named best actress at Cannes, for her performance in the Academy Award-winning *The Official Story* (1985). While she continues to do Spanish-language films, she has earned acting credits in the United States for *Gaby, A True Story* (1987) about a woman with cerebral palsy, *Cousins* (1989), starring Ted Danson, an American version of the French *Cousin/Cousine* (1975), *Vital Signs* (1990), a cliché-ridden medical student stint, and *One Man's War* (1991, British film made for cable) about Joel Filiartiga, a

Paraguayan activist doctor who tried to bring human rights abuses in his homeland to international attention.

Before he died in 1992, Néstor Almendros had become one of the world's foremost cinematographers. Among the works he filmed were *The Wild Racers* (1968), *Gun Runner* (1968), *Ma nuit chez Maud/My Night at Maud's* (1969, French production director Eric Rohmer), *L'enfant sauvage/The Wild Child* (1970, French production, director François Truffaut), *Le genou de Claire/Claire's Knee* (1971, French production, director Eric Rohmer), *L'histoire d'Adèle/The Story of Adele H.* (1975, French production, director François Truffaut), *Kramer vs Kramer* (1979), *Sophie's Choice* (1982), *Billy Bathgate* (1991), and *Days of Heaven* (1979) for which he won a 1979 Academy Award in cinematography. He codirected two films in the 1980s, *Improper Conduct* (1984) and *Nobody Listened* which itemized the torture of homosexuals and other renegades in Castro's Cuba.

María Conchita Alonso debuted in *Fear City* (1984) and established herself in Hollywood with her role in *Moscow on the Hudson* (1984) opposite Robin Williams. Her work as an actress includes *A Fine Mess* (1986), an unsuccessful Blake Edwards comedy, *Touch and Go* (1986), *Extreme Prejudice* (1987) starring Nick Nolte in yet another undistinguished border drug film, *The Running Man* (1987) starring Arnold Schwarzenegger, *Colors* (1988), a gang film directed by Dennis Hopper and starring Robert Duvall, *Vampire's Kiss* (1988), *Predator 2* (1990), and *McBain* (1991), an adventure film involving a team of mercenaries attempting to overthrow a Central American dictator.

Trini Alvarado debuted in pictures at the age of eleven in *Rich Kids* (1979) by Robert Young about two kids going through puberty. Alvarado has done considerable work in television and films including *Mrs. Soffel* (1984), starring Diane Keaton and Mel Gibson, about a woman who helps two prisoners escape, *Times Square* (1980), *Sweet Lorraine* (1987) about a small Catskill hotel past its prime, *Satisfaction* (1988), *American Blue Note* (1989), *The Chair* (1989), *Stella* (1990) opposite Bette Midler in an undistinguished remake of the 1937 *Stella Dallas*, and *The Babe* (1992) starring John Goodman as Babe Ruth.

Pedro Armendáriz did a few films in the 1960s before he died in 1963 including *Francis of Assisi* (1961) and *Captain Sinbad* (1963).

Desi Arnaz had an appearance in *The Escape Artist* (1982, starring Raúl Julia and Terri Garr).

Brazilian director Hector Babenco became famous for *Pixote* (1981, Brazilian production), a chilling drama of an abandoned ten-year-old street criminal who pimps, sniffs glue, and murders three people before the finale, and for *Kiss of the Spider Woman* (1985, U.S.-Brazilian production) about a gay man and a political activist locked together in a South American prison cell. Babenco established himself in the United States with *Ironweed* (1987) and *At Play in the Fields of the Lord* (1991).

Spanish actor Antonio Banderas has been one of the favorite actors of Spanish director Pedro Almodóvar. The following Almodóvar films, all released in the United States with English subtitles, featured Banderas: *Labyrinth of Passion* (1983), *Law of Desire* (1986), *The Matador* (1988), *Women on the Verge of A Nervous Breakdown* (1988), and *Tie Me Up! Tie Me Down!* (1990). Banderas was also seen in a Spanish film with English subtitles, *The Stilts* (1984, director Carlos Savrat). *The Mambo Kings* (1992) was his first English-language role, and he played Tom Hanks'ss lover in the 1993 AIDS-related film *Philadelphia*. He will be in the forthcoming *Interview With the Vampire*.

Steven Bauer (Steven Echevarría) was the character of Rocky in the program *Qué pasa U.S.A.* and had a principal part in *Scarface* (1983). He starred in *Thief of Hearts* (1984), and starred or had principal parts in *Running Scared* (1986), *The Beast* (1988) about a Soviet tank in Afghanistan, *Gleaming the Cube* (1989) about skateboarding and murder, *A Climate for Killing* (1991), *Drive Like Lightening* (1991, made for cable), and *Sweet Poison* (1991). On television he was in the miniseries *From Here to Eternity*, and in the TV film *The Camerena Story* he was Kiki

Camarena, the Mexican American narcotics agent whose murder had international consequences.

Robert Beltrán starred in Haskell Wexler's ill-fated *Latino* (1985) about the Nicaraguan war and has had roles in *Night of the Comet* (1984), a satire about the end of the world, the Paul Bartel's comedies *Eating Raoul* (1982) and *Scenes from the Class Struggle in Beverly Hills* (1989), the highly regarded *Gaby, A True Story* (1987) about a brilliant woman incapacitated by cerebral palsy, *Streethawk* (1986), *To Die Standing* (1990), and *Kiss Me a Killer* (1991).

Rubén Blades, the highly talented singer-composer-musician-lawyer and prospective future Panamanian statesman debuted with the awful boxing film, *The Last Fight* (1983) but gained recognition on the screen as cowriter and star of *Crossover Dreams* (1985). He has had a considerable number of roles in films such as *Fatal Beauty* (1987), a bomb featuring Whoopi Goldberg, *Critical Condition* (1987) with Richard Pryor and Rachel Ticotin, and *Homeboy* (1988) featuring Mickey Rourke as an aging alcoholic boxer. In *Dead Man Out* (1988), Blades played the lead as an inmate going crazy waiting execution. He also had parts in *The Milagro Beanfield War* (1988), *Disorganized Crime* (1989), *The Lemon Sisters* (1989), *Mo' Better Blues* (1990), *Predator 2* (1990), *The Two Jakes* (1990), *Crazy from the Heart* (1991), *The Super* (1991), starring Joe Pesci as a slumlord, *The Josephine Baker Story* (1991, U.S.-British cable TV film), and *One Man's War* (1991, British). He also did the notable documentary, *AIDS: Changing the Rules.*

"Cantinflas" (Mario Moreno) played in *Pepe* (1960) as a glorified manual laborer who pines for the blonde Americana (Shirley Jones) but never gets close. Instead he is reunited with his beloved horse who he calls "my son." The comedian returned to Mexican films for good.

Despite a number of inferior roles, Julie Carmen, an impressive actress who did well in *Gloria* (1980), a notable film starring Gena Rowlands escaping from the Mafia, and in *The Milagro Beanfield War (1988)*, is getting attention and plenty of work. She has done some television, including *Falcon Crest* and quite a bit of film including *Can You Hear the Laughter? The Story of Freddie Prinze* (1979), *Last Plane Out* (1983) about the final days of the Somoza regime, *The Penitent* (1988), *The Neon Empire* (1989), a bomb about Las Vegas gangsters adapted from a four-hour cable TV production, *Paint it Black* (1989), a disappointing thriller never released theatrically, about a sculptor struggling against an unscrupulous gallery owner, *Fright Night Part II* (1989), and *Kiss Me a Killer* (1991) in which she starred along with Robert Beltrán. She plays a Puerto Rican CIA chief in *Curaçao* (1993).

Barbara Carrera, a Nicaraguan model, made her debut in the 1970s with *The Master Gunfighter* (1975) and has appeared in a number of notable films and several bombs. She has appeared in *Embryo* (1976); *The Island of Dr. Moreau* (1977); *When Time Ran Out . . .* (1980); *Condorman* (1981, British production, distributed by Disney); *Masada* (1981), a spectacular and notable TV film featuring Peter O'Toole and based on the famous battle of Masada during the Roman domination of the Holy Land; the James Bond vehicle *Never Say Never Again* (1983), as Fatima Blush, a notable sexy villainess; *Lone Wolf McQuade* (1983, starring Chuck Norris and David Carradine), about a maverick Texas Ranger trying to punish the leader of a gun-smuggling ring; *Wild Geese II* (1985, British), about a mercenary hired to free Nazi Rudolf Hess from his imprisonment in Berlin's Spandau prison; *Love at Stake* (1987), where she steals the show in a supporting part as a sexy witch in this parody of Salem witch hunts; *Loverboy* (1989); and *The Wicked Stepmother* (1989), a bomb that was Bette Davis's last appearance in film.

Elpidia Carrillo got an opportunity to attain recognition opposite Jack Nicholson in the awful potboiler *The Border* (1982) and did excellent work in *Salvador* (1986, directed by Oliver Stone and starring James Woods). In addition, she appeared in *Beyond the Limit* (1983), an undistinguished adaptation of Graham Greene's *The Honorary Consul*, *Predator* (1987), and *The Lightning Incident* (1991, cable TV film), a laughable flick about a baby kidnapped by voodoo cultists determined on revenge.

Henry Darrow, who did a lot of television in the 1960s and 1970s, notably *The High Chaparral* series, and was in *Badge 373* (1973), saw considerable action in the films, usually in cops, convicts, and drugs-type films including *Attica* (1980), an excellent depiction of the prisoner uprising, *In Dangerous Company* (1988), *L.A. Bounty* (1989), and *The Last of the Finest* (1990). He had an important role in Jesús Treviño's *Seguín* (1982).

Danny de la Paz had roles as a Chicano in *Boulevard Nights* (1979) and *American Me* (1992). He also appeared in *Barbarosa* (1982) and *The Wild Pair* (1987) about FBI agents bringing drug-dealing racists to justice.

Dolores del Río's first Hollywood role since the 1940s was the 1960 Elvis Presley film, *Flaming Star* where she played an American Indian mother; Presley, in his best film plays a half-breed Indian who must choose sides when his mother's people go to war. Recalling her roles during this period, she observed that Hispanics, if they worked at all, tended to play Native Americans because of the popularity of Westerns in the 1960s. On the other hand "the few Hispanic characters in Hollywood were often played by Hollywood stars. Even less suitable ones like Paul Newman or Janet Leigh" (Hadley-García, p. 168). In addition to *Flaming Star,* Dolores del Río had roles in *Cheyenne Autumn* (1964) and *The Children of Sánchez* (1978), her last film. She had a cameo role in *More than a Miracle* (1967) starring Sophia Loren and Omar Sharif.

Rosana de Soto appeared in the Chicano production, *The Ballad of Gregorio Cortez* (1982) and subsequently crossed over into Hollywood via *La Bamba* (1987) and *Stand and Deliver* (1988). She was Dustin Hoffman's non-Hispanic wife in *Family Business* (1989).

Steven E. de Souza, partially of Hispanic descent, is a movie scriptwriter who worked on, among other films, *Die Hard* (1988), *Die Hard 2* (1990), and *48HRS.* (1982), and has written one of the scripts for the legally embattled, possibly forthcoming *Beverly Hills Cop III.*

Héctor Elizondo, who had previously won an Obie for his role as a Puerto Rican locker room attendant in the off-Broadway play *Steambath,* made his debut in 1971 with Burt Lancaster in *Valdez is Coming.* Elizondo, primarily in character roles, has proven to be a major, enduring talent in films for both theatrical and television distribution. In the 1970s, he did *The Taking of Pelham 1-2-3* (1974) about the hijacking of a New York City subway train, *Report to the Commissioner* (1975), a well-done urban police department film that also represented Richard Gere's film debut in a small part as a pimp, *The Dain Curse* (1978, TV film), and *Cuba* (1979), an adventure/love story set during the fall of Batista in 1959. Beginning in 1980, his film career further accelerated with *American Gigolo* (1980), *Young Doctors in Love* (1982), *Honeyboy* (1982, TV film), starring Erik Estrada and Morgan Fairchild and featuring a repast of boxing clichés of the poor-boy-makes-it genre, *The Flamingo Kid* (1984), an appealing teen comedy-drama, *Private Resort* (1985), a teen comedy starring Johnny Depp, *Out of the Darkness* (1985, TV film, starring Martin Sheen), a notable movie about the capture of the notorious New York City serial killer, Son of Sam, *Nothing in Common* (1986, starring Tom Hanks and Jackie Gleason), *Leviathan* (1989), *Power, Passion, and Murder* (1987, TV film, starring Michelle Pfeiffer), *Pretty Woman* (1990), with the aging Richard Gere this time purchasing a hooker, *Forgotten Prisoners* (1990, TV film), about the inhumane conditions in a Turkish prison, *Frankie and Johnny* (1991), *Chains of Gold* (1991, TV film), about a crusading social worker searching for his young friend kidnapped by a drug-dealing gang, and *Necessary Roughness* (1991), about a motley group of losers banding together to create a winning football team.

In the area of musical composition, Emilio Estefan, husband of Gloria Estefan, has produced the scores of numerous financially successful films including *Top Gun* (1986) and *Three Men and a Baby* (1987). He is one of the highest-earning Hispanics in the field of entertainment.

Emilio Estévez, Martin Sheen's son, who uses the original family surname in part because of his blond hair and blue eyes, has secured many roles in mainstream pictures. He has become recognized as a major talent as an actor and now also writes screenplays and directs films. He was in *Tex* (1982, starring Matt Dillon), an excellent coming-of-age adventure about the struggles of two teenage brothers growing up in the Southwest without parental guidance, appeared in *The Outsiders* (1983, director Francis Coppola) and *Nightmares* (1983), and first achieved recognition in *Repo Man* (1984). He had principal roles in *The Breakfast Club* (1985), a bold and innovative teen film, and *St. Elmo's Fire* (1985), and starred in the notable coming-of-age film *That Was Then . . . This is Now* (1985, costarring Craig Sheffer), *Maximum Overdrive* (1986), *Stakeout* (1987, costarring Richard Dreyfuss and Madeleine Stowe), and *Young Guns* (1988). *Nightbreaker* (1989, cable TV film released theatrically by Warner) had Martin Sheen and Emilio Estévez playing the same character in the 1950s and 1980s respectively. It is a strong and prescient film about a naive doctor who witnesses the U.S. government's use of the military as guinea pigs in 1950s atomic tests in Nevada. The script is based on Howard Rosenberg's novel, *Atomic Soldiers.* Estévez's career has continued full pace in the 1990s: *Men at Work* (1990), *Young Guns II* (1990), *Freejack* (1992, Warner Brothers, starring Mick Jagger and Anthony Hopkins, with Esai Morales in a supporting role), a weak science-fiction thriller, *Another Stakeout* (1993, starring Richard Dreyfuss), and *The Mighty Ducks* (1993), which was sufficiently popular that a newly formed hockey team, in Anaheim, California, was named after the film team. Estévez wrote, directed (with some assistance from Robert Wise), and starred in *Wisdom* (1986, also starring Demi Moore), a box office and artistic failure primarily because of an inferior script about a recent graduate who couldn't find work because of a long-ago felony and who, in his frustration, commits bank heists to aid the plight of American farmers. A moderately better effort at writing and directing by Estévez was *Men at Work* (1990) in which he and real-life brother Charlie Sheen play garbage collectors whose freewheeling lifestyle is interrupted by an environmental plot.

Erik Estrada debuted with a switchblade in the Pat Boone film *The Cross and the Switchblade* (1972) and followed it with *The New Centurions* (1972, starring George C. Scott and Jane Alexander), a well-done police drama. He became widely recognized in the role of Frank "Ponch" Poncherello, the motorcycle-riding star of TV's *CHiPS* (1977-83). He has done considerable film work, unfortunately mostly in low-budget, sexploitation, drug, or mercenary films. His credits include the Western *The Longest Drive* (1976); *Fire!* (1977); *Honeyboy* (1982), in which a poor boy makes good as boxer with Morgan Fairchild as the honeygirl; *Hour of the Assassin* (1986), where he plays a character who has been hired to kill the president of fictional San Pedro and who must be stopped by a CIA agent played by Robert Vaughn; the sexploitation films *Caged Fury* (1989) and *Do or Die* (1991, also starring *Playboy* centerfold Roberta Vásquez); *Guns* (1990), as a sneering gunrunner opposite *Playboy* centerfold Dona Speir; *The Last Riders* (1990), where the Slavers motorcycle club seeks revenge on one of its own; *Night of the Wilding* (1990); and *Spirits* (1990) in which he plays a doubting priest facing off evil. More recently Estrada has been making foreign films including the Mexican movie *Juana la cubana* (1992). He's scheduled to appear in *The Final Gold*, a Canadian film due for U.S. release, and he has a starring role in the Mexican soap opera, *Dos mujeres y un camino.*

Emilio "El Indio" Fernández had acting roles in a number of films, many of them directed by Sam Peckinpah. His credits during this period included *The Night of the Iguana* (1964) as a bartender, *The Reward* (1965), *The Appaloosa* (1966), *Return of the Seven* (1966), *A Covenant with Death* (1967), *The War Wagon* (1967), *The Wild Bunch* (1969) as evil General Mapache, *Pat Garrett and Billy the Kid* (1973), *Bring Me the Head of Alfredo García* (1974), *Lucky Lady* (1975), *Under the Volcano* (1984), and *Pirates* (1986).

During this period José Ferrer did numerous films including *Lawrence of Arabia* (1962), *The Greatest Story Ever Told* (1965), *Ship of Fools* (1965), *Enter Laughing* (1966), *Cervantes* (1967, French-Italian-Spanish production, also known as *Young Rebel*), *The Big Bus* (1976), *The Private Files of J. Edgar Hoover* (1977), a tame soap opera done before the Hoover revelations, *The Sentinel* (1977), *Zoltan–Hound of Dracula* (1977), *Fedora* (1978), *The 5th Musketeer* (1979), *Natural Enemies* (1979, starring Louise Fletcher), a well-done domestic murder drama, *Pleasure Palace* (1980), about a casino, *Gideon's Trumpet* (1980, TV film starring Henry Fonda), a well-made drama about a man denied legal counsel because he could not afford one, *The Big Brawl* (1980), a Kung Fu comedy, *Berlin Tunnel 21* (1981), *A Midsummer Night's Sex Comedy* (1982), *To Be or Not to*

Be (1983), *Bloodtide* (1984), about bizarre rituals on a Greek island, *The Evil that Men Do* (1984), *Dune* (1985), *Strange Interlude* (1988, a PBS production, starring Glenda Jackson), *A Life of Sin* (1990), and *Old Explorers* (1990). José Ferrer also directed *Return to Peyton Place* (1961) and *State Fair* (1962).

Mel Ferrer did a variety of films during the period including one with José Ferrer. His credits include *Sex and the Single Girl* (1964), *The Fall of the Roman Empire* (1964, starring Sophia Loren and Alec Guinness), which was a cut above other films within the classical epic genre, *El Greco* (1966, Italian-French production) reducing the painter's life to soap opera, *Brannigan* (1975) featuring John Wayne traveling to London to bring back a fugitive, *Eaten Alive* (1977), *The Norseman* (1978), *Guyana: Cult of the Damned* (1979), *City of the Walking Dead* (1980), *Emerald Jungle* (1980, Italian production) about a woman who searches for her sister in the Amazon and finds cannibal tribes instead, *Lili Marleen* (1981, German production, distributed in German with English subtitles, director Rainer Werner Fassbinder, starring Giancarlo Giannini), an interesting film about a Nazi wartime song idol, *One Shoe Makes it Murder* (1982, TV film) depicting Ferrer as a crime boss hiring Robert Mitchum to find his wayward wife played by Angie Dickinson, *Seduced* (1985, TV film starring Cybill Shepherd, with José Ferrer as well) about a politician embroiled in sex and murder, and *Revenge* (1990, starring Kevin Costner, Anthony Quinn, and Madeleine Stowe, with John Leguizamo), a dull mix of the slick and the sordid that was a box office failure. Ferrer gained wide exposure in the role of a lawyer in the television series *Falcon Crest*.

Spanish director Jess (Jesús) Franco has done numerous low-budget horror and soft pornographic films, in which he sometimes appears as an actor. Among these films are *Castle of Fu Manchu* (1968), *Count Dracula* (1970, starring Herbert Lom and Klaus Kinski), *Deadly Sanctuary* (1970, starring Jack Palance and Klaus Kinski), *Venus in Furs* (1970, starring Klaus Kinski), *A Virgin among the Living Dead* (1971), *Women in Cell Block 9* (1977), *Demoniac* (1979), *Jack the Ripper* (1979), *Ilsa, the Wicked Warden* (1980), *Bloody Moon* (1981), and *Erotikill* (1981).

Andy García achieved star status in 1990s. A Havana native who grew up in Miami Beach, he had a small part in the baseball movie *Blue Skies Again* (1983) and worked as a newspaper reporter turned crazed killer in *The Mean Season* (1985). He turned in an excellent performance as a villain in *8 Million Ways to Die* (1986). García also costarred in *Clinton and Nadine* (1987, TV film, with Ellen Barkin), before earning widespread recognition as the upright FBI agent in Brian de Palma's *The Untouchables* (1987). In 1988, he completed *American Roulette*, a spy thriller; was an official of the Educational Testing Service in *Stand and Deliver;* and, in 1989, he played another sincere police officer in the box office failure *Black Rain*. With his appearances in *The Godfather Part III*, *Internal Affairs* (he cowrote the script of the latter) and *A Show of Force*, 1990 was his breakthrough year. More recently he was in *Hero* (1992, Columbia, with Dustin Hoffman and Geena Davis) and *Jennifer Eight* (1992, Paramount, with John Malkovich).

Thomas Gómez (Sabino Tomás Gómez) was in *Summer and Smoke* (1961) playing the father of the dance hall girl played by Rita Moreno, *Stay Way, Joe* (1968, starring Elvis Presley, also with Katy Jurado), which reinforced stereotypes about contemporary Indians, and *Beneath the Planet of the Apes* (1970).

With the death of Chris-Pin Martin in 1953, Pedro González González (Ramiro González González), born in Aguilares, Texas, 1925 (García Riera, 1988, Vol. III, 145), replaced him in sidekick roles, less frequently seen beginning in the 1960s. Like his animated counterpart, Speedy González, he played a loquacious, nervous and jumpy type, almost contradicting the more traditional economy of words, gestures, and movement of the lower class, rural Mexican. He appeared in *The Adventures of Bullwhip Griffin* (1967) and in *Hostile Guns* (1967) where he is a poor goat thief thrown into an American jail where he really learns to do business. He also had parts in *Hook, Line and Sinker* (1969) and *The Love Bug* (1969).

José González González, brother of Pedro, was in *The Mermaids of Tiburon* (1962), *For Love or Money* (1963), and *The Aqua Sex* (1965).

Evelyn Guerrero was the apt comic foil in the Cheech and Chong films, including *Cheech and Chong's Next Movie* (1980), *Cheech and Chong's Nice Dreams* (1981), and *Things are Tough All Over* (1982).

Rita Hayworth did a few films in the 1960s and 1970s including *The Happy Thieves* (1961), *Circus World* (1964), *The Money Trap* (1966), *The Poppy Is Also a Flower* (1966), *Head* (1968), a film written by Jack Nicholson and Bob Rafelson for the rock group The Monkees, *The Naked Zoo* (1970), *Road to Salina* (1970), and *The Wrath of God* (1972).

León Ichaso directed *El Super* (1979), *Crossover Dreams* (1985), *The Take* (1990, TV film), a *Miami Vice* copycat, and several episodes of the television series, *Miami Vice.*

Marabina Jaimes won an Emmy Award for Best Host or Moderator of a TV Series for her work for KCET's *Storytime*. The show has been picked up nationally by PBS for 1994 distribution.

Neal Jiménez established himself as a screenwriter and most recently as a director. His credits as a screenwriter include *Where the River Runs Black* (1986), *River's Edge* (1986), and *For the Boys* (1991). Recently he wrote and debuted as codirector of the semiautobiographical film *The Waterdance,* about a young novelist (played by Eric Stoltz) who becomes a paraplegic after an accident and learns to adjust to a multiethnic rehabilitation center. The film also stars Wesley Snipes, William Forsythe, and Elizabeth Peña. He has written the screenplay for Robert Redford's upcoming release *Dark Wind,* based on the novel of Tony Hillerman.

Raúl Julia first became well-known for Shakespeare and other classical stage roles and in 1971 he debuted in small parts in *The Organization, Been Down So Long It Looks Like Up to Me,* and *Panic in Needle Park* (which also launched Al Pacino's career). In the 1970s, Julia appeared in *The Gumball Rally* (1976) and *Eyes of Laura Mars* (1978). Beginning in the 1980s, Julia has been one of the most productive Hispanic actors, appearing in *Tempest* (1982), *One from the Heart* (1982), *The Escape Artist* (1982), *Compromising Positions* (1985), *Kiss of the Spider Woman* (1985), *The Morning After* (1986), *Florida Straits* (1986), *Trading Hearts* (1987), *The Alamo: Thirteen Days to Glory* (1987, TV film), *The Penitent* (1988), *Tango Bar* (1988), *Tequila Sunrise* (1988), *Moon Over Parador* (1988), *Romero* (1989), *Frankenstein Unbound* (1990), *Havana* (1990), *Mack the Knife* (1990) *Presumed Innocent* (1990), *A Life of Sin* (1990), *The Rookie* (1990), *The Addams Family* (1991), and *Addams Family Values* (1993). Many of the productions described above are Hispanic-focused. Some of them, such as *The Penitent,* which evoked the *penitentes* of New Mexico and their reenactment of Christ's crucifixion, and *Florida Straits,* an HBO production about escaping Cuba by boat, are quite obscure. Others, including *Romero* in which Julia plays the slain archbishop of El Salvador, are likely to be enduring films. Julia costarred in the notable *Kiss of the Spider Woman* (1985) from the novel by Argentine Manuel Puig. He played a political prisoner sharing a cell with an apolitical gay man. Julia has worked in Puerto Rican productions or coproductions including *Tango Bar* (1988) and *La gran fiesta* (1987).

Katy Jurado played character roles in *One-Eyed Jacks* (1961), starring and directed by Marlon Brando, *Barabbas* (1961), *Smoky* (1966), *A Covenant With Death* (1967), and *Stay Away, Joe* (1968), subsequently moving into television films. In the 1970s, she had roles in *Pat Garrett and Billy the Kid* (1973), *The Children of Sánchez* (1978), and was the mother in the Paul Rodríguez television sitcom, *a.k.a. Pablo.*

Fernando Lamas appeared in a few less than memorable films such as *The Lost World* (1960), *A Place Called Glory* (1966, German production), *Kill a Dragon* (1967), *Valley of Mystery* (1967), *The Violent Ones* (1967), *100 Rifles* (1969), *Backtrack* (1969), *Murder on Flight 502* (1975, TV film), *Powderkeg* (1976, TV film), the pilot for the mid-1970s television series, *The Bearcats,* and the best of the lot, *The Cheap Detective* (1978), a parody of *The Maltese Falcon,* in which he had a supporting role.

Lorenzo Lamas (son of Fernando Lamas and Arlene Dahl) has been in film and television since his teenage years, appearing in *Take Down* (1978), a comedy about wrestling, *Body Rock* (1984), a box office failure about break dancing in the South Bronx, *Snake Eater* (1989), *Snake*

Eater 2, The Drug Buster (1989), *Night of the Warrior* (1990, also with Arlene Dahl), a kick-boxing film, *Final Impact* (1991), another kick-boxing film, and *Killing Streets* (1991). Lamas has done considerable work on television including *Falcon Crest, California Fever,* and *Secrets of Midland Heights.*

John Leguizamo has had parts in *Casualties of War* (1989), *Die Hard 2 (1990), Revenge* (1990), *Regarding Henry* (1991), and *Whispers in the Dark* 1992); he starred in *Super Mario Brothers* (1993) about two Brooklyn plumbers who try to save a beautiful princess in an alternate universe where people evolved from dinosaurs, and was in *Carlito's Way* (1993, Universal, directed by Brian De Palma and starring Al Pacino), a film about the rise and fall of a Puerto Rican criminal. He costarred in *Hangin' with the Homeboys* (1991, director Joseph B. Vásquez), an excellent low-budget film, comparable in quality to John Singleton's *Boyz N the Hood* (1991). He also had a semiregular role on the television series *Miami Vice.* Leguizamo is also well-known for his comic performances including *Spic-O-Rama* (HBO one-man comic show) and *Mambo Mouth* (the script of the latter was published in 1993). Leguizamo is the winner of an Obie and Outer Critics Circle Award.

Margo appeared in *Who's Got the Action* (1962).

Richard "Cheech" Marín began as part of the comedy team "Cheech and Chong" in 1970, bringing their stoned and hippy routines to the screen with *Cheech and Chong's Up in Smoke* (1978), the highest grossing film of the year. In succession the comedy duo did *Cheech and Chong's Next Movie* (1980), *Cheech and Chong's Nice Dreams* (1981), *Things are Tough All Over* (1982), *Yellowbeard* (1983), and *Cheech and Chong's the Corsican Brothers* (1984). After the duo split up in 1985, Cheech Marín extended his range considerably, appearing in *After Hours* (1985, director Martin Scorsese), a notable, bizarre, and brutal dark comedy that takes place in SoHo, New York City; *Echo Park* (1986), about show business hopefuls living in one of Los Angeles's seedier neighborhoods; *Rude Awakening* (1989) about draft dodgers of 1969 who return from Central America in 1989; *Ghostbusters II* (1989); *Troop Beverly Hills* (1989); *Far Out Man* (1990, director Thomas Chong), a box office failure in which he did a cameo; and *Shrimp on the Barbie* (1990). His most significant Hispanic-focused production has been *Born in East L.A.* (1987), which he wrote and directed and in which he starred.

A Martínez (Adolf Martínez III) played the role of Juan Nepomuceno Seguín in the film by Chicano director Jesús Salvador Treviño, *Seguín* (1982), costarred in *Hunt for the Night Stalker* (1989, TV film also released as *Manhunt: Search for the Night Stalker),* based on the pursuit of serial killer Richard Ramírez, and starred in *Powwow Highway* (1988), an interesting comedy treating the serious subject of the mistreatment of American Indians on reservations. His primary credits have been in television including *Santa Barbara, Storefront Lawyers, The Cowboys, Centennial, Born to the Wind, Cassie & Company, Whiz Kids,* and *L.A. Law.*

Rachel McLish (formerly Rachel Elizondo), a bodybuilder born in Harlingen, Texas, of Mexican parents, debuted in the documentary *Pumping Iron II: The Women* (1985) and costarred with Oscar winner Louis Gossett, Jr. in *Aces: Iron Eagles III* (1992), yet another film about busting drug dealers, this time in Peru.

Bill Meléndez has become one of the top independent animators in Hollywood. Bill Meléndez Inc. does a great deal of work for the *Peanuts* cartoons of Charles Schultz.

Ramón Menéndez has won recognition for his directing of *Stand and Deliver* (1988) and recently directed and cowrote *Money for Nothing* (1993), featuring John Cusack as an out-of-work longshoreman who's down on his luck and finds $1.2 million which ends up turning him into a small-time criminal. His girlfriend is played by Debi Mazar.

Ricardo Montalbán was in *Let No Man Write My Epitaph* (1960), *Desert Warrior* (1961), *Hemingway's Adventures of a Young Man* (1962), *Love is a Ball* (1963), *Rage of the Buccaneers* (1963), *Cheyenne Autumn* (1964), *The Singing Nun* (1965), *The Money Trap* (1966), *Alice Through the Looking Glass* (1966), *Madame X* (1966), *Blue* (1968), and *Sol Madrid* (1968); was an Italian lover in *Sweet Charity* (1969); and appeared in *Escape from the Planet of the Apes* (1971), *Conquest of the*

Planet of the Apes (1972), *The Train Robbers* (1973), *Joe Panther* (1976), *Fantasy Island* (1977, TV film that launched the series), *Return to Fantasy Island* (1977), *Mission to Glory* (1979, also starring César Romero), a box office and critical failure about Spanish padre Francisco Kino who helped develop California in the late seventeenth century, *Star Trek II: The Wrath of Khan* (1982), and *The Naked Gun* (1988). His career was greatly aided by his starring in the long-running television series, *Fantasy Island* (1978-84).

Rosenda Monteros, a Mexican actress who had been in *Villa!* (1958) had a supporting role in *The Magnificent Seven* (1960); was in *Tiara Tahiti* (1962, British production) and *The Mighty Jungle* (1964), and in *She* (1965, British) she played the second female lead to Ursula Andress. In 1969, she had a role in the film *Popi* starring Alan Arkin as a Puerto Rican widower struggling to support his young sons. The film was able to spawn a brief TV series that starred Héctor Elizondo.

Esai Morales played Ritchie Valens's disturbed half-brother in *La Bamba* (1987) and gave a stirring performance. His first role was opposite Sean Penn in *Bad Boys* (1983), where he was superb as the sworn Hispanic enemy of the Anglo juvenile delinquent. He also has appeared in *Great Love Experiment* (1984), *L.A. Bad* (1985), *The Principal* (1987), featuring James Belushi versus the school thugs, *On Wings of Eagles* (1988), *Bloodhounds of Broadway* (1989), a Damon Runyon tale with Madonna, *Naked Tango* (1991, script by Manuel Puig, with Fernando Rey in a supporting role) about the tango underground of 1920s Buenos Aires, and *Ultraviolet* (1992); he has a principal part in the forthcoming film *Rapa Nui* about the culture and ecology of Easter Island.

Rita Moreno, to date the only Hispanic actress to win an Oscar, earned her award for her supporting role in *West Side Story* (1961) which, unfortunately, promoted the careers of mostly non-Hispanics, including Natalie Wood and George Chakiris in the roles of Hispanic characters. Moreno went on to do a supporting role in an adaptation of Tennessee Williams's *Summer and Smoke* (1961), and she had roles in *Samar* (1962) about the inhumane treatment of Philippine inmates, *Cry of Battle* (1963, starring Van Heflin), another Philippine action film, *Marlowe* (1969), as a stripper who helps solve a criminal case, *The Night of the Following Day* (1969), an unsuccessful film starring Marlon Brando, *Popi* (1969), *Carnal Knowledge* (1971), in which she had a cameo role, *The Ritz* (1976), where she did a memorable role as a no-talent Puerto Rican singer in a bathhouse, *The Boss' Son* (1978), *Happy Birthday, Gemini* (1980), *The Four Seasons* (1981), a notable film about four stages of friendship among three middle-aged couples, *Life in the Food Chain* (1991), and *Age Isn't Everything* (1991). She has done considerable television work and won Emmys as best supporting actress on a variety show for *The Muppet Show* (1977) and as best actress in an appearance on a dramatic show for *The Rockford Files* (1978).

Rick Nájera, one of the founders of the successful comedy troupe Latins Anonymous now works as a writer on Fox's *In Living Color*. He has produced and stars in his own short, comic film, *Pain of the Macho*.

Gregory Nava, who won recognition for the outstanding film he directed, *El Norte* (1983), also directed *A Time of Destiny* (1988, Columbia) a revenge film which was poorly received despite a strong cast including William Hurt, Timothy Hutton, and Francisco Rabal.

Manuel R. Ojeda appeared in The Last Rebel (1961) and The Queen's Swordsmen (1963).

Edward James Olmos debuted in *Aloha, Bobby and Rose* (1974) in which Anglos accidently involved in a murder run away to Mexico, and he starred in *Alambrista!* (1977), an independent Chicano feature and one of the best films to date to evoke the U.S.-Mexico border. He did a reprise of his theatrical role of the *pachuco* in *Zoot Suit* (1981), a critical success but box office failure; was cast in lesser roles in *Wolfen* (1981), *Virus* (1982), and *Blade Runner* (1982) in which he played a memorable part as an origami-practicing detective; and then played the lead in the Chicano production *The Ballad of Gregorio Cortez* (1982). He also had the role of General Santa Anna in the Chicano production *Seguín* (1982, director Jesús Salvador Treviño). He achieved national recognition in the role of Lieutenant Martin Castillo in the television series, *Miami Vice*, beginning in 1984. His admirable performance in *Stand and Deliver* (1988) earned him a nomination for the Academy Award. He also acted in *The Nightingale* (1983), a fairy tale with Mick Jagger and Barbara Hershey, *Saving Grace* (1986), directed by Robert Young, about a pope incognito among Italian peasants, *Triumph of the Spirit* (1989) as a Gypsy in a World War II concentration camp, *Maria's Story* (1990), and *A Talent for the Game* (1991, director Robert Young). He directed and starred in *American Me* (1992), a story of Chicano gang culture.

Pina Pellicer was in the Mexican film *Macario* (1960) and played the lead in *One-Eyed Jacks* in 1961, the year she committed suicide.

Elizabeth Peña debuted in *El Super* (1979, director León Ichaso, in Spanish with English subtitles, reportedly the first Spanish-language film to be shot in New York City) about the trials of a homesick exiled Cuban who labors as an apartment house superintendent in Manhattan. She made a name for herself in the 1980s in *They All Laughed* (1981, director Peter Bogdanovich), *Crossover Dreams* (1985) with Rubén Blades, *Down and Out in Beverly Hills* (1986), *Batteries Not Included* (1987), *La Bamba* (1987),*Vibes* (1988) starring Cyndi Lauper and Jeff Goldblum, *Blue Steel* (1990), *Jacob's Ladder* (1990), and *The Waterdance* (1992). On television she was in the series *Tough Cookies* and *I Married Dora*.

Spanish actor Julio Peña appeared in *The Happy Thieves* (1961), *The Revolt of the Slaves* (1961), *The Castilian* (1963, Spanish production), *Kid Rodelo* (1966), *Minnesota Clay* (1966), *Web of Violence* (1966), *Falstaff* (1967), *The Hellbenders* (1967), *Savage Pampas* (1967), *One Step to Hell* (1969), and *El Condor* (1970).

Rosie Pérez was in an episode of the television series *21 Jump Street*, appeared in Spike Lee's *Do the Right Thing* (1989) as an unwed Puerto Rican mother, and in an HBO film, *Criminal Justice* (1990), where she played a crack-addicted prostitute. Pérez had a brief appearance as a screechy puertorriqueña in *Night on Earth* (1992, director Jim Jarmusch), an offbeat, episodic film about four cabdrivers in four different countries and their oddball encounters. She costarred with Woody Harrelson in *White Men Can't Jump* (1992), which won her national recognition, and was in *Untamed Heart* (1993, starring Christian Slater and Marisa Tomei). In *Fearless* (1993, Warner, director Peter Weir), opposite Jeff Bridges, she appears as a young mother coping with the loss of her baby in a plane crash. Her work in *Fearless* garnered her an Academy Award nomination in the Best Supporting Actress category. She will appear in the forthcoming *Cop Tips Waitress $2 Million* with costars Bridget Fonda and Nicolas Cage.

Lou Diamond Phillips, an actor born in the Philippines who is of partial Hispanic descent, first came to prominence as Ritchie Valens in *La Bamba* (1987). He subsequently distinguished himself as a calculus-proficient gang member in *Stand and Deliver* (1988). His considerable credits include *Harley* (1985), *Dakota* (1988), *Young Guns* (1988), *Disorganized Crime* (1989), *Renegades* (1989), *The First Power* (1990), *A Show of Force* (1990), *Young Guns II* (1990), and *Ambition* (1991).

Anthony Quinn was one of very few long-standing Hispanic actors whose career expanded during the 1960s and 1970s. In fact, Quinn was able to move away from his Latin image of the 1950s (e.g.,*Viva Zapata, Ride Vaquero!*) to portray a variety of exotics. He had a role in the hit *The Guns of Navarone* (1961), played a biblical character in *Barrabas* (1961), an Arab in *Lawrence of Arabia* (1962), the title role of *Zorba The Greek* (1964), a Russian pope in *The Shoes of the Fishermen* (1968), an Italian in *The Secret of Santa Vittoria* (1969), and back to a Greek in the excellent *A Dream of Kings* (1969), which takes place in the Greek community of Chicago, and *The Greek Tycoon* (1978). He also had Hispanic roles in *Behold a Pale Horse* (1964), a post-Spanish Civil War story of politics and violence, *Guns for San Sebastian* (1968), *The Children of Sánchez* (1978), and *High Risk* (1981) as a sleazy bandit leader in Colombia. Additional credits during the period include: *Heller in Pink Tights* (1960), the moving *A High Wind in Jamaica* (1965), *Lost Command* (1966), *The Magus* (1968), *R.P.M. (Revolutions Per Minute)*, 1970, director Stanley Kramer, in which Quinn plays a liberal professor who becomes president of the university amid student unrest, *A Walk in the Spring Rain* (1970, costarring Ingrid Bergman), *Across 110th*

Street (1972), *The Don is Dead* (1973), *The Destructors* (1974), yet another drug dealer film, *The Con Artists* (1977), *The Message (Mohammad, Messenger of God)*, 1977, where Quinn plays Mohammad's uncle, *Caravans* (1978), *The Salamander* (1981), *Lion of the Desert* (1981), *Regina* (1983, Italian production), *African Rage* (1985), *Ghosts Can't Do It* (1990), *Revenge* (1990), Spike Lee's *Jungle Fever* (1991), and *Only the Lonely* (1991).

Francesco Quinn, son of Anthony Quinn and Jolanda Addolari, has been in *Quo Vadis?* (1985, Italian television production), *Platoon* (1986), *Indigo* (1989), and *Priceless Beauty* (1989).

Chita Rivera was in a supporting role as a dance-hall hostess in *Sweet Charity* (1969). She also had a supporting role in *Mayflower Madam* (1987, TV film) starring Candice Bergen as Sydney Biddle Barrows, a descendent of the Mayflower and classy madam. She played Dick Van Dyke's secretary girlfriend on the original Broadway production of *Bye Bye Birdie* but the 1963 film featured Janet Leigh in a "Mexican wig" as the character of Rose de León.

Jorge Rivero was in *Rio Lobo* (1970), *Day of the Assassin* (1979), *Priest of Love* (1981), *Target Eagle* (1982), *Counterforce* (1987), and *Fist Fighter* (1988).

Comedian Paul Rodríguez was in *D.C.Cab* (1983), starred on the television series *a.k.a. Pablo* (1984), and has done a number of films since including *Miracles* (1986), *Ponce de León and the Fountain of Youth* (1986), *Quicksilver* (1986), *The Whoopee Boys* (1986), *Born in East L.A.* (1987), and *Made in America* (1993).

Robert Rodríguez cofinanced, wrote, directed, filmed, and edited *El Mariachi* (1993) with the intention of selling it to the Spanish video market. However, when an agent saw the film it was circulated to the major studios. All the studios bid for the rights, and Columbia, which also has a contract with John Singleton, seemed most appealing to Rodríguez. The young director was given a two-year, three-picture deal with Columbia and he hopes to do an *El Mariachi* trilogy.

Gilbert Roland's best role of the 1960s was as an American Indian in John Ford's last Western and only pro-Indian film, *Cheyenne Autumn* (1964) costarring Ricardo Montalbán and Dolores del Río. He was also in *Samar* (1962), *The Reward* (1965), *The Poppy is Also a Flower* (1966), *Any Gun Can Play* (1968), and *The Ruthless Four* (1969). In the 1970s, he appeared in *Islands in the Stream* and *The Black Pearl* (both 1977). He also appeared in *Barbarosa* (1982).

Phil Román, the president of Film Roman does the animation for *The Simpsons* and other projects include *Garfield and Friends*, *Bobby's World* on Fox and the Pizza Hut mascot, Big Foot. Film Roman recently did its first feature film, *Tom and Jerry: The Movie*, which has been successful in Europe and is scheduled to open in the United States in 1994. A forthcoming animation project for educational television is *The Way Things Work*, featuring the character of Dr. Celia, a Hispanic scientist who explains scientific principles.

César Romero, who had a cameo role in *Pepe* continued to obtain roles, appearing in *Ocean's Eleven* (1960), *Seven Women from Hell* (1961), *If A Man Answers* (1962), *Donovan's Reef* (1963), *We Shall Return* (1963), *A House is Not a Home* (1964), *Marriage on the Rocks* (1965), *Sergeant Deadhead* (1965), *Two on a Guillotine* (1965), *Batman* (1966), *Hot Millions* (1968), *Skidoo* (1968), *How to Make It* (1969), *Madigan's Millions* (1969), *Midas Run* (1969), *A Talent for Loving* (1969) where he appears as a Mexican landowner who tricks footloose Richard Widmark into marrying one of his daughters, *Latitude Zero* (1970), *The Red, White and Black* (1970), *Sophie's Place (Crooks and Coronets)*,1970, *Now You See Him, Now You Don't* (1972), and *The Proud and the Damned* (1973). However, he achieved more recognition in the 1960s as the Joker in the TV *Batman* series. In the 1970s, he did two formula Disney comedies, *The Computer Wore Tennis Shoes* (1970) and *The Strongest Man in the World* (1975). In the 1980s, he appeared in the television series *Falcon Crest* in the role of Peter Stavros, a Greek billionaire, in *Lust in the Dust* (1985), a parody of Westerns, and in *Simple Justice* (1989).

Charlie Sheen, younger brother of Emilio Estévez and son of Martin Sheen, made his first appearance as an extra in *Apocalypse Now* (1979), was in *Red Dawn* (1984), and attracted attention for his role as a precocious fourteen-year-old boy who falls in love with the new girl in town in *Lucas* (1986). He has since emerged as one of the leading actors of his generation, best known for his roles in *Platoon* (1986), set in Vietnam, and *Wall Street* (1987), about greed and unscrupulous financial trading, also featuring Martin Sheen, both directed by Oliver Stone. Additional acting credits include *The Boys Next Door* (1985), *Ferris Bueller's Day Off* (1986), *No Man's Land* (1987), *Three for the Road* (1987), *Young Guns* (1988), *Eight Men Out* (1988) directed by John Sayles, *Major League* (1989), *Men at Work* (1990), *Navy Seals* (1990), *The Rookie* (1990), *Hot Shots!* (1991), *Cadence* (1991, director Martin Sheen), about a prejudiced stockade commander who forces a new, white prisoner to spy on his black cellmates, *Hot Shots II* (1993), and *The Three Musketeers* (1993). He will appear in *Fixing the Shadow* in 1994.

Martin Sheen debuted on film in *The Incident* (1967) about drunken hoods who terrorize New York subway passengers. He went on to star status, reprising his stage role in *The Subject Was Roses* (1968) about a young veteran's troubled relationship with his parents, and appeared in the antiwar film *Catch-22* (1970) and in a television landmark, *That Certain Summer* (1972), the first TV movie to convey a homosexual theme. He did another notable TV film, *The Execution of Private Slovik* (1974), about the only American soldier (World War II) executed by the American government since the Civil War. Additionally, he was in *The Andersonville Trial* (1970, TV film), *No Drums, No Bugles* (1971), *Rage* (1972), *Catholics* (1973), *Badlands* (1974) about a killing spree in the 1950s, *The Missiles of October* (1974, TV film), *The Little Girl Who Lives Down the Lane* (1976, starring Jodie Foster), in which he played a child molester, *Sweet Hostage* (1976), *The Cassandra Crossing* (1977), the notable Vietnam war film directed by Francis Ford Coppola, *Apocalypse Now* (1979), *The Final Countdown* (1980), *Loophole* (1980), *That Championship Season* (1982), *Gandhi* (1982), *Enigma* (1982), *The Dead Zone* (1983), *Kennedy* (1983, TV miniseries), *Man, Woman and Child* (1983), *Firestarter* (1984), *The Guardian* (1984), *Out of the Darkness* (1985, TV film also starring Héctor Elizondo), *The Fourth Wise Man* (1985, TV film), *News at Eleven* (1985), *Consenting Adults* (1985, TV film), *Samaritan: The Mitch Snyder Story* (1986, TV film), *Shattered Spirits* (1986, TV film), *The Believers* (1987), *Conspiracy: The Trial of the Chicago 8* (1987, TV film), *Siesta* (1987), *Wall Street* (1987, starring Charlie Sheen), *Judgment in Berlin* (1988), *Da* (1988), *Beverly Hills Brats* (1989), *Beyond the Stars* (1989), *Cold Front* (1989), *Nightbreaker* (1989, also starring Emilio Estévez) about the effects of nuclear tests on military personnel in Nevada in the 1950s, *The Maid* (1991), and *Touch and Die* (1991, also starring René Estévez). Martin Sheen made his directing debut in 1991 in the Republic Pictures film *Cadence* starring himself and sons Charlie Sheen and Ramón Estévez and won an Emmy for directing the TV special *Babies Having Babies*, in which he worked with his daughter René Estévez. He also had a role in the television miniseries *Gettysburg* (1993) produced by Esparza-Katz for the TNT cable channel.

Jimmy Smits won an Emmy award and gained wide exposure as Victor Sifuentes on the *L.A. Law* television series and was seen in *Running Scared* (1986), starring Billy Crystal and Gregory Hines as wisecracking detectives, *The Believers* (1987), a New York City voodoo cult movie starring Martin Sheen, and *Vital Signs* (1990), a medical school drama. He costarred as a Mexican revolutionary with Jane Fonda and Gregory Peck in *Old Gringo* (1989). In 1991, he appeared in *Fires Within* (Pathé) a romantic drama about Cuban exiles in America, and *Switch* (Warner) in a comedy role as the friend of a man who comes back to life in the body of a woman.

Madeleine Stowe, who is half Costa Rican, was in *The Nativity* (1978, TV film) about Joseph and Mary, *Stakeout* (1987), *Worth Winning* (1989), *Revenge* (1990), *The Two Jakes* (1990), *Closet Land* (1991, director Radha Bharadwaj), an interesting, minimalist sort of film that depicts the torture and interrogation of suspects by an unnamed government, *Unlawful Entry* (1992), *The Last of the Mohicans* (1992, Fox), and *Another Stakeout* (1993). Her latest film is *Blink* (1994).

Rachel Ticotin made her debut in *Fort Apache, the Bronx* (1981) and played the enigmatic Melina in Arnold Schwarzenegger's *Total Recall* (1990). Her acting credits include *King of the Gypsies* (1978), *Critical Condition* (1987), *One Good Cop* (1991), *Prison Stories: Women on the Inside* (1991, TV miniseries), and *F/X II: The Deadly Art of Illusion* (1991). She was production assistant for *Dressed to Kill* (1980) and *Raging Bull* (1980).

David Valdés is a director and producer. His credits as assistant director include *Firefox* (1982), *The Outsiders* (1983), and *Rumble Fish* (1983). He was producer or executive producer of *Bird* (1988), *Unforgiven* (1992) and *A Perfect World* (1993). He was the director of *In the Line of Fire* (1993).

Daniel Valdez, brother of Luis Valdez had the lead in *Zoot Suit* (1981).

Luis Valdez, director, playwright, and screenwriter is a major example of the "Hispanic Hollywood" phenomenon. In addition to his independent, Chicano productions (see following chapter) he was the director of *Zoot Suit* (1981), which closely followed the theatrical version that had been so successful in Los Angeles. Valdez wrote and directed *La Bamba* (1987) evoking the life and career of Ritchie Valens. This film was tremendously successful in both mainstream and Hispanic markets. It was the first major film that was simultaneously produced and distributed in both English and Spanish.

Mexican actress Isela Vega was in *Rage* (1966, U.S.-Mexican production) about a misanthropic doctor, played by Glenn Ford, who contracts rabies and races across the Mexican desert to get help, *The Deadly Trackers* (1973), *Bring Me the Head of Alfredo García* (1974), *The Streets of L.A.* (1979), and *Barbarosa* (1982).

Raquel Welch (Raquel Tejada) debuted in *A House is Not a Home* (1964) and gained considerable attention for her role in *Fantastic Voyage* (1966), then attained star status with such films as *One Million Years B.C.* (1966), *100 Rifles* (1969), *Myra Breckinridge* (1970), *Bluebeard* (1972), and *The Three Musketeers* (1974). Other credits include *A Swinging Summer* (1965), *Shoot Loud, Louder . . . I Don't Understand* (1966) opposite Marcello Mastroianni, *Bedazzled* (1967, British production), an excellent updating of the Faust legend also starring Dudley Moore, *Bandolero!* (1968), *Lady in Cement* (1968), and *The Biggest Bundle of Them All* (1968). She had a cameo appearance in *The Magic Christian* (1970), a film starring Peter Sellers and Ringo Starr, *Fuzz* (1972), *Hannie Caulder* (1972), *Kansas City Bomber* (1972), *Restless* (1972, Greek production), *The Last of Sheila* (1973), *The Four Musketeers* (1975), *The Wild Party* (1975), *Mother, Jugs and Speed* (1976) opposite Bill Cosby, *The Legend of Walks Far Woman* (1982) as an American Indian heroine, and *Scandal in a Small Town* (1989, TV film).

In addition to his roles in a number of important Chicano productions, actor Richard Yniguez appeared in *Boulevard Nights* (1979) and *Jake Spanner Private Eye* (1989, TV film).

Daphne Zúñiga is probably best known for her role as John Cusack's reluctant traveling companion in Rob Reiner's *The Sure Thing* (1985), an update of Frank Capra's *It Happened One Night* (1934) about two college students who don't get along and travel cross-country together. She was in Lucille Ball's first dramatic telefilm, *Stone Pillow* (1985), played Princess Vespa in Mel Brooks's *Spaceballs* (1987), was the leading lady in *The Fly II* (1989), and had roles in *The Dorm That Dripped Blood* (1981), *The Initiation* (1983), *Modern Girls* (1986), *Last Rites* (1988), *Staying Together* (1989), *Gross Anatomy* (1989), and *Prey of the Chameleon* (1992, TV film). Zúñiga has a recurring role in Fox television's *Melrose Place*.

Frank Zúñiga has directed *The Golden Seal* (1983), *The Wilderness Family, Part II* (1978), and *Fist Fighter* (1988).

Notes

[1]García Riera (1988, III, 151) points out that many of the Italian actors in these films had their names changed for foreign distribution. For example, Ignazio Spalla became Pedro Sánchez, and Guiliano Gemma was turned into Montgomery Wood. In 1964, the film publicity produced for *Per un pugno de dollari* (U. S. release, *A Fistful of Dollars*) billed director Sergio Leone as Bob Robertson. The films themselves were dubbed into English or Spanish for local distribution.

[2]It also gave impetus to other Westerns made in Europe of the nonsadistic kind. The most notable of these was *Viva María!* (1965, French-Italian coproduction, director Louis Malle), mostly a pretext to bring together the two most famous French actresses of the period, Brigitte Bardot and Jeanne Moreau. It had two beautiful entertainers stuck in revolutionary San Miguel (but clearly Mexico) around the turn of the century.

7

The Emergence of U.S. Hispanic Films

As we have seen in the previous chapter, the emergence of Chicano, Puerto Rican, and other U.S. Latino cinema followed as a natural, even inevitable consequence of the Civil Rights movement, particularly the introduction into and training of a cadre of Hispanic professionals in the industry, who worked both inside established channels to create more genuine Hollywood Hispanic-focused films and outside of them to produce independent U.S. Latino cinema. As Chicano/Chicana and other Latino/Latina actors, filmmakers, and other professionals entered the industry and received their apprenticeships through the production of documentaries on varied subject matter, their sensitivities inevitably turned to the Hispanic experience, primarily because the Hispanic story was there, beckoning and untold. As Treviño put it with respect to the Chicano cinematic phenomenon, "As a by-product of this '60s activism and organizing it became increasingly evident that if a truer story was to be told then Chicanos would have to be the ones to tell it" (Treviño, 1982, 171).

In the previous chapter we reviewed mostly the mainstream product, including the films of the "Hispanic Hollywood" category. Here we focus on the independent or semi-autonomous U.S. Latino cinema.

During the late 1960s and early 1970s, the film industry, among others, became the target of both national and local civil rights groups. Following on the success of the NAACP in having the industry open more jobs to blacks, the League of United Latin American Citizens, the Mexican American Legal Defense and Educational Fund, ASPIRA of America, the National Council of La Raza, and others urged similar consideration for Hispanics. As a result, several individuals who would become renown got their start in the film industry as activists. The now noted producer, Moctesuma Esparza was one of the "L.A. Thirteen" "indicted on conspiracy charges in the March 1968 blowouts in East L.A. high schools, [and subsequently] organized the UCLA Media Urban Crisis Coalition program, which recruited thirteen ethnic minorities" (Noriega, 1992, 142). Luis Valdez, the founder of El Teatro Campesino during the Delano grape strike made an early, natural, militant activist transition to film, producing *I Am Joaquín* (1969) based on Rodolfo "Corky" Gonzales's notable poem. Activism was particularly intense in the Los Angeles area where various individuals began to organize Latino media groups such as CARISSMA and JUSTICIA. In 1969, a group of Hispanic actors, led by Ricardo Montalbán, organized NOSOTROS, a group devoted to protesting the kinds of roles Hispanics were forced to play and to working to better the image of Hispanics in Hollywood films. At the same time that constituency-based organizations were pressing Hollywood, government statistics were confirming the extent of United States Hispanic underrepresentation in the industry. In 1969, a U.S.

Equal Employment Opportunity Commission report found that only 3 percent of the work force at major Hollywood studios was "Spanish surnamed." Similar statistics prevailed in commercial television and, even more amazing, public broadcasting was shown to have compiled an even worse record of less than 1 percent Mexican or Chicano employees. As Jesús Treviño observed (1982, 171), the major studios responded with token gestures to employ more Chicanos, primarily by means of internship programs; television responded primarily through its creation of low-budget, off-hours community interest "talk" shows; and the universities (particularly UCLA and the University of Southern California) participated with special admissions programs.

In a certain sense, the emergence of Latino cinema was unexpected—at least by industry executives. Prodded by the courts, by certain sectors of society such as college students, and above all by the Civil Rights movement, particularly the Hispanic constituency-based organizations, the film corporations did hire Latinos, but for general work in the profession and not necessarily for the production of Latino films. The creation of U.S. Latino films was not possible until the condition of entry and training of Latino professionals was fulfilled; but those very Latino films also subverted the status quo values of the industry itself.

Noriega has suggested that from the very first introduction of U.S. Latinos into the film and television industry, the situation that those individuals faced taught them a most crucial lesson, namely "how to subvert the discursive parameters for mass media so that Chicano filmmakers could work within and yet against the industry and its conventions" (1992, 142). One of the channels for this phenomenon of working both within the system and against it was in television projects. The newly minted Latino apprentices often turned to television projects, producing minority public affairs shows that reported on various protests but which also explained them to mainstream audiences, empathized with them, legitimated them, and promoted their underlying ideals.

One of the more innovative shows was *Reflecciones* (KABC-TV in Los Angeles, 1972-73), in which Luis Garza, Susan Racho, and David García mastered the objective discourse of reportage in order to pioneer a new form of television, the political documentary series, which protested the Vietnam War, advocated a farmworkers' union, and exposed the criminal legal system (Noriega, 1992, 142). Another important show was Jesús Salvador Treviño's *Acción Chicano*. The documentary *Carnalitos* (1973) by Bobby Páramo was produced under the show's sponsorship.

The Civil Rights movement had an effect on acting roles as well, although tokenism here still prevailed. Significant Hispanic parts had to wait until filmmakers (directors, producers, and scriptwriters especially) would create them. With respect to acting roles, beginning in the mid-1960s many Hispanics appeared in all sorts of films that were not specifically focused on Hispanics including *Bob and Carol and Ted and Alice* (1969), *The Goodbye Girl* (1972), *Blume in Love* (1973), *Dog Day Afternoon* (1975), *The Marathon Man* (1976), *The Big Fix* (1978), *Grease* (1978), *The Changeling* (1979), *Back Roads* (1980), *9 to 5* (1980), *Whose Life is it Anyway?* (1981), and many others. Unfortunately as Carlos Cortés (1985) points out, these bit characters usually come off as nothing more than stick furniture, functioning as maids, bank tellers, secretaries, cops, a drug dealer or two, and with notable exceptions, such as the stalwart nurse in *Whose Life is it Anyway?* and the bad madam in *Back Roads,* they seldom do more than take up space, look Latin, and spout either Spanish or stereotypically accented English.

By 1974, the method of working within the system as well as against it had taken a markedly more institutional quality as student protests waned, partially with the defusing of the Vietnam War issue, as some Chicanos rose through the system, and as some volunteer organizations disbanded. JUSTICIA, for example, organized by Ray Andrade, Pete Rodríguez, and Bob Morones at California State University at Los Angeles, outlived its viability because it had been successful in its initial goals, helping to bring about locally Chicano-produced television shows including *Acción Chicano* (KCET-TV), *Reflecciones* and *Unidos* (KABC-TV), and *Impacto* (KNBC-TV); because as a community protest group it lacked funding; and because much of its mission was subsequently subsumed into the Latino Consortium and the Los Angeles Chicano Cinema Coalition.

In 1974, the Latino Consortium was created, with its institutional base in the PBS-affiliate, KCET-TV, Los Angeles. The Consortium "served as a national syndicator of Latino-themed programming to public television. According to the first (and current) executive director, José Luis Ruiz, the Latino Consortium owes its survival to its institutional status, which helped it secure the long-term funding and organizational continuity that the other volunteer groups lacked" (Noriega, 1992, 142).

The mid- and late 1970s were also the period that witnessed the emergence of a few manifestos or testimonials on what Chicano/Chicana film is or ought to be (see Noriega 1992) including "Ya Basta Con Yankee Imperialist Documentaries!" by Cine-Aztlán (1974), "Towards the Development of a Raza Cinema" by Francisco X. Camplis (1975), "Notes on Chicano Cinema" by Jason C. Johansen (1979), and Sylvia Morales's 1979 interview which appears in Noriega (1992) as "Filming a Chicana Documentary (1979)". Noriega (1992, xiii) has described the first manifestos as both affiliating Chicano cinema to the Chicano civil rights movement and New Latin American Cinema. Sylvia Morales extends the project to the expansion of Chicano/Mexican history to include women marginalized or obscured in that history as well as feminist and related goals.

In 1978, less than 10 years after the founding of NOSOTROS, the Los Angeles Chicano Cinema Coalition was founded; its philosophy had evolved from protesting Hollywood's exploitive tendencies to responding to two concerns: "the need to evolve a Chicano cinema esthetic, and the need to create an alternative to the 'commercial' influence of Hollywood film. . . . " (Treviño, 1982, 176). The group had as its primary goal to promote the growth and development of a Chicano cinema esthetic that would work on behalf of Chicano efforts toward social justice and allied concerns.

Chicano Cinema Productions

The Chicano film period is preceded by a handful of films. *Flight* (1960, independent production directed by Louis Bispo) starring Efraín Ramírez, Esther Cortez, María González, and Andrew Cortez is based on the well-known Chicanesque short story by John Steinbeck which was in circulation in secondary school texts during the period. It depicted a young Chicano who kills a drunk in a Monterey, California, bar and runs into the hills where he is hunted down and killed. This is a crude and inexpertly acted film, one that does not have the benefit of trained filmmakers yet, but a notable precursor.

The documentary *Huelga* (1967), about the strike against the grape growers in Delano, is not a Chicano production (it was written and produced by Mark J. Harris and directed by Skeets McGrew). The film got attention from *Variety* (Oct. 4, 1967) because it screened at the New York Film Festival and was exhibited on educational television. Another non-Chicano film which can be considered a precursor is *The Young Animals* (1968, director Maury Dexter, see previous chapter), especially since the final scene has a high school student body picketing the school on behalf of Mexican Americans.

The first Chicano productions were in television, including talk shows, soap operas, and other programs such as *Canción de la raza; ¡Ahora!, Unidos, Reflecciones, Acción Chicano, Impacto, The Siesta is Over,* and *Bienvenidos.* The networks also did some important documentary films about Mexican Americans within the context of migrant farmworkers that also provided work for Hispanics: *Harvest of Shame* (1960, CBS), *Hunger in America* (1968, NBC), and *Migrant* (1970, NBC).

The major exception to this point of entry was the case of Luis and Daniel Valdez, founders of El Teatro Campesino, who should be recognized as producers of the first Chicano film, the 1969 adaptation of the epic poem, *I Am Joaquín,* by Rodolfo "Corky" Gonzales. It is quite fitting that the first Chicano film would convert the following verses into kinesis:

> They frowned upon our way of life
> and took what they could use.
> Our art,
> our literature,
> our music, they ignored—
> so they left the real things of value
> and grabbed at their own destruction
> by their greed and avarice. (Gonzales, 1972, 70)

Noriega (1991, np) points out that even copyrighting was a subject for what he judges "the most powerful Chicano film ever made."

> One sign of the film's rasquachismo or underdog aesthetics is its irreverence toward the copyright, which gives legal protection to property, something Chicanos have rarely been able to take for granted. *I Am Joaquín* challenges the copyright in assigning it to a collective, El Teatro Campesino, rather than an individual. But it is the C/S (short for Con Safos) at the film's end that subverts the copyright. When placed at the end of an artistic expression, Con Safos signifies "forbidden to touch, or the same will happen to you," a kind of Chicano copyright. Con Safos gives the film a discursive framework within which to speak on its own terms, a framework within and yet in opposition to the legal structure of mass media. (Noriega, 1991, np)

By the early 1970s, Chicanos were producing and directing a series of politically aware documentaries on the Chicano experience. Among the most significant of these are David García's *Requiem-29: Racism and Police Repression Against Chicanos* (1971), which described the East Los Angeles riot and the circumstances surrounding the suspicious death of Chicano reporter Rubén Salazar; Jesús Treviño's *América Tropical (1971),* about the whitewashing of a Siqueiros mural in Los Angeles; Jesús Treviño's *Yo soy chicano* (1972), the first Chicano film to be nationally televised and to deal with the Chicano movement from its roots in pre-Columbian history to the activism of the Chicano present; José Luis Ruiz's *Cinco vidas* (1972), which glosses the lives of five Chicanos and Chicanas of varied background and experiences; Jesús Treviño's *La raza unida* (1972), which covered the 1972 national convention of the Raza Unida party;

Ricardo Soto's *A la brava* (1973), describing the condition of Chicano *pintos* at Soledad prison; Rick Tejada-Flores's *Sí se puede* (1973), which records César Chávez's twenty-four-day fast in Arizona to protest proposed antistrike legislation; *Los desarraigados/The Uprooted* (1973, director Francisco X. Camplis) about the United States immigration policies and use of imported labor, focusing on a woman and her family; José Luis Ruiz's *The Unwanted* (1974), depicting the difficulties of the *indocumentado* population; Ricardo Soto's *A Political Renaissance* (1974), which examines the contemporary emergence of Chicano political power; and Severo Pérez's *Cristal* (1975) about Crystal City, "Spinach Capital of the World" and birthplace of the Raza Unida party.

The earliest Chicano cinema also includes the film adaptation of one of the finest Teatro Campesino *actos, Los vendidos* (1971), which depicts in a highly comic way a number of Chicano stereotypes. Subsequently, this group's *La gran carpa de los rasquachis* (1976) was produced for public television with critical success under the title *El corrido*. The early period also includes Jeff Penichet's *La vida* (1973), which describes a family of poverty-stricken Mexicans who survive by scavenging the trash left by American tourists in a small village in Baja California. *Carnalitos* (1973), directed by Richard Davies and produced by Bobby Páramo and Jesús Treviño, was the first Chicano-made film about gang members and *pintos* (prison inmates). It exposes the degree to which Hollywood and the press has stereotyped these groups and it allows the *pintos* to speak for themselves and to advise their *carnalitos* or little brothers.

In the years since 1975 the pace of Chicano documentary cinema has accelerated enormously. Scores of films have been produced and this is yet another area of Latino film that requires a book of its own. What follows are brief notations of some of the most significant documentary productions since 1975.

AIDS

Using the telenovela style, *Ojos que no ven . . .* (1987, director José Gutiérrez) is an educational video about AIDS and its impact in a Latino barrio. *Face to Face with AIDS* (1988, director Socorro Valdez) uses the soap opera format to depict a Latino community and family dealing with the myths, prejudices, and realities surrounding AIDS.

The AIDS Test (1989, director José Vergelin) helps people make informed choices on choosing to test for the HIV virus. *At Risk* (1989, producer Daniel Matta, director Warren Asa Maxey), based on an original stage play by Carlos Morton, portrays a variety of issues, prejudices, and misconceptions about AIDS.

Vida (1990), directed by Lourdes Portillo, is about a single Latina who confronts AIDS and finds a new sense of her self and awareness of her sexuality. *Who Killed Freddy Fulano?* (1990, director Jorge Sabez) is a motivational piece intended to prompt discussion regarding the risks of taking drugs and engaging in high-risk sexual behavior. *Between Friends* (1990), directed by Severo Pérez, examines the transmission of AIDS through unprotected sex and drug abuse. *Mi hermano* (1990), directed by Edgar Michael Bravo, tells the story of an immigrant family facing the AIDS-related death of its eldest son. *(In)Visible Women* (1991, directors Ellen Spiro and Marina Alvarez) is about four Latina women coping with HIV. *Lights of Hope* (1991, director Rita Guajardo Lepicier) is about the role of the Catholic Church in the AIDS crisis.

Anthropological and Folkloric

Among the most notable documentaries of the anthropological or folkloric type are Esperanza Vázquez and Moctesuma Esparza's *Agueda Martínez* (1977), nominated for an Academy Award in 1978, and Michael Earney's *Luisa Torres* (1981). Both documentaries depict the life styles of elderly women in northern New Mexico. Also outstanding are Les Blank's *Chulas fronteras* (1976) and its sequel, *Del mero corazón* (1979), which beautifully evoke the *norteña* or *conjunto* music prevalent in the Texas-Mexico border area and throughout the Southwest. Homer A. Villarreal's *Expression: The Miracle of Our Faith* (1978) is on the practices of *curanderismo* in San Antonio and elsewhere in south Texas; Daniel Salazar's *La tierra* (screened at the 1981 San Antonio festival) describes the Chicano lifestyle in Colorado's San Luis Valley; and Luis Reyes's *Los Alvarez* (screened at the 1981 San Antonio festival) depicts the hopes and dreams of a family living in California's Salinas Valley.

Ray Téllez's *Voces de yerba buena* (screened at the 1981 San Antonio festival) traces the Hispanic historical foundations of the San Francisco area and evokes the contemporary Latino influence in the area today; Ken Ausubel's *Los remedios: The Healing Herbs* (screened at the 1983 San Antonio festival) is a review of herbal medicine in the Southwest; Rhonda Vlasak's *Between Green and Dry* (screened at the 1983 San Antonio festival) examines the impact of accelerated economic change in the New Mexican village of Abiquiu; Paul Espinosa's *The Trail North* (1983) follows Dr. Robert Alvarez and his ten-year-old son Luis as they re-create the journey their familial ancestors made in coming to California from Baja California; Toni Bruni's *Los vaqueros* (screened at the 1983 San Antonio festival) is about Chicano cowboys, particularly those who participate in the Houston Livestock Show and Rodeo.

Producer/director Jack Ballesteros created *Mt. Cristo Rey* (screened at the 1984 San Antonio festival), a documentary about a priest in a small mining community near El Paso and how he erected a huge sandstone cross and statue of Christ. Toni Bruni's *Long Rider* (1986) is an English language version of her 1983 *Los vaqueros*. *Folklórico* (1987), directed by Joseph Tovares, treats the rise of Mexican folkloric dance in the Southwestern United States and its use as an ethnic symbol by Chicanos. *Vaquero: The Forgotten Cowboy* (1987, director Hector Galán) traces the American cowboy to the Mexican American vaquero. *Los Piñateros* (1987, director Severo Pérez) treats the traditional craft of making piñatas in San Antonio. Director Miguel Pendás captures the traditional Day of the Dead celebration in modern Mexico and also introduces vintage footage of Diego Rivera, Frida Kahlo, and Leon Trotsky discussing the attitudes toward death in technologically advanced societies versus Mexico in *Day of the Dead* (1987). *Corridos! Tales of Passion and Revolution* (1987), written and directed by Luis Valdez and starring Linda Ronstadt, brings to life some of Mexico's most beloved folk ballads.

Birthwrite (1989, Jesús Salvador Treviño, director, and Luis Torres, producer) is a docudrama that re-creates the theme of growing up and self-identity in a number of U.S. Hispanic writers; and *Del Valle* (1989), directed by Dale Sonnenberg and Karl Kernberger, evokes traditional and popular Mexican and New Mexican music performed in the central Río Grande valley of New Mexico. *La ofrenda* (1989), directed by Lourdes Portillo and Susana Muñoz, is about the filmmakers' relationship to the history and present-day celebrations of the Day of the Dead. *Anima* (1989) is an expressionistic film that explores the Day of the Dead and the relationship of death to everyday life.

Nopalito's Milagro (1992, director Franco Ontiveros) is the story of a small prickly pear cactus and its encounter with a curandera. *Regeneration* (1992), directed by Jeffrey Reyna, describes a young Chicano's confrontation with a stubborn old farmer and as a result, with his own culture and historical heritage. Director Jorge Sandoval depicts a Chicano musician who encounters a *curandera* one night in *City of Passion* (1993), a film that focuses on cultural beliefs and folklore and Chicano music. *Santa Sanidad/Spiritual Healer* (1993), directed by Horacio Rodríguez, is a film, available in either Spanish or English, that evokes the problems that occur when a traditional spiritual healer dabbles in New Age thinking.

Art, Culture, Literature, Music, and Allied Topics

Numerous documentary films have been produced that either describe or highlight Chicano art, poetry, music, culture, and the like. Among the more notable are José Valenzuela's *Chicano Poetry–Segundo encuentro* (1978), about a gathering of writers and artists in Sacramento; Juan Salazar's *Entelequia* (1978), which evokes the life and poetry of Ricardo Sánchez, ex-convict and current Ph.D.; William Greaves's *In Search of Pancho Villa* and *Voice of La Raza* (both screened at the 1978 San Antonio festival), the former an interview with Mexican American actor Anthony Quinn about the Mexican Revolution and contemporary United States politics and social change and the latter also with Anthony Quinn and, in addition, Rita Moreno and other vocal members of the Hispanic community concerned with issues of discrimination, culture, and language. Sabino Garza's *La llorona* (screened at the 1978 San Antonio festival) is a film depiction of the traditional folk tale. Chale Nafus's *Primo Martínez, santero* (screened at the 1979 San Antonio festival) is about a young man in Austin, Texas, who carves statues of the Virgin Mary from wood.

Francisco Torres's *Chuco* (1980) and Joe Camacho's *Pachuco* (1980), treat the 1941 Zoot Suit riots in Los Angeles through the art of José Montoya. Efraín Gutiérrez's *La onda chicana* (screened at the 1981 San Antonio festival) is a review of a 1976 Chicano concert featuring Little Joe y la Familia, Los Chanchos, La Fábrica, and other groups. Juan Salazar's *Mestizo Magic* (screened at the 1981 San Antonio festival) is about a fantasy trip through Aztlán exploring the world of Chicano art from its ancient past through its living musicians, sculptors, painters, dancers, and writers. Keith Kolb's *Southwest Hispanic Mission* (screened at the 1981 San Antonio festival) treats noted Chicano art historian Jacinto Quirarte who describes the technology and esthetics of mission buildings. Teena Brown Webb's *¡Viva la causa!* (screened at the 1981 San Antonio festival) depicts the popular wall mural movement in Chicago.

Paul Venema's *Barrio Murals* (screened at the 1983 San Antonio festival) documents the creation of the Cassiano Homes murals in San Antonio's Westside. Gary Greenberg's *Dale Kranque: Chicano Music and Art in South Texas* (screened at the 1983 San Antonio festival) profiles leading Texas Chicano musicians and artists. Beverly Sánchez-Padilla's *In Company of José Rodríguez* (screened at the 1983 San Antonio festival) is a visual history and conversation with the founder and artistic director of La Compañía de Teatro de Albuquerque. Sylvia Morales's *Los lobos: And A Time to Dance* (screened at the 1984 San Antonio CineFestival) is a documentary on Los Lobos including segments of a live performance, interviews with the musicians and montages that evoked their fusion of music forms. *Rasgado en dos* (screened at the 1984 San Antonio CineFestival), directed by Alan McGlade, features the poetry of Alurista, Gina Valdés, Rubén Medina, and Patrick Ojeda.

Jesse Treviño: A Spirit Against All Odds (1985, producer/director Skip Cilley) is a stirring documentary about one of San Antonio's best known artists who, while serving in Vietnam, lost a right arm and shattered his left leg yet was still able to pursue his career. *Hip Hop: The Style of the 80s* (1987), directed by Abe Cortez, evokes breakdancing, graffiti, visual art, and rap music among Chicanos, Puerto Ricans, and African Americans. In *Hispanic Art in the U.S.A.: The Texas Connection* (1988), director Betty Maldonado portrays seven Texas artists among the thirty artists around the country represented in the important exhibit "Hispanic Art in the United States—30 Contemporary Painters and Sculptors."

Popol Vuh (1989), directed by Patricia Amlin, is an animated film of the Sacred Book of the Quiche Maya. Lourdes Portillo and Susana Muñoz have produced and directed *La ofrenda: The Days of the Dead* (1989), an exploration of the pre-Hispanic roots of *El día de los muertos* and the social dimensions of death. *The Other Side of the Coin* (1989), producer/director Sean Carrillo, evokes the work of three East Los Angeles visual and literary artists: Simone Gad, Marisela Norte, and Diana Gamboa.

With respect to Diego Rivera, special mention should be made of a much earlier film, the Detroit Institute of Art's haunting *Rivera: The Age of Steel,* which describes Diego Rivera's extraordinary Detroit murals of the 1930s and the equally extraordinary political reactions that this art aroused in the automobile and allied industries. A new contribution to the same topic is *Rivera in America* (1988), produced and directed by Rick Tejada-Flores, who traces the artist's stay in the United States during the 1930s and examines the works he did there. *Frida Kahlo: A Ribbon Around a Bomb* (1990), produced by Cora Cardona and directed by Ken Mandel, depicts the life of Mexican artist Frida Kahlo through archival footage together with pivotal performances from a play based on her diary produced by Teatro Dallas.

Border Brujo (1990), directed by Isaac Artenstein, depicts performance artist Guillermo Gómez-Peña as he transforms himself into fifteen personas in an effort to exorcise the demons of a dominant culture. In *Las tandas de San Cuilmas (Los Carperos)* (1990), producer and director Jorge Sandoval documents a contemporary Chicano play which pays homage to the traveling theater or "carpas" of the 1930s and 1940s. *The Pastorela: A Shepherd's Play* (1991, director Luis Valdez) aired on PBS during the 1991 Christmas season.

The Aztlán Chronicles (1992, first selection), directed by Daniel Jacobo, features Luis Valdez as he discusses the importance of indigenous culture (additional selections will revolve around varied aspects of the Chicano/Chicana experience). *Tejano State of the Art* (1992, director Roy Flores) explores the evolution of Tejano music from the 1920s through the Americanized rock and roll era. *The Texas Tornados* (1992, director Daniel Jacobo) films a live concert by this famous musical group at the pier in Santa Monica. In *Dos por dos* (1993), director David Zamora Casas films his work as a performance artist exploring stereotypes ranging from gays in the military to customs of the cultura chicana. *Fascinating Slippers* (1992-93, director Juan Garza) documents the creation of an art piece by Glugio "Gronk" Nicandro for the San José, California Museum of Art. *Luiseño Christmas* (1993, director Isaac Artenstein) is based on Native American artist James Luna's live performance piece; the artist calls friends, family and present and former lovers excusing himself from their Christmas celebrations.

Chicana Topics

In the area of Chicana studies mention must be made of Conchita Ibarra Reyes's *Viva: Hispanic Woman on the Move* (screened at the 1979 San Antonio festival), which looks at the recent successes and the continuing struggles of Hispanic women. Lourdes Portillo's *Después del terremoto* (1979) is a pioneering example of the use of the telenovela to treat issues related to immigration (the earthquake referred to is one that affected the Nicaraguan community) as well as gender politics within the barrio, particularly among immigrants.[1] Julio Rosetti's *La mujer, el amor, y el miedo* (screened at the 1981 San Antonio festival) is concerned with the needs of battered *raza* women; and Barbara Wolfinger's *Chile pequín* (screened at the 1983 San Antonio festival) is about a college-educated Chicana whose values clash with the more traditional ones of her family home town.

Sylvia Morales's *Chicana* (1979) traces the traditional, historically imposed, and emerging roles of Mexicanas and Chicanas from pre-Columbian times to the present. This presentation of 500 years of Mexicana/Chicana history provides a corrective to the implicitly male-oriented nationalism of the early films including *I Am Joaquín*. Elvira M. Alvarado's *Una mujer* (screened at the 1984 Eastern Michigan University festival) is an interview with a Chicana in Los Angeles who speaks out about rape and sexual assault. *Date Rape* (1989), directed by Jesús Treviño, is a made-for-television program that examines the dilemma faced by a young woman after she is raped by the most popular high school senior. *My Filmmaking, My Life* (1990), produced and directed by Patricia Díaz, is the inspirational life story of Matilde Landeta, a filmmaker who worked her way up from a script girl to producer/director in the Mexican film industry during the 1940s. *The Trouble with Tonia* (1990), produced by Juan Garza and Lynda Martínez and directed by Juan Garza, is a comic melodrama in a world of soap operas and false expectations. In *Las nuevas tamaleras* (1991), producer/director Betti Maldonado evokes the tradition of making Christmas tamales and how a new generation of women come together in la tamalada to share time together.

In Frances Salomé España's *El espejo/The Mirror* (1991), the filmmaker presents herself fragmented as an absurd testimonio on her life in East Los Angeles. In addition to Salomé, other Chicanas using "experimental video to transform cultural narratives include Betty Maldonado *(Night Vigil,* 1982), Beverly Sánchez Padilla *(The Corrido of Juan Chacón,* 1990), Sandra P. Hahn *(Replies of the Night,* 1989; *Slipping Between,* 1991), S. M. Peña *(Crónica de un ser,* 1990; *Dark Glasses,* 1991; *Dionysius' Ox,* 1991), and T. 'Osa' Hidalgo de la Riva *(Mujería: The Olmeca Rap,* 1991)" (Noriega, 1992, 163).

¡Adelante Mujeres! (1992), directed by Mary Ruthsdotter and produced by the National Woman's History Project, evokes the history of Chicana women over five centuries. *Talking Back* (1992, director Renate Gangemi) examines the filmmaker's own experience as a domestic with that of other Latin American women; the film attempts to break this sector's invisibility and silence due to its economic and political status. *Tanto tiempo* (1992, director Cheryl B. Leader) is about a mother and daughter who abandon their heritage to adapt to an American lifestyle; confronted by their past, they rediscover their heritage. *Three Generations of a Latino Family* (1992, director Paul Bonín Rodríguez) depicts Irene Garza, the victim of abusive marriages, twice divorced and the mother of three grown sons, who leaves her job and goes to college. *Mujeres*

de cambio (1993, director Susana Ortiz) is a multigenerational examination of societal expectations toward and roles of women.

Chicano (Liberated Male) Topics

Pain of the Macho (1992), directed by Daniel Jacobo, is a satire on machismo and other myths of the Latin Lover. It was written by Rick Nájera, one of the writers from the television show *In Living Color*. *El mundo L.A.: Humberto Sandoval, Actor* (1992), directed by Harry Gamboa, Jr., is a documentary/performance project that presents the views, expressions, and existence of the individual Chicano male.

Children's Films

The Bike (1991, producer/director Gary Soto) is about a boy's first bike ride through his neighborhood that turns out to be a goofy odyssey where he encounters magicians, dancing girls, and a bully. In *Guelita Loli* (1992), directors Nancy Rodríguez and Jesús de la Torre describe a world of both mystery and insight for a young girl as her grandmother passes on the tradition of storytelling to her. In *El regalo de Paquito* (1993, director Luis Avalos) a young boy learns a Christmas lesson of commitment to his family as a result of his parents' financial setbacks.

Education, Including Bilingual and Health Education

The Chicano experience in public education has been an important topic and concern of *raza* filmmakers. Documentaries on bilingual education include the series by Adolfo Vargas, *Una nación bilingüe* (1977), *Bilingualism: Promise for Tomorrow* (1978), and its sequel, *Consuelo ¿Quiénes somos?* (1978), one of the best of its genre, perhaps because of the excellent screenwriting by Rudolfo Anaya. Elaine Sperber's *Overture* (screened at the 1981 San Antonio festival) uses the school setting to explore the potential for friendship and antagonism between Vietnamese and Chicanos living in a hostile urban environment. In addition, José Luis Ruiz's *Guadalupe* (1975) is a screen adaptation of the play of the same title by El Teatro de la Esperanza; it is a docudrama about conditions in Guadalupe, California, especially the deplorable educational situation.

Southwestern Bell's, *America's Time Bomb: The Hispanic Dropout Rate* (1986), narrated by Edward James Olmos, is an instructive documentary on the dropout rate among Latino students. It includes an interview with then mayor of San Antonio, Henry Cisneros. *Eres lo que comes* (1987), directed by Socorro Valdez Barajas, is a docudrama about an unmarried, pregnant teenager who with the help of a nutritionist takes control of her health and her pregnancy. *Dreams of Flying* (1989), directed by Severo Pérez, focuses on a young Latina's desires to enter college against the wishes of her father.

Gangs, Youth, Drugs, Orphans, and Domestic Violence

The circumstances of gangs specifically and youth generally have been the subject of Efraín Gutiérrez's *El Juanio* (screened at the 1979 San Antonio festival), about the drug problems (mostly paint sniffing) faced by youngsters in the barrios of San Antonio. Ray Téllez's *Joey* (1980) evokes the problems of identity and of adolescence of a sixteen-year-old Chicano youth; Terry Sweeney's *Streets of Anger, Streets of Hope* (screened at the 1981 San Antonio festival) is an interview documentary where members tell what attracts them to gangs; and Pat Connelly's *El grito de las madres dolorosas* (1981) is one of the most moving accounts of gang violence (in unincorporated East Los Angeles) and what a church brother teamed together with a group of concerned mothers attempted to do about it. Director Bill Jersey's *Children of Violence* (1984 screening at San Antonio festival), treats four brothers in the Oakland, California, barrio. *Dolores* (1989), produced and directed by Pablo Figueroa, portrays the problem of domestic violence within the Latino community.

Jesús Salvador Treviño won the Directors Guild of America award (1989) in the dramatic daytime show category for his CBS Special, *Gangs*. This film is about a young man who returns to the barrio only to learn that his fourteen-year-old brother has become a member of the gang he once led. *Distant Water* (1990), directed by Carlos Avila, is a moving film about a ten-year-old boy and his friends growing up Chicano in the 1940s and 1950s in Los Angeles. The young Chicano takes a personal stance against the segregated swimming pools of Los Angeles in the 1940s.

The Addict (1991), directed by Rogelio A. Lobato, treats the effects of violence on young adults. In *Chill Out* (1991), director Michael Coin has actors Edward James Olmos, Lou Diamond Phillips, and others talk one-on-one to teenagers about suicide and indirect suicide when people put themselves in dangerous situations such as drinking and driving, taking drugs, and joining gangs. *The Ballad of Tina Juárez* (1992), directed by Juan A. Uribe, is a docudrama about a young Mexican girl who, after being forced to leave the orphanage, walks north to the Texas-Mexico border, tragically finding her parents too late for a family reunion. Director Carlos Solís, Jr. depicts Chicano gangs and their attitudes in East Los Angeles in *Homeboys* (1992). *Los Carnales* (1992-93), directed by Alejandro Hinojosa, is about a young Chicano torn between his family and his friends who have begun to engage in gang-related activities.

Gay and Lesbian Topics

A History of Violence (1991), directed by Danny G. Acosta, is a montage about the problems experienced by a gay man and his community. *Mujería: Primitive and Proud. Part I* (1991), *Part II* (1992), directed by T. "Osa" Hidalgo de la Riva, is about the story of an Olmec character, Eagle Bear, who accidently comes across time and space to be reborn into the Chicana lesbian spirit of Eagle Bear. *After the Break* (1992, director Mary Guzmán) is about a multicultural lesbian therapy group that experiences personality clashes. *Both* (1993), directed by Vic de la Rosa, is a painful, honest story about a romance between two San Francisco men living with HIV.

History

Jeff and Carlos Penichet's *El pueblo chicano: The Beginnings* and *El pueblo chicano: The Twentieth Century* (both 1979) are panoramic overviews of Chicano cultural roots and contemporary issues. Warren Haack's *Dead in the Sierra* (screened at the 1978 San Antonio festival) is about the legendary nineteenth-century social bandit, Joaquín Murrieta. Ralph Madariaga's *Incident at Downieville* (1979) is about the first documented case in the history of California (1851) of the execution of a woman of Mexican origin (following a trial of dubious impartiality). *Royalty in Exile* (1986), directed by Daniel Jacobo, is about a pachuco of the 1940s and a vato of the 1950s who despite their recognition of an illustrious Hispanic history face a reality where they have no money, no land, and no voice in the legal and social processes. In *A Mosque in Time* (1989), director Edin Vélez presents the architectural space of the Great Mosque of Córdoba as well as the contrasting use of the building by Islamic and Christian patrons. In *History of Mexican Los Angeles: Social and Cultural History, 1781-1990s* (1991), producer/director Antonio Ríos-Bustamante traces the history of Los Angeles's Mexican community. *The Hunt for Pancho Villa* (1993), produced by Hector Galán and Paul Espinosa, written by Paul Espinosa, and directed by Hector Galán, is about Pancho Villa's raid on Columbus, New Mexico, in 1916 and the failed efforts of the U.S. government to capture him.

Immigration

Esperanza (1985), directed by Sylvia Morales, is a drama about two children whose mother is picked up by immigration police. *Maricela* (1986, Richard Soto, producer and Christine Burrill, director) is the story of a young Salvadoran girl who emigrates to Los Angeles with her mother to find a new home and a better life. In *Yolanda/De nuevo* (1988), director Severo Pérez tells the story of an unwed mother in Mexico who is forced to leave her native country and illegally enters the United States. *The Foundling* (1991), directed by William Franco, is about a refugee from El Salvador, desperate, pregnant, and recently widowed, who becomes the victim of a baby-selling ring when she attempts to cross the border into the United States. Directors Jesse Lerner and Scott Sterling describe the racial violence against immigrants organized by a number of nativist groups along the U.S.-Mexican border in *Natives* (1991). *Refugees* (1991, producers/directors Miguel Pendas and Howard Petrick) is about the nearly one million people, about one fifth of the population of El Salvador, who have fled their country to come to the United States only to find that the fear of the death squads and torture have been replaced by unemployment, homelessness, and "illegal" status.

Low Riding

Alicia Maldonado and Andrew Valles's *The Ups and Downs of Lowriding* (screened at the 1981 San Antonio festival) is an investigation of lowriding through the eyes of the cruisers themselves, the general public, and the police department. Rick Tejada-Flores, producer/director of *Low 'N Slow: The Art of Lowriding* (screened at the 1984 San Antonio festival), both explains the lowriding phenomenon and makes a case for it as as an important form of modern industrial folk art. *Rag Top Ralph* (1984), directed by Juan Garza, is about Ralph Carrillo, the "World Champion Low Rider Hopper." *Low and Slow–San Antonio Lowriders* (1991), directed by Michael Mehl, speaks to the issues of work, ethics, car clubs, and public misconceptions about lowriding.

Politically Focused and Labor Union Films

On the matter of politics and the emerging Chicano political movement, i.e., unions and strikes, a number of valuable films have been produced. These include Marsha Goodman's *Not Gone and Not Forgotten* (screened at the 1983 San Antonio festival), which depicts how the community of Pico Union in Los Angeles successfully fought the mayor, the city council, and powerful business interests in order to maintain the integrity of its neighborhood; Richard Trujillo's *Tixerina: Through the Eyes of the Tiger* (1983), an interview with Reies López Tixerina reviewing the famous courthouse riot of 1967 in Tierra Amarilla and akin events; National Education Media's *Decision at Delano* (screened at the 1982 Eastern Michigan University festival), which documents the historic Delano grape-worker's strike; and the Centro Campesino Cultural's *El Teatro Campesino* (screened at the 1982 Eastern Michigan University festival), which traces the Teatro from its beginnings in the fields boosting the morale of striking farmworkers and winning over *esquiroles* to its present role as a theater committed to social change.

Paul Espinosa and Isaac Artenstein's extraordinary documentary *Ballad of an Unsung Hero* (1984) evokes the political consciousness of an earlier era, depicting the life history of the remarkable Pedro J. González, a pioneering radio and recording star who was thrown into jail on trumped-up charges by the Los Angeles District Attorney's office in the midst of the Great Depression. Co-producers/directors, Jesús Salvador Treviño and José Luis Ruiz's *Yo soy/I Am* (1985) reviews the progress that Chicanos have made during the last two decades in politics, education, labor, and economic development and summarizes the variety of ways that Chicanos are responding to contemporary challenges. Diana Costello, producer, and Matthew Patrick, director's *Graffiti* (1986) is about a nocturnal wall sketcher in a militaristic South American country. Paul Espinosa, producer, Frank Christopher, director's *The Lemon Grove Incident* (1986) is a docudrama that examines the response of the Mexican American community in Lemon Grove, California, to a 1930 school board's attempt to segregate their children into a special school.

A Quiet Revolution: Christian Base Communities of Latin America (1988), directed by Audrey L. Glynn, is a moving film about small groups of poor and marginalized Latin Americans confronting social problems with the help of liberation theology. The film also contains an interview with the great Peruvian philosopher and liberation theologian, Gustavo Gutiérrez. *Watsonville on Strike* (1989), producer/director Jon Silver, describes an eighteen-month strike by cannery workers that virtually paralyzed a rural California town. Marilyn Mulford and Mario Barrera's *Chicano Park* (1989) is a compelling and moving visual history of the struggle of one community, Barrio Logan, to stake out a place for itself in the metropolis of San Diego. The film shows the process through which Logan residents begin to effect positive changes in their lives and their community by using the richness of their cultural heritage as the basis around which to educate themselves to gain political power. *Los mineros* (1990), produced and directed by Hector Galán, is a wonderful film about the Mexican American miners whose labor battles spanned nearly half-a-century from 1903 to 1946 and shaped the course of Arizona history.

Sin fronteras (1991), directed by Cheche Martínez and Colin Jessop, is a denunciation of police brutality against borderland communities. *Tierra o muerte* (1991, director Carolyn Hales) is about the local residents of a remote New Mexico valley who set up an armed camp to stop a subdivision while a group of shepherds turn to civil disobedience in a desperate bid to find pasture for their flocks. In *Por la vida* (1992), director Olivia Olea depicts the thousands of immigrants who sell goods on the streets of Los Angeles and the discrimination that they and other members of the Latino community are confronted with. *Pollution Knows No Borders* (1992, director Linda Cuellar) describes the tragic deaths of babies born with medical problems in the Lower Río Grande Valley and the conscious inattention to these problems on the part of industry, the medical profession, and tourism.

Psychological or Spiritual Insights

I'll Be Home for Christmas (1990, director Robert Díaz LeRoy) depicts Robert O'Hara (formerly Roberto Herrera) who comes to terms with the solitude and anger he felt as a child when his father died in prison. *The Air Globes* (1990), directed by Patricia Cardoso, evokes childhood dreams, desires, and innocence during a Christmas recollection. *How Else Am I Supposed to Know I'm Still Alive* (1991-92), written by Evelina Fernández and directed by José Luis Valenzuela, is about two middle-aged

Chicanas who help each other through mid-life crises and obtain a deeper appreciation of friendship. Starring Lupe Ontiveros and Angela Moya, it won best film at the 17th Annual San Antonio CineFestival.

Always Roses (1990, director Luis Avalos) is a about a twelve-year-old boy who develops a sense of pride in himself when his parents send him to stay with his grandparents for the summer. Nancy de los Santos's *Breaking Pan With Sol* (1992) takes place during the protagonist's thirtieth birthday, and depicts interactions with family, friends, and boyfriend; the character ultimately realizes the strength she needs can only come from herself. *Pebble in the Pond* (1993, directors David Peña and Cristella Rocha) is about a successful young man who only transcends his spiritual emptiness through the intercession of a spiritual healer in the old neighborhood he had left behind.

Quincentennial (1492-1992) Related

In *Herencia y esperanza* (1991), director Gayla Jamison traces the westward movement of Spanish colonization from the time of Columbus to the settlement of New Spain. *1492 Revisited,* (1992, director Paul Espinosa) features art work from an exhibition entitled "Counter Colonialismo" which offers an alternative perspective on the quincentenary celebration. *Autodescubrimiento: 1492-1992* (1992), directed by Rodrigo Betancur, is a multicultural, multilingual evocation of Hispanic, Anglo, and indigenous society. In *Una Historia/A History* (1992), directors Dan Boord and Luis Valdovino use a bilingual board game as a central metaphor of Western history to evoke 500 years of power, discrimination, genocide, and greed.

Undocumented Workers, Farmworkers, and Migrant Workers

The plight of *indocumentados* (undocumented workers) and migrant labor generally has seen extensive filmic treatment over the last decade and a half, including Ricardo Soto's films *Cosecha* (1976), about migrant labor, *Migra* (1976), on the arrest of *indocumentados, Al otro paso* (1976), on the economy of the border, and *Borderlands* (1983), which once again explores the complex interrelations of the Mexico-United States border. Jesús Carbajal and Todd Darling's *Año Nuevo* (screened at the 1979 San Antonio festival and the 1981 winner of the Eric Sevareid Award for Best Information Program, Academy of Television Arts and Sciences) is about the nearly unprecedented court struggle by twenty-two undocumented workers against their employer, the Año Nuevo Flower Ranch; and Jim Crosby's *Frank Ferree: El amigo* (screened at the 1983 San Antonio festival) depicts this man from Harlingen, Texas, known as the Border Angel, who spent most of his adult life in an untiring effort to aid the poor and dispossessed along the Texas border with Mexico. Special mention needs to be made of the Learning Corporation of America's *Angel and Big Joe,* an Academy Award winner for short dramatic film, starring Paul Sorvino, which depicts the friendship and ultimate parting of a migrant worker youth and a lonely Anglo telephone repairman. The United Farm Workers' *The Wrath of Grapes* (1986) is a documentary that depicts the plight of California farmworkers exposed to deadly pesticides.

There Goes the Neighborhood (1987), directed by Severo Pérez, explores the conflicts among long-time residents of neighborhoods with new immigrants from Latin America and elsewhere. *In the Shadow of the Law* (1987, producer Paul Espinosa, director Frank Christopher) is about the many struggles of four families who have lived illegally in the United States for many years. *Miles From the Border* (1987), directed by Ellen Frankenstein, centers around a family twenty years after they have migrated from

Zacatecas, Mexico, to the racially divided town of Fillmore, California, the first city in California to pass a resolution making English the official language. Producer/director Susan Ferris has used historical footage, clippings, interviews, and other realia to trace the history of the farmworkers' union and to chronicle the experiences of Mexican farmworkers in California in *The Golden Cage: A Story of California's Farmworkers* (1989). Paul Espinosa has produced and directed *Vecinos desconfiados/Uneasy Neighbors* (1989), evoking the growing tensions between the migrant worker camps and affluent homeowners in the San Diego area. *Farmworkers Diary* (1990), directed by Paul Shain, provides an inside view of a day in the life of Chicano farmworkers at a farm labor camp in central California.

In *Aquí se puede* (1991), directors Melissa Young and Mark Dworkin present the difficult conditions experienced by farmworkers and their families in the state of Washington. *Un cielo cruel y una tierra colorada* (1991), directed by Leopoldo Blest Guzmán, is about three friends living and working the fields in California who return to Mexico to visit their families and return again to Los Angeles different but wiser men. *Yo trabajo la tierra* (1991), produced and directed by Adán M. Medrano, the founder of the San Antonio CineFestival, is an intimate portrait of a farmworking family and reveals the day-to-day toils and simple pleasures of summer workers in the Midwest.

World War II

Memories of Hell (screened at the 1983 San Antonio festival) describes the suffering of some eighteen hundred New Mexico soldiers who fought in the Philippines, many of them survivors of the 1941 Bataan Death March. Alfredo Lago's *The Men of Company E* (screened at the 1983 San Antonio festival) recounts the bravery and tragedy in Italy during World War II of the all-Latino Unit of the United States 5th Army from El Paso, Texas. *Hero Street U.S.A.* (1985), produced and directed by Mike Stroot, is a dramatic story of how, beset by unrelenting discrimination, the Mexican American community of twenty-two families of the town of Silvis, Illinois, set out to establish itself firmly as all-American and in the process contributed eighty-seven sons to war, eight of whom died in battle. *Valor* (1989, producer/director Richard Parra, narration by Ricardo Montalbán) relates the contributions of Al Ramírez (awarded four Bronze Stars) and other Mexican Americans during World War II as well as the discrimination they experienced which provided background for the establishment of the American GI Forum.

Other Films

Other significant documentaries relating to various aspects of the Chicano community need to be noted. Mercedes Sabio's two-part *Wealth of a Nation–Hispanic Merchants* (both screened at the San Antonio festival, 1981) are about Hispanic businesses both in the barrio and outside of Hispanic neighborhoods. Dale Sonnenberg's and Joseph Tovares's *Barbacoa, Past, Present, Future* (screened at the 1983 San Antonio festival), is on how this food is produced, distributed, and consumed. *My Sin is Loving You* (1988), directed by Esther Durán, is about a housewife who escapes the drudgery of her life by entering the melodramatic world of a television soap opera. *Futures* is an educational program directed by Eric Sherman. In the episode "Agriculture" (1990), master teacher Jaime Escalante and actor Jimmy Smits educate young adults in that field, and in "Cartography" (1990), Edward James Olmos and Jaime Escalante explore contemporary approaches to the art of map making. *Corazón de Vegetable* (1992), directed by Abel Cornejo, is about a vegetarian who falls in love with a meat-eating butcher and is torn between her sophisticated beliefs and her primordial lust.

Chicano Features

Attempting to define the corpus of Chicano features is a complex task. If one focuses on independent productions, produced outside of the studios, the following films emerge, with their directors, including those of Efraín Gutiérrez whose works unfortunately have become inaccessible and whose contributions have fallen into obscurity: *Los vendidos* (1972), the first independent production and an adaptation of one of the finest of El Teatro Campesino's *actos, La Vida* (1973, Jeff Penichet), *Please Don't Bury me Alive!/Por favor ¡No me entierren vivo!* (1977, Efraín Gutiérrez), *Alambrista!* (1977, Robert M. Young), *Amor Chicano es para siempre/Chicano Love is Forever* (1978, Efraín Gutiérrez), *Only Once in a Lifetime* (1978, Alejandro Grattan), *Raíces de sangre* (Mexico, 1978, Jesús Salvador Treviño), *Run, Junkie/Tecato, Run* (1979, Efraín Gutiérrez), *The Ballad of Gregorio Cortez* (1982, Robert M. Young), *Seguín* (1982, Jesús Salvador Treviño), *Heartbreaker* (1983, Frank Zúñiga), *El Norte* (1983, Gregory Nava, independent production in association with American Playhouse), *Stand and Deliver* (1988, Ramón Menéndez, independent production released first by Warner Brothers prior to its PBS airing), *Break of Dawn* (1988, Isaac Artenstein), *La carpa* (1992, Carlos Avila, released through PBS), and *El Mariachi* (1993, Robert Rodríguez, released by Columbia Pictures). Hollywood has made much Horatio Alger public relations about "boy wonder" Robert Rodríguez's $7,000 film, how it has brought in over $1.8 million, and how he is now at work on a sequel, the second installment of what he hopes will be a trilogy. This $5 million budget film is allegedly to be in the same homemade style without Columbia Pictures interference. "*. . . y no se lo tragó la tierra/. . . And the Earth Did Not Swallow Him*" is a film project from the novel written by Tomás Rivera and published in 1971, and a co-production between KBPS-TV San Diego and director/writer Severo Pérez. The producer is Paul Espinosa. The film was about to be premiered at the time of this writing.

To this list, which is notable for its paucity of productions since 1988, we should add several of the "Hollywood Hispanic" films (combining Hispanic expertise and often control with Hollywood production values and distribution) which are more closely affiliated with Chicano independent film than with the average Hollywood production that makes use of Chicano material. These include *Zoot Suit* (1981, Luis Valdez), *La Bamba* (1987, Luis Valdez), *Born in East L.A.* (1987, Cheech Marín), and *American Me* (1992, Edward James Olmos), starring Pepe Serna and Danny de la Paz. Noriega (1992, 147) calls *The Milagro Beanfield War* (1988, Robert Redford) a "Chicano-Latino" film as well. In my view it is more of a Hollywood film with Chicano content as is *Bound by Honor* (also distributed as *Blood In, Blood Out,* director Taylor Hackford, 1993).

The key criteria for defining a Chicano feature no longer revolves around the film's nature as an independent film rather than one produced with the involvement of the studios or mainstream production companies. Independence in itself is a relative term since most Chicano films described in that way were funded by such entities as the Corporation for Public Broadcasting, the National Endowment for the Humanities, the Public Broadcasting System, or foundations, including in the case of *Stand and Deliver,* the Atlantic Richfield Foundation, and the National Science Foundation, a federal agency. These entities also exercise control although in a more complex or subtle fashion than what is exercised by Hollywood. For example, *Seguín* was originally conceived as the first part of a series, but it was cancelled by the National Endowment for the Humanities, in part because of politics and in part because of protests within the Chicano community about the positive treatment accorded to the principal protagonist who, according to historian Rudy Acuña (a member of the advisory board for the film), was a slaveholder who did not deserve the good treatment he received in the film.

How then to sort out what may legitimately be defined as Chicano films from others? We need to fall back on two other criteria. One is control over the material, whether or not that material is produced within Hollywood. The Hollywood Chicano films *Born in East L.A.*, *Zoot Suit*, *La Bamba*, and *American Me* qualify as such because they were mostly controlled by Chicanos. The other criterion, an admittedly subjective and ambiguous one that requires analysis and argumentation on the part of the film scholar, is the authenticity or relevancy of the material itself, including the ability of the film to transcend formulas and box-office exploitiveness. The term transcend is used advisedly since almost all films including the most authentic must be pitched for sales and will use character types to some degree (see Williams, 1985).

Authenticity is not only an element of content but of artistry as well. Recently Noriega (1991, 1992) has pointed out some of the innovations of Chicano film, which sometimes have been misunderstood by mainstream reviewers and misused to downgrade the film in question. Noriega's analysis of these characteristics as well as my own are offered here, not as a list of elements that authentically Chicano films need to have, for such a usage would be unwarranted since it would create an orthodoxy blocking innovation in the future—the artistry of Chicano and other U.S. Latino film needs to be open ended. However, the appearance of these elements does affect a number of Chicano features and documentaries and are useful in helping to understand the peculiar qualities of Chicano filmic artistry.

The Deconstruction and Subversion of Hollywood Genres and Formulas. Many Chicano films turn established formulas and genres on their heads. *El Norte* is not merely the alternative, but in fact the antithetical border immigration film. *Raíces de sangre* and *Born in East L.A.* function in a similar capacity. *The Ballad of Gregorio Cortez* is the Chicano Western, it subverts both the classical Western and the bandido, bad Mexican, or greaser films. *Zoot Suit* is the Chicano "answer" to Latin musicals and gang films. *Seguín* is the Chicano "answer" to the Anglo glorification of the Alamo. *Stand and Deliver* creates a contradictory calculus to all of the gang and rip-up-the-school by Latino hoodlums films.

The Innovative Use of Spanish and English (and Sometimes Indigenous Languages). This element, called code switching by linguists, is incorporated in films such as *El Norte, La Bamba, Raíces de Sangre, Born in East L.A.,* and numerous others as a fundamental aspect of the film. In these films, the fullest appreciation of the work, the channel, as it were, at its maximum frequency, can be attained only by the bilingual, multicultural viewer. The plot itself of The Ballad of Gregorio Cortez (see Gutiérrez-Jones, 1992) revolves around a linguistic discrepancy between Spanish and English. This element has developed so much that the more innovative Anglo directors such as Taylor Hackford in Bound by Honor have honored the Chicano film by imitating it.

The Innovative Use of Chicano Music. The corrido or ballad as well as other traditional and hybrid forms have been significant expressions of both the Chicano movement and its film. And, as Noriega has pointed out (1991), the most provocative and popular Chicano feature films have been either musicals such as *Zoot Suit,* musical biographies like *La Bamba,* musical parodies such as *Born in East L.A.,* or about music as resistance, including *Ballad of Gregorio Cortez* and *Break of Dawn.* Music in these works often situates us within a Chicano cultural space, using diverse styles to express both Chicano culture and cultural conflict with Anglo culture. Although less extensively, Chicano art, food preparation, graffiti, slang, and mannerisms also extend into Chicano films.

The Innovative Use of Mise en Scène *and of Montage.* Noriega (1991, np, 1992, 173ff) has made a valuable analysis of Chicano filmic techniques, concluding that the *mise en scène* of Chicano cinema, the "putting of the scene" of the Chicano experience, involves for the first time a screen space "filled not just with Chicano 'images' but with the aural and visual texture of our culture: the music, languages, home altars, food preparation, neighborhoods." Similarly Chicano montage has often served to temporally extend the *mise en scène.* For example, numerous Chicano documentaries "begin with a montage sequence that outlines the history of the Chicano experience, starting at some point between the Conquest and the Mexican Revolution, and lead up to the particular moment to be documented. These films acknowledge the de facto horizon of expectations for films about Chicanos and attempt to resituate the text—but not without a sense of irony" (Noriega, 1991, np; 1992, 173).

Chicano feature films have contrasted greatly with contemporaneous films about Chicanos made by Hollywood directors and producers, even as they have shared some themes, situations, or genres such as the problems at the U.S.-Mexican border, the Western genre, or teenage groups. Some of the salient characteristics of Chicano film not usually seen in the Hollywood product, in addition to a meticulous attention to the actual cultural and social conditions of Chicano life and the use of Spanish to produce a bilingual film with considerable switching between languages, are the recuperation of Chicano history (in period pieces), close attention to the political dimensions of the topics that are cultivated on screen, commitment to dealing with issues above considerations of box office, and a willingness to employ considerable numbers of Hispanic actors and Hispanic production people. Chicano pictures feature plots that may or may not appeal to the mainstream audience but are definitely designed for Chicano filmgoers. They feature Hispanic actors in genuine situations, usually filmed on location in authentic settings, and speaking or singing in a natural, often bilingual environment. A noticeable recent example of this type of authenticity is *La carpa* (1992), directed by Carlos Avila, produced by Michael Zapata, written by Carlos Avila and Edit Villarreal, and starring Enrique Castillo, Rick Coca, Danny de la Paz, Jaime Gómez, William Márquez, Karla Montana, Lupe Ontiveros, Bel Sandre, and Herbert Siguenza. The film is about the arrival of the *carperos,* traveling musicians and comics, and the impact they have on a small town during a tense moment.

In contrast to the conventional Hollywood pap of the border, Chicano productions such as *Raíces de Sangre, Alambrista!, El Norte,* and *Break of Dawn* (1988), Isaac Artenstein's film about a radio announcer and singer deported to Tijuana, have all evoked the situation at the border with sociological depth and creative distinction. Written, directed, and photographed by Robert M. Young and produced by Michael Hausman and Irwin Young, *Alambrista!* is the story of Roberto, a migrant worker who crosses the border illegally and soon discovers that the United States is not the land of opportunity he thought it was. *Born in East L. A.,* despite the criticism of it by the mainstream as loosely strung together skits, has been rightly acknowledged by Noriega (1991) and Fregoso (1990, 1993)[2] as an authentically Chicano evocation and subversion of the immigration issue as well as California's English-Only initiative. The quality of Latino verisimilitude, heightened by the bilingual (or in the case of *El Norte,* trilingual) script, have caused these movies to stand head and shoulders above their Hollywood contemporaries such as *Blood Barrier, The Border,* or *Borderline.*

Chicano "Westerns" have differed markedly from the Hollywood version. Both *Seguín* (1981, Jesús Treviño) and *The Ballad of Gregorio Cortez* (1982, Moctesuma Esparza and Robert M. Young) have been fundamentally involved with the recuperation of lost (or rather, suppressed) aspects of Chicano history, and have evoked politically charged elements of that history. *The Ballad,* about social hero Gregorio Cortez wrongly accused of stealing a horse, is also a stirring evocation of false assumptions and cultural and linguistic misunderstandings, since the fatal encounter with Anglo law enforcers arises out of their misunderstanding of the difference between *caballo* (stallion) and *yegua* (male).

Seguín is a Chicano Alamo story, the first in the history of the cycle, which dates to as early as 1911 (see chapter 4) to elaborate a Chicano perspective. The 1911 *The Immortal Alamo* and the 1915 *The Martyrs of the Alamo* began this cycle of films, generally presenting Mexicans as ineffective fighters, able to triumph only through vast superiority of numbers, certainly not through skill. With the 1953 *The Man from the Alamo,* the 1955 *The Last Command,* the 1960 *The Alamo,* and the 1986 television docudrama, *The Alamo: 13 Days to Glory,* the basic view remains of heroic Anglos killing masses of Mexicans before succumbing to overwhelming odds "although these latter-day movies do better human balance, with some Mexicans even emerging as real people" (Greenfield and Cortés, 1991, 50). In contrast, *Seguín* depicts a *tejano* who out of complex social circumstances fights at the Alamo with the Anglos against the Mexicans, leaves before the final siege, becomes mayor of San Antonio during the early days of the Texas Republic, is discriminated against by Anglos, and subsequently fights with Santa Anna on the side of the Mexicans in the Mexican-American War.

Luis Valdez's productions, *Zoot Suit* (1981) and *La Bamba* (1986), as well as *Stand and Deliver* (1988, Ramón Menéndez, Tom Musca, and Edward James Olmos) and *Hangin' with the Homeboys* (1991, Puerto Rican producer/director Joseph P. Vásquez), set in New York, all deal with various aspects of Chicano or Puerto Rican juvenile and domestic life in the United States. Valdez's two works, both of which have an important historical dimension, are fine examples of Chicano filmmaking, with Hollywood support and distribution. The Chicano juvenile films are light years away, or rather, ahead of Hollywood product such as *Streets of L.A.* (1979) and *Walk Proud* (1981). The Hollywood films are usually exploitive in their approach (although *Bound by Honor* is an exception, a much stronger Hollywood film, probably because it benefitted from Chicano expertise including the scripting of Jimmy Santiago Baca). Whether the Chicanos in these films are a menace to whites or to themselves, it is strictly the prospect of violence and its sensationalistic description on screen that carries these Hollywood juvenile films.

In contrast, *American Me* is a highly violent film; it shares that characteristic with Hollywood gang films. However, its grim, cautionary message to Chicanos, whether accepted by potential gang members or not, is the antithesis of commercial exploitation.

In fact, pursuing its message in a relentlessly downbeat fashion, the film actually sacrificed box-office potential to its message, earning a review in *Variety* in March 1992 as "one of the grimmest films produced by a major studio in recent memory." It should be noted, and *American Me* is a case in point, that what might be authentically Chicano can also stereotype with respect to other ethnic groups. The Mafia-related scenes in this film are notably cliché.

Even further afield from the Hollywood product marketed for youth, *Stand and Deliver* is a stirring story that barely even evokes gang violence. It is primarily about the extraordinary Bolivian mathematics teacher Jaime Escalante who helps Hispanic high school students in East Los Angeles learn college-level calculus and get admitted into selective universities.

Puerto Rico's Contributions to the Film Industry and Puerto Rican Films

Both the film industry in Puerto Rico and Puerto Rican films deserve considerable more attention than they have been given to date, and this coverage attempts to redress that circumstance to the degree possible in an overview of this sort. Puerto Rican film dates at least from 1916 with the establishment of the Sociedad Industrial Cine Puerto Rico by Rafael J. Colorado and Antonio Capella (in 1912 Juan Emilio Viguié Cajas took the first known shots in Puerto Rico, of Ponce). This production company's first work had a *jíbaro* focus and was titled *Por la hembra y el gallo* (1916), which was followed by *El milagro de la virgen* and *Mafia en Puerto Rico*. Because of a lack of funds and competition from U. S. film, the Sociedad Industrial was bankrupted and no prints of its films are known to exist, although there are still photographs of *Por la hembra y el gallo*. In 1917, another company, Tropical Film Company, was organized with participation by well-known Puerto Rican literary figures Luis Lloréns Torres and Nemesio Canales. Although its existence terminated with the entry of the United States into World War I, it did produce *Paloma del monte*, directed by Luis Lloréns Torres. In 1919, the Porto Rico Photoplays company was organized and produced *Amor tropical* (1920) with American actors Ruth Clifford and Reginald Denny, a melodrama produced for the North American market but which failed to penetrate that distribution system, causing the company to go bankrupt.

Juan Emilio Viguié Cajas purchased the equipment of Photoplays and began a long and productive filmmaking career in Puerto Rico, primarily based on doing newsreels for continental U.S. enterprises such as Pathé, Fox Movietone, and MGM. Among his works were films on Charles A. Lindbergh's trip to Puerto Rico in 1927, and the San Ciriaco hurricane of 1928. He did many documentaries for the government (the first of which in 1920 was *La colectiva* about the tobacco industry) and for private entities. His film *Romance tropical* (1934) was the first Puerto Rican feature of the sound period. Written by the poet Luis Palés Matos, it depicts a lovesick young musician who attempts to seek his fortune at sea in a tiny boat. It debuted at the Paramount in Santurce but was not financially successful. It was the only feature that Viguié did. No copies of the film remain.

On the other hand, Rafael Ramos Cobián, who owned the largest chain of movie theaters in Puerto Rico backed some productions, mostly in Mexico, including *Mis dos amores* (1938), with Puerto Rican actress Blanca de Castejón and Mexican Tito Guízar, and *Los hijos mandan* (1939), with Blanca de Castejón and Arturo de Córdova.

With the exceptions described above, film languished in Puerto Rico until after World War II. In 1949, the island government established a production facility in Old San Juan. In that year, Luis Muñoz Marín decided to support film production on the island in order to carry out some of the reforms, especially agricultural and industrial, for which he was seeking strong support. He outlined his idea in the preamble of the Act of 1949 establishing the Division of Community Education which produced a series of films in Puerto Rico from the 1940s to the 1960s:

> The goal of community education is to impart basic teaching on the nature of man, his history, his life, his way of working and of self-governing in the world and in Puerto Rico. Such teachings addressed to adult citizens meeting in groups in the barrios, settlements and urban districts, will be imparted through moving pictures, radio, books, pamphlets and posters, phonographic records, lectures and group discussions. The object is to provide the good hand of popular culture with the tool of basic education. (Cited in English translation in *Films With a Purpose,* 1987.)

Administered by the División de Educación de la Comunidad (which was part of the Departamento de Instrucción Pública), the Old San Juan production facility produced sixty-five shorts and two features by 1975, the year of publication of its last catalog. It counted on the cooperation of many of the best Puerto Rican graphic artists (Homar, Tony Maldonado, Eduardo Vera, Rafael Tufiño, Domingo Casiano, and others) and writers (René Marqués, Pedro Juan Soto, Emilio Díaz Valcárcel, Vivas Maldonado, and others). The unit also made considerable use of North American expertise, particularly Edwin Rosskam (screen writer), Jack Delano, a longtime resident of Puerto Rico (director), Benji Donniger (cameraman), and Willard Van Dyke (director). Generally these films, because they were produced by a unit of government responsible for education, had a pedagogical or didactic quality. *Los peloteros* (1951) is generally thought to be the best film from this period. It was directed by Jack Delano and based on a script by Edwin Rosskam and featured Ramón Ortiz del Rivero (the celebrated comedian Diplo) and Miriam Colón. The premise revolves around the activities of a group of children trying to buy baseball uniforms and equipment. This was also the first full-length feature film produced by the Puerto Rican Division of Community Education.

Among the other important social films that came out of the crucible of the Division of Community Education were *Las manos del hombre* (1952), written and directed by Jack Delano, a documentary about the dignity and value of different kinds of manual labor. *El puente* (1954), directed by Amílcar Tirado, is about a community that solves the overflowing of a river by building a bridge. *El santero* (1956), written by Ricardo Alegría and directed by Amílcar Tirado, is a documentary about a devoted santero struggling to compete with mass-produced commercial plaster images. *Ignacio* (1956), directed by Angel F. Rivera, is a dramatic adaptation of the book *Los casos de Ignacio y Santiago* written by René Marqués about the timidity in a Puerto Rican man from the countryside and how he overcame his problems and began to speak his mind. *El cacique* (1957), written by Emilio Díaz Valcárcel and directed by Benji Donniger, depicts the way a rural community deals with an authoritarian and greedy community leader. *El yugo* (1959), written by Pedro Juan Soto and directed by Oscar Torres, is the story of a fishing village and the way it formed a cooperative to free itself from the exploitation of the middle man. *Juan sin seso* (1959), written by René Marqués and directed by Luis Figueroa, was a satire about the undue influences of advertising. *El hombre esperado* (1964), written by Emilio Díaz Valcárcel and directed by Luis A. Maisonet, is a biopic about the life and work of José Pablo Morales, writer and politician who struggled against an exploitive system imposed by the Spanish Governor, General Pezuela. *La quiebra* (1964), written by Pedro Juan Soto, based on two short stories by Miguel Meléndez Muñoz, is about a country man who can't keep his small farm going and ends up bankrupt.

Of special interest were films dedicated to the role and treatment of women in Puerto Rican society, particularly in the countryside, and the very positive message those films contained. Such films included *Modesta* (1956), directed by Benji Donniger, which showed the physical abuse that women suffered in the Puerto Rican countryside. Modesta decides that she will not take the abuse any longer and she physically attacks her husband with a stick. Soon all the women of the community learn of Modesta's revolt and they unite to demand cooperation and fair treatment from their husbands. This film won first prize in the 1956 Venice Film Festival. *¿Qué opina la mujer?* (1957), written by René Marqués and directed by Oscar Torres, is a documentary that opens with a dramatization of the poor way that women are treated in Puerto Rico. The narrator turns then to interviews to prove the benefits and the need for women to participate in the development of the society. Interviewees include First Lady Inés Mendoza de Muñoz Marín, historian Margot Arce de Vázquez, and social worker Dr. Rebecca Goldberg. *Gena la de Blas* (1964), directed by Luis A. Maisonet and based on a short story by José Luis Vivas Maldonado, tells the story of a country woman, Gena, whose husband, Blas, and older son display a macho attitude towards her and deny her the right to participate in the affairs of the farm and the community. After Blas suffers an accident, Gena must run the farm herself. With the help of her sons, neighbors, and her own intelligence, she turns out a good coffee crop and her husband is forced to change his attitude about the role of women in society.

Aside from the Community Education films, Viguié Film Productions, founded in 1951 by Juan Emilio Viguié hijo and the journalist Manuel R. Navas, became the first large Puerto Rican film production company. In 1953, the writer Salvador Tió became a partner of the company, which had its own studio and laboratory in Hato Rey (which has now become part of the Conservatorio de Música). Many filmmakers received their training here or with the División de la Educación de la Comunidad. The company produced both commercials and documentaries for the government and private firms. In 1962, the company was associated with the brothers, Roberto and Marino Guastella and what emerged ultimately, in 1974 was Guastella Film Producers, currently the largest producer in Puerto Rico. Unfortunately, no film laboratory currently exists in Puerto Rico; however, footage is sent to New York.

Beginning in the 1950s, the production of film features accelerated somewhat. A group of investors and actors head by Víctor Arrillaga and Axel Anderson produced a few films under the Producciones Borinquen. *Maruja* (1959) was the most successful, premised on the love life of a barber's wife, and starring Marta Romero and a number of well-known actors and actresses from Puerto Rican television. A number of films were produced in Puerto Rico by North American filmmakers for the continental market (*Machete* [1958] is the best known, primarily for its sexuality).

Coproduction with Mexican interests began during the 1960s but led to no more than the repetition of old Mexican formula films with Puerto Rican settings. Among the films that were produced were *Romance en Puerto Rico* (1961, which has the distinction of being the first Puerto Rican color film), *Bello amanecer* (1962), *Lamento bo-*

rincano (1963), *Mientras Puerto Rico duerme* (1964, about the drug problem), *El jibarito Rafael* (1966, about Rafael Hernández), and *Fray Dollar* (1970). Most of the major actors (and directors) were not Puerto Rican but Mexican or other Latin American nationalities.

In 1964, television producer Paquito Cordero organized Pakira Films, and with financial backing from Columbia Pictures it made a number of films based on the appearances of the television comedian, Aldaberto Rodríguez (Machuchal). These films, including *El alcalde de Machuchal* (1964), *Millonario a-go-go* (1965), *El agente de Nueva York* (1966), and *El curandero del pueblo* (1967) were financially successful. The company also produced its own Mexican formula films, called "churros" by the Mexican industry, such as *En mi viejo San Juan* (1966), *Luna de miel en Puerto Rico* (1967), and *Una puertorriqueña en Acapulco* (1968). In New York, *El pueblo se levanta* (1968) was produced by the Third World Newsreel collective. The film focuses on the Puerto Rican community of East Harlem and the activities and philosophy of the Young Lords Party.

Several films based on criminals who had captured the popular imagination were produced by Anthony Felton, a Puerto Rican resident of New York. Popular for a while, the public eventually tired of these films with very low budgets and production values and earthy language and titillating situations: *Correa Coto, iasí me llaman!* (1968), *La venganza de Correa Coto* (1969), *Arocho y Clemente* (1969), *La palomilla* (1969), and *Luisa* (1970).

In the 1970s, the number of Mexican coproductions with Puerto Rico declined significantly, primarily because of political changes in the Mexican film industry (see Treviño, 1979). Among the few that were done are *Yo soy el gallo* (1971), featuring Puerto Rican singer, José Miguel Class, *La pandilla en apuros* (1977), *iQué bravas son las solteras,* featuring *vedette* Iris Chacón, and *Isabel La Negra* (1979), by Efraín López Neris, the first superproduction by Puerto Rican standards, featuring José Ferrer, Henry Darrow, Raúl Julia, and Miriam Colón. This last film is about a notorious madam of a Ponce brothel and was filmed in English. However, the production was both an artistic and financial failure.

While the number of features declined, the number of documentaries increased greatly in the 1970s, spurred in part by the intense political climate of Puerto Rico and also by the emergence of Puerto Rican filmmakers working in the continental United States, particularly in Boston, New York, and Philadelphia. A number of *talleres cinematográficos* were established. Notable among them was Tirabuzón Rojo which produced *Denuncia de un embeleco* (director, Mario Vissepó), *Puerto Rico* (1975, Cuban Film Institute and Tirabuzón Rojo, 1975), a socioeconomic analysis of present-day Puerto Rico from an *independentista* point of view, and *Puerto Rico: paraíso invadido/Puerto Rico: Paradise Invaded* (1977, Alfonso Beato, director), an examination of the history and present-day reality of Puerto Rico from an *independentista* perspective. Independent filmmakers produced *The Oxcart* (1970, José García Torres), a short (20 minute) portrayal of the migration of a Puerto Rican family that is based on the famous play by René Marqués; *Culebra, el comienzo* (1971, Diego de la Texera); *La carreta* (1972, José García, Spanish-language version of *The Oxcart*); *Los nacionalistas /The Nationalists* (1973, José García Torres, director) which surveys the activities of the Puerto Rican Nationalist Party during the 1950s with a special focus on Don Pedro Albizu Campos; *La vida y poesía de Julia de Burgos* (1974); *Destino manifiesto* (1977); *A la guerra* (1979, Thomas Sigel, director), an ode to the Puerto Rican community's war against cultural and racial discrimination in the form of a poem read by its author, Bimbo Rivas; and *The Life and Poetry of Julia de Burgos* (1979, José García Torres, director, Spanish-language version in 1974), a docudrama on the life and work of the great Puerto Rican poet.

In the 1980s, a number of features were produced including *Una aventura llamada Menudo* (1983, Orestes Trucco), featuring the famous young musical group. This film was one of the biggest box office successes in Puerto Rican history, however, its sequel, *Operación Caribe* (1984) with another very popular juvenile group, Los Chicos, was a financial flop. Also produced, all in 1986 were *Reflejo de un deseo* (Ivonne María Soto, director), about the director's mother, a poet; *Nicolás y los demás* (Jacobo Morales, director), a variation on the eternal triangle theme; and *La gran fiesta* (Marcos Zurinaga, director). The first two were low budget vehicles, done in 16 mm. and blown up to 35 mm. They were not financially nor artistically successful. On the other hand, *La gran fiesta* (producer, Roberto Gándara, director Marcos Zurinaga) has been a watershed in Puerto Rican film. Produced with a high budget by local standards (about $1 million), and boasting excellent production values, this period piece with strong political dimensions, evokes the handing over of the San Juan Casino to the United States military in 1942 amidst considerable turmoil about the possibility of a Nazi invasion, the status of Puerto Rico, and changing attitudes among the upper classes, particularly growers and merchants. This financially successful film was also the first to be produced under the new Ley de Sociedades Especiales (Ley 8, July 19, 1985), which was designed to spur filmic production.

Among independent filmmakers, primarily with financial support of the Fundación Puertorriqueña de las Humanidades, the number of documentaries were on the increase in the 1980s, among them *Retratos* (1980, Stewart Bird, director) which chronicles the life stories of four individuals from New York's Puerto Rican community in their attempts to adjust to life in America; *Puerto Rico: Our Right to Decide* (1981, Stanley Nelson, director), featuring interviews with people from various walks of life on Puerto Rico's current problems and aspirations for its political future; *Puerto Rico: A Colony the American Way* (1982, Diego Echeverría, director), an examination of the island's economic relationship with the United States; *La operación* (1982, Ana María García, director) about the sterilization of Puerto Rican women; *El arresto* (1982, Luis Antonio Rosario Quiles, director) which dramatizes a major event in the history of the Puerto Rican independence movement; *Ligía Elena* (1983, Francisco López), a color animation that criticizes consumerism, snobbery, and racism, set to a salsa song by Rubén Blades; *Manos a la obra: The Story of Operation Bootstrap* (1983, Pedro Rivera and Susan Zeig), an examination of the economic development plan undertaken in the 1950s called "Operation Bootstrap"; *La herencia de un tambor* (1984, Mario Vissepó) about Afro-Caribbean music; *Luchando por la vida* (1984, José Artemio Torres) about Puerto Rican tobacco workers; *Luis Muñoz Marín* (1984, Luis Molina), a biography of the noted governor; and *Corretjer* (1984, Antonio Segarra), a portrait of the noted poet and politician. *Los Sures* (1984), directed by Diego Echeverría, is a portrait of one of New York City's poorest neighborhoods and the gritty survival of five of its Puerto Rican residents. *La fiebre de irse,* directed by Alex Griswold (screened at the 1984 San Antonio CineFestival), is about the plight of a mainland Puerto Rican caught between the necessity of a steady income and the need to return home to the island.

El cetí (1985), Taller de Cine La Red, is about a small Puerto Rican fish, the effects of pollution on its life cycle, and the various legends about it that have been passed from generation to generation by the local fishermen. *Baquiné para un maestro* (1985), directed by Kino García, documents the funeral of the well-known Puerto Rican musician, Rafael Cortijo.

La batalla de Vieques/The Battle of Vieques (1986, Zydnia Nazario) examines the U.S. Navy's control and use of the small island of Vieques; *Tufiño* (1986, Ramón Almodóvar) evokes the life and work of this painter; *Raíces eternas* (1986, Noel Quiñones) describes the history of Puerto Rico since the discovery; *Cimarrón* (1986, Luis Antonio Rosario), is a short fiction about a black slave who escapes his owner's manor and searches for his wife and child in Puerto Rico;

Machito (1986 Carlos Ortiz) is an excellent biographical film that follows Machito's career as well as the evolution of Latin jazz from the Cuba of the 1920s to contemporary New York City. *The House of Ramón Iglesias* (1986), directed by Luis Soto, is about a Puerto Rican father who decides to return to the island after having lived in the United States for over nineteen years, with very painful results. *Have You Seen La Nueva Mujer Revolucionaria Puertorriqueña?* (1987), directed by Lisa Rudman, permits us to visit with four Puerto Rican women incarcerated for their involvement in the Puerto Rican independence movement. They discuss why they chose to be "armed fighters for independence," and what this choice has meant for them as women and mothers. *30 de agosto* (1987, director Emilio Rodríguez Vásquez) depicts the history of the abuses of the FBI, allegedly creating charges against sixteen Puerto Ricans of conspiring to rob $7 million from the Wells Fargo Company in Hartford, Connecticut, in order to intimidate and discredit advocates of Puerto Rico's independence. *Life in the G* (1988), directed by Joan Jubela, is about a Puerto Rican whose Brooklyn neighborhood is going through gentrification. *Una historia de los Reyes Magos* (1988, Producciones Rodadero) is an animation that brings to life a Puerto Rican story inspired by the tradition of the Magi. *Brooklyn Freestyle* (1988), directed by Héctor Sánchez, is about a young Puerto Rican who explores freestyle bicycling as an alternative to drugs for the teenagers in his Brooklyn, New York, community. *Working a Dream: Puerto Rican Theater in the South Bronx* (1988), directed by Diana Corya, is about the first permanent Puerto Rican theater group; the South Bronx is seen in a broader social, historical, and political context. *Sabios árboles, mágicos árboles* (1988, Puerto Rico Conservation Trust) is an animation that deals with the importance of trees and with man's relationship to nature; *Las plumas del múcaro* (1989, Puerto Rico Animation Workshop) is an animated Puerto Rican folk tale from the oral tradition. *Myrna Báez: Los espejos del silencio* (1989), directed by Sonia Fritz, is a profile of a Puerto Rican painter and graphic artist. *Plena is Work: Plena is Song* (1989), directed by Pedro Rivera and Susan Zeig, traces the roots of Plena, the Puerto Rican blend of African and Spanish idioms through the work of Cortijo, Canario, Ismael Rivera, and César Concepción. *AIDS in the Barrio: Eso no me pasa a mi* (1989), directed by Peter Piella and Frances Negrón, explores the spread of AIDS in Philadelphia's Puerto Rican community through an analysis of sexism, homophobia, and drug use.

Casita Culture (1990), directed by Cathe Neuku and narrated by Willie Colón, is about the casitas that are indicative of the cultural survival of the Puerto Rican community within New York City. *The Bell* (1990), directed by Noel Quiñones, tells the story of a slave-owning family cursed by a mysterious tragedy. The film is based on an original nineteenth-century story written by Cayetano Coll y Coste. *The Salt Mines* (1990), produced and directed by Susana Aiken and Carlos Aparicio, is about a community of homeless people who live along the Hudson River where the New York City Sanitation

Department stores its out-of-service trucks and excess garbage. Producer and director Noel Quiñones offers a comic portrayal of a middle-aged man's confrontation with his excesses in *San Juan Story* (1990). The thirty-minute film stars Jacobo Morales and Rosana de Soto. *Visa For a Dream* (1990, producer/director Sonia Fritz) exposes the hardships of life in the Dominican Republic as told by Dominican women who have immigrated to the neighboring island of Puerto Rico. *Puerto Rico: Arte e identidad* (1991), produced by Myrna Báez and J. A. Torres Martino and directed by Sonia Fritz, is a historical look at Puerto Rican cultural and political identity through its visual arts. Directors Vincent Cafarelli and Candy Kugel created the animated film *Fast Food Matador* (1991) about a New York City coffee shop delivery boy. *Gagá* (1992), directed by Héctor Méndez-Caratini, documents the religious ritual undertaken by a young boy as he passes into manhood. *Images of Faith* (1992), directed by Rebecca Marvil, depicts the venerable tradition of using hand-carved santos in the religious practices of Puerto Rico. *Loíza* (1992), directed by Héctor Méndez-Caritini, is on the famous Puerto Rican town's celebration of its feast day. In *Adombe: La presencia africana en Puerto Rico* (1992), director Edwin Reyes explores the historical and cultural African presence in Puerto Rico. *Once Upon a Time in the Bronx* (1993), directed by Ela Troyano, is a docudrama based on the lives, work, and neighborhood of the Spanglish rap group, Latin Empire.

Among the more recent feature films, Puerto Rican filmmaker Joseph B. Vásquez's *Hangin' with the Homeboys* (1991, independent production distributed by New Line Cinema) is an exceptional film. It was the cowinner of a screenwriting award at the Sundance Film Festival. *Homeboys* evokes the coming of age of four young male friends, two Puerto Rican, two African American, out on the town during a night in which their futures and relationships with each other are tested. *The Sun and the Moon* (1987, independent production, director Kevin Conway) was a box-office and critical failure, begun by and starring María Norman and Mila Burnette, actors of Puerto Rican descent, and also featuring José Ferrer. The film is about a chic Manhattanite fed up with her lifestyle and cheating husband who moves in with relatives in the South Bronx and organizes tenants. *Tango Bar* (1988), directed by Marcos Zurinaga, who also directed *La gran fiesta*, starring Raúl Julia, Valeria Lynch, and Rubén Juárez, is the story of three once popular dancers reunited to recreate their floor shows of ten years past. This Argentinian-Puerto Rican coproduced tango musical follows the history of the dance from its origins to the present, against the political backdrop of Argentina. *Cuentos de Abelardo* (1990), directed by Luis Molina-Casanova, is a feature length film that provides us with three uniquely Puerto Rican short stories by Abelardo Díaz Alfaro.

Cuban American and Other U.S. Latino Films

Guillermo Cabrera Infante (1985) and David R. Maciel (1993) trace the origins of Cuban cinema in the United States to the 1960s and the arrival in this country of disaffected Cuban exiles after the triumph of the Cuban Revolution. A key element in this, according to Maciel (1993, 329) was the prohibition in 1961 of the documentary *PM*, a film subsidized by the independent literary magazine, *Lunes de Revolución,* which depicted the Cuban proletariat alienated from the revolutionary process. While considerable time had to pass between the period when the Cuban filmmakers left Cuba and the production of films in this country, recently such production has greatly accelerated.

Two episodes of the series *Heatwave,* directed by Ledith P. Lugo have been dedicated to Paquito D'Rivera, the Cuban-born alto saxophone Latin jazz musician, and Mongo Santamaría, one of the best-known North American Afro-Cuban musicians. Both of these profiles were screened at the 1984 San Antonio CineFestival. *Photo Album* (1986), directed by Enrique Oliver, is an affectionate remembrance of the filmmaker's experience as a young immigrant from Cuba. *Three by Three* (1986), directed by Calgero Salvo, is a docudrama about an "undesirable" arriving in San Francisco from Mariel, Cuba. The film deals with Castro, Cuba, gay life, and racism. In *Cuba/USA* (1988), director Wayne Salazar describes the lives of three Cuban artists living in New York. *Hecho en Cuba* (1989), directed by Umberto Sagramoso, is a documentary on Cuban music that goes from the African rhythms that gave it birth to contemporary sounds. Graciela I. Sánchez has produced and directed *No porque lo diga Fidel Castro/Not Because Fidel Castro Says So* (1988) which is an insightful look into gay life in Cuba, evoking both traditional and more contemporary attitudes.

Americas/The Americans (1992), directed by Peter Bull and Joseph Tovares, is a portrait of Miami's Cuban Americans focusing on this group's economic power, anticommunist sentiments and reactions to the English-only versus bilingualism political conflicts. *Souvenirs* (1992), directed by José Peláez, is docudrama that explores the experience of growing up Cuban in the United States and the problems faced by all young Latinos who must learn to live in two separate cultures at once. In *Cuba Va: The Next Generation* (1993), directors Gail Dolgin and Vicente Franco give a candid and polemical look at Cuba's future from the dynamic perspective of its youth, including both committed socialists and disillusioned dissidents. *No es fácil* (1993), directed by Neal A. Escobar, tells how a Cuban family which has left the island is able to adjust to life in the United States, with particular focus on the younger generations of Cuban immigrants.

The first Cuban American full-length feature film is *El Súper* (1979, director León Ichaso, in Spanish with English subtitles). Elizabeth Peña debuted in this film about the trials of a homesick exiled Cuban who labors as an apartment house super in Manhattan. This is reportedly the first Spanish-language film to be shot in New York City. An island Cuban film, *Lejanía* (1985, released also as *Parting of the Ways,* director Jesús Díaz Rodríguez) has affected the Cuban American population inasmuch as its theme centers on the ties that exist between the Cubans on the island and their relatives who chose to immigrate, principally to the United States.

Films by and/or about other U.S. Latino groups or about Latinos in the border region are also being produced. *The Return of Rubén Blades* (1985), produced and directed by Robert Mugge, is a music documentary about the passion and commitment, art and politics of the well-known singer, songwriter, and actor; and producer Eduardo Aguiar's *Federico García Lorca in New York* (1986) is an evocation of the Spanish writer's experiences and work set in New York. *Los que se van* (1991), directed by Adolfo Dávila, is a Mexican documentary that focuses on the alienation experienced by Mexican immigrants in search of a better life in the United States. . . . *Dear Teresa* (1992), directed by July Melo, is about a Dominican who enters illegally into the United States and confronts the often deceitful reality of his new homeland to make his own way. *Esta noche* (1992), directed by Alex Vargas, is about a Latino from an unnamed Latin American country who was a former member of a death squad and now lives in San Francisco. He begins to obsess about a young neighbor who reminds him of another woman whom he had tortured and murdered and who continues to haunt his memory. *De mujer a mujer* (1993), produced and directed by the membership of the Mujeres Indígenas Productions (San Antonio, Texas), focuses on the sexual beliefs, practices, and the debunking of taboos of several Indo/Afro/Hispano American women.

Notes

[1]Fregoso (1992, 195) takes me to task for "failings" with respect to Lourdes Portillo. I quote from her bilious passage: "Portillo herself has been one of our most misunderstood and distorted film practitioners. Male critics simply don't known what to make of her. She has been called a Nicaraguan filmmaker by Gary Keller in his introduction to the first Chicano cinema anthology (1985). Assuming that only a man could conceive of a national activist film association, Keller also forgot to mention that Portillo was one of the founders of Cine Acción." These remarkably silly comments do bring up one issue, the ethnic identity of filmmakers, that is worth discussing. Before doing so, however, let me dispense with inaccuracies. First, I didn't think it necessary or important to refer to any founders of Cine Acción, male or female. And I still don't. Fregoso merely makes an issue of this to pursue her own frivolous agenda. As for calling Portillo Nicaraguan, I never did this. I don't know what her nationality is. Here is exactly what I wrote in Keller (1985, 52): "Not only have the last ten years (1975-1984) witnessed a surge of Chicano-focused documentaries but also the establishment of a corpus of dramatic films, both shorts and features. Among the significant short dramatic works of the last ten years we need to include . . . Lourdes Portillo's *Después del terremoto* (1979), winner of the Diploma of Honor, Cracow, Poland, in 1979, a portrayal of the Nicaraguan community in the United States responding to the aftermath of an earthquake back home . . ." Why does Fregoso falsely create a citation for me about Portillo's ethnicity and falsely claim I've "forgotten" to recognize Portillo in a second way? Because the truth ought not get in the way of her missionary zeal which is to create in Lourdes Portillo, together with Sylvia Morales and Esperanza Vásquez, the representatives of Chicana "counteraesthetics." (In order to have Esperanza Vásquez meet the ideological quotient she happens to conveniently fail to mention that the film *Agueda Martínez* is by Esperanza Vásquez and horrors! a man!, Moctesuma Esparza). Counteresthetes need to counter oppressors and if oppressors don't exist, Fregoso has no problem at all creating them out of ideologically vapid air! In yet another place (1990-91, 85) she claims that Chicanas have been excluded or marginalized from film festivals and from what she calls the "canon" no less! of film criticism, namely the one humble book at that time, Keller (1985). This is no less a straw dog since the "canon" in question contained papers by Cordelia Candelaria, Sylvia Morales, Yolanda Julia Broyles, Guadalupe Ochoa Thompson, Rosa Linda Fregoso, and others knowledgeable about Chicana film. In fact this ludicrous and egregious claim is contradicted by perpetrator Fregoso herself who in 1993, p. 152 suggests that "for discussion of stereotypes of Chicanas" a reader should consult three specific articles and no others. All three, by Cordelia Candelaria, Sylvia Morales, and Carlos Cortés are in my very same book which she denigrates as excluding Chicanas! Returning to the ethnicity of filmmakers, I do want to note that in my scholarly work on Latino/Latina cinema, I have not been particularly concerned with the ethnic identity of the filmmakers. I don't have trouble recognizing Portillo as doing Chicana film, or Robert Young for that matter. Ethnicity of the filmmaker is a factor but not an overriding one. This is in contrast to others who have preferred to use the concept of Chicanesque/chicanesca to categorize Chicano-focused work by non-Chicanos.

[2]While Fregoso (1990, 1993) has interesting insights into *Born in East L.A.,* her obeisance to ideology sometimes gets in the way, causing her to make patently wrong analyses. Notably in her review of *Born in East L.A.,* having decided that this is a genuine and valuable Chicano film (which it is), she goes to absurd and myopic lengths to sanitize the work as a worthy paragon for left-leaning feminists (which in some places it is not). She goes on and on citing Emily Hicks, Mikhail Bakhtin, "grotesque realism," etc. about the opening sequences, never facing up to the raunchiness of them and instead claiming that the film "deploys the enigmatic image of the French woman in order to

universalize the parody of Chicano voyeurism" (1993, 51), that the woman is an "enigmatic image" and similar comments (49, 51). She simply fails to come to terms with these images in their own salaciousness which provide a very natural continuity between Cheech's earlier film persona and his subsequent persona in *Born in East L.A.* The antidote to Fregoso's false platitudes of universal Chicano voyeurism is to be found in Christine List's (1992) article on Cheech and Chong, which shows us that after all it *is* possible to be both titillating and countercultural, *make a pitch* for the box office with all sorts of salacious and juvenile humor *and* be subversive. The Cheech in *Born in East L.A.* still is the same horny, earthy, unrefined guy who in *Up in Smoke* says about his girlfriend, "I hope she hasn't eaten. I got something for her. Tube steak smothered in underwear," and who runs to the toilet after eating Mexican food holding his buttocks and muttering, "Come on, cheeks, stay together." That he is the same guy is a fundamental aspect of *Born in East L.A.* which was intended to cross over to a larger audience, and did so with some success. The audience that Cheech had always catered to in the first place was one of hippy, countercultural types, Chicano and otherwise, not elitist theoretical tergiversators of humor into ideologically correct channels.

Works Cited

This list is made up primarily of works cited in this book. The general bibliography appears in the companion volume, *A Pictorial Handbook of Hispanics and United States Film.*

Adams, Les, and Buck Rainey. *Shoot-em-Ups, The Complete Reference Guide to Westerns of the Sound Era.* New Rochelle, NY: Arlington House, 1978.

Admari, Ralph. "The House that Beadle Built, 1859-1869." *American Book Collector* 4 (November 1933): 223-225.

"American Me." *Variety,* March 10, 1992, 2, 29.

Balshofer, Fred J., and Arthur C. Miller. *One Reel a Week.* Berkeley: University of California Press, 1967.

Barbour, Alan G. *Cliffhanger: A Pictorial History of the Motion Picture Serial.* Secaucus, NJ: Citadel Press, 1977.

Barbour, Alan G. *Days of Thrills and Adventure.* New York: Macmillan, 1970.

Bataille, Gretchen M., and C. Silet. *The Pretend Indians: Images of Native Americans in the Movies.* Ames, IA: Iowa State University Press, 1980.

Biberman, Herbert. *Salt of the Earth: The Story of a Film.* Boston: Beacon Press, 1965.

Bilbao, Elena, and María Antonieta Gallart. *Los chicanos.* Mexico City: Ed. Nueva Imagen, 1981.

Bishop, W.H. "Story-Paper Literature." *Atlantic* 44 (September 1879): 387.

Blades, Rubén. "The Politics Behind the Latino's Legacy." *The New York Times,* April 19, 1992, Section H31.

Bogle, Donald. *Toms, Coons, Mulattoes, Mammies, and Bucks: An Interpretative History of Blacks in American Film, 1900-1941.* New York: Viking Press, 1973.

Bowser, Eileen, ed. *Biograph Bulletins 1908-1912.* New York: Farrar, Straus and Giroux, 1973.

Bowser, Eileen, ed. *Film Notes.* New York: The Museum of Modern Art, 1969.

Bowser, Eileen. *The Transformation of Cinema, 1907-1915.* Vol. 2 of Charles Harpole, gen. ed., *History of the American Cinema.* New York: Charles Scribner's Sons, 1990.

Burgin, Victor, James Donald, and Cora Kaplan, *Formations of Fantasy.* New York: Routledge, 1989.

Burns, E. Bradford. *Latin American Cinema: Film and History.* Los Angeles: Latin American Center, 1975.

Burton, Julianne. "Marginal Cinemas and Mainstream Critical Theory." *Screen* 26, no. 3 (1985): 18-21.

Cabrera Infante, Guillermo. "Cuba's Shadow." *Film Comment* 21 (1985): 49-58.

"Caja de sorpresas." *Tiempo,* March 30, 1945, 39.

Candelaria, Cordelia. "Film Portrayals of La Mujer Hispana." *Agenda* 11, no. 3 (June 1981): 32-36.

Cárdenas, Don, and Suzanne Schneider, eds., *Chicano Images in Film.* Denver, CO: Denver International Film Festival, 1981.

Cham, Mbye B. *Critical Perspectives on Black Independent Cinema.* Cambridge, MA: MIT Press, 1988.

Cohen, Sarah Blacher. *From Hester Street to Hollywood: The Jewish American Stage and Screen.* Bloomington, IN: Indiana University Press, 1986.

"Connecting with the American Experience: An Interview with Luis Valdez." *Hispanic Business,* July 1987, 10-13.

Connor, Edward. "The Genealogy of Zorro." *Films in Review,* Aug.-Sept. 1957, 330-333, 343.

Contreras Torres, Miguel. *El libro negro del cine mexicano.* Mexico: Editora Hispano-Continental Films, 1960.

Corliss, Richard. "Born in East L.A.: Hollywood Can Be a Tough Town for Non-Anglos." *Time,* July 11, 1988, 66-67.

Cortés, Carlos E., "Chicanas in Film: History of an Image." In *Chicano Cinema: Research, Review, and Resources,* edited by Gary D. Keller. 94-108. Binghamton, NY: Bilingual Review/Press.

Cortés, Carlos E. "Chicanos y medios masivos de comunicación." *Plural,* Enero 1993, 50-59.

Cortés, Carlos E. "*The Greaser's Revenge* to *Boulevard Nights:* The Mass Media Curriculum on Chicanos." In National Association for Chicano Studies, *History, Culture, and Society: Chicano Studies in the 1980s.* Ypsilanti, MI: Bilingual Press, 1983.

Cortés, Carlos E. "The History of Ethnic Images in Film: The Search for a Methodology." In *Ethnic Images in Popular Genres and Media,* special issue of *MELUS, The Journal of the Society for the Study of the Multi-Ethnic Literature of the United States* 11, no. 3 (Fall, 1984): 63-77.

Cortés, Carlos E. "The Immigrant in Film: Evolution of an Illuminating Icon." In *Stock Characters in American Popular Film,* Volume 1 of *Beyond the Stars,* edited by Paul Loukides and Linda K. Fuller, 23-34. Bowling Green, OH: Bowling Green State University Popular Press, 1990.

Cortés, Carlos E. "Italian-Americans in Film: From Immigrants to Icons." In *Italian-American Literature,* special issue of *MELUS, The Journal of the Society for the Study of the Multi-Ethnic Literature of the United States* 14, nos. 3-4 (Fall-Winter, 1987): 107-126.

Cortés, Carlos E. "The Role of Media in Multicultural Education." *Viewpoints in Teaching and Learning* 56, no. 1 (Winter 1980): 38-49.

Cortés, Carlos E. "The Societal Curriculum: Implications for Multiethnic Education." In *Education in the 80s: Multiethnic Education,* edited by James A. Banks, 24-32. Washington, DC: National Education Association, 1981.

Cortés, Carlos E. "Who is María? What is Juan? Dilemmas of Analyzing the Chicano Image in U.S. Feature Films." In *Chicanos and Film: Essays on Chicano Representation and Resistance,* edited by Chon A. Noriega, 83-104. New York: Garland Publishing Co., 1992.

Cripps, Thomas. *Slow Fade to Black: The Negro in American Film, 1900-1942.* New York: Oxford University Press, 1977.

deCordova, Richard. *Picture Personalities: The Emergence of the Star System in America.* Urbana, IL: University of Illinois Press, 1991.

De los Reyes, Aurelio. *Cine y sociedad en México, 1896-1930.* México: Instituto de Investigaciónes Estéticas, UNAM, 1981.

De los Reyes, Aurelio. *Los orígenes del cine en México.* México: Colección SEP 80, 1983.

Delpar, Helen. "Goodbye to the 'Greaser': Mexico, the MPPDA, and Derogatory Films, 1922-1926." *Journal of Popular Film and Television* 12 (1984): 34-41.

Dibbell, Julian. "Notes on Carmen." *Village Voice,* October 29, 1991, 43-45.

Dixon, Wheeler W. *The "B" Directors: A Biographical Directory.* Metuchen, NJ: Scarecrow Press, 1985.

Doane, Mary Anne. "Film and the Masquerade: Theorizing the Female Spectator." *Screen* 23, nos. 3-4, (September/October 1982): 74-87.

Dockser, Amy, Edward James Olmos, and Tom Bower. "Making Sure There Are Alternatives: The Ballad of Edward James Olmos, Tom Bower, and Gregorio Cortez." *Imagine* 1, no. 1 (Summer 1984): 1-9.

Enciclopedia del cine mexicano. México: Publicaciones Cinematográficas, 1955.

Erens, Patricia. *The Jew in American Cinema.* Bloomington, IN: Indiana University Press, 1984.

"Esparza/Katz Skeds Seven Pix in 16 Months With $68 Mil Slate," *Variety* 228, no. 55 (August 21, 1990).

Everson, William K. *The Bad Guys: A Pictorial History of the Movie Villain.* New York: The Citadel Press, 1964.

Everson, William K. *A Pictorial History of the Western Film.* New York: The Citadel Press, 1969.

Ewen, Stuart, and Elizabeth Ewen. *Channels of Desire: Mass Images and the Shaping of American Consciousness.* Minneapolis, MN: University of Minnesota Press, 1982.

Fernández, Enrique. "Spitfires, Latin Lovers, Mambo Kings." *The New York Times,* April 19, 1992, H1, H30.

Films with a Purpose: A Puerto Rican Experiment in Social Film, April 23-May 3, 1987. Museum of Modern Art, The Collective for Living Cinema, New York University, El Museo del Barrio. The Bronx Museum of Art, El Instituto de Cultura Puertorriqueña. New York: Exit Art, 1987.

Finch, Christopher. *The Art of Walt Disney: From Mickey Mouse to the Magic Kingdom.* New York: Harry N. Abrams, Publ., 1973.

Flori, Monica. "A Selected and Annotated Filmography on Latin American Women." *Third Woman* 2, no. 2 (1984): 117-21.

Ford, Charles. "Paramount at Joinville." *Films in Review,* November 1961, 541-550.

Frase-Blunt, Martha. "Everything's Rosie." *Hispanic,* April 1993, 14-16.

Fregoso, Rosa Linda. "*Born in East L.A.* and the Politics of Representation." *Cultural Studies* 4, no. 3 (October 1990): 264-280.

Fregoso, Rosa Linda. *The Bronze Screen: Chicana and Chicano Film Culture.* Minneapolis: University of Minnesota Press, 1993.

Fregoso, Rosa Linda. "Chicana Film Practices: Confronting the Many-Headed Demon of Oppression." In *Chicanos and Film: Essays on Chicano Representation and Resistance,* edited by Chon A. Noriega, 189-204. New York: Garland Publishing Co., 1992.

Fregoso, Rosa Linda. "La quinceañera of Chicana Counter Aesthetics." *Centro: Boletín del Centro de Estudios Puertorriqueños* 3, no. 1 (Winter 1990-91): 87-91.

Fregoso, Rosa Linda. "*Zoot Suit* and *The Ballad of Gregorio Cortez.*" *Crítica* 1, no. 2 (Spring 1985): 126-31.

"French-Spanish Versions for 20 Paris Pictures." *Film Daily,* September 5, 1930.

French, Warren. "The Cowboy in the Dime Novel." *Texas Studies in English* 30 (1951): 219-234.

Friar, Ralph E., and N.A. Friar. *The Only Good Indian.* New York: Drama Book Specialists, 1972.

Friedman, Lester D. *Hollywood's Image of the Jew.* New York: Frederick Ungar Publishing, 1982.

Friedman, Lester D., ed. *Unspeakable Images: Ethnicity and the American Cinema.* Urbana, IL: University of Illinois Press, 1991.

Fusco, Coco. "The Latino 'Boom' in Hollywood." *Centro de Estudios Puertorriqueños Bulletin* 2, no. 8 (1990): 48-56.

Gabler, Neal. *An Empire of Their Own: How the Jews Invented Hollywood.* New York: Crown Publishers, 1988.

Gabler, Neal. "The Jewish Problem." *American Film* 13, no. 9 (July/August 1988): 37-44.

Gansberg, Alan L. "The Dealmakers: Methods, Money, Movies!" *Hispanic Business,* July 1991, 32-37.

Gansberg, Alan L. "Raúl Julia: One of the Busiest Actors in America." *Hispanic Business,* July 1992, 48-52.

García, Guy. "Frente a frente con Edward James Olmos." *Más,* Marzo-Abril 1991, 59-64.

García, Guy. "A Tale of Two Movies." *Premiere,* April 1992, 38-42.

García, Juan R. "Hollywood and the West: Mexican Images in American Films, 1894-1983." In *Old Southwest, New Southwest,* edited by Judy Nolte Lensink. Tucson: Tucson Public Library, 1988.

García, Kino. "Puerto Rico: Hacia un cine nacional." *Centro de Estudios Puertorriqueños Bulletin* 2, no. 8 (1990): 80-90.

García Riera, Emilio. *El cine mexicano.* México, D.F.: Ediciones Era, 1963.

García Riera, Emilio. *Emilio Fernández, 1904-1986.* Guadalajara: Ed. Universidad de Guadalajara, 1987.

García Riera, Emilio. *Historia del cine mexicano.* México: SEP/Foro 2000, 1986.

García Riera, Emilio. *Historia documental del cine mexicano 1926/1966.* 9 vols. México: Ediciones Era, 1969-1987.

García Riera, Emilio. *Howard Hawks.* Guadalajara: Ed. Universidad de Guadalajara, 1988

García Riera, Emilio. *Mexico visto por el cine extranjero.* Vol. 1, *1894/1940;* Vol. 2, *1906/1940, Filmografía;* Vol. 3, *1941/1969;* Vol. 4, *1941/1969, Filmografía.* México, D.F. Ediciones Era, 1987-1988.

Gonzales, Rodolfo "Corky". *I Am Joaquín/Yo soy Joaquín.* New York: Bantam Books, 1972.

Greenberg, Bradley S., Michael Burgoon, Judee K. Burgoon, and Felipe Korzenny, *Mexican Americans and the Mass Media.* Norwood, NJ: Ablex, 1983.

Greenberg, Bradley S., and Pilar Baptista-Fernández. "Hispanic Americans: The New Minority on Television." In *Life on Television: Content Analysis of U.S. TV Drama,* edited by Bradley S. Greenberg, 3-12. Norwood, NJ: Ablex Publishing Corporation, 1980.

Greenfield, Jeff. *Television, the First Fifty Years.* New York: Crescent Books, 1981.

Greenfield, Gerald Michael, and Carlos E. Cortés. "Harmony and Conflict of Intercultural Images: The Treatment of Mexico in U.S. Feature Films and K-12 Textbooks." *Estudios Mexicanos* 7, no. 2 (1991): 45-56.

Gunning, Tom. *D. W. Griffith and the Origins of American Narrative Film.* Urbana, IL: University of Illinois Press, 1991.

Gunning, Tom. "The Narrator's Incision: The Legacy of Griffith's Biograph Films." Unpublished paper for the colloquium on D. W. Griffith at the Université de Paris, n.d. Available in the files of the Museum of Modern Art, New York City.

Gunning, Tom. "Weaving a Narrative: Style and Economic Background in Griffith's Biograph Films." *Quarterly Review of Film Studies,* Winter 1981, 11-21.

Gutiérrez-Jones, Carl. "Legislating Languages: *The Ballad of Gregorio Cortez* and the English Language Amendment." In *Chicanos and Film: Essays on Chicano Representation and Resistance,* edited by Chon A. Noriega, 219-232. New York: Garland Publishing Co., 1992.

Hadley-Freydberg, Elizabeth. "Prostitutes, Concubines, Whores and Bitches: Black and Hispanic Women in Contemporary American Film." In *Women of Color: Perspectives on Feminism and Identity,* edited by Audrey T. McCluskey, 46-65. Bloomington, IN: Women's Studies Program, Indiana University, 1985.

Hadley-García, George. *Hispanic Hollywood: The Latins in Motion Pictures.* New York: The Citadel Press, 1990. Simultaneous Spanish-language version, *Hollywood Hispano.*

Hansen, Miriam. *From Babel to Babylon.* Cambridge: Harvard University Press, 1991.

Hanson, Patricia King, exec. ed. *The American Film Institute Catalog of Motion Pictures Produced in the United States. Feature Films, 1911-1920.* Berkeley: University of California Press, 1988.

Hanson, Patricia King, exec. ed. *The American Film Institute Catalog of Motion Pictures Produced in the United States. Feature Films, 1931-1940.* Berkeley: University of California Press, 1993.

Hart, John Mason. *Revolutionary Mexico: The Coming and Process of the Mexican Revolution.* Berkeley: University of California Press, 1987.

Harvey, Charles M. "The Dime Novel in American Life." *Atlantic Monthly* 100 (July, 1907): 44.

Haskell, Molly. *From Reverence to Rape: The Treatment of Women in the Movies.* New York: Holt, Rinehart and Winston, 1974.

Havránek, Bohuslav. "The Functional Differentiation of the Standard Language." In *A Prague School Reader on Esthetics, Literary Structure and Style,* edited by Paul L. Garvin. Washington, DC: Georgetown University Press, 1964.

Hayden, Sterling. *Wanderer.* New York: Knopf, 1963.

Iglesias, Norma. *Entre yerba, polvo y plomo: lo fronterizo visto por el cine mexicano.* Tijuana: El Colegio de la Frontera Norte, 1991.

Iglesias, Norma. "La visión de la frontera a través del cine mexicano." In *Times of Challenge: Chicanos and Chicanas in American Society,* edited by National Association for Chicano

Studies, 125-133. Houston: University of Houston Mexican American Studies Program, 1988.

Iglesias, Norma. *La visión de la frontera a través del cine mexicano.* Tijuana: Centro de Estudios Fronterizos del Norte de México, 1985.

International Motion Picture Almanac, 1928-1945. New York: Quigley Publishing Co., 1928-1945.

Jacobs, Lewis. *The Rise of the American Film: A Critical History.* New York: Harcourt Brace and Company, 1939.

Jenks, George C. "Dime Novel Makers." *Bookman* 22 (October 1904): 112.

Jiménez, Lillian. "From the Margin to the Center: Puerto Rican Cinema in the United States." *Centro de Estudios Puertorriqueños Bulletin* 2, no. 8 (1990): 28-43.

Jiménez-Rueda, Julio. "El cine sonoro: Otra opinión sobre la cuestión del lenguaje español y las películas habladas—el problema fundamental." *La Opinión,* January 14, 1930, 14.

Johansen, Jason C. "El cine chicano, redefiniendo su crecimiento." In *Suplemento Cultural de La Opinión,* November 16, 1980.

Johanssen, Albert. *The House of Beadle and Adams and Its Dime and Nickel Novels: The Story of a Vanished Literature.* 2 vols. Norman: University of Oklahoma Press, 1950.

Johnson, Randal, and Robert Stam, eds., *Brazilian Cinema.* New Jersey: Associated University Presses, 1982.

Johnston, Claire. "Femininity and the Masquerade: Anne of the Indies." In *Psychoanalysis and Cinema,* edited by E. Ann Kaplan, 64-72. New York: Routledge, 1990.

"Joinville Makes 110 in 12 Languages." *Film Daily,* August 26, 1930.

Katz, Ephraim. *The Film Encyclopedia.* New York: Thomas Y. Crowell, 1979.

Kazan, Elia. "Letters to the Editor." *The Saturday Review,* 35 (April 5, 1952): 22.

Keller, Gary D., ed. *Chicano Cinema: Research, Reviews, and Resources.* Binghamton, NY: Bilingual Review/Press, 1985.

Keller, Gary D., ed. *Cine chicano.* México, D.F.: Cineteca Nacional, 1988.

Keller, Gary D. "Film." In *The Hispanic-American Almanac,* edited by Nicolás Kanellos, 543-594. Detroit: Gale Research, Inc., 1993.

Knight, Alan. *The Mexican Revolution.* 2 vols. Cambridge: Cambridge University Press, 1986.

Koszarski, Diane Kaiser. *The Complete Films of William S. Hart: A Pictorial Record.* New York: Dover Publications, 1980.

Koszarski, Richard. *An Evening's Entertainment: The Age of the Silent Feature Picture, 1915-1928.* Vol. 3 of Charles Harpole, gen. ed., *History of the American Cinema.* New York: Charles Scribner's Sons, 1990.

Kotz, Liz. "Unofficial Stories: Documentaries by Latinas and Latin American Women." *Centro de Estudios Puertorriqueños Bulletin* 2, no. 8 (1990): 58-69.

Krafsur, Richard P., exec. ed. *The American Film Institute Catalog of Motion Pictures. Feature Films, 1961-1970.* New York: R. R. Bowker Company, 1976.

Lamb, Blaine P. "The Convenient Villain: The Early Cinema Views the Mexican American." *Journal of the West* 14 (October 1975): 75-81.

Latino Film and Video Images. Special Issue. *Centro* 2, no. 8 (Spring 1990). Centro de Estudios Puertorriqueños, Hunter College/CUNY.

Latinos and the Media. Special Issue. *Centro* 3, no. 1 (Winter, 1990-91). Centro de Estudios Puertorriqueños, Hunter College/CUNY.

Leab, Daniel J. *From Sambo to Superspade: The Black Experience in Motion Pictures.* Boston: Houghton-Mifflin, 1975.

Levine, Paul G. "Remember the Alamo? John Wayne Told One Story. PBS's Seguín Tells Another." *American Film,* Jan.-Feb. 1982, 47-48.

List, Christine. "Self-Directed Stereotyping in the Films of Cheech Marín." In *Chicanos and Film: Essays on Chicano Representation and Resistance,* edited by Chon A. Noriega, 205-218. New York: Garland Publishing Co., 1992.

López, Ana M. "Are All Latins from Manhattan?: Hollywood, Ethnography, and Cultural Colonialism." In *Unspeakable Images: Ethnicity and the American Cinema,* edited by Lester D. Friedman, 404-424. Urbana, IL: University of Illinois Press, 1991.

Maciel, David R. "Braceros, Mojados, and Alambristas: Mexican Immigration to the United States in Contemporary Cinema." *Hispanic Journal of Behavioral Sciences* 8 (1986): 369-385.

Maciel, David R. *El Norte: The U.S.-Mexican Border in Contemporary Cinema.* San Diego, CA: Institute for Regional Studies of the Californias (San Diego State University), 1990.

Maciel, David R. "Latino Cinema." In *Handbook of Hispanic Cultures in the United States: Literature and Art,* edited by Francisco Lomelí, 312-332. Houston: Arte Público Press and Instituto de Cooperación Iberoamericana, 1993.

Martin, Mick, and Marsha Porter, *Video Movie Guide 1993.* New York: Ballantine Books, 1992.

"Mexico Bars Any Film of Charlie's or Doug's [Fairbanks], Punishing for Kidding Country in Past Pictures." *Motion Picture World,* January 27, 1923.

Michener, Charles. "Black Movies." *Newsweek* 80 (October 23, 1972): 74.

Miller, Jim. "Chicano Cinema: An Interview with Jesús Treviño." *Cineaste* 8, no. 3 (1978).

Miller, Randall M., ed. *The Kaleidoscopic Lens: How Hollywood Views Ethnic Groups.* Englewood, NJ: Jerome S. Ozer, 1980.

Miller, Tom. "Salt of the Earth Revisited." *Cineaste* 13, no. 3, (1984): 31-36.

Mindiola, Jr., Tatcho. "El corrido de Gregorio Cortez: The Challenge of Conveying Chicano Culture Through the Cinematic Treatment of a Folk Hero." *Tonantzin,* November 1986, 14-15.

Monroy, Douglas. "'Our Children Get So Different Here': Film, Fashion, Popular Culture and the Process of Cultural Syncretization in Mexican Los Angeles, 1900-1935." *Aztlán, A Journal of Chicano Studies* 19, no. 1 (Spring 1988-90): 79-108.

Monsiváis, Carlos. "Cantinflas: de la esencia popular al moralismo pedagógico." Prensa Hispana, Junio 17, 1993, 2, 6, 8-9. Rep from *Proceso,* No. 860, 26 de abril de 1993.

Monsiváis, Carlos. "The Culture of the Frontier: The Mexican Side." In *Views Across the Border: The United States and Mexico,* edited by Stanley R. Ross. Albuquerque, NM: University of New Mexico Press, 1978.

Monsiváis, Carlos. "De México y los chicanos, de México y su cultura fronteriza." In *La otra cara de México: el pueblo chicano.* edited by David R. Maciel, 1-19. Mexico, 1977.

Monsiváis, Carlos. "¡Orale, arriba! de Speedy González a don Juan." *La cultura en México,* supplement of *Siempre,* Feb. 7, 1979.

Mora, Carl J. *Mexican Cinema: Reflections of a Society, 1896-1980.* Berkeley, CA: University of California Press, 1982. Revised edition, 1990.

Morsberger, Robert E., ed. *Viva Zapata! (The Original Screenplay by John Steinbeck).* New York: Viking Press, 1975.

Mottet, Jean. *D. W. Griffith: Colloque international sous la direction de Jean Mottet.* Paris: Editions L'Harmattan (Publications de la Sorbonne), 1984.

Munden, Kenneth W., exec. ed. *The American Film Institute Catalog of Motion Pictures Produced in the United States. Feature Films, 1921-1930.* New York: R. R. Bowker Company, 1971.

Murillo, Fidel. "Dolores del Río se ha negado a filmar una cinta denigrante." *La Opinión,* May 24, 1931.

Musser, Charles. *The Emergence of Cinema: The American Screen to 1907.* Vol. 1 of Charles Harpole, gen. ed., *History of the American Cinema.* New York: Charles Scribner's Sons, 1990.

Musser, Charles. "Ethnicity, Role-playing, and American Film Comedy: From *Chinese Laundry Scene* to *Whoopee* (1894-1930)." In *Unspeakable Images: Ethnicity and the American Cinema,* edited by Lester D. Friedman, 39-81. Urbana, IL: University of Illinois Press, 1991.

"Must Talkies Stay at Home." *Literary Digest,* December 29, 1930.

"Myrtle González Dead," *Los Angeles Times,* October 23, 1918, part II, 1.

Nash, Jay Robert, and Stanley Ralph Ross, *The Motion Picture Guide*. New York: R. R. Bowker Company (first 12 vols, publ. 1987, succeeding guides published annually).

National Film Archive Catalogue: Silent Fiction Films, 1895-1930. London: British Film Institute, 1966.

Nericcio, William Anthony. "Of Mestizos and Half-Breeds: Orson Welles's *Touch of Evil.*" In *Chicanos and Film: Essays on Chicano Representation and Resistance,* edited by Chon A. Noriega, 189-204. New York: Garland Publishing Co., 1992.

Nesteby, James R. *Black Images in American Films, 1896-1954*. Washington, DC: University Press of America, 1982.

Niver, Kemp R., ed. *Biograph Bulletins, 1896-1908*. Los Angeles: Locare Research Group, 1971.

Niver, Kemp R. *D. W. Griffith: His Biograph Films in Perspective*. Los Angeles: John D. Roche, Inc., 1974.

Niver, Kemp R. *Early Motion Pictures: The Paper Print Collection in the Library of Congress*. Washington, DC: Library of Congress, 1985.

Niver, Kemp R. *The First Twenty Years: A Segment of Film History*. Los Angeles: Locare Research Group, 1968.

Niver, Kemp R. *Klaw and Erlanger Present Famous Plays in Pictures*. Edited by Bebe Bergsten. Los Angeles: Locare Research Group, 1976.

Niver, Kemp R. *Motion Pictures from the Library of Congress Paper Print Collection, 1894-1912*. Berkeley, CA: University of California Press, 1967.

Noriega, Chon. "Chicano Cinema and the Horizon of Expectations: A Discursive Analysis of Film Reviews in the Mainstream, Alternative and Hispanic Press, 1987-1988." *Aztlán, A Journal of Chicano Studies* 19, no. 2 (Fall 1988-90): 1-32. Published earlier as *Chicano Cinema and the Horizon of Expectation: a Discursive Analysis of Recent Reviews in the Mainstream, Alternative and Hispanic Press*. (SCCR Working Paper No. 30). Stanford, CA: Stanford Center for Chicano Research, 1990.

Noriega, Chon, ed. *Chicanos and Film: Essays on Chicano Representation and Resistance*. New York: Garland Publishing Co., 1992. Reprinted 1992 by University of Minnesota Press.

Noriega, Chon. "Citizen Chicano: The Trials and Titillations of Ethnicity in the American Cinema, 1935-1962." *Social Research* 58, no. 2 (Summer 1991): 413-438.

Noriega, Chon, "Essay." In "*Cine de Mestizaje:* The National Latino Film and Video Festival, 1991." New York: El Museo del Barrio, 1991 (pamphlet, unpaginated).

Noriega, Chon. "In Aztlán: The Films of the Chicano Movement, 1969-79." *Whitney Museum of American Art,* pamphlet no. 56, January 9-27, 1991.

Noriega, Chon. *Working Bibliography of Critical Writings on Chicanos and Film* (Working Bibliography Series, no. 6). Stanford, CA: Mexican-American Collections, Stanford University Libraries, 1990.

Nuiry, Octavio Emilio. "The Hollywood-Washington Connection." *Hispanic,* October 1993, 15-22.

O'Connor, John E. *The Hollywood Indian: Stereotypes of Native Americans in Film*. Trenton: New Jersey State Museum, 1980.

O'Connor, John E. "TV: Seguín: True Tale of the Texas Revolution." *New York Times,* Arts/Entertainment, January 26, 1982.

Ordóñez, Elizabeth J. "La imagen de la mujer en el nuevo cine chicano." *Caracol* 5, no. 2 (October 1978): 12-13.

Pearson, Edmund. *Dime Novels: Or Following an Old Train in Popular Literature*. Boston: Little, Brown, 1929.

Pearson, Roberta. "The Modesty of Nature: Performance in Griffith's Biographs." Ph.D. dissertation, New York University, 1986.

Peiss, Kathy. *Cheap Amusements: Working Women and Leisure in Turn-of-the Century New York*. Philadelphia: Temple University Press, 1986.

Pérez, Richie. "From Assimilation to Annihilation: Puerto Rican Images in U.S. Films." *Centro de Estudios Puertorriqueños Bulletin* 2, no. 8 (1990): 8-27.

Pérez Turrent, Tomás. "La bamba." *El Universal,* December 29, 1987, 1, 4.

Pettit, Arthur G. *Images of the Mexican American in Fiction and Film.* College Station, TX: Texas A&M University Press, 1980.

Pettit, Arthur G. "Nightmare and Nostalgia: The Cinema West of Sam Peckinpah." *Western Humanities Review* 29 (Spring 1975): 105-22.

Pinto, Alfonso. "Hollywood's Spanish Language Films," *Films in Review* 24, no. 8 (October 1973): 474-483.

Pinto, Alfonso. "Lupe Vélez, 1909-1944." *Films in Review,* November 1977, 513-24.

Pinto, Alfonso. "Mona Maris." *Films in Review* 31, no. 3 (November 1977): 146-159.

Pitt, Leonard. *The Decline of the California.* Berkeley: University of California Press, 1966.

Rainey, Buck. *Heroes of the Range: Yesterday's Saturday Matinee Movie Cowboys.* Metuchen, NJ: The Scarecrow Press, 1987.

Rainey, Buck. *The* Shoot-Em-Ups *Ride Again. A Supplement to* Shoot-Em-Ups. Metuchen, NJ: The Scarecrow Press, 1990.

Ramírez, Arthur. Review of *Chicano Cinema,* by Gary D. Keller. *The Americas Review* 14, no. 3-4 (1986): 160-61.

Ramírez, Gabriel. *El cine de Griffith.* Mexico City: Ed. Era, 1972.

Ramírez, Gabriel. *Lupe Vélez: la mexicana que escupía fuego.* México: Cineteca Nacional, 1986.

Ramírez Berg, Charles. "*Bordertown,* the Assimilation Narrative and the Chicano Social Problem Film." In *Chicanos and Film: Essays on Chicano Representation and Resistance,* edited by Chon A. Noriega, 33-52. New York: Garland Publishing Co., 1992.

Ramírez Berg, Charles. *Cinema of Solitude: A Critical Study of Mexican Film, 1967-1983.* Austin: University of Texas Press, 1992.

Ramírez Berg, Charles. "Stereotyping in Film in General and of Hispanics in Particular." *Howard Journal of Communications* 2, no. 3 (Summer 1990): 286-300.

Ramsaye, Terry. *A Million and One Nights.* New York: Simon and Schuster, 1926.

Reyes, Luis. "Hispanic-American Cinema Lights Up the Silver Screen." *Hispanic Times,* Oct.-Nov. 1981, 28-29.

Reyes de la Maza, Luis. *Memorias de un pentonto.* Mexico City: Ed. Posada, 1984.

Reyes de la Maza, Luis. *Salón Rojo.* México: Ed. Cuadernos de Cine, Dirección General de Difusión Cultural, UNAM, 1968.

Richard, Jr., Alfred Charles. *The Hispanic Image on the Silver Screen: An Interpretive Filmography from Silents into Sound, 1898-1935.* New York: Greenwood Press, 1992.

Richardson, F.H. *Motion Picture Handbook, 1910.* New York: Moving Picture World, 1910.

Ringgold, Gene. *The Films of Rita Hayworth.* Secaucus, NJ: The Citadel Press, 1974.

Ríos-Bustamante, Antonio. "An Idea Whose Time Has Come." *Caminos* 5, no. 7 (July-Aug. 1984): 39-41.

Ríos-Bustamante, Antonio. "Latino Participation in the Hollywood Film Industry, 1911-1945." In *Chicanos and Film: Essays on Chicano Representation and Resistance,* edited by Chon Noriega, 21-32. New York: Garland Publishing Co., 1992.

Ríos-Bustamante, Antonio. "Latinos and the Hollywood Film Industry, 1920s to 1950s." *Americas 2001* 1, no. 4 (January 1988): 18-21.

Rivera, Lucas. "Mambo King of Comedy." *Hispanic,* March 1992, 11-15.

Riviere, Joan. "Womanliness as Masquerade." In *Formations of Fantasy,* edited by Victor Burgin, James Donald, and Cora Kaplan, 35-44. New York: Routledge, 1989.

Roberts, Shari. " 'The Lady in the Tutti-Frutti Hat': Carmen Miranda, a Spectacle of Ethnicity." *Cinema Journal* 32, no. 3 (Spring 1993): 3-23.

Robinson, Cecil. *Mexico and the Hispanic Southwest in American Literature.* Tucson: University of Arizona Press, 1977.

Robinson, Cecil. *With the Ears of Strangers: The Mexican in American Literature.* Tucson: University of Arizona Press, 1969.

Robinson, Henry Norton. "Mr. Beadle's Books." *Bookman* 60 (March 1929): 22.

Roeder, Jr., George H. "Mexicans in the Movies: The Image of Mexicans in American Films, 1894-1947." Unpublished manuscript, University of Wisconsin, 1971. (Highly faded copy in possession of G. D. Keller.)

Roffman, Peter, and Jim Purdy. *The Hollywood Social Problem Film.* Bloomington: Indiana University Press, 1981.

Rosen, Irwin C. "The Effect of the Motion Picture 'Gentlemen's Agreement' on Attitudes Toward Jews." *Journal of Psychology* 26 (1948): 525-36.

Rosen, Marjorie. *Popcorn Venus: Women, Movies and the American Dream.* New York: Coward, McCann and Georghegan, 1973.

Rosenfelt, Deborah Silverton. *Salt of the Earth.* Old Westbury, NY: The Feminist Press, 1978.

Rosenzweig, Roy. *Eight Hours for What We Will: Workers and Leisure in an Industrial City, 1870-1920.* Cambridge: Cambridge University Press, 1983.

Sadoul, Georges. *Louis Lumière.* Paris: Collection Cinéma d'aujourd'hui, Editions Seghers, 1964.

Saragoza, Alex M. "The Border in American and Mexican Cinema." *Cultural Atlas of Mexico-United States Border Studies.* Edited by Raymond Paredes. Los Angeles, CA: UCLA Latin American Center Publications, 1990.

Saragoza, Alex M. "Mexican Cinema in the United States, 1940-1952." In National Association for Chicano Studies, *History, Culture and Society: Chicano Studies in the 1980s.* Ypsilanti, MI: Bilingual Press, 1983.

Schickel, Richard. *D. W. Griffith: An American Life.* New York: Simon and Schuster, 1984.

"Screen Credit for Dubbed Voices by UA." *Variety,* November 27, 1929.

Sklar, Robert. *Movie-Made America: A Cultural History of American Movies.* New York: Random House, 1975.

Stam, Robert, and Spence, Louise. "Colonialism, Racism, and Representation: An Introduction." *Screen* 24, no. 2 (1983).

Stanfield, Peter. "The Western, 1909-14: A Cast of Villains." *Film History* 1 (1987): 97-112.

Stanley, Robert H., and Charles S. Steinberg. *The Media Environment: Mass Communications in American Society.* New York: Hastings House, 1976.

"Sylvia Morales: Faith Even to the Fire." *Booklist,* December 15, 1992.

Tafolla, Carmen. *To Split a Human: Mitos, Machos y la Mujer Chicana.* San Antonio, TX: Mexican American Cultural Center, 1985.

Taylor, Frank J. "Leo the Caballero." *Saturday Evening Post,* July 6, 1946, 26.

Thomas, Bob. "Chico Day." *Action,* January-February 1971, 19-21.

Thompson, Frank. *Alamo Movies.* East Berlin, PA: Old Mill Books, 1991.

Tibbetts, John, and James M. Welsh. *His Majesty the American: The Films of Douglas Fairbanks.* New York: Barnes, 1977.

Torres, José Artemio. "Cine." In *Puerto Rico A-Zeta,* edited by Lucas Morán Arce. Barcelona: Ediciones Nauta, S.A., 1987.

Treviño, Jesús Salvador. "Chicano Cinema." *New Scholar* 8 (1982): 167-173.

Treviño, Jesús Salvador. "Lights, Camera, Action." *Hispanic* 5 (August 1992): 76.

Treviño, Jesús Salvador. "The New Mexican Cinema." *Film Quarterly* 32, no. 3 (1979).

Vanderwood, Paul J. "An American Cold Warrior: *Viva Zapata!*" In *American History/American Film: Interpreting the Hollywood Image*, edited by John E. O'Connor and Martin A. Jackson, 183-201. New York: Frederick Ungar, 1979.

Vanderwood, Paul J., ed. and introd. *Juárez* (film script). Madison, WI: Univ. of Wisconsin Press, 1983.

Veloso, Caetano. "Caricature and Conqueror, Pride and Shame." *New York Times,* October 20, 1991, sec. H, 34.

Wall, Howard Lamarr. *Motion Pictures, 1894-1912 [Identified from the Records of the United States Copyright Office].* Washington, DC: Library of Congress, 1953.

Walley, Wayne. "*La Bamba* Wakes Up Hollywood: Hispanic Market Potential Pondered." *Advertising Age,* August 10, 1987, 41.

Wellek, René, and Austin Warren. *Theory of Literature.* 3d Edition. New York: Harcourt Brace and World, 1956.

Williams, Linda. "Type and Stereotype: Chicano Images in Film." In *Chicano Cinema: Research, Reviews, and Resources,* edited by Gary D. Keller, 59-63. Binghamton, NY: Bilingual Press, 1985.

Williams, Linda. "Type and Stereotype: Chicano Images in Film." *Frontiers: A Journal of Women's Studies* 5, no. 2 (Summer 1980): 14-17.

Wilson II, Clint C., and Félix Gutiérrez. *Minorities and Media: Diversity and the End of Mass Communication.* Beverly Hills, CA: Sage, 1985.

Woll, Allen L. "Bandits and Lovers: Hispanic Images in American Film." In *The Kaleidoscopic Lengs: How Hollywood Views Ethnic Groups,* edited by Randall M. Miller, 54-72. Englewood, NJ: Jerome S. Ozer, 1980.

Woll, Allen L. "Hollywood's Good Neighbor Policy: The Latin American Image in American Film, 1939-1946." *Journal of Popular Film* 3 (Fall, 1974): 283-5.

Woll, Allen L. *The Latin Image in American Film.* Los Angeles: Latin American Center, University of California, 1977.

Woll, Allen L. "Latin Images in American Films." *Journal of Mexican History* 4 (1974): 28-40.

Woll, Allen L. Review of *Chicano Cinema,* by Gary D. Keller. *Journal of American Ethnic History* 6, no. 1 (Fall 1986): 111-112.

Woll, Allen L., and Randall M. Miller, eds., *Ethnic and Racial Images in American Film and Television: Historical Essays and Bibliography.* New York: Garland Publishing Co., 1987.

Wood, Robin. "The American Nightmare: Horror in the 70s" and "Normality and Monsters: The Films of Larry Cohen and George Romero." Chapters 5 and 6 in *Hollywood from Vietnam to Reagan.* New York: Columbia University Press, 1986.

Yacowar, Maurice. "Aspects of the Familiar: A Defense of Minority Group Stereotyping in Popular Film." *Film Literature Quarterly* 2, no. 2 (Spring 1974): 129-39.

Ybarra Frausto, Tomás. "The Chicano Alternative Film Movement." *Centro de Estudios Puertorriqueños Bulletin* 2, no. 8 (1990): 44-47.

Zeitlin, Ida. "Sous American Sizzler." *Motion Picture,* September 1941.

Zinman, David. *Saturday Night at the Bijou.* New Rochelle, NY: Arlington House, 1973.

Zoglin, Richard. "Awaiting a Gringo Crumb." *Time,* July 11, 1986, 76.